CAPITAL OFFENCE

CAPITAL OFFENCE

Why Some Benefit at *Your* Expense

PAUL MUSSON

UNICORN

First published by Unicorn
an imprint of the Unicorn Publishing Group, 2025
Charleston Studio
Meadow Business Centre
Lewes BN8 5RW

www.unicornpublishing.org

All rights reserved. No part of this publication may be reproduced, stored in or introduced into a retrieval system, or transmitted, in any form or by any means (electronic, mechanical, photocopying, recording or otherwise), without the prior written permission of the copyright holder and the above publisher of this book.

Every effort has been made to trace copyright holders and to obtain their permission for the use of copyrighted material. The publisher apologises for any errors or omissions and would be grateful to be notified of any corrections that should be incorporated in future reprints or editions of this book.

© Paul Musson, 2025

10 9 8 7 6 5 4 3 2 1

ISBN 978-1-917458-04-7

Cover: Unicorn
Typesetting: Vivian Head

Printed in Malta by Gutenberg Press

CONTENTS

	Introduction	7
CHAPTER 1	Money: Why Does It Exist?	16
CHAPTER 2	Evolution of Money	31
CHAPTER 3	Some Economics	51
CHAPTER 4	Fun With Money	69
CHAPTER 5	GDP Part 1	79
CHAPTER 6	GDP Part 2	95
CHAPTER 7	Capital	111
CHAPTER 8	The Natural Rate of Interest	122
CHAPTER 9	The Neutral Rate of Interest	133
CHAPTER 10	Government Part 1	142
CHAPTER 11	Government Part 2	159
CHAPTER 12	Inflation: What Causes It?	176
CHAPTER 13	Inflation: Higher Than You Think	194
CHAPTER 14	The Wealth Effect	213
CHAPTER 15	Housing Part 1	219
CHAPTER 16	Housing Part 2	231
CHAPTER 17	Corporate Culture	237
CHAPTER 18	Stock Markets: Setting the Scene	250
CHAPTER 19	Stock Markets: Some of the Basics	257
CHAPTER 20	Stock Markets: A Few More Things	268
CHAPTER 21	Stock Markets and Executives	273
CHAPTER 22	Stock Markets and Policymakers	282
CHAPTER 23	Stock Markets and Quantitative Easing	293
CHAPTER 24	What's Wrong With Capitalism? Part 1	308
CHAPTER 25	What's Wrong With Capitalism? Part 2	322
CHAPTER 26	How We Got Here	334
CHAPTER 27	How Do We Fix Things?	350
	Conclusion	360
	Acknowledgements	368
	Index	370

INTRODUCTION

THE WORLD IS becoming increasingly divided and angry, and many view our economic system as being unfair. And in some ways, they are right. People are having to take on ever-increasing amounts of debt just to get by; meanwhile, a small per centage of the population are making out like bandits, as evidenced by skyrocketing wealth inequality. I don't believe that this was ever the plan, and although policymakers are largely responsible, they didn't intentionally get us into this mess.

Why This Book?

The financial system and how the economy works can be very complex and intimidating subjects. However, once the terminology is decoded into everyday language and you start at the beginning, taking it one step at a time, you can start to get a good understanding about how the economy really works; the shroud that hides what's really going on is slowly lifted, exposing all sorts of economic fallacies and received wisdom that isn't. This was my goal in writing this book: to empower people by helping them understand what's going on so that they can have a voice and contribute to positive change.

René Descartes: Divide each difficulty into as many parts as is feasible and necessary to resolve it.[1]

Some Housekeeping

You'll notice that I ended that last sentence with an endnote, which means that at the end of each chapter there will be some added information on the subject at hand. Throughout the book I attempt to keep things as simple as possible by avoiding financial industry jargon, however, occasionally I'll include some stuff that's a bit more complicated in an endnote. I may also include references to a book that's related to the subject at hand. Regardless, it's not necessary for you to read the endnotes to understand the message of this book. But hopefully, you'll be encouraged to read them or at least give them a try.[2]

The Road to Hell is Paved With Good Intentions
For many years, much of the value of your savings has been confiscated from you and the purchasing power of your income diminished without your knowledge or consent. And, importantly, this has been deliberate because those responsible for the confiscation actually believed that, longer term, it would be for your own good. It's not. The beneficiaries of this confiscation are largely those in power and the wealthy. Although I do believe that the motives of those responsible for this are *largely* well-intentioned, in some cases, their hubris blinds them with respect to the unethical, destructive and divisive consequences of their actions. The reason this theft has been going on for so long and, indeed, is accelerating, is that most people don't understand how it's happening. Ironically, many people believe that they actually benefit from the actions that ultimately rob them of their wealth. (I'll be using the words *wealth*, *savings* and *capital* interchangeably throughout this book. We all have capital.)

Face The Music
On reading that last paragraph, you may have decided that you don't believe it, or don't want to believe it. You may even feel that, even if it were true, the impact is minimal and as long as you mind your own business and do the right thing, then you are unlikely to be negatively impacted in any significant way and so it's not worth worrying about. *Nothing could be further from the truth.* In fact, it is this belief that makes the wealth confiscation that much easier. Everyone is significantly impacted by this, and there is simply no escaping it. Even worse is that, ultimately, this will be about much more than the confiscation of wealth, as the potential ramifications for all of us will be particularly dire unless we do something about it. I don't claim to have any solutions that offer an easy way out of this mess – for the very simple reason that there aren't any. No one likes hearing this sort of thing, and no one likes being the bearer of bad news – or at least most people don't. But of course, whether the news is good or bad, you will want to know what's going on. For instance, if your doctor discovered you had cancer, you would want him or her to tell you right away. Being aware of the problems and facing head on the tough battle ahead is your only chance of survival, and facing it head on is what we must now all do.

The maths of the situation is beyond dispute, and the only question will be do we do the right thing by finally facing reality and sharing the pain together, or do we continue digging a hole and deluding ourselves with respect to the error of our ways. It's always good to remember the First Law of Holes: *If you find yourself in a hole, stop digging.* Unfortunately, whether we continue digging or stop, we have a tough task ahead of us. However, proactively dealing with the issue sooner would, ultimately, result in less suffering and a greater chance that we can again start moving forward together in a very constructive way.[3] The delusional, digging-faster route, which feels better in the short term, is, ultimately, considerably more painful and dangerous in the long term. So far, policymakers have chosen the latter course, but only because we allow and encourage them to do so.

You may think that I'm simply using sensationalist tactics to grab your attention. I wish this were so. You can simply look around you on a day-to-day basis to see the deep divides that separate many people and nations. Fortunately, many are gradually coming to understand that something is wrong with the rules of engagement; that the world is increasingly becoming a case of Us vs. Them; and that change is necessary. While I don't profess to understand all of the reasons why the world has become so divided, in this book I will endeavour to explain carefully what I believe to be a significant contributor to what ails us all: the stealthy, or covert, confiscation and redistribution of wealth from the many to the few. Indeed, it's not that anyone is breaking the law (for the most part); it's that the rules and the system are structurally flawed. The result has been growing wealth disparity, slowing economic productivity growth, and a monumental explosion in global debt.

Making the Correct Diagnosis

Although people are becoming increasingly aware that things aren't working as they should – or at least as they used to – it's a challenge to understand why. And the reason it's a challenge to understand what's going on is because economics, like any industry, or field of study, speaks in a different language. Economic commentary is often riddled with words or concepts that the average person doesn't understand, and so it's easy to conclude that what is being discussed is far beyond one's comprehension.

It's not.[4]

This book is a humble attempt to help those who have never studied economics to understand what's going on and to put them in a position to be heard and make a difference. The good news is that people are becoming increasingly aware that they are being conned and are, thus, waking up and more open than ever to studying this subject. However, due to the complex language and the theft being two or three steps removed from the perpetrators' actions, most people go through life oblivious to how the value of their savings/capital/wealth is being taken from them. The risk then becomes that what ails the global economy is misdiagnosed and, thus, the wrong medicine is prescribed.

Our current economic system is increasingly functioning as a wealth redistribution (i.e. gain at the expense of others) and capital consumption/destruction mechanism rather than one of true wealth creation in which all participants benefit. Wealth is not only being redistributed within this generation, but to this generation from the next. Unless we make the necessary changes to right the ship, this will be the first time in modern history that the next generation will not be better off than the one that preceded it.

Back To Basics

The seeds of this book were sown during the runup to the Global Financial Crisis (GFC) in the mid-2000s. As a professional investor, I was becoming more and more frustrated with how policymakers were not only setting the stage for reckless behaviour but were actively encouraging it. And in my opinion, their motives were clear. I became even more frustrated with the policy response to the GFC, which effectively bailed out the reckless behaviour by encouraging even more of the very same and has continued to do so to this day, long after the *emergency* had passed. Ever since then, my spare time has been taken up with studying economic philosophy, as I wanted to go back to the beginning to understand how things worked. Focusing on principles and fundamentals rather than symptoms helps one to anticipate potential consequences that are two or three steps removed from today's actions (second- and third-order effects).

Over the last fifteen years I have come to discover that the principles that underly my investment style are very similar to those that form the basis of a healthy and sustainable economic system; in fact, they are principles by which I had learned to live my life long before I even knew I wanted to become an investor. It's not about having a strong intellect but intellectual honesty, patience, independent thought, hard work and a do-no-harm attitude with respect to living your life.

Clearly Communicating

As an investor, I have been practicing effective communication with my clients for many years. My goal when discussing a subject is always to educate rather than impress. If you're impressed with a presentation but don't understand it, I believe that one of three things is going on:

1. The speaker just doesn't care whether or not you understand what they're saying.
2. The speaker doesn't know what they're talking about and is attempting to conceal the fact.
3. The speaker knows what they're talking about, but they want to keep you in the dark.

In the second and third cases, the speaker might purposefully use complicated terminology to confuse and intimidate the listener into silence.

I believe that many politicians have become victims of fallacious economic doctrine that is espoused by the something-for-nothing crowd. Often, the prescribed solutions give politicians the easy way out and *appear* to be beneficial in the immediate short term, while blinding them to the longer-term consequences from which today's younger generation and future generations will suffer.

It's everyone's right to understand why certain policy decisions are being made, even if most people won't agree with those decisions. And making sure others understand why you are doing something is often an opportunity for you yourself to understand what it is you are doing, and why. Albert Einstein is purported to have said that if you can't explain something to a six-year-old, then you don't understand it yourself. And Walter Bagehot (pronounced 'badge-it'), the great British economics journalist from the 1800s, said, writing about the money market, '…that it is the writer's fault if what he says is not clear'.[5] These brilliant people understood the importance of clear communication. I believe that many of today's smart people don't communicate clearly because their motives differ enormously from people like Einstein and Bagehot. But I believe that can change. I hope that this book will help by giving you some of the tools necessary to better understand why policymakers behave the way they do. And then you will be in a position to effect change and make the world a better place.

I never studied economics in school, apart from the basic courses; thus, I had no axe to grind, or thesis/reputation/philosophy to defend, when I embarked on my own journey of understanding what was wrong with the way our economy was working. But I did start from a position of face-the-music, do-no-harm, long-term, second-order-effect kind of thinking. I also started knowing how important clear communication was and that, often, in this regard, less is more. It's much more difficult to write a concise explanation than a long one because the exercise demonstrates whether or not you really know what you're talking about; the temptation is often to write down a whole bunch of stuff and hope that the truth is buried somewhere within it. I always like to remind myself of the line by Blaise Pascal, 'I would have written a shorter letter, but I did not have the time.'[6]

Putting your thoughts down on paper is usually a very humbling experience; all of the things you were so certain about in your mind, are all of a sudden a little more open to questioning once they're in a place for the whole world to see. Most importantly, it's a great opportunity to learn, and I have taken many twists and turns along the way from when I started writing this book six years ago.

Hubris

One of the main issues is that many policymakers and economists seem to think that they know best how much of your capital you should be spending or saving and what prices you should be paying. In some ways, it's as if they suffer from a version of Hero Syndrome that has them unable to resist taking credit for fixing things that didn't need fixing. We've all experienced this in the workforce – an authority figure can't stand the fact that things seem to be working perfectly fine without them, so they intervene to re-establish their supposed *worth* to the organisation and, thus, justify their existence – and salary. In other ways, it's similar to control-freak parents who attempt to steer every aspect of their children's lives because they 'know what's best for them'. Although in both cases the actions are well intended, they each suffer from a common denominator: hubris.

Show Me the Money

The foundations of a flourishing economy are the products and services that result from savings and investments combined with human ingenuity and hard work, that is, the production of stuff over time. And then having in place a fair mechanism for exchanging those products and services. As you are already aware, the mechanism for exchanging the results of productive efforts is money, but this mechanism has been distorted to such a grotesque degree that it is leading us into an economic system that is decidedly unfair with a few benefiting at the expense of everyone else. I believe that our current monetary system imposes needless hardship on most of the population; thus, it is a moral issue. And if we don't fix it soon, not only will things get significantly worse, but even the top one per cent will, ultimately, suffer. Longer term, it's in everyone's interest to do away with the wealth-confiscating monetary system that is starting to threaten the very fabric of our society. Understanding what money is will make it easier to understand how the system works against you. And the more people who understand what's going on, the greater chance we have of changing things for the better.

Setting The Scene

An economic system can work to its full potential only if it is based on property rights, decentralised power and freedom; something the Founding Fathers and authors of the US Constitution knew all too well. However, over the last few decades, our rights and freedoms are being increasingly trampled upon by a powerful minority who believe that their actions are for the greater good.

They're not.

Before getting started, I'll say right from the outset that I'm not suggesting there is some sort of global conspiracy of rich and powerful people conspiring to keep themselves rich and the rest poor. I'm also not saying that there isn't such a conspiracy; I really don't know. But the point is there doesn't need to be a conspiracy for you to be angry about what is happening in the world today. I believe many policymakers are well intentioned and actually believe that their actions are in the best interest of most people. Unfortunately, many of them are doing more harm than good. However, they are not the ones who will suffer the consequences of their actions. It's the rest of society that suffers – and that suffering will continue to grow in severity until people awaken to what is going on and demand change.

In my opinion, although there are many fallacious theories about what is truly needed for an economy to function to its full potential, a large part of what ails today's economy is the lack of a true understanding of the concept of money. And so, we'll start with that subject. It's not nearly as straightforward as most people think, and most people don't understand how money is created and what it truly represents. This lack of understanding is what has enabled policymakers (for centuries) to secretly confiscate the wealth of the citizenry and to even delude themselves regarding the real and harmful effects of their actions.

After discussing money, other important issues, for example, inflation, interest rates, what drives housing prices and stock markets higher and what really drives an economy forward will be easier to understand. We'll take it slowly and use analogies where possible to help you better your understanding of the issues at hand.

Time is short. Unfortunately, it's already too late for some. But we need to make a difference while we still can before the population rises up in justified anger and condemns the economy to perpetual stagnation, or worse.

I make no claim to originality in this book apart from most of my analogies. I have simply rearranged some economic concepts that have been put forward over the last couple of hundred years by very capable people who were interested in the pursuit of truth. I've attempted to make the story flow from one chapter to the next, so it is important to read them in order, as they do tend to build on each other. And as economics is a social science, like psychology, rather than a natural science, like chemistry, all of my statements in this book should be considered my opinion – and, of course, any errors are completely my own.

Faith in People

My experience has taught me that people are much smarter and more capable than most so-called experts give them credit for. However, either through hubris or a desire for control, some policymakers believe that only they are smart enough and therefore have the right to control things that they believe are well beyond our comprehension. This book is targeted to all of those who are frustrated with the current state of affairs yet have the passion, desire and ability to make a difference. I humbly and sincerely hope that this book will make the whole subject of economics less intimidating, and, more than anything, I hope it will encourage you to discover your own path on the way to truth and, in so doing, contribute to the achievement of a truly fair, compassionate and free world.

ENDNOTES

[1] Rene Descartes was a French philosopher and scientist from the seventeenth century.
[2] Just checking.
[3] The best opportunity to deal with the issues, so far, was during the Global Financial Crisis of 2008/2009. However, that opportunity was wasted.
[4] Note that once you get deep into the weeds that certain aspects of economics can become very complicated indeed, but you don't need to get lost in the intricacies in order to understand the basic principles.
[5] *Lombard Street: A Description of the Money Market*, p. 1.
[6] Blaise Pascal was a French scientist and philosopher during the 1600s. Another apt quote of his is 'Justice without force is powerless; force without justice is tyrannical.'

CHAPTER 1

MONEY: WHY DOES IT EXIST?

Before discussing subjects such as interest rates, inflation, housing and how stock markets work – and how all of these things increasingly serve the transfer of wealth from one part of society (mainly lower income families, the middle class, pensioners, and the next generation) to another part (primarily the top 1%), it's important to start from the very beginning. And that all starts with the concept of money.

What is Money?
Ask people what they think money is and what it means to them and you're bound to get a wide array of different and often very emotionally charged answers. I've been asking this question for quite some time now, and I still find it fascinating listening to people's thoughts on money. I used to own a brewpub, and I remember one day asking a couple of our regular customers what money meant to them. An hour and a half later, the discussion was still raging, with other regulars and staff joining in the conversation. Sometimes, I'd get a very short and passionless answer. No matter what people had to say, I always found the answer interesting, as it would often tell me something about that person. At other times, it was quite eye-opening in that I would learn something new on the subject or see it from a different perspective. Sometimes you can learn a lot by asking very simple questions. The trouble is, it's sometimes embarrassing asking simple questions, as it can make you sound like an idiot. I've always liked this quote from Bruce Lee: A wise person can learn more from a foolish question than a fool can from a wise answer.[1]

Before reading any further, ask yourself what money means to you and then write it down. Don't be afraid to be brutally honest; you don't have to show it to anyone if you don't want to. Put down the first thing, and anything, that comes to mind.

OK, now that you've given it some consideration, let me share with you what some other people have had to say on the subject. Some of them simply blurted out the first thing that came to their minds. Here are a few examples:

- Savings
- Security
- Safety
- Power
- Greed
- Freedom
- Fame
- Stress
- Root of all evil
- Inheritance
- Pyramid scheme
- Gold
- Opportunity
- Control

Other people were more descriptive, while others were wary that my question might be some sort of trap and, thus, it might have taken them a few days to get back to me. Still others felt intimidated or were worried that they wouldn't have the right answer. Of course, I attempted to assure these people that any answer about what money means to them was right as long as it was honest. Here are some of those responses:

- Something you use to buy things with.
- I'm a plug-away kind of guy. For me money is security, comfort and no worries. Helps to deal with the ever-present wolf at the door. Then you can make yourself happy.
- I never figured out what money was because I never made enough of it.
- Those who make money know what it is while those who are given it don't.
- Money forces or influences you to make decisions.
- Any time I think of money I think about it in a negative way.
- I don't think about how much money I have but how much I need.
- The best feeling is that I know that I earned it.
- Money is what runs our world.

- Money is something I don't have.
- Money is the necessary evil in a capitalist nation.
- Money is the key to happiness.
- Money is security but it should be generosity.
- It can remove the burden of worrying.
- Money is freedom to do what you want.
- Money is very much a means to an end.
- Money will always factor into major life decisions but, hopefully, only ever as a consideration rather than the main driving force.
- Money is a universal means of energy transfer [there's always one show-off ☺].
- Money is something you get to buy stuff.
- I work my butt off to make as much money as possible. To me, it's the lifeline that helps us live better. If we have a lot of it, we will be able to live well without worrying. I was raised to have a very strong work ethic so we could make a lot of money, so to me, it's a very important part of living well.
- Give me back the gold standard when the price of gold was fixed, which backed our money. At least then I could understand its value and feel that money in the bank would be there in the future.

You'll notice that one person mentioned that money was the root of all evil. I'm sure you've heard others say the same thing. However, money is not at the root of what ails our society; rather, a lack of understanding of what money actually represents, how it is created, and how its value is taken from you is contributing to a two-tier economic system of haves and have-nots.

All the perplexities, confusions, and distresses in America arise, not from defects in their constitution or confederation, not from a want of honor or virtue, so much as from downright ignorance of the nature of coin, credit, and circulation.[2]

– John Adams

It doesn't have to be that way; indeed, for many years, it wasn't. Over time, and all over the world, societies, independently of each other, adopted some sort of money system because it helped to facilitate the exchange of what those societies were producing. This worked because the money could be trusted – at least, trusted significantly more than it can be today – and that trust led to an economic system that was based largely on real and fair rewards for efforts that were really worth something and that contributed to the general well-being of society. In past years, a strong currency was considered a reflection of the strength of an economy; thus, 'sound as a pound'.[3]

Those days are largely over.

> Lenin[4] is said to have declared that the best way to destroy the Capitalist System was to debauch the currency (Ed. note: lower the value). By a continuing process of inflation (Ed. Note: printing money, or increasing the money supply), governments can confiscate, secretly and unobserved, an important part of the wealth of their citizens. By this method they not only confiscate, but they confiscate arbitrarily; and, while the process impoverishes many, it actually enriches some.
> – John Maynard Keynes[5]

Compounding the difficulties in the comprehension of money is the fact that many in charge either don't seem to understand the concept of money themselves, or they do understand it, but deliberately use complex terminology to keep you in the dark.

> The study of money, above all other fields in economics, is one in which complexity is used to disguise truth or to evade truth, not to reveal it.[6]
> – John Kenneth Galbraith

Most of us get up every day and go to work for around half of our waking hours so that we can earn money with which we can then purchase the necessities, and luxuries, of life. We save some of our money so that at a certain age we can be in a position to no longer have to work – so that we will have enough money to live out the rest of our days in comfort. As earning money is hard work, we sometimes imagine easier ways of making it happen: winning the lottery, hitting it big in Las Vegas, or discovering a treasure hoard.

Apathy

Some people, on being told that our monetary system redistributes their wealth to others without their consent, will simply shrug their shoulders and get on with their lives. I think it may be because they can't see the theft happening and so they simply don't believe it. Or perhaps people believe it may be partially true but it would take far too much effort to figure out how it's happening; and, even then, how could they stop it? However, if instead you told someone that over the next twelve months their business partner would secretly steal five per cent of their profit; or their bank would confiscate five per cent of their savings; or a clerk in the store would short-change them; or the store would charge them a higher price for a product than what was listed; or a family member would take part of their inheritance; or they would be ripped off in any other ways that people can be ripped off – then they would be outraged.

How wealth is secretly taken from the citizenry is a real scourge on our society; it is a violation of property rights, which makes it a moral issue. And the scourge is much worse than you think, as much of the wealth that is confiscated from you goes to the rich. And that is why wealth disparity has been increasing for many years, that is, the results of much of your hard work and productive efforts that you have left after taxation go to someone else.

Before I get into explaining exactly what money is, you should know that there are differences of opinion as to how money originated. However, I am going to discuss money from what's called the commodity theory point of view. What this theory means is simply that money evolved over the years from people trading different commodities with each other. I think discussing money in this way makes things much more intuitive and will help you understand the true concept of money. Regardless of how money came to be, I don't believe it really matters; the basic principles of what money is are the same no matter how it originated. Although, for some reason, some people think that because money may have originated in a different manner, it legitimizes authorities taking your wealth from you.

It doesn't.

So, what is money? On a daily basis, we consume various goods and services to satisfy our many needs and wants. Anything from drinking coffee, to reading news online, to watching online videos, to filling up the car with gas, to purchasing clothes, to going out for dinner, to going for a haircut. However, for the most part, others will not provide these goods and services free of charge. They will expect to get paid for whatever it is they are providing you, and because they're getting paid, the transaction is not a gift but an exchange. The exchange involves a good or service on one side and money on the other. That is, you use some of your money to *buy* goods and services from others, and they accept money for the goods and services that they *sell* to you. I know this all sounds rather obvious, but have you ever thought why others are so willing to accept your cash for all of the valuable goods and services that they have to offer you? The answer, of course, is that they believe your money has value and they can use that money to buy goods and services from other people.

But why, or how, is it that money has value, and how is the exact level of that value determined? For instance, why is ten dollars enough to buy you a cheeseburger and fries but not enough to buy you a car?

Barter

Let's go back to the beginning. Before money came along, people were likely self-sufficient in that they probably provided themselves with everything they needed. For example, they found or hunted their own food and made their own shelter and clothes. It was probably a pretty meagre existence, but because everyone provided for themselves, there was no need to exchange things with each other. However, societies became more developed through something called *division of labour*, which simply means that instead of one person doing everything, jobs are divided up into separate tasks. For instance, in an ancient society, perhaps some people would hunt, others would grow crops, and others would make clothes and shelter.[7] This would then necessitate these people exchanging goods with each other, which is known as barter (or direct exchange).

A system of barter simply means that people produce goods and/or services and then trade (barter) those goods and/or services with each other to satisfy their respective needs and wants. I don't believe there is any official record of a large society operating under the barter system for the very simple reason, as you will see, that it would be impossible to do so. However, I'm sure all of you have participated in some sort of bartering at some point in your life. Perhaps your parents always made you a ham and cheese sandwich for your school lunch, and your friend's parents always made them a tuna sandwich.

After a while, you might have started getting sick of eating ham and cheese sandwiches every day, and so you might have decided to make a deal with your friend. Thus, you gave them your ham and cheese sandwich in exchange for their tuna sandwich. That's bartering. You probably didn't try to sell your sandwich and then use the proceeds to buy a sandwich from someone else. That's because, at that age, most kids don't have money – I know I didn't. Or perhaps you might have traded baseball cards, or a bike for a skateboard, or whatever. The point is that, because there was no money in the economic system of an elementary school room or playground, kids naturally resorted to the only method of exchange that was available to them: barter. So, it's likely that very small and unsophisticated societies started out with a system of barter, and only once money became established as a medium of exchange was it possible for those societies to flourish.

Let's look how the barter system might have worked, and all the problems it presented – and how money solved these problems. Let's assume there was a small village many years ago called Barterville. In this village there may be a blacksmith making axes, a baker making bread, a chicken farmer providing eggs, a cobbler making shoes, and a horse breeder selling horses.[8]

We'll start by looking at things from the blacksmith's perspective. Assume you are the village blacksmith and you want to get some food or clothing. You go to the local market. To entice other people to give you what you want, you'll probably need to give them something that they want in return. So, you will have first had to produce an axe to give yourself *purchasing power* (also known as the *means of payment*) with which you could enter the marketplace and exchange it with someone else for the items you wanted. Of course, back in the day, a blacksmith may have instead decided to enter the market wielding the axe in a threatening manner and taking things by force. That's another form of obtaining something without giving something in return (something for nothing, or, rather, at the expense of someone else), and we'll see later how, in today's money system, the abuse of property rights has taken on proportions that even a marauding blacksmith could scarcely imagine.

Anyway, let's say you decide not to hack people to pieces. Instead, you attempt to exchange your axe with someone else for whatever goods they have to offer. Perhaps you wanted some eggs. You would approach the chicken farmer and ask her if she would be willing to exchange some of her eggs for one of your axes. Obviously, she would be willing to go ahead with the exchange only if she needed an axe. Fortunately for you, the chicken farmer does need an axe, and so the two of you make an exchange (an axe for eggs), and you both go home happy.

Now assume that, about a month later, you fancy acquiring some more eggs. You make another axe and set off for the market for another exchange with the chicken farmer. The only problem is that the chicken farmer tells you she's not willing to make the exchange because she doesn't need another axe. This doesn't mean that you won't be able to obtain any eggs, although it does make things a bit tricky and requires a little ingenuity on your part.

You remember hearing about a dispute the other day – the chicken farmer wanted to trade some eggs for a new pair of shoes, but the cobbler is allergic to eggs and would not make the trade. Fortunately for you, you discover that the cobbler needs an axe. The cobbler gives you two pairs of shoes for your axe. You then go back to the chicken farmer who gladly exchanges eggs with you for one pair of shoes. Not only have you obtained the eggs you needed, you also have one pair of shoes leftover that you can use in exchange for something else. Perhaps you previously exchanged an axe for bread from the baker and so now you can offer them a pair of shoes in exchange for bread. This form of trade is called indirect exchange; you're exchanging an axe for a pair of shoes so you can then use the shoes to exchange for eggs and bread.

The Problems Money Solves

This is all fine and dandy; however, the next time you go to the market with an axe to exchange for eggs and bread you'll need to find another person who needs an axe that also makes stuff that the chicken farmer and baker need. Even if they both wanted another pair of shoes, that likely wouldn't help you, as the cobbler probably doesn't need another axe. So, you wander around the market trying to find people who need an axe and who also make things that are appealing to the chicken farmer and baker. And every time you go to the market it will become increasingly more difficult to make an exchange that will ultimately result in you walking home with eggs and bread.

Coincidence of Wants

This is the *first problem* with a barter economy: For an exchange to take place, both parties have to want what the other has to offer. This is called a *coincidence of wants* or a *double coincidence of wants* (same thing as far as I know). What it means is simply that an exchange in a barter economy can only take place between two people if each person has what the other wants. Therefore, the chicken farmer will only exchange eggs with you if she needs an axe, or whatever else it is you have to offer her in exchange.

This is the first problem that money solves. If you want to purchase something from someone else, you no longer have to worry about the other person wanting whatever good or service you have to offer in return. For instance, if you are a doctor and want bread, you don't have to wait until the baker gets sick so you can provide her with healthcare services in exchange for bread; you simply pay for the bread using money. This makes life considerably less complicated. Imagine if we were still in a barter economy and a brain surgeon needed a new filter for her furnace (or the seller of furnace filters needed brain surgery).

Unit of Account

The *second problem* with a barter economy is deciding how much of each thing to exchange in any transaction so that both parties will feel that they got a fair deal. For instance, how many dozen eggs is fair compensation for the time, expertise and materials that were required to make your axe? What about bread and shoes? We can envisage a barter economy with the following agreed-upon prices:

1 axe = 20 dozen eggs
1 axe = 2 pairs of shoes
1 axe = 100 loaves of bread

As you can see, listing the prices of goods in the form of other goods starts to get very complicated, even when there are only four goods involved. For instance, one pair of shoes costs ten dozen eggs and fifty loaves of bread, while one dozen eggs costs five loaves of bread. Imagine how complicated things would be in a large economy with millions of different goods being exchanged. For instance, how many kitchen chairs would you have to produce to take a flight to Florida?

This is the second problem that money solves, and it does this through something called *unit of account*. What it means is simply that all goods are priced in terms of money rather than other goods. Of course, all goods and services are still implicitly priced in terms of all other goods and services, but it's not necessary to know what those prices are; all you need to know is the *money price*. For instance, if the money price of a dozen eggs is five dollars and that of a pair of shoes is fifty dollars, then you could also say that the egg price of a pair of shoes is ten dozen eggs (10 dozen eggs x $5 = $50 = one pair of shoes). But with money, you don't need to know that.

Divisibility

The *third problem* with the barter system arises when you have products that you can't divide into small-enough sums to make small purchases. Notice above that we priced one axe in terms of eggs (20 dozen), shoes (2 pairs) and bread (100 loaves). But that price is only of interest to the chicken farmer, the cobbler and the baker. How do we price eggs, shoes, and bread in terms of axes? It would look like this:

    1 dozen eggs   = one-twentieth of an axe
    1 pair of shoes = half an axe
    1 loaf of bread = one-hundredth of an axe

The obvious problem here is if you are an egg farmer and the blacksmith only wants one dozen eggs from you, what are you going to do with one-twentieth of an axe? It's not as though it would be one-twentieth as effective as a whole axe; it wouldn't even *be* an axe (unless it was super small). Likewise, if a horse breeder fancied a loaf of bread, she couldn't realistically trade with the baker, because she might deem a fair trade to be one thousand loaves of bread in return for one horse and most of the loaves would go mouldy long before she had a chance to eat them. And it doesn't make much sense to attempt to equate the cost of a couple of loaves with, say, a horse's ear. With money, the blacksmith and the horse breeder can use cash to purchase the exact number of items, such as eggs, that they require and not the number of eggs that would equate to one axe or one horse.

Portability

Portability is the *fourth problem* that money solves. A blacksmith on a shopping trip can hardly be expected to walk around with a bunch of axes, nor a horse breeder with a couple of horses in tow. The beauty of money is that the full value of ten axes or a couple of horses can be carried in one's pocket.

Store of Value

Storing your products for future sale or consumption is the *fifth problem* that money can solve. (This presumes we have honest money, which we don't; much more on this later.) For instance, a baker may want to bake a lot of loaves today and save them to purchase other goods and services sometime in the future, or perhaps even to fund her retirement. However, after a few days the bread will start to go stale and the baker won't be able to exchange them for anything. So, bread serves as a poor store of value; that is, the baker's breadmaking efforts cannot be stored in that bread for more than a few days – after that, it loses its value. Money, on the other hand, is a good *store of value*.

Fungibility

Perhaps one more thing worth mentioning here about the characteristic of money. Money is fungible, meaning that one part of a certain commodity is exactly the same as another. For instance, suppose you stored a one-gallon tank of gasoline in your neighbour's garage and then one day your neighbour ran out of gas for their lawnmower and used yours. The next day your neighbour drove to the gas station to refill the tank. When you needed to retrieve your gallon of gas from your neighbour, you wouldn't care that it wasn't the actual gas you had originally put in the tank. All you care about is that there is a gallon of gas in the tank, because gas is fungible (assuming it's the same octane). Commodities such as water, wheat, copper and gold are also all fungible. Likewise, if you deposit a fifty-dollar bill in your bank account and six months later withdraw the same amount from an ATM, you don't expect it to be the same fifty-dollar bill you deposited.

Thus, all of these problems associated with a barter economy are solved by money:

1. *Coincidence of wants*: You can sell your goods to someone who produces stuff for a living that you would never consider buying.
2. *Unit of Account*: All goods are priced in terms of money.
3. *Divisibility*: Money can be used to buy any product of any worth no matter how large or how small.

4. *Portability*: Money is easy to carry around – and most of it is now in digital form, which makes it easily accessed through things like bank cards.
5. *Store of wealth*: You can use money to store the value of the goods you produce or services you provide.
6. *Fungibility*: All money is treated equally when used by people to buy and sell goods and services.

The Role of Money

As mentioned in the introduction, the heart of a vibrant and growing economy is not the money but all of the people producing goods and services. Money is simply used to exchange the hard work and ingenuity of people. Another way of thinking about it is that you could have an economy without money (albeit a small one), but you couldn't have one without goods and services. And your ability to pay for any good or service should be a result of you first producing a good or service for someone else. For example, if you make socks for a living and you want to go to the movies, then you might have to first make and sell two pairs of socks in order to pay for the movie. On the other hand, if you own a movie theatre and you need a couple of pairs of socks, you would first need to sell a ticket to someone who wanted to watch a movie and then use that money to buy the socks. It is extremely important to understand that each person had to first produce or offer something to another person in order to obtain the wherewithal to buy something from someone else. Things are first produced and then sold to someone in exchange for money; it's an indirect exchange (an economic good for money) rather than a direct exchange (one economic good for another, e.g. socks for a movie). Using money to exchange all of the things that are produced in an economy makes life considerably easier for us all and helps the economy to function. But the money, in and of itself, has little to no value.[9]

Means of Payment

I like the way economist Frank Shostak clarifies things. The things you produce – bikes, bread, socks, movies – are the *means of payment*. The fact that you have produced something now gives you the wherewithal to go out and exchange whatever it was you produced for something that someone else has produced. And what they have produced is, of course, their means of payment, that is, they are able to buy what you have produced because they, too, have produced something. But rather than through direct exchange (barter), the transaction is done indirectly through money – the *medium of exchange*. Money doesn't make the world go round; that's done by the hard work and ingenuity of billions of people who create goods and services. Money is used to facilitate the exchange of all that stuff, all of that hard work. And it's the hard work and ingenuity that give us all purpose.[10]

> *Happiness is not in the mere possession of money; it lies in the joy of achievement, in the thrill of creative effort.*
> – Franklin D. Roosevelt

Nothin' From Nothin' Leaves Nothin'

Another way I like to think about it: it's like the college diplomas that you see hanging on the office walls of professionals. The diploma, in and of itself (i.e. the cost of the ink and paper and the process of printing and framing), is not worth much. However, it's worth a lot because of what it signifies: all of the years of study and learning it took to earn that diploma. Of course, you could simply go out and buy a framed diploma, but it wouldn't mean that you've learned anything or have anything of value to offer a potential employer or customer. And you might get away with doing that for a while and effectively earn something for nothing before you're found out as a fraud. However, it's important to remember that you can't get something for nothing, despite the fact that many policymakers and economists seem to have convinced themselves, and try to convince you, that you can. If you have obtained something without providing something else in return, then your gain came at someone else's expense. The bottom line: an unearned diploma is worthless.

How comfortable would you be visiting a doctor whose diplomas on their wall were simply printed? The only thing those diplomas would represent is fraud. Likewise, paper money has no real value except that it represents the goods and services that were produced in order to acquire it. Therefore, it should be obvious that the wealth (capital) created in an economy is the amount of stuff that is being produced on a daily basis, not the amount of money that is printed to indirectly exchange that stuff. You could triple the amount of money in an economic system and not increase the value of goods and services one iota. Similarly, you could print a bunch of college diplomas, but it wouldn't increase the number of doctors, lawyers or engineers in our economy. Not only that, but it would also significantly hamper our economy, as consumers and employers would grow to distrust college diplomas. This is not unlike our current situation with money. And while a fake diploma may enable you to get something for nothing for a while (at someone else's expense), it wouldn't be long before you were found out as a fraud and possibly face severe consequences. On the other hand, the something-for-nothing myth that results from printing money has been going on for decades and at great expense to those who can least afford it – with none of the perpetrators facing any consequences.

Our economy could not function without money and the indirect exchange that it makes possible. However, there is a downside to using money: it gives others the opportunity to take your wealth (capital) from you without your knowledge or consent. Money – or at least the authorities charged with controlling the supply of it – needs to be trusted.[11] You would then be confident that the capital you have produced and temporarily stored up in the medium of exchange (i.e. your money) would be safe. Unfortunately, that has not been the case for a very long time, and things have become significantly worse in recent years. It would be like if you were to make ten bikes and then store them for safe keeping so that you could purchase a new fridge and stove at some time in the future, and then, when you go to retrieve the bikes, you find that five of them are no longer there. As you will soon see, it's not as if those bikes have simply vanished into thin air; someone else has them.

ENDNOTES

[1] Bruce Lee was an iconic figure of the 1960s and 1970s who was a martial arts expert and actor. He died tragically young in 1973, aged thirty-two.
[2] John Adams in a letter to Thomas Jefferson, 25 August 1787. *Founders Online*.
[3] The pound is Britain's currency.
[4] Lenin, or Vladimir Lenin, led a revolution against the Czar of Russia in 1917 and was the first leader of the communist state known as the Soviet Union. As communism was, more or less, the opposite of capitalism, it should be noted that he is said to have believed the best way to destroy capitalism was to debauch the currency. Any communist can take comfort in not having to figure out a way to destroy the currencies of Western states, as the debauchery is now happening from within.
[5] *The Economic Consequences of the Peace*, John Maynard Keynes. New York, Harcourt, Brace and Howe, 1920.

[6] John Kenneth Galbraith, *Money: Whence It Came, Where It Went*, Boston, Houghton Mifflin Company, 1975.
[7] Division of labor also means dividing up tasks within certain jobs. So, in terms of shelter, one person may be a bricklayer, another a glazier, another an electrician and so on.
[8] Many people have used these sorts of analogies over the years.
[9] Note that back when money was gold, it did indeed have value.
[10] Frank Shostak, *The Problem With the Velocity of Money*. Mises.org. December 17, 2018.
[11] Note that in the past there were examples where authorities did not issue money; instead, people would bring their gold or silver to government or private mints to be minted into coins. Also, private banks would issue their own banknotes that represented gold or silver coins in their vault. This latter system was not like what many misinformed people today claim it was: wildcat banking, which refers to a lightly regulated and fraudulent banking system. For more on this see George Selgin and Larry White.

CHAPTER 2

EVOLUTION OF MONEY

It is well enough that people of the nation do not understand our banking and monetary system, for if they did, I believe there would be a revolution before tomorrow morning.

– Henry Ford

Commodity Money

For hundreds of years, money was in the form of coins that were made with gold, silver or some other sort of metal. In short, it was a *commodity* money; it was actually worth something in and of itself – the value of the metal that was used to mint the coin.[1]

Although gold and silver were the most common forms of commodity money, there were many other kinds of commodities that functioned as money, and not all of them were metal; for example, buttons, tobacco and shells were also used. Each of these commodities started off with their own inherent value before being used as a type of money used for its exchange value. Obviously, some of these commodities would have served better as money than others, but the mere fact that the less-desirable ones once functioned as a form of money indicates that they were the best option available at the time and that they helped the economy to function better.

A relatively recent example of a commodity money being adopted comes from R.A. Radford. He was a prisoner of war during the Second World War. In 1945 he wrote an article titled 'The Economic Organization of a P.O.W. Camp'. In the article, he explains that because the prisoners didn't have any money, they had to adopt a commodity medium of exchange. The story went something like this. Soldiers who were captured and put in POW camps would receive Red Cross packages which contained various food items such as tea, biscuits, cheese, tins of sardines and chocolate. As you might expect, each prisoner would have preferences for certain food items. Perhaps one prisoner didn't like cheese but loved chocolate. He might then attempt to exchange his cheese with another prisoner who preferred cheese to chocolate. As you know, this is a barter system, and it comes with all of the problems that we discussed in Chapter 1. However, also in the care packages were cigarettes, and prisoners found that these commodities were able to play a similar role to that of money. They solved the issue of requiring a coincidence of wants; they were a useful unit of account (things became priced in terms of cigarettes); most if not all things were valued more than one cigarette so they didn't need to be divisible (even then, the cigarettes probably weren't filtered, so you could have cut them in half); they were portable; and they were fungible. They were probably not a great long-term store of value (they might get wet or crumpled or, literally, go up in smoke), but given the circumstances, a long-term store of value was not really needed. It therefore stands to reason that cigarettes would become a form of money in POW camps. And, as far as I know, they did so not because some government official decreed that they should. So even if you didn't smoke, you would want to obtain cigarettes because they enabled you to buy products from other prisoners. Any prisoners fortunate enough to make it home probably never used cigarettes again as a form of money, because there would then have been better options available to them.[2]

Silver and Gold

Over time, gold and silver came to be the primary commodities for money, with gold becoming preeminent. A gold coin's worth was dictated by how many grams of gold it contained rather than a random number stamped on the coin. Because of this, it was difficult for policymakers to influence how much money was in the economy, and it prevented them from secretly extracting wealth from the citizenry. They could still do it, but it would happen at a much slower rate than it does today, as it was much more difficult to do so. One example from ancient times of debasement happening over many years was of a Roman silver coin called the denarius that was introduced around 211 BC. At its introduction, it weighed 4.6 grams and the silver content ranged from 95 to 98 per cent. By AD 241 the weight of the coin was reduced to 3.4 grams, and only 48 per cent of it was silver.[3] So the silver content in the coin went from 4.5 grams down to 1.6 grams. You might think that policymakers reducing the silver content in the denarius by 65 per cent over time was highway robbery – and it was. However, it was still a far cry from how your capital is taken from you in our modern age. The 65 per cent decline in the silver content of the denarius happened over 452 years, which meant that the average annual debasement was only 0.2 per cent. Today, the debasement of the currency in your pocket or bank account or your wages happens at a far greater rate than that experienced by the denarius. Commodity monies were a great benefit to society and a great inconvenience for governments because wealth could not be so easily siphoned off from the citizenry.

Money Names

The history of money being made from precious metals is evidenced today in the names of our money. The word 'dollar' is derived from the *thaler*, which was a silver coin minted in Europe hundreds of years ago. The British Pound used to represent one pound of silver (240 silver pennies[4]). Eventually, the US Dollar and the British Pound came to be defined as representing a certain weight of gold. For example, in 1925, one ounce of gold was worth $20.67, this meant that the value of a dollar would have been equal to around one-twentieth of a troy ounce, or 1.5 grams of gold.[5] The British Pound in 1925 was worth almost five times as much as the US Dollar ($4.87 in USD terms). Its value was equivalent to that of 7.3 grams of gold; thus, another way of thinking about the value of the British Pound versus the US Dollar is that in 1925 the Pound represented almost five times as much gold as that of the Dollar.

Gold

The US used to have what was called a classical gold standard for about a hundred years (1815 to 1914). During this time, you could actually take your paper money to the bank and ask for its equivalent value in gold. Imagine that. Today, of course, it's a completely different story. There is no underlying commodity that backs the value of money – which is why your wealth is so easily taken from you.

Technically, you could still go to the bank today and purchase gold with your money, but the amount of money you will need to purchase gold changes constantly, and over longer periods of time the price steadily increases. As just noted, back in the 1920s you could exchange $20.67 for one ounce of gold. By the year 2024, it would cost you approximately $2,500. So, if you had $10,000 back in 1925 and, instead of holding on to the cash you decided to convert it into 483 ounces of gold ($10,000 ÷ $20.67 = 483), today you would be able to sell that gold for $1,207,500. That's $1,197,500 more than if you had just held on to the $10,000 in cash. And the majority of this discrepancy is not because gold has appreciated in value but because money has depreciated in value.

How the value of money and gold evolved over time:

1925
Money: $10,000
Gold (483 ounces) = $10,000

2024
Money: $10,000
Gold (483 ounces) = $1,207,500

The average annual compounded return on your gold investment would have been around 5%.

So, gold held its value much better than money. However, the money was likely sitting in a bank account so let's assume you earned 3% interest per year on your savings. Here's how much your money would have grown since 1925:

2024
Money: $186,589
Gold (483 ounces) = $1,207,500

However, both these numbers assume no taxes. With a savings account, the interest you earn is taxed every year, thus diminishing the effect of compounding.[6] For gold, you are only taxed when you sell your gold and recognise a capital gain (i.e. the money you made on your gold investment).[7]

So, if we assume interest income in your bank account is taxed each year and the capital gain on gold is taxed at 20% when you sell it in 2024, the value of $10,000 of money earning 3% interest and of 483 ounces of gold would be as follows:

Money by 2024 at 3% Interest
Money: $104,640
Gold: $966,000

Even if you had managed to somehow earn 5% interest every year, you would still be worse off after tax than if you had held gold:

Money by 2024 at 5% Interest
   Money: $485,625
   Gold: $966,000

Only if you had managed to earn 6% on your savings for 99 years would your money then be worth more than gold in 2024. Good luck with that.

(Note that this is not a recommendation to drain your bank account and invest all of your money in gold. We're finally able to earn a modicum of interest on our savings after having effectively received nothing for fifteen years. However, that can change quite quickly.[8] I have some gold in my savings, but if you are considering such an investment, I highly recommend that you speak with a professional investment advisor.)

Another way of looking at how differently the respective values of gold and the dollar have tracked is by looking at what each would have been able to purchase in 1925 compared to 2024. In 1925, a gallon of milk cost 56 cents.[9] Compare that to around $3.94 in 2024.[10] So, in 1925, given that an ounce of gold was worth $20.67, you could have spent one ounce of gold or $20.67 to buy 37 gallons of milk ($20.67 ÷ $0.56 = 37). By the year 2024, that $20.67 in cash would buy you about 5 gallons of milk ($20.67 ÷ $3.94 = 5), but one ounce of gold would buy you 635 gallons ($2,500 ÷ $3.94 = 635). But again, if you had earned 3% per annum on your $20.67 in your savings account, then in 2024 you would have had $216 after taxes (assuming a 20% tax rate). At $3.94 a gallon, you would be able to buy 55 gallons of milk in 2024, or 580 fewer gallons than you could with your gold.[11]

True Money

Because of the difficulty in manipulating the money supply when it was gold, that form of money was a much more stable currency than what we have today. The quantity of money in the system would only increase as more gold was discovered somewhere in the world and then be brought into the country and minted into coins. Although there were some periods of higher inflation caused by an increase in the money supply as new gold discoveries were made, by and large, the global supply of gold increased at a fairly slow and steady rate. According to Mark Skousen (Chapter 8 'The Theory of Commodity Money: Economics of a Pure Gold Standard' in *The Structure of Production*), over the last hundred years, gold supplies have increased at an annual rate of about 1 to 3 per cent.

The United Kingdom was on the gold standard from 1821 to 1914. Over that time, overall prices actually fell by an average of 0.05 per cent per annum.[12] Meanwhile, when the US was on the gold standard from 1879 to 1914, the inflation rate was 0.006 per cent[13] – essentially zero. In fact, in the latter part of the 1800s, prices in the US actually fell, on average, as the amount of stuff being produced grew at a rate faster than that of the money supply: a state known as good deflation which we'll look at later.

The bottom line is that money used to be a very trustworthy medium of exchange. Over time, all over the world, and independently of each other, societies adopted commodity money systems usually based on gold, because such systems helped to facilitate the honest exchange of what those societies were producing.

Banks Evolve[14]

As more people used money, they needed a safe place to keep their money. Banks originated by offering to safely store peoples' money in a vault and they would charge a fee for these services. Over time, banks evolved to an institution that would lend out your stored money to other people. Then, banks started producing banknotes, which looked like the paper money we have today. These notes represented the gold that the banks held in their vaults, so at any time you could take a banknote to the bank and demand the equivalent amount in gold. Banknotes were a great innovation because they meant that people no longer had to carry around their gold coins. But, of course, banknotes were easier to forge.

Banks also started offering customers chequing services whereby people who had money deposited in a bank could write a cheque for payment of goods rather than going to the bank every time they needed money.

Over time, fewer and fewer people holding banknotes would come to their banks to redeem their gold. Most of the gold was just sitting in vaults doing nothing. When they realised this, the banks started lending out more banknotes than there was gold in their vaults. This was the beginning of *fractional reserve banking*, which essentially means that banks would only hold a fraction of the gold in their vaults as reserves against all of the banknotes that they had issued.[15]

There were problems with this banking system from time to time, particularly when too many people would bring their banknotes to the bank and exchange them for gold. However, the system generally worked very well for long periods.[16] And there was little inflation because the amount of money in the system was still largely dependent on how much gold was mined each year and minted into coins – and that amount increased at a very slow rate.

Over time, banks were prevented from issuing their own banknotes and today all currency in the United States is issued by its central bank, the Federal Reserve. And bank reserves are no longer gold; instead, they consist of currency and electronic reserves created by the central bank.

Today, we still have a fractional reserve banking system, but instead of holding a fraction of banknotes issued, banks hold a fraction of their reserves (I go through a simplified example soon). For instance, if you deposit $10,000 into your bank, then your bank could lend out 90% of that to someone else.[17] Again, this system works fine as long as everyone doesn't want access to all of their money at the same time. Think of that scene in *It's A Wonderful Life* where everyone rushes to Bailey Bros. Building and Loan to withdraw all of their money.

The Money Supply

So, what is money today? There are various definitions of money. Let's quickly look at three of them in the US context.

Monetary Base (M0)

There are two parts to the monetary base:

- All currency (bills and coins) held by banks or people.
- Bank reserves held by commercial banks in their bank accounts at the central bank. (We'll come back to this soon.)

M1
There are also two parts to M1:

- All the currency held by people.
- Money deposited in chequing accounts.

M2
And there are three parts to M2:

- M1
- Time deposits at banks of less than $100,000.
- Retail money market funds.[19]

To keep things simple, we'll talk about M1, which is all the dollar bills and coins that people have in their possession or in safety deposit boxes, as well as deposits in their chequing accounts at their banks.

Coins and paper currency are printed or stamped and put into circulation through the commercial banking system by a country's central bank. These are some of the major central banks:

- United States: The Federal Reserve (the Fed)
- European Union: The European Central Bank (ECB)
- Japan: Bank of Japan (BoJ)
- England: Bank of England (BoE)
- Switzerland: Swiss National Bank (SNB)
- Canada: Bank of Canada (BoC)
- Australia: Reserve Bank of Australia (RBA)

In the United States, most of the currency is by far in the form of $100 bills, which totaled $1.7 trillion in 2020; $20 bills are the second most common at $235 billion. Total bills in circulation were just over $2 trillion. Over the last twenty years, the value of notes in circulation has increased at a rate of 6.6 per cent per annum. According to Ruth Judson of the Federal Reserve, approximately half of US currency circulates outside of the United States.

However, a significant majority of the money supply is in deposit form in banks, with only around 10 per cent being in the form of dollar bills and coins. And because banks actually create deposits, at first blush, it seems that the banking system is responsible for most of the money created in our system. Let's look at how commercial banks increase M1 (the money supply) every time they lend money.

Money Creation

You will often hear economists say that money is *lent into existence* by commercial banks. Is this true? Well, it depends on your definition of money. Also, the commercial banks are not at liberty to lend into existence as much as they'd like to.

Let's go through it step by step.

First, assume that you have $10,000 and, also, that you are the only one in the economy that has any money. The situation would look like this:

Economy
You = $10,000.

With me so far? :)

Now let's say you deposit your $10,000 into your bank. We'll call it Bank A. Total money in the economy has not changed, except that it's now in your bank account instead of under your mattress. And you have a deposit receipt for $10,000 which represents your $10,000 in Bank A.

This $10,000 is a liability of Bank A because it owes you $10,000.

Another way of thinking about it is that there is an asset of $10,000 that you have in the form of a deposit in Bank A and a liability of $10,000 that Bank A has because it owes you that much, that is, you have effectively lent the bank $10,000.

Economy

Deposits	Liabilities
Your deposit in Bank A: $10,000	Bank A owes you: $10,000

Bank Reserves

Your deposit in Bank A is also called a bank reserve, and it can now lend it to someone else. Remember that banking evolved into fractional reserve banking, and, up until the global COVID pandemic, banks in the United States were required to hold reserves of 10% on demand and chequing accounts. Since then, all reserve requirements have been eliminated, but we'll stick with the 10% reserve ratio rule, because using it makes it easier to understand what's going on.

With a 10% reserve ratio, Bank A can't lend all of your money to someone else; it is required to keep some of it in its vault in case you want to access some of it. In this case, Bank A is only required to retain $1,000 ($10,000 × 10%) of your $10,000 deposit in its vault. It can lend out the other $9,000 ($10,000 × 90%).

Let's assume that your bank lends $9,000 of your deposit to Jack the Cobbler, who also has an account at Bank A. The Bank simply credits his account with $9,000.

So now let's look at how much money (M1) is in the banking system.

	Deposits
Your Deposit in Bank A	$10,000
Jack's Deposit in Bank A	$ 9,000
Total Deposits	$19,000

Total deposits in the economy have gone up from $10,000 to $19,000 or an increase in the money supply of $9,000. So just by making a loan to Jack, Bank A increased the money supply by $9,000.

Clearing Cheques

Now Jack uses that $9,000 to buy equipment from the Shoe-In Equipment Company. He pays using a cheque from Bank A. On receiving the $9,000 cheque, the Shoe-In Company deposits it in its own bank, Bank B. Then Bank B will let Bank A know that it received one of its cheques for $9,000 and will ask Bank A to send over the $9,000 of reserves to Bank B to clear the cheque. Now let's look at how much money (M1) is in the banking system.

	Deposits
Your Deposit in Bank A	$10,000
Shoe-In Deposit in Bank B	$ 9,000
Total Deposits	$19,000

By spending his money on equipment, Jack did not increase the money supply. Total deposits in the economy have not gone up and instead there was a transfer of deposits from Bank A to Bank B.

Re-lending Money

However, the money supply increase doesn't stop there, because Bank B is now allowed to lend out 90% of the $9,000 deposit it's holding on behalf of the Shoe-In Company. Perhaps Bank B lends out $8,100 ($9,000 × 90%) to Sheila, who uses the money to purchase some hardware for her business from the IT Equipment Company. Bank B retains 10% of the deposit ($900) in its vault ($9,000 × 10% = $900). The IT Equipment Company then deposits that $8,100 in its bank account at Bank C. Once Bank C receives the cheque, it informs Bank B that it has one of its cheques for $8,100 and asks Bank B to send over $8,100 of reserves to clear the cheque. The total amount of money, represented by total deposits in the economy, just went up again. It looks like this:

	Deposits
Your Deposit in Bank A	$10,000
Shoe-In Deposit in Bank B	$ 9,000
IT Equipment Company Deposit in Bank C	$ 8,100
Total	$27,100

But again, the number of reserves has not increased.

So, we started off with your $10,000 that was deposited in Bank A, but because the bank was able to lend 90% of your deposit out to someone else, that resulted in another deposit in Bank B, which in turn lent out 90% of its deposit, which ended up in Bank C. This process can continue until your original deposit of $10,000 is transformed into total deposits in the banking system of $100,000. Thus, with a 10% reserve requirement in a fractional reserve banking system, a deposit in a bank can create a tenfold increase in the money supply. This type of money is called fiduciary media and it is not fully backed by some form of reserve money. In this case, the $100,000 is backed by your $10,000 deposit and thus is only backed 10% by reserves; although the total amount of deposits increased, the reserves didn't.

Gold Coins as Reserves

Because the deposits increased significantly but the reserves didn't, you have a lot of people laying claim to the same amount of reserves. This works as long as everyone doesn't want all of their money back at the same time. I'll use gold coins to help make things clearer. We'll add a gold coins column to the tables above.

So, first, you deposit 10,000 gold coins worth a dollar each into Bank A, which looks like this:

	Deposits		Gold Coins
Your Deposit in Bank A	$10,000	Bank A Vault	10,000

But then Bank A lends out 90% of those gold coins, 9,000 of them, to Jack the cobbler, and keeps 1,000 in their vault as the 10% reserve. Then Jack writes a cheque for 9,000 gold coins and uses it to pay for the equipment from the Shoe-In Equipment Company. On receiving that cheque, Shoe-In deposits it in its bank account at Bank B. Bank B then clears the cheque by sending it over to Bank A and asking for the 9,000 gold coins, which it then deposits in its vault.

So now the total amount of deposits (M1) and gold coins in the system would look as follows:

	Deposits		Gold Coins
Your Deposit in Bank A	$10,000	Bank A Vault	1,000
Shoe-In Deposit in Bank B	$ 9,000	Bank B Vault	9,000
Total Deposits	$19,000	Total in Bank Vaults	10,000

Thus, the total deposits (M1) in the banking system have increased to $19,000, but the total number of gold coins is still only 10,000: 1,000 in Bank A and 9,000 in Bank B. As a result, you and the Shoe-In Company both lay claim to the same 9,000 gold coins.

When the IT Equipment Company makes a sale to Sheila, the situation looks as follows:

	Deposits		Gold Coins
Your Deposit in Bank A	$10,000	Bank A Vault	1,000
Shoe-In Deposit in Bank B	$ 9,000	Bank B Vault	900
IT Equipment Company Deposit in Bank C	$ 8,100	Bank C Vault	8,100
Total Deposits	$27,100	Total In Bank Vaults	10,000

You, Shoe-In, and the IT Equipment Company have total deposits of $27,100, but there are still only 10,000 gold coins in the economy; and the same holds for when total deposits get to $100,000. Thus, commercial banks are not lending gold coins into existence but, instead, they are lending deposits into existence – with multiple people thinking they have a claim on the same gold coins. Again, this all works fine as long as everyone doesn't want their gold coins back at the same time. Essentially what you have is the same money being lent, spent and re-lent. You had real resources of 10,000 gold coins that you didn't want to spend today and thus you have lent them to someone else to use in the meantime.[20]

With millions of people in the banking system, it was extremely rare that everyone would want all of their money back at the same time; therefore, if run prudently, the system of fractional reserve banking with money backed with gold worked just fine and there was little inflation.[21] From time to time, the banking system did get into trouble, and so central banks were created with the ability to literally print money and backstop the system.[22]

Today's Bank Reserves

In today's banking system, gold coins no longer serve as reserves. Instead, reserves are created by the central bank. For instance, in the above example, if the reserves of $10,000 had been pyramided into $100,000 of loans, the banking system would not be able to make any more loans. Thus, it wouldn't be able to increase the money supply (M1). The US commercial banking system is restricted in how much it can increase M1 by the amount of reserves that are in the system, and the Federal Reserve is the only entity that can increase reserve.[23]

Some say that commercial banks can make loans and increase M1 even if they don't have the reserves to back them up. This is true, but, eventually, the reserves will need to be found to back up such loans.

For instance, assume Bank D didn't have any reserves, and its client Sam the Fishmonger wanted to borrow $10,000 to purchase a new fridge for his fish shop from the Cool Fridge Company. Bank D could electronically create a $10,000 deposit in Sam's bank account, which means that the money supply (M1) just increased by $10,000 without any new reserves being created. However, this situation will only persist if one of three things happens. One, Sam would need to leave that money in his bank account and not spend it; thus, he can't buy the new fridge. Two, if he does spend that $10,000, then the Cool Fridge Company would need to hold on to the cheque from Sam and not deposit it in its bank (Bank E). Or three, if the Cool Fridge Company did deposit the cheque in its account at Bank E, then that bank would have to hold on to the cheque and not send it to Bank D for clearing. As you might expect, the odds of any of these things happening are essentially zero.

If Bank E did present the $10,000 cheque to Bank D but Bank D didn't have any reserves to send to Bank E, Bank D would be insolvent.[24] To avoid insolvency, Bank D would need to find $10,000 in reserves that it can send to Bank E. This is why, ultimately, the central bank has the final say on how much money there is in the system. On the other hand, if the Federal Reserve increases the amount of reserves and banks don't create new loans, then the money supply will not increase.

Is Fractional Reserve Banking Inflationary?

So far, we have seen that when people deposit their money in a bank, it creates reserves that the bank can then use to lend to others. For instance, when you deposited your $10,000 gold coins in Bank A, the banking system could pyramid a total of $100,000 of loans on that deposit of $10,000.

However, there would be no increase in the amount of *real resources* (gold coins). If you decide not to spend your gold coins, your bank will lend them to someone else to spend. And then if the company deposits them into its bank, they will in turn be lent out to someone else, and so on.

Not everyone can spend the total $100,000 in loans at the same time. A person can only borrow and spend money after someone else has borrowed and spent.[25] In the above example, if we think about it in terms of gold coins, Sheila could only borrow $8,100 worth of gold coins from Bank C once Jack the Cobbler had spent his $9,000 in gold coins and Shoe-In Equipment Company had deposited them into Bank C. And note that each time the money was spent, one real resource (gold coins) was exchanged for another real resource (e.g. shoemaking equipment).

For this reason, it might be that that fractional reserve banking is not inflationary. In the example above, what increased was the number of deposits but not the number of gold coins. And not everyone is spending all of those coins at the same time. The fact is, they couldn't. Every time someone spends money they have borrowed from the bank what they are effectively spending are gold coins that someone else has put aside. A real resource of a gold coin is being used to purchase another real resource in the form of equipment or something else.

If for whatever reason everyone decided they wanted to spend their money at the same time the whole banking system would collapse as the gold coins that had been lent were recalled by all of the banks that had lent them out. The amount of deposits (M1) would collapse back to the original $10,000 gold deposit, that is, the money supply would shrink by 90% from $100,000 to $10,000.

I believe that the only inflationary aspect of the US monetary system is the Federal Reserve's creation of reserves.

No Golden Handcuffs

When reserves were based on a real commodity such as gold, it was rare that those reserves could be increased rapidly. However, today, the banking system has morphed into something quite different, and the main reason for that is that money is no longer based on a real resource. Back in the day, a strong currency was deemed essential to honest trade, with descriptive terms such *as good as gold or sound as a pound*. However, over a period of around forty years, the United States, and by extension, the rest of the world, cut all ties between money and gold[26] resulting in what's now called a fiat currency standard.

With a fiat standard, there is no commodity of value that backs the paper money or the banks' reserves. For instance, when you hold a $100 bill in your hand you know that the value of the paper and the ink that was used to make that bill is not worth $100. In fact, according to the Federal Reserve, in 2020 the cost to produce a $100 bill was 19.6 cents. Most of the reserves for banks are in electronic form and pretty much cost nothing. Because reserves are no longer representative of how much gold is in the economy, they can be created at will by central banks. So, when a central bank wants to increase the money supply it prints reserves electronically, and with that money it buys assets from commercial banks, and those reserves are deposited in the commercial banks' accounts that they hold at the central bank. The commercial banks can then start making loans backed by those reserves, and this is what causes inflation: money is printed out of thin air rather than borrowed from someone else.

> *I see in the near future a crisis approaching which unnerves me and causes me to tremble for the safety of my country. Corporations (of banking) have been enthroned, an era of corruption in high places will follow, and the money power of the country will endeavor to prolong its reign by working upon the prejudices of the people until the wealth is aggregated in a few hands and the Republic destroyed.*[27]
>
> – Abraham Lincoln

Fiat Currency

The definition of fiat is *by decree* or *by law*. In other words, our money today has value only because the government says it does. You might wonder how something like a fiat money, which is essentially worthless, became the accepted medium of exchange (money). Well, it wasn't really accepted; rather, it was forced upon the people by the government by their making that fiat money *legal tender*. Legal tender means that if someone is in debt to you, you must accept legal tender fiat money from that person when they want to repay the loan. In addition, you must pay your taxes with legal tender (try paying your taxes with bitcoin[28] and see what happens), so you really have no choice but to use it as a medium of exchange. With a fiat standard of money, its supply can be increased much more rapidly because it doesn't require the discovery of new gold. Instead, it just needs someone to push a few buttons and print more of it.

Money Supply Contraction

Whenever someone pays back a loan the total number of deposits goes down. For instance, if Bank A lent you $10,000 for one year, they would do so by creating a $10,000 deposit in your bank account. Assume that you spend that $10,000 and then over the rest of the year you save up $10,000, which you deposit in your bank account. At the end of the year, when you use that $10,000 in your bank account to pay back the loan, the liability you had to the bank is now zero (i.e. you've paid off your loan). But your $10,000 deposit has also gone (i.e. total deposits in the banking system went down). However, there is no real issue with deposits contracting each time a loan is repaid as there are usually more loans being issued (deposits created) by banks than there are loans being repaid (deposit contraction). If the reverse were true, it would mean that less of the saved money in banks was being borrowed and put to productive use and that would not be good.

Money Supply Growth

From 1961 to 1971, the year the US went off the gold standard, the monetary base increased at an average annual rate of 5.2%.[29] The average rate of growth since 1971 has been 8.4%.[30] Over the two-year period from the onset of COVID in March 2020 to March 2022, the monetary base increased by 58%.[31] I believe that rapid increases in the base money engineered by central banks is what accounts for the vast majority of inflation – or, more accurately, price increases.

Another form of money creation is quantitative easing, which is a more recent phenomenon. I discuss this in a later chapter, but I believe that quantitative easing was implemented to drive asset prices higher rather than increase bank lending, and, for the longest time, this newly created money was sort of trapped within capital markets.[32] And, although it didn't directly lead to high price inflation, it inflicted great harm on the productive capacity of the economy as well as leading to grotesque levels of wealth disparity and monumental government debt.

How Much Money is Enough?

Many policymakers will tell you that an economy cannot grow unless the money supply increases. I don't believe this is true, as there have been prior instances of significant economic growth with very little or no growth in the money supply, as we saw earlier with the gold standard examples of the UK and the US (i.e. the money supply increased very slowly, yet both economies saw an explosion in production).

Because policymakers continuously increase the amount of money in the system, that money relentlessly loses its value. A recent example of the impact of rapidly increasing the money supply over many years occurred here in Canada. Back in 2013, the government stopped minting pennies. So much money had been printed over the years that pennies had become practically worthless and too expensive to produce.

Of course, there are differences of opinion regarding the benefits or consequences of policymakers increasing the money supply. Needless to say, governments think it is a great idea.

Others believe that there should be no change in the money supply. The great nineteenth-century British classical economist David Ricardo believed that the correct amount of money in an economy was whatever it was at that moment and that it should not change. We have seen that there have been long periods where very slow increases in the money supply were associated with very strong economic growth. With more stuff being produced than money being created, the units of money become more valuable, thus allowing the stuff to be sold at lower prices. As an economy grows, it doesn't need to run out of a medium of exchange (money), because as the money becomes more valuable, smaller and smaller denominations of the existing money could be used. So rather than the Canadian penny being discontinued because it couldn't buy anything, it would rise in value such that the Canadian mint could start producing half-pennies and perhaps even quarter-pennies. (In the United Kingdom, there used to be such a thing as a farthing, which was a quarter of a penny.)

I haven't found any proof that a rapidly rising money supply is good for an economy; in fact, I think that history shows the exact opposite to be true: that the amount of money rising quickly destroys an economy's ability to function properly. It also redistributes wealth within a society.

We still have more to discuss about money, but before we do that, it's important to discuss some basics about how an economy works. We'll look at that in the next chapter.

ENDNOTES

[1] There is evidence that credit transactions may have taken place before people adopted money as a medium of exchange. For instance, a person may have lent ten bushels of wheat in return for receiving a pig a year later. However, this seems to have essentially been another form of barter, but with a time lag.

[2] However, if we remain on the current path, we may end up being better off adopting a monetary system based on the cigarette standard.

[3] Denarius. *Wikipedia*.

[4] Pounds, Shillings and Pence. Royalmintmuseum.org.uk.

[5] A troy ounce of gold is equivalent to 31.1 grams. Therefore, based on the 1925 value of gold given above, the value of a dollar would have equalled that of 31.1 grams ÷ $20.67 = 1.5 grams of gold. Note: A troy ounce is slightly different from a regular (imperial) ounce and is only used to measure the weights of precious metals; imperial ounces were used to measure everything else. (For instance, a troy ounce of gold is 31.1 grams, while a regular ounce of flour weighs 28.3 grams.)

[6] Note that the tax system unfairly punishes lower-income earners who would typically save by keeping their money in the bank, thus having the interest earned taxed each year. Higher-income earners typically invest in stocks and real estate, both of which are tax-advantaged. The answer to this unfairness is not to take away the tax advantages of stocks and real estate but to reduce the tax disadvantage of saving money in your bank.

[7] A capital gain happens when you sell an asset at a price higher than that for which you bought it. So, if you bought a stock for $10 and it appreciated in value to $25, then when you sell it at that price, you have made a capital gain of $15. The $15 gain is subject to a tax called a capital gains tax, but the rate of that tax is typically lower than your personal tax rate.

[8] Some feel that policymakers will continue with a policy of financial repression as the only way to get out of this mess. I hope that they don't, but if they do, your chances of earning any kind of real return on your savings will be zero and, in fact, you will be losing capital.

[9] Retail Prices, 1890 to 1925: Bulletin of the United States Bureau of Labor Statistics, No. 418.

[10] St Louis Federal Reserve.

[11] If you had managed to earn 5% interest each year, then by 2024, your money would have bought you 255 gallons of milk – still 380 fewer gallons than the ounce of gold would have got you.

[12] O'Donoghue, Goulding, and Allen, 2004. *From Better Money: Gold, Fiat, or Bitcoin?* by Lawrence H. White, 2023, pp. 49–50.

[13] Johnston and Williamson 2014a: From Better Money Gold, Fiat, or Bitcoin? By Lawrence H. White 2023, page 50.

[14] Here I will focus on how things progressed in the United States.

[15] This first started with goldsmiths in England in the 17th century.

[16] In particular, see George Selgin on the Scottish (1700s and 1800s) and Canadian banking systems.

[17] This assumes a 10% reserve requirement which no longer exists.

[18] *It's a Wonderful Life* is one of my favourite movies, but, as others have pointed out, the bank run on Bailey Bros. Building and Loan highlights the importance of banks being able to honour their obligations to their depositors. However, the business did survive; its solvency

was threatened only once George Bailey's bungling Uncle Billy lost $8,000 (around $128,000 in today's money). I believe that those in favour of fractional reserve banking would point out that it was things like these (i.e. ineptitude or poor government regulations) that usually undid a fractional reserve bank. Note that the antagonist, the mean old Henry F. Potter, might not have been someone you'd want to invite over for Christmas dinner and listen to him talk about all of the people he has evicted from their homes because they couldn't pay their mortgage, or that he effectively stole $8,000 when Uncle Billy inadvertently handed it to him. But his shareholders/depositors slept well knowing that their savings were being managed prudently (i.e. not by Uncle Billy).

[19] Source: https://www.federalreserve.gov/faqs/money_12845.htm.

[20] Economist George Selgin believes that fractional reserve banking is not inflationary and I believe this might be the reason why. See his paper Banks Are Intermediaries of Loanable Funds. Cato Working Paper No. 80. March 18, 2024.

[21] For a vigorous defence of fractional reserve banking see George Selgin. For just as vigorous an attack on the subject, see Jesús Huerta de Soto (*Money, Bank Credit, and Economic Cycles*). And for a good debate on the subject, see George Selgin and Robert Murphy on YouTube ('Does Fractional Reserve Banking Endanger the Economy? A Debate').

[22] Central banks first came into being primarily for fiscal reasons (mainly to help governments finance their wars; the Bank of England in 1694 and the Bank of Amsterdam in 1609). Once fractional reserve banking became dominant, central banks were needed as a lender of last resort during those periods when everyone *did* want all of their money back. According to Walter Bagehot, central banks were supposed to lend freely on *good* collateral at *punitive* rates (the opposite of what the Federal Reserve has done i.e. lend freely on *bad* collateral at *easy* rates). And when the world went to a fiat money system in 1971, an entity was needed to restrict the growth of the money supply, which could now be created at will. Central banks receive a failing grade in terms of maintaining the purchasing power of money, but they get an A+ from governments for funding their deficit spending.

[23] Note that people can increase bank reserves if they deposit cash they are holding into their banks, but the increase as the result of such deposits is minimal.

[24] Banks will often make loans and then go look for the reserves and possibly borrow them from other banks or from the central bank.

[25] Unless the commercial bank obtains new reserves from the central bank or by borrowing them from another bank.

[26] First in 1933, with President Roosevelt making it illegal for citizens to hold gold, and then in 1971, with President Nixon fully taking the world off the gold standard.

[27] Archer H. Shaw, *The Lincoln Encyclopedia,* New York, Macmillan, 1950, quoting from a letter dated 21 November 1864 from Abraham Lincoln to Colonel William F. Elkins.

[28] Many people store their capital in bitcoin as a way to escape the ravages of central banks printing money. Its price can be very volatile. I don't currently own any, but I can understand why many people do.

[29] Federal Reserve Bank of St. Louis

[30] Ibid.

[31] Ibid.

[32] Capital markets coordinate those who have capital to lend or invest with those who require capital to put to productive use. I discuss capital markets later in the book.

CHAPTER 3

SOME ECONOMICS

Some things that should not have been forgotten were lost. History became legend and legend became myth.
— Galadriel in 'The Lord of the Rings: The Fellowship of the Ring'

Progress is cumulative in science and engineering, but cyclical in finance.
— James Grant

UNLIKE THE HARD sciences of chemistry and physics, where knowledge grows over time, in economics it ebbs and flows.[1] Over the last number of decades, it has been ebbing more than flowing. Much of what economists a couple of hundred years ago had discovered with respect to how an economy really works has either been forgotten or purposely papered over. Instead, economics has become based on ideology, sometimes called normative economics (i.e. economists proffer economic doctrine as they wish things to be rather than as they are).

In this chapter I'll discuss a few economic basics that I hope will help you understand how an economy works based on firm economic principles rather than on wishful thinking. One of the key things to do is to separate money from what is really going in an economy. Then it will be clearer the role that money plays and how it can be abused by whoever controls how much money is in the system. While money and banking are essential parts of what's required for an economy to thrive, they really are only meant to play a supporting role in what leads to productivity growth and greater human welfare. Not only that, but money can distort in our own minds what we think is necessary for a strong, sustainable, and fair economy, and it also makes it much easier for some policymakers to convince others, and themselves, that you can get something for nothing.

You can't.

Finally, the form of money we have today enables policymakers to transfer wealth within society without the permission of its citizenry, and, today,

much of that redistribution of wealth benefits those who don't need it.
The value in an economy resides in the things that are being produced rather than the amount of money in the system. A growing and improving economy requires the investment of real resources.

An Island Economy

Let's look at a desert island to help explain how an economy works.[2] Assume that there are three of you on this island. You are adept at scooping fish out of the water with your bare hands and can catch three fish per day. Shirley is great at climbing trees and is able to collect three coconuts per day. Jane is in great shape and is able to climb a steep hill every day to collect three litres of water from a mountain spring. There is no money in this island economy, but with only three people, it doesn't really matter. It's fairly easy to exchange goods directly with each other. You all agree to swap one item with each other every day. You catch three fish per day. You keep the first one for yourself and then exchange the second for a coconut from Shirley and the third for a litre of water from Jane. An obvious but extremely important point here is that each of you had to produce something before you could demand something from the others. The importance of this point to how an economy functions cannot be overstated. This is related to Say's Law or Say's Law of Markets, which was proposed by French economist Jean-Baptiste Say in the early 1800s. Say said that the production of one thing immediately created demand for something else.[3] So, in our island economy, by catching fish you are now able to demand a coconut from Shirley and fresh water from Jane. Likewise, by collecting a coconut, Shirley is in a position to demand a fish from you. This all seems fairly straightforward, but it's true only if you're producing something that someone else wants, and in the desired quantity. For instance, if you caught slugs, your supply of slugs would not create demand for coconuts, because Shirley has no intention of eating any slugs. If you were to catch a hundred fish a day, they wouldn't all create demand for coconuts or water; this is because you'd be catching more fish than Shirley or Jane wished to consume.

The Invisible Hand

So, supply creates demand as long as the right things are being supplied, and in the right quantity. Incredibly, this is what happens in the global economy billions or trillions of times on a daily basis. This is controlled by what economist Adam Smith called the *invisible hand*[4], effectively the self-interest of anyone producing or working in an economy. For instance, in our island economy, you don't catch fish just so you can hand them over to Shirley and Jane; you catch them because you expect to receive something for them in return – your desire for coconuts and water drives you to catch fish. Of course, it's nice to be able to give some fish away for free to those who aren't able to collect coconuts or water, but to be able to do that, you need to take care of your own needs first, and this happens through the production of goods that are valued by others and, thus, exchanged with them. The beauty of all of this is that no one needs to be coerced into doing anything; it's all completely voluntary. If you want to acquire more things made by others, you have to produce more things that are valued by others. The efficiency of the invisible hand is destroyed when certain people attempt to control the marketplace by pushing it in a direction different from the one determined by the needs, wants, choices and preferences of those doing all the work and who have *skin in the game*.

Skin in the game simply means that it's your capital at risk of loss, not someone else's. Governments never have skin in the game because all of the capital they put at risk comes from taxpayers. The importance of skin in the game cannot be overemphasised.

> *It is not just that skin in the game is necessary for fairness, commercial efficiency, and risk management: skin in the game is necessary to understand the world.*[5]
>
> – Nassim Taleb

If people make rational decisions and thus do only what they believe to be in their self-interest, then policymakers moving things in a different direction (the visible hand) will not be doing so in everyone's best interests. Not only that, but those policymakers can only move the economy in a different direction, by taking resources away from those who have created them (i.e. you) and redistributing those resources to the areas that policymakers have decided are more deserving.

Free Choice

Of course, this is not to suggest that everyone necessarily loves what they do for a living or even feel that they have a choice. For instance, parents with young children likely feel they have no choice but to work in order to provide for their families. However, ultimately, the decision to work (and, perhaps, where to work) or produce (and what to produce) resides with each and every one of us. Some of us are fortunate to love what we do for a living; others are not. Many may feel they're not earning anywhere near what they deserve (probably most of us). For instance, you may feel that you should be paid more than one coconut for each fish you exchange with Shirley. However, if Shirley doesn't agree with you, then you're out of luck. Maybe you need to catch a tastier fish, or trap lobsters instead. That might induce Shirley to hand over two of her coconuts. The foundations of a thriving economy are people *voluntarily* deciding to produce things that they believe other people will value and then voluntarily exchanging those things via the medium of exchange called money. As long as this is happening in a society that enjoys safety, property rights and contract law, then you are a long way towards what you need for an economy to thrive and prosper. Human spirit, ingenuity, curiosity and intelligence takes care of the rest.

Introducing Money

Now let's introduce money into our small island economy. Assume each of you has two dollars – a total of six dollars on the island. Because each of you was willing to exchange one of your items for one of the other items in the island economy, it stands to reason that they would all have a similar money price. Given that there is a total of six dollars on the island it makes sense to price each product at one dollar.[6] Every day, you use your two dollars to buy a coconut and a litre of water. Now you have no money. But, every day, Shirley and Jane each buy a fish from you for a dollar, leaving you once again with two dollars. So now you have been able to consume a fish, a coconut and a litre of water, and still have two dollars in your pocket at the end of the day. Shirley and Jane also consume what you consume and are left with two dollars each.

Now, suppose that Shirley is a former central banker. She is tired of living on the same diet every day. She believes that, if only there were more money on the island, you'd all be able to purchase more things to eat. Like many politicians and economists, she believes that growing the money supply (inflation) is necessary for an economy to grow. She's convinced that more money will magically increase the number of items being produced on the island. So, Shirley gets your and Jane's permission to print another six dollars and divide them evenly amongst yourselves. Now, instead of having two dollars, you all have four dollars each to spend.

Quite obviously, the island economy did not all of a sudden become twice as wealthy because the amount of money doubled. True, the residents think they are twice as wealthy because they have twice as much money as they did the day before. However, the productivity of the economy has not changed; total production per day is still three fish, three coconuts and three litres of water. Increasing the amount of money in the system did not teach you how to catch more fish or help Shirley to climb trees better or increase Jane's fitness level so she could make two trips per day to the spring. As a result of twice as much money chasing the same amount of goods, the prices of those goods will simply adjust higher to reflect the new amount of money in the system; the prices will double. And, despite the fact that you start each day with $4 instead of $2, you can still only buy one coconut and one litre of water and eat one fish.

In this example, the only impact of doubling the money supply was the doubling of prices on the island. There were no other effects or consequences. Therefore, the impact of increasing the amount of money on the island was *neutral*.

As you will see later, when policymakers rapidly increase the money supply, its impact on the economy is not neutral. Not only does it reduce the productive capacity of the economy, but it also facilitates the theft of productive effort from some and gives it to others. Those who get the money first benefit the most and those who get it last are hurt the most.[7]

Competition

Note that each industry on the island only has one producer, which means there is no competition. As a result of the lack of competition, each resident is quite comfortable with their situation, and they don't feel the need to figure out how to improve their capacity to produce more stuff or what new stuff to produce.

'So what?' you might say. 'As long as they're happy, why not continue as they are?' Except that perhaps one day the fish might move on, a disease might kill the palm trees, or the freshwater spring might dry up. Such a tragedy happened in Ireland in the mid-1800s. At the time, the Irish population's diet was heavily dependent upon potatoes. For a period of seven or eight years, a disease infected the potato crops, resulting in mass starvation; approximately a million people died.

Entrepreneurs

Of course, a more diverse economy is just one of the benefits of a free market system in which exchange is completely voluntary and not coerced. Another thing to note is that, in the real world, most of us don't need to worry about trying to improve our own productive output. Yes, we may go to school, train in some field, or gain experience that will make us more valuable workers for our employers. But we don't necessarily have to directly invest our savings and put them at risk in order to try and come up with innovative ideas or better, more efficient ways of producing things. Investment over time and risk-taking is being done by the owners of capital and entrepreneurs. These people put their own capital at risk and invest the time necessary to innovate and improve productivity so that consumers will buy their products. These entrepreneurs are the real change makers in our society. The entrepreneur's capital represents previous contributions that they or others have made to society that they have saved up in the form of money. Perhaps they worked as an employee for another company and received an hourly wage and instead of spending all of their weekly pay cheque, they decided to save ten per cent of it to build up a sum of capital. They then decided to risk their previous efforts saved up in the form of money by starting a new business. If they are successful, they will reap the benefits; but if they are unsuccessful, they could potentially lose all of their capital.

We can indirectly contribute to productivity growth by investing our savings in the stocks of companies. One issue with this is that, when deciding what to do with the capital, the decision-makers (i.e. the executives of the company) don't have as much skin in the game as entrepreneurs. For large corporations, most of the skin belongs to the shareholders rather than those running the business. However, there are still many great corporate executives out there running businesses. Unfortunately, some corporate executives are not great and are willing to swing for the fences because there's not much downside if they fail.[8]

If entrepreneurs want to grow their businesses, they typically can't do it on their own; they need to hire employees. But employees don't need to risk losing anything to benefit from what the entrepreneur is doing. Employees are paid an hourly wage in return for work, and they don't have to put up any of their own capital. Importantly, in most instances, employees don't have to wait until the products they are helping to produce are sold before they get paid. The entrepreneur pays the employees in advance of the product selling. And employees get paid whether or not the product even sells – even if the company is ultimately unsuccessful. Of course, if the company is not successful, then those employees will eventually be laid off, but then they can go and work for another entrepreneur who seems to be having success.

If an entrepreneur is very successful and the business grows to a significant size, then they will have to hire professional managers to help run the business. Being an entrepreneur and running a large business requires a different skill set, and good entrepreneurs don't always make good managers If you look at the largest companies in the world today, many of them were founded many years ago by entrepreneurs, and they have been run for many years by professional managers. Many of these managers/executives are extremely talented, continuing the entrepreneurial spirit of the founders. Others are what I like to call career executives.

So, people play different roles in the success of a business: entrepreneur, capital provider, management, employee. However, only the first two put their capital at risk. Thus, they are the only ones who risk losing a significant amount of their capital. Or, conversely, *earning* a significant amount of capital. But as we have seen, these capital providers and entrepreneurs are only rewarded if consumers will voluntarily purchase the goods the entrepreneur is producing. The entrepreneur, capital provider and consumers all benefit, as well as the employees of the company, and the managers.

Fair Share: Employees and Customers

Managing a business is not easy. Typically, it requires years of post-secondary education, as well as long hours at the office. As a result, management is usually paid significantly more than the other employees. However, the amount of total compensation for some executives has soared to obscene levels. Well-run businesses with an eye on the long term will often reward their employees commensurately with the success of the business, with some form of profit-sharing – although not enough firms do this.

If Company A comes up with a successful new innovation and is making a lot of money, other companies will then attempt to enter that market to compete for some of that abundant profitability. The new competition will likely take customers away from Company A, which would then necessitate a response from that company. First, they might lower their prices to be more competitive, which lowers the company's profitability. Next, Company A may decide to invest in more efficient production processes (lower their production costs) and thus boost their profitability once more. Or Company A might invest in innovation and attempt to either improve their product or come up with new ones and win the customers back that way.

So, competition encourages companies to save and invest more in their business to be either more efficient, more innovative, or both. The great thing about this from the point of view of us consumers is that, despite the fact that we don't need to take on risk by investing our capital, we benefit from the efforts of all of those who do. It also makes it difficult for companies to earn high levels of profitability for extended periods of time. Consumers benefit from this competition and investment by continually having new products to buy and being able to purchase previous innovations at lower prices. This is the way things are supposed to work, but, unfortunately, there is a lot of unfairness in today's economic system. However, the problems are not a result of a free market system based on savings, investment and competition; rather, they exist because the system has been grossly distorted.

Competition

Let's go back to our island economy and introduce a little competition. Assume that all of a sudden, Bill shows up on the island, and he's just as good at climbing trees as Shirley. There is now competition in the coconut industry and, therefore, both Shirley and Bill will be incentivised to find cheaper or more efficient ways of collecting coconuts – Shirley, so she can drop her prices and continue to sell her two coconuts per day, and Bill, so he can undercut her and take over the market.

For instance, if Bill tied a bunch of sticks together, perhaps he could now use it to dislodge the coconuts off a tree rather than having to climb it.[9] He would then have more coconuts to sell per day and could, thus, reduce his price and take market share away from Shirley. In response, Shirley might devise an even more efficient stick than Bill's and collect more coconuts than him (or hit him over the head with it). She would then be in a position to set her price lower than Bill's and, thus, keep the market to herself. Because both Shirley and Bill improved their productivity and because there was competition in the industry, the supply/production of coconuts increased, and the price of coconuts fell. Thus, our island economy is better off.

Now this would be a problem for Shirley and Bill if there were ongoing monopolies in fish and water, as they would still only be able to purchase one item of each no matter how many coconuts they were to offer in exchange (although they could eat more coconuts). Of course, that would be good for you and Jane because each of you would be able to purchase more coconuts for each fish and litre of water, respectively.

Fortunately for Shirley and Bill, more people show up and start to compete in fishing and in the collection of water. Because of this new competition, you and Jane are incentivised to devise tools to produce more stuff each day. Perhaps you make a fishing net that enables you to catch a hundred fish per day instead of three. Likewise, your competitor is catching more fish. Meanwhile, more coconuts and water are being brought to market. People start looking for new things to supply to the island economy. They use their ingenuity to collect or build things they think the others might value and thus be willing to exchange for the stuff that they have collected or made. Yes, there are more people to feed on the island, but because of productivity improvements, there is now far more food per person, and everyone benefits.

Saving and Investment

An important aspect of the island economy's productivity improvement is investment. Each person needed to invest time and capital to make productivity improvements. But to make the necessary investments, each person would have needed to save some of what they were already producing, because investment requires some delay of current consumption. For instance, it might have taken you two days to make the net. Over that period, you would not have had time to fish by hand; for two days, you would not have had any fish to eat or trade for coconuts and water. For a couple of days before making your net, you decided not to eat the coconuts you had exchanged for fish and, instead, you saved them. You also decided to drink only half a litre of water each day. It wasn't easy eating and drinking less than usual for two days before you started making the net, but you were confident that this would lead to much greater consumption in the future. When you're busy making your net and unable to fish, at least you have a coconut to eat each day and half a litre of water to keep you going. Of course, Shirley and Jane are unable to exchange for fish over this two-day period, but they can eat more coconuts and drink more water. After two days, your net is complete and you will now able to catch a hundred fish per day.

Saving capital (forgoing some consumption today) and then investing that capital over time is what results in productivity improvements and greater consumption in the future. Importantly, though it wasn't demonstrated in this example, the population of our island economy did not need to increase for the economy to grow.[10] (Reasonable rates of population growth are generally a good thing, but they are not a requirement for a growing economy.)

This is how a market system is supposed to work. People use their own ingenuity, efforts and savings (capital) to come up with better ways of doing things (i.e. of making things at lower costs). Other people, and successive generations, then make improvements on those improvements, and, thus, the productive capacity of the economy constantly improves over time, resulting in more and better stuff being produced with fewer resources. This enables producers to lower the prices of their products and take market share from other producers. This, in turn, encourages other producers to also become more productive so they can lower the prices of their products and compete more effectively.

The natural tendency in a freely functioning market system is deflation or falling prices. The fact that, instead, we have prices continuously rising is a result of governments printing money and increasing the money supply at a rate faster than entrepreneurs can improve the productive capacity of the economy. When they do that, the benefits of investment and productivity growth are transferred from you to someone else.

The Sovereign Consumer

In economics, the consumer is said to be *sovereign*. This means that, ultimately, consumers decide the fates of companies. Consumers have this power because they are free to choose which products they buy and what prices they're willing to pay for those products. If companies can't satisfy the consumer, then they will not survive. Those best able to satisfy the customer will be the most successful. That is, companies don't succeed by being the best at *taking* from their customers.

Real vs. Nominal

The more investment that takes place in an economy, the more productive it becomes and the more stuff that can be produced at lower cost. So, the sovereign consumer is better off (becomes wealthier) even if their wages don't grow, because the price of everything keeps going down. As we discussed earlier, your wealth is determined not by how much money you have but how much stuff your money can buy. If your wages double but the prices of all the stuff you want to buy also double, then you are no better off. Even worse is when our wages rise more slowly than the prices of the stuff we buy. To put it in economic jargon, wages might rise in *money* terms (also known as *nominal*), but if prices of things are rising faster than wages, then wages are falling in *real* terms.

A quick example will help explain. Assume you earn $10 an hour and a small pizza costs $10. That means that you have to work for an hour; assuming no taxes (cue laughter) in order to purchase a small pizza. However, now assume that your wages double to $20, but the price of the pizza triples to $30. Despite the fact that your wages went up in money or nominal terms to $20, they dropped in real terms, because now, after working for an hour, you don't have enough money to buy a pizza. You now have to work for an hour and a half. Putting it into percentages, your wages increased by 100 per cent in nominal terms but decreased by 33 per cent in real terms (your one hour of labour can now only buy two-thirds of a pizza).

Capital and Time

Productivity improvements require investment of capital and time. When Shirley wanted to compete with Bill in the coconut industry, she had to stop climbing trees to collect coconuts and instead devote her time and human capital into using resources to make a tool with which to dislodge the coconuts. Generally speaking, the more capital and time that is invested, the more productive a society becomes. However, a big problem occurs in a world where people increasingly value things right now (consumption) as opposed to later (savings): there is less investment than there should be. Another problem is that people don't see the great things that would have happened had they forgone some consumption and, instead, saved more.[11]

Investment leads not only to productivity improvements but, through innovation, to better and new products. For instance, think how electronic products such as televisions and smartphones have improved over the years. Or how cars and e-commerce have evolved, making our lives more enjoyable. Or how we don't have to go to a video store anymore to pick up a movie (which itself was an improvement on what was available before that); instead, we can stream it at home. Perhaps the most uncomfortable thing about investment is that it takes time and is risky – there is no guarantee of success. The time aspect means one needs to delay consumption today in order to have the chance of consuming more in the future.

Time Preference

In economic terms, someone who has a very high preference for consuming today is said to have a *high time preference*. A person more amenable to delaying consumption is said to have a *low time preference*. As you might imagine, people are widely dispersed along the time preference spectrum. Generally speaking, however, the lower the average time preference of a society, the more capital is saved and invested and the more wealth is created over time. Conversely, in a society with a higher average time preference, less capital is saved and invested and more of it is consumed, and, thus, wealth generation is reduced. Effectively, people with higher time preference will forgo higher consumption in the future for more consumption today, while people with lower time preference will willingly consume less today so they can consume more in the future. In the long run, people who have a low time preference are able to consume more in aggregate than people who have a high time preference.

The Benefits of Failing

As consumers, we all benefit from competition. Yes, some companies and entrepreneurs will lose to other companies and entrepreneurs, but there are two things to note. First, companies that are losing market share are incentivised to invest more into their business to better compete for the consumer. Secondly, the owners will typically have been successful before starting these businesses and were in a position to willingly take the time and risk required to become even more successful. Of course, many entrepreneurs lose everything, but they obviously think it's a risk worth taking, because they do it voluntarily. Perhaps they had a dream of doing something exciting or were tired of working for someone else and considered the risk of losing some or all of their capital to be worth it.

I am directly familiar with the restaurant industry, because I used to own a brewpub. Although I wasn't involved in running the business, I would meet with my pub partners on Saturday mornings to discuss tactics and strategies to drive sales. It was a great experience. However, despite the sterling efforts of all involved, for a number of reasons, the business was a failure financially. But in my case, it was money I could afford to risk. The fact of the matter was that other restaurants and pubs in the area were providing better customer value propositions than we were, and the sovereign consumers were voting with their feet by dining more often at those other establishments. That's capitalism. We were not able to provide a customer value proposition good enough to attract enough customers to turn a profit. The result? We eventually closed our doors. We then sold our assets. Perhaps we'll invest the proceeds in another venture in which we will hopefully do a better job that enables us to keep our doors open. Or not.

This is how the free-market system is supposed to work; the sovereign consumer decides your fate, and, ultimately, everyone is better off. The winners (the ones providing the best customer value proposition) are profitable and are able to reinvest in their business to continue wooing their customers, or perhaps even improve their customer value proposition still further or expand and hire more people so they can offer the same great value to more people. Of course, some people go through economic hardship when their businesses fail, but the thing to do is pick themselves up and try again or get a job working for someone else. I don't think anyone would argue that the central bank should have provided our brewpub with interest-free and, ultimately, forgivable loans, at taxpayer expense, so we could keep our business going. Had such assistance been given us, we may have been able to lower our prices to be more competitive, thus forcing our competitors to lower their prices, perhaps to the point where no one would be making any money. Then there would be less excess capital to reinvest in (what used to be) the winning businesses. Plus, why should the central bank feel it's entitled to transfer wealth from you, the consumer, to us so we can continue to provide a product that, through your actions, you have already told us you don't want?

Short-Circuiting the System

That's the way things are supposed to work. However, for many years, policymakers have stepped in to bail out poor business models and it has accelerated over the last twenty years. Central banks have started bailing out basket-case, value-destroying companies by driving interest rates to zero or even negative and printing trillions of dollars, which steals value from the rest of the society. These companies don't produce enough value on their own, so the central banks transfer your hard-earned capital to them to keep them afloat – to continue their capital-destroying ways. These companies, known as zombies, are increasing in number. Keeping zombie companies alive by driving interest rates to zero or giving them government (taxpayer funded) handouts destroys the capital within industries that would have otherwise been available for investment and, thus, improvements in productivity. If this practice continues, it will result in the eventual zombification of our entire economy.

Better things made more efficiently means that the standard of living should be constantly improving for all of us and each successive generation should be better off than the one preceding it. However, for many of today's younger generation, life is not getting easier, and many of them feel that it will be very difficult to achieve the same sort of lifestyle as that enjoyed by their parents. And, spoiler alert: it's not because the younger generation is lazy or suffers from feelings of entitlement.

Broken Window Fallacy

In 1850, a famous French economist, Frédéric Bastiat, introduced the broken window fallacy to help dismantle the belief that war, or a natural disaster that causes destruction, is, ultimately, good for the economy. The thinking by many back then – like today – was that if things needed to be rebuilt, the resulting construction would spur economic activity leading to the creation of wealth for society. Believe it or not, you still see this sort of thinking when a hurricane is expected to hit an area of the United States. Commentators will often say that the rebuild after the devastation will be a boost to the local economy. It's kind of crazy when you think about it. How can the destruction of buildings be a good thing? But as you may know, or as you will see later, GDP (final spending/consumption) is used by many economists and politicians to determine whether an economy is creating wealth. By this thinking, if spending in the economy increases, that is a sign of a healthy economy. If spending to repair damage caused by a hurricane, results in GDP increasing, one can understand why some people might think that destruction of buildings and infrastructure boosts the economy. People and businesses will have to spend some of their capital, and governments will spend taxpayers' capital to fix houses, factories and roads. And as spending is included in the calculation of GDP, but destruction is not, spending to rebuild will boost GDP.

But, of course, on an overall basis, destruction is very bad for an economy. How could it not be? Any sane person should simply be able to stop there and get on with more important things without needing to delve into it any further. However, the presence of complicated charts and formulas constructed by some economists necessitate more thought to lift the shroud of deceit behind the idea that natural disasters and wars are good for an economy. Part of the confusion arises from the fact that, while destruction is not good for an overall economy, some people benefit from crises; but, of course, they are benefiting only because someone else's capital was destroyed.

The broken window fallacy goes something like this. When you arrive at your bike shop one morning, you discover that the front window has been broken. Perhaps the locals had lost faith in the US paper dollar[12] and were desperate to get their hands on any hard asset they could find for use in barter, and so they threw their local central banker through your shop window so they could steal your bikes. You call Glen from the local window repair company. He comes over to fix the window and charges you $1,000. Note that in this instance, the window repair company doesn't need to hire another person and train them in the art of fixing windows. They just send over one of their existing service people to take care of it, or perhaps Glen himself does the job. Hardly any companies operate at full capacity, and so destruction of limited proportions simply results in higher profits for the entrepreneurs of the industries that do the repairs. Glen's service personnel won't benefit if they are on a salary, but they may earn more money if they're required to work overtime.

Regardless, let's look at what just happened. You had capital in the form of a window that you had previously paid for as well as capital of $1,000 in your bank account. Your capital in the form of a window was destroyed. Then Glen the Glazier replaced the window, but you had to give him your capital of $1,000 that was in your bank. So now you, again, have capital in the form of a window, but you no longer have $1,000 of capital in the bank. That is, you have suffered capital destruction of $1,000. However, Glen, now has an additional $1,000 of capital in his bank account.

So, before your window was broken, we had the following situation:

- One window in your bike shop.
- $1,000 in your bank account.

And, after the broken window:

- One window in your bike shop.
- $1,000 in Glen the Glazier's account.

So, net – net – there was no increase in capital in the local community, and it would be tempting to say that the whole thing was simply a redistribution of wealth ($1,000 from your bank account to Glen's) that made you poorer and someone else wealthier. However, society is worse off, because the time and capital that could have been spent on adding to the economy instead needed to be used to replace what had been destroyed.

When talking about the broken window fallacy, some would point out that you now have $1,000 less to spend. Perhaps you were saving that money to buy a new television. If so, now the seller of televisions is harmed because you can't buy what you had been saving up for. However, the glazier now has your $1,000, and he may be planning on spending that money on something else, perhaps even a television. Thus, from my understanding, a broken window generates economic activity through spending, and GDP rises because of that. However, no net wealth is created; instead, there is a net destruction and a redistribution of wealth within the economy. However, by simply focusing on the *symptom* of GDP, or final spending, one can see how someone could be fooled into thinking that natural disasters or wars might be just what the economy needs to get it back on its feet. One can even imagine a severe hurricane causing significant damage to an area, and, upon hearing that the resulting repairs were causing local GDP to go through the roof, a politician might be tempted to take credit for the hurricane. An economy grows wealthier over time when it creates more capital than is consumed and/or destroyed.

How Much Should People Earn?

One final comment before returning to the concept of money. For many years, there have been people who claim that companies should pay their employees enough so that they can buy the products that they are producing. At first, it may seem intuitive, without thinking too carefully, that if the employees can't afford to purchase a company's own products, then the company won't be able to sell anything it produces. However, that depends on what the company is producing. Should a worker at Ferrari earn enough so that they can purchase one of their cars? All of us should be compensated based on our contribution to the final product. In a free market where there is easy access to information and employees can easily change jobs, then anyone who feels that they're not being fairly compensated can switch employers. I would expect that, generally speaking, most people are paid a fair approximation of their contributions. However, I'm sure that some people are not, as the hassle of changing jobs and/or moving allows some companies to get away with not paying their employees their fair share. On the other side of the spectrum, there are some instances where executives of corporations make far more than their contributions. I'll deal with that later. Okay, now that we've discussed a few things about the economy, it's time to return to money.

ENDNOTES

[1] F. A. Hayek, *A Tiger by the Tail: The Keynesian Legacy of Inflation*, p. 34.
'I cannot help regarding the increasing concentration on short-term effects – which in this context amounts to the same thing as concentration on purely monetary factors – not only as a serious and dangerous intellectual error, but as a betrayal of the main duty of the economist and a grave menace to our civilization. To the understanding of the forces that determine the day-to-day changes of business, the economist has probably little to contribute that the man of affairs does not know better. It used, however, to be regarded as the duty and the privilege of the economist to study and to stress the long-run effects apt to be hidden to the untrained eye, and to leave the concern about the more immediate effects to the practical man, who in any event would see only the latter and nothing else. The aim and effect of two hundred years of continuous development of economic thought have essentially been to lead us away from, and "behind", the more superficial monetary mechanism and to bring out the real forces that guide long-run development.

...It is not surprising that Mr. Keynes finds his views anticipated by the mercantilist writers and gifted amateurs: Concern with the surface phenomena has always marked the first stage of the scientific approach to our subject. But it is alarming to see that after we have once gone through the process of developing a systematic account of those forces which in the long run determine prices and production, we are now called upon to scrap it, in order to replace it by the short-sighted philosophy of the businessman raised to the dignity of a science. Are we not even told that "since in the long run we are all dead", policy should be guided entirely by short-run considerations? I fear that these believers in the principle of *après nous le déluge* may get what they have bargained for sooner than they wish.'

2 Many others have used this scenario over the years.

3 This theory has been controversial ever since it was first stated over two hundred years ago. In fact, a misquote of Say's Law was used by John Maynard Keynes in his watershed book *The General Theory of Employment, Interest and Money*, published in 1936. This misquote, or straw man, helped Keynes convince politicians, and many economists, that demand, not supply, is what drives a healthy economy. This line of thinking has helped get us to the precarious situation of exploding debt, wealth disparity and social unrest in which we now find ourselves. For a thorough and excellent analysis of Say's Law see Steven Kates's *Say's Law and the Keynesian Revolution*.

4 Adam Smith was a Scottish economist from the 1700s whose most famous book was *An Inquiry into the Nature and Causes of the Wealth of Nations* in 1776, commonly referred to as *The Wealth of Nations*.

5 From Nassim Taleb's book *Skin in the Game: Hidden Asymmetries in Daily Life*, Random House, 2018, p. 3.

6 These exchanges happen not because each of you values a fish as equal to a coconut and a litre of water. You value a fish more than anything else, but once you've consumed it, rather than another fish, you would prefer to have a coconut and a litre of water. Therefore, you exchange with Shirley and Jane because you now value more what they have than what you have. And Shirley and Jane are exchanging with you for the same reasons. The economic term for this is subjective marginal utility.

7 This is known as the Cantillon Effect.

8 This has, in part, led to the financialisation of our economy through short-term decision-making that seems to be focused more on symptoms than fundamentals. We discuss this in more detail later.

9 I'm borrowing these sorts of examples from others who have written about this stuff.

10 The money supply did not need to grow, either.

11 This scenario is often referred to as an unprovable counterfactual which is related to a phrase from the great French economist Frédéric Bastiat: '**That which is seen, and that which is not seen.**' In other words what we see are the results of a decision, but what we don't see are the results that would have happened if a different decision had been made. 'Counterfactual' simply means what it says: 'counter to the actual facts of what happened and what is.' It's impossible to know exactly what would have happened had different decisions/directions been made in the past. For example, saying that your life would have been better had you studied one subject at school rather than another is an unprovable counterfactual. Likewise, saying that you would have been happier if you had different friends, or wealthier if you had taken that other job, are all things that you can't prove, because there is no way of knowing in which direction your life would have gone had those other things happened. Of course, this is often used by people to serve their own ends. For instance, rather than admit any role in contributing to a debt-plagued economy with growing wealth disparity and falling productivity growth, many policymakers will tell you that things would have been far worse had they not printed trillions of dollars bailing out Wall Street and transferring your wealth to asset owners. However, as it becomes increasingly more obvious that, instead of things getting better, like the central banks said they would, things continue to get worse in terms of more debt and more wealth disparity, through deductive reasoning, one is able to see what is not seen and realise that things only get better for the very few who benefit from central bank policies.

12 Perhaps after QE 12.

CHAPTER 4
FUN WITH MONEY

So far, we've looked at why money exists and how it facilitates the exchange of things that people are producing, that is, the real economy. Then we explored how money evolved from coins that were minted into a definite weight of a precious metal such as gold or silver into a fiat currency backed by nothing. We then took a little bit of a detour to talk about the economy. In this chapter, we'll touch on few more things about the concept of money that will help make more sense of the chapters that follow.

Money is Not the Economy
As a reminder, money is not the economy. It is what is used to exchange all of the goods and services being produced in the economy: it is a medium of exchange. It also serves other secondary functions. It is a unit of account and, importantly, a store of value of the results of your efforts.

Money is desirable for these reasons. While both money and the production of goods and services are what make the world go around, only an increase in the amount of goods and services being produced (coming from saving and investment) creates economic prosperity. Rapidly increasing the money supply does nothing to foster sustainable economic growth. It merely redistributes wealth and destroys it over the long term.

All the money in the world would not drive an economy forward if people stopped producing things. The only thing money would then be good for then would be to redistribute the diminishing pile of previously produced things. (More and more, we are moving towards this state of affairs). A simple way of thinking about it would be if you were stranded on a desert island and discovered a treasure chest containing a million dollars, that money would be of no use to you (apart from setting it on fire to keep warm, perhaps) unless you survived long enough to be rescued and thus had the opportunity to spend it. Given that your priority would be survival and finding food and building shelter, you'd probably much prefer to have found an axe and a fishing net in that chest. If you were alone on a desert island there would be no function for money to play.

Money: A Store of Value

The amount of money in the system represents, in effect, the value of goods and services that people have produced and have decided to store temporarily in that form. For instance, let's go back to the community from Chapter 1 and assume there is $1,000 in circulation: the blacksmith and the baker both have $50, and the horse breeder has $900. What does that money represent? Fifty dollars' worth of axes, fifty dollars' worth of bread, and $900 worth of horses produced and sold by the blacksmith, baker and horse breeder, respectively. The blacksmith might have made five axes and sold them for $100 each, thus receiving $500. Perhaps he then decided to spend (consume) $450 of that money, leaving $50 to be spent at another time. Thus, he has the value of half an axe stored up in the form of money. Of course, he may have decided to store the value of his axes in forms other than money. For instance, he may have decided to consume only $350. Of the remaining $150, perhaps he decided to use $100 to purchase a small painting, not because he liked it but because he thought it might be a good store of value, that is, he was confident he would be able to re-sell the painting in the future and get his $100 back.[1] After buying the painting, he had $50 left. Thus, the value of the blacksmith's efforts in producing axes would be stored up in a painting worth $100 and $50 of money.

Saved Money is Still Spent

Some people complain that savers don't deserve to earn interest on their savings because they should be spending their money (consuming) to support the economy. They argue that by not spending their money, savers are keeping their productive efforts out of the economy, to the detriment of other people. This way of thinking is wrong because of a confusion between money and real resources and what happens to money that is saved and invested rather than consumed, as well as a misunderstanding of what's required to drive an economy forward.

You receive money for the real resources you helped to produce. Whether you spend your money, put it in a bank account, or tuck it under your mattress, the real resources that you helped to produce are still out there in the economy doing their thing. If you produce a bike and sell it for $500 and simply keep the money in your pocket, the real resource you produced, the bike, is still out there being used by someone. Complaining that you should immediately go out and spend your $500 to purchase a real resource that someone else produced is nonsensical. Spend your $500 on something only if you value a real resource more than you do the $500 in your pocket. You are under no obligation whatsoever to spend your money.

What happens if you don't spend your money? First, we'll assume that you put it in your bank account. Your $500 can now be lent to others who want to borrow money, perhaps to invest it in their business. Thus, by your forgoing consumption today, your money is being put to use (spent) by someone else to help grow the economy. If, instead, you had spent your money on a consumer good, your capital would be gone – you would have consumed your capital and it would no longer be available for investment.

Although consumption is the ultimate end game for all investment, you can't have consumption without investment. The more investment there is today, the more consumption there will be in the future.

Hoarding

Now consider what happens when, instead of putting your $500 in your bank account, you hide it under your mattress. In economics, this is known as hoarding. Your money is now unavailable for someone else to borrow and invest. However, given that around 90 per cent of the money in our system is in digital form and only 10 per cent is in physical form such as banknotes and coins, then at any given time, only a very small fraction of the total money supply is being hoarded. Let's consider what would happen if people started hoarding more of their physical money. The money in circulation being used as a medium of exchange would decrease and, assuming no change in output (stuff being produced in the economy), the prices of the real resources would fall, that is, each unit of money would store more real resources. And as money began to become more valuable, this might encourage the hoarders to start spending their cash.

Stable Money Supply

Another fascinating thing about money is that as long as there is enough of it for people to transact with, there is no need to attempt to calculate what the optimal amount of money should be. What's key for an economy to function most optimally and most fairly is that the amount of money in the system remains relatively constant or grows very slowly. As the economy, through saving and investment, becomes more productive over time – that is, more stuff is being produced – then the prices of that stuff will necessarily fall. The result is that over time your savings and your wages can purchase more. This is how we should all be benefiting from a system that becomes more productive over time, and our kids should be better off than us, and their kids better off than them, and on into the future. It used to be that way, but now it has stopped, even reversed, such that, at this moment, our kids can't hope to be nearly as prosperous as we have been. And the great injustice is that much of the prosperity of my generation was not earned. We were simply lucky to benefit from monetary policy that transferred to us wealth that was, is and will be created by others – in large part, by our kids and immigrants. This is entirely due to the amount of money being pumped into the system at a prodigious rate and the bailing-out of bad behaviour.

As mentioned earlier, if the amount of money in an economy was increased and it was evenly split amongst the people, then there would be no transfer of wealth. Instead, the prices of all things would simply adjust upwards. If there is less money in the system, then the prices of goods would drop.

For instance, in our village example above, we had axes at $100 each. And assume that a loaf was worth $1 and a dozen eggs $5. But instead of there being $1,000 in our economy, say there was only $100. In that case, the prices of everything in the economy would come down by a factor of ten, like this:

Axe:	$10
Loaf:	$0.10
Dozen Eggs:	$0.50

But note that although the *prices* of everything have fallen by a factor of ten, there has been no decline in the *value* of the products. If you are a baker, you can still buy one axe for fifty loaves of bread just as it was when everything was priced ten times higher. Another way to think about it is that you still have to commit the same amount of time and effort to bake the same number of loaves required to buy one axe; nothing has changed. That's because value is determined not by money but by the efforts and productivity of people. This is related to the saying by famed investor Warren Buffett, that 'Price is what you pay, value is what you get.'

Other Stores of Value

As mentioned earlier, you can store the value of your efforts in things other than money. In fact, you can store it in all sorts of things, but perhaps the most widely used store of value for most people apart from money is housing.[2] When you buy a house, you usually do it with borrowed money, and you pay off the mortgage in monthly instalments to the bank over twenty-five to thirty years. Over time, you make a living producing a good or a service that others value, and you receive money in return. Whatever you made that was provided to someone else is now stored up in the form of money. You then take some of that money to pay down your mortgage and, thus, effectively transfer the value of what you produced from money to your house. If you make and sell bikes, then if over the years you manage to pay back the mortgage, you can look at the value of your house as representing many of the bikes you made over the years. Thus, the value of much of what you added to society is stored up in that house.

Most people feel confident about the safety and sustainability of the wealth that they have stored up in a house, in large part because central banks can't print houses like they can money. On the other hand, central banks can, and do lower, interest rates, which benefits you as a homeowner because lower financing costs drive the price of your house higher. However, there is a great injustice here: when interest rates are dropped, homeowners obtain value free of charge from someone else. So, not only is the value of many of your bikes stored up in the value of your house, but the value of a lot of what other people produced also effectively gets stored up there, too. Ideally, if a nurse was buying your house there should be a fair exchange of bikes for nursing service, but because central bankers have driven the price of your house through the roof, the nurse has to transfer to you twice as much nursing service, that is, work twice as long as they would otherwise have had to work, to pay the price. Of course, the house-seller has not done anything illegal, but that still doesn't mean it's fair. Through the dropping of interest rates by the central bank, value has been redistributed from one part of society to another – in this case, from those who don't own a house to those who do. I'll discuss exactly how this works in the chapter on housing.

Money Destruction
Here's another way to think about what money really represents – and what

it doesn't. First of all, imagine that we're in a world in which the money supply remains constant (cue laughter). Secondly, imagine that one day a billionaire takes $10 billion of their cash and piles it into their backyard. What does that pile of money represent? Ten billion dollars of productive efforts, some of it by the billionaire.[3]

What would happen if, in a fit of madness, the billionaire decided to set that whole pile of cash on fire?[4] Obviously, the billionaire would be $10 billion poorer, or, better phrased, $10 billion less wealthy. But what about looking at it from the perspective of the broader economy. What's that impact? There would be $10 billion less money in the economic system, but no real value would disappear, apart from the value of the paper on which the money has been printed. (At 19.6 cents per hundred-dollar bill and 100 million hundred-dollar bills, that equates to $19.6 million.) And I suppose the fire might have made a small contribution to global warming. On the plus side, the billionaire could have invited over a few neighbours to enjoy the spectacle.

So, if there's very little impact on the broader economy and the billionaire is out $10 billion of value or purchasing power, what happened to that purchasing power? Obviously, it must have ended up somewhere else. In burning the money, the billionaire has committed a great humanitarian act by transferring $10 billion in value or purchasing power to everyone who holds money.

To help with the concept, assume that before the billionaire burnt their money, there was a total of $20 billion in the economy, used as a means of exchange and store of value. After the billionaire burns their money, the amount of money in the economy has been cut in half and, thus, money prices of assets, goods and services would also eventually be halved. Therefore, whatever money you hold would double in purchasing power and, thus, it would buy twice as much as it would have before that $10 billion went up in smoke.

Remember that money in itself does not create value. Value is created by people making and doing things (i.e. creating capital). Money just helps move that capital around. So just because the economy's money supply is cut in half doesn't mean that it now takes someone twice as long to make a bike or build a home or give a massage. The prices of everything in society will fall, but the value of everything remains the same. So, the money price of your house may fall, but when you sell it, the money you receive will buy more than it would have before the billionaire's fit of madness.[5]

But the one thing that wouldn't be reduced in money terms is the value of debt outstanding, and that's because a loan is a unique form of financial asset that is contractual in nature. For instance, if you lend someone $1,000, the nominal value of your loan will not change according to the laws of supply and demand. Someone else out there has signed a contract to pay you back $1,000 at some point in the future.[6]

If the money supply is halved, the real value of debt increases significantly, which makes it more difficult to repay. Thus, by burning their money, the billionaire causes two massive redistributions of wealth within society. First, as we have seen, value will be redistributed from them to anyone else who is holding cash. And secondly, value has been transferred from anyone who owes money (borrower or debtor) to anyone who has lent money (lender or creditor). Obviously, if a reduction in the money supply transfers wealth from borrowers to lenders, then of course the opposite must also be true, that is, an increase in the money supply will transfer wealth from lenders to borrowers. In an inflationary environment created by an increasing supply of money, value is extracted from people's savings and wealth and is also redistributed from anyone who is owed money to anyone who owes money . And given that governments have monumental levels of debt, you're starting to get a sense as to why governments are always so keen to expand the money supply so quickly.

Of course, if the world's money supply were to halve, it would lead to a global financial catastrophe. Even a small sustained decrease in the money supply today could topple the financial system, given how much debt is outstanding. As far as I am aware, no one is calling for a reduction in the money supply, just a cessation of its rapid growth.

Stable Money Principle

People who lend money will know that money is being printed and will therefore attempt to offset the annual decline in the value of money by charging borrowers a higher rate of interest. However, for many years, central banks were printing so much money and buying so many assets to drive interest rates down, that lenders couldn't get fairly compensated for the decreasing value of the money that was being used to pay back their loans (see the chapters on interest rates).

I'm not necessarily advocating in this book for a gold standard, despite the fact that I think the world would be a much better place for it. I believe that the starting point matters and that the current fiat fractional reserve banking system cannot be replaced overnight without causing significant dislocations. However, I believe we should move *towards* the principle of a gold standard (hard currency) by slowly, over time, removing the governments' and central banks' abilities to manipulate the supply of money in the system. I really don't know how long an ideal adjustment period would be. If you ask policymakers, they'll first tell you it's a bad idea. But if they did agree with you, they would likely recommend a ridiculously lengthy adoption period (say, fifty years) in the hope that the whole idea would eventually fizzle away. Obviously, it needs to happen sooner rather than later.

It's possible that the current system will, all on its own, provide the very calamity needed to effect change quickly, but, just as it was for the last crisis in 2008/2009, that opportunity would probably be wasted. Regardless, the only way to change our current monetary system, whereby people's capital is slowly and secretly confiscated from them by the policymakers, is for the people to demand that the government stop rapidly increasing the money supply.[7] And in my opinion, whether this new system is a gold standard or a fiat currency that cannot be easily manipulated doesn't really matter. (Actually, the latter might be preferable, if such a system could ever be devised – and trusted.) The economist Milton Friedman believed that a tightly controlled fiat system would be a lot more efficient than the costs of operating with a gold standard. A gold standard requires all the cost, time and effort of digging up gold in one part of the world and shipping it thousands of miles, only to be re-buried in another part of the world. (The United States keeps most of its gold buried deep in the ground at Fort Knox, Kentucky.[8]) On the other hand, Lawrence H. White makes a good case for returning to a gold standard and says that the costs of doing so would be far less than many claim.[9]

Regardless of whether we have a fiat or gold monetary system, it's important that it be hard money whose supply cannot be rapidly increased. As well, there must be strict rules governing what the government is allowed to do in times of *emergencies*. What constitutes an emergency is, of course, subjective, and emergencies always seem to be used by policymakers as excuses to break the rules. Bottom line: the ability of policymakers to easily manipulate the money supply must be removed.[10]

Don't Blame Money

Money is not evil – it is merely a medium of exchange. Evil is a human/moral trait. There is absolutely nothing wrong with the concept of money itself, but there is a lot wrong with how the money system is abused by some who control it and some who use it. Imagine there is no such thing as money and we are living in a barter system where you can only acquire things by directly exchanging one thing for another. You make bikes, which you use to exchange for the necessities of life and the odd luxury. You start working longer hours producing more bikes because you want to have a bigger house, or a nicer car, or take a trip to Europe. To have the means (i.e. the bikes that you can exchange for these items), it's necessary to forgo some leisure time, and maybe you don't get to spend as much time with your family because you're spending more time in the bike shop. Obviously, making more bikes at the expense of leisure activity or family time is a personal decision. Yes, perhaps your family will suffer because you're not around as much and perhaps you're no fun at cocktail parties because all you talk about is bikes. But how does that make bikes evil?

> *Do not impute to money the faults of human nature.*
> – John Wesley

ENDNOTES

[1] Or even more if he had the good fortune of the artist meeting their maker shortly after the paining was bought; the value of a painting often rises once the artist has passed on.

[2] Other forms in which people might store value include stocks, bonds, precious metals, art and exotic cars.

[3] Most billionaires have certainly contributed a lot to society, and I'm sure most of them are decent people. However, for some of them, their wealth far exceeds their actual contributions. Which means that part of their wealth was actually produced and owned by someone else before it was redistributed by central banks to those billionaires.

[4] Dr Robert Murphy discusses this sort of stuff a lot. He helped me in my understanding of these concepts, but he is not responsible for any errors I may have made.

[5] While the value of your money savings would go up, over time your wages or salary would slowly adjust downward to reflect the reduced money supply in the economy. Companies would see the prices of their products or services cut in half and so if the employee wages and salaries stayed where they were before the billionaire torched their money, the companies would be losing a lot of money. Therefore, your income would eventually be cut in half, but because the prices of what companies produce would also be cut in half, you would be able to buy the same amount of stuff with your reduced money income.

[6] Of course, the amount of funds available to be lent out will affect interest rates, and we'll discuss that later on. Also, the current money price of the loan you made can go up and down depending on what interest rates are doing (if interest rates rise, the value of a bond goes down, and vice versa), but as long as you hold it for the length of the contract and the borrower pays you back (i.e. doesn't default), then you'll get back the full money price of your loan.

[7] Related to this is preventing central banks from manipulating interest rates.

[8] One would have thought that Keynesian economists would be very much in favour of all the hole-digging jobs that re-adopting the gold standard would create.

[9] Lawrence H. White, *Better Money: Gold, Fiat, or Bitcoin*. Cambridge University Press 2023.

[10] Many view the cryptocurrencies that have sprung up as hard currency alternatives to soft currency fiat. Of course, they are not widely held (yet), which is a requirement for something to be defined as money. And I suspect that their very success could bring about their demise, as it would likely elicit a response from policymakers. However, I applaud the spirit of cryptocurrencies.

CHAPTER 5

GDP PART 1

IN THIS CHAPTER, I'll describe what GDP is and how it is used to measure the strength of an economy. Then I'll explain why I believe it is often a very misleading measure of the underlying health and productive capacity of an economy, that is, its ability to produce wealth for its citizens. And, finally, we'll look at how focusing on GDP can lead policymakers into making decisions that will diminish an economy's productive capacity over time.

Definition

GDP stands for Gross Domestic Product and the U.S. Bureau of Economic Analysis (BEA) describes it as 'A comprehensive measure of U.S. economic activity. GDP measures the value of the final goods and services produced in the United States (without double counting the intermediate goods and services used to produce them). Changes in GDP are the most popular indicator of the nation's overall economic health.'

On the surface, this makes a lot of sense. By adding up everything produced in a country over a year, you get a sense of not only what a country's economy (i.e. its people) is able to produce but also what the people in that country were able to buy. The more an economy is able to produce, the more its people will be able to use that stuff as means of payment to buy other things. As we discussed with Say's Law, the ability to buy things depends on the ability to produce things. If someone is not able to produce anything, then they are not in a position to purchase anything, because they don't have any capital to offer in exchange.

Intermediate Spendings

You'll notice in the above BEA definition of GDP that *intermediate* goods and services are excluded to avoid double counting. Assume that your bike company sold a bike for $500. That would be included in the GDP number. Or, looking at it another way, a person spent $500 on a good produced by the economy and that was a final sale, that is, the customer bought the bike to ride it (effectively, to 'consume' it over a number of years), not to re-sell it to someone else. However, when you were making the bike, you had to purchase items that were needed to make the bike – things such as metal for the frame, gears, tyres, and spokes. Say you spent $400 on those things. This is intermediate spending. If your intermediate spending were included in the calculation, then it would look as if the economy had produced $900 worth of stuff. But it hadn't. It only produced a $500 bike. Obviously, the frame, gears, tyres and spokes that you purchased are part of the bike, not separate from it.

Companies also make final purchases. For example, when your company buys a pump to inflate the tyres before you sell the bike, that purchase is included in GDP. It was a final purchase; you didn't buy it to re-sell it.

Some GDP Basics

There are three broad methods for calculating GDP, three different ways of looking at the same thing, as they all come up with pretty much the same number: the Production Approach, the Income Approach and the Expenditure Approach. When you think about it, it makes perfect sense that these three numbers should amount to the same thing. As discussed, something can only be purchased with something else that has already been produced. Therefore, it stands to reason that the Production and Expenditure approaches should give the same number. Also, your income is based on other people using the stuff that they have produced, after they have exchanged them for money, to buy things from you or your company. Thus, income equals production equals expenditure. I am going to focus on the Expenditure Approach (final spending) for calculating GDP.

There are four categories of final spending:

1. Personal consumption expenditure
2. Business investment
3. Government spending
4. Net exports of goods and services

Note that government salaries are included in GDP, because by employing people, the government is purchasing service from them in return for pay. Therefore, if the government were to hire thousands of employees to just goof off and push around paper clips all day, their salaries would be added to GDP. In other words, such an increase in the number of government employees would suggest that the productive capacity of the economy had increased when, in fact, no such thing had happened – rather, it just got worse. If, on the other hand, a private company were to hire thousands of employees to do nothing, their salaries would not be added to GDP. However, governments would still like this scenario, because, although their salaries would not be included in GDP, those employees would likely spend the money the company is paying them to do nothing and, thus, they will boost consumption in the economy and contribute to GDP growth. But, obviously, the productive capacity of the economy did not increase, in fact it just went down, because now the company has less to invest in its business to produce more stuff.

As you might expect, the four categories of final spending do not contribute equally to the GDP number. According to the BEA, US GDP for 2023 was broken down as follows:

- GDP: $27.4 trillion
  - Personal consumption expenditure: $18.6 trillion
  - Gross private domestic investment: $4.8 trillion
  - Government consumption expenditures and gross investment: $4.7 trillion
  - Net exports of goods and services: -$0.8 trillion

On a per centage basis, it looks like this:

- GDP: 100%
  - Personal consumption expenditure: 67.9%
  - Gross private domestic investment: 17.5%
  - Government consumption expenditures and gross investment: 17.2%
  - Net exports of goods and services: -2.9%

As you can see, consumer spending makes up more than two-thirds of GDP. What you can also see, which should worry you significantly, is that government spending is similar to that of business investment. Not only that, but only part of government spending is captured in the GDP figure.

Transfer payments such as Social Security and unemployment benefits are not included but instead are largely captured in GDP once those government transfers are spent by consumers. If you include those transfer payments, then government spending is considerably higher than business investment. According to the International Monetary Fund[1], total government spending (including transfer payments) in the United States has grown significantly over the years in not only absolute terms but also as a per centage of the economy.

Government spending as a per centage of GDP over the years:

1900:   2.7%
1950:   13.4%
2015:   35.2%

Spending

Okay, so you might think that this all makes sense and that it's perfectly reasonable for policymakers to monitor the growth of GDP and to believe that the most important factor in driving economic growth is consumer spending. However, this is wrong. Because no one can spend unless things have first been produced, and so, by definition, the most important thing in ensuring an economy can grow is saving, investment and production – not consumption. In other words, it's saving and investment that allows consumption to occur, not consumption that allows saving and investment to occur. Another thing to note is that the vast majority of the capital that the government spends is consumed rather than invested, and the government sources all of its capital from the private sector. Therefore, the larger the government is as a per centage of the economy, the more capital is consumed and, thus, the less capital there is available for the private sector to invest. And, thus, the less productive is the economy.

Because final spending can occur only if there has been sufficient saving and investment, GDP is more a symptom of what is going on in an economy than the fundamental driver. And because policymakers focus more on the symptom of GDP, it can be an extremely misleading measure of the overall health of the economy. This demonstrates a classic error that many people make: they measure what they are able to, or what is easy, rather than what really matters.[2]

GDP Analogy

For many years, I have been using the following analogy with my clients to help explain the hazards of focusing solely on GDP to gauge the productive health of an economy.

Every year, your neighbour buys a more expensive car, puts another addition on to the house, and goes on an even more expensive vacation. This is your neighbour's final spending, or their GDP, and as it's growing every year, policymakers would simply assume that your neighbour's productive capacity must be in good health. Indeed, if your neighbour was increasing their spending every year because their business was producing more and more of the stuff that other people valued, and your neighbour was reinvesting in their business to produce even more stuff in the future, then you would likely have confidence that their final spending (GDP) could continue to grow.

Your neighbour's business has been successful because each year they have been taking a lot of the profit of the business and reinvesting it back into the company to make it even more productive. However, if your neighbour's personal spending started to increase faster than their company could increase its productivity, then there would be less capital available to reinvest in the business. I've seen this happen many times, and I think that the reason some fall into this trap is that when companies first reduce the amount of money they reinvest in their business, there is initially no change in the company's productive capacity or competitive position. Therefore, in the short term, it looks as if your neighbour has figured out how to invest less in their business and spend more on fun stuff. They believe they can have their cake and eat it, too, which is central to the socialists' something-for-nothing mentality. As a result of underinvesting in their business, your neighbour's final spending initially picks up and, thus, their rate of GDP growth accelerates; that is, lower investment has resulted in higher GDP.

However, over time, due to the reduced reinvestment in the business, both the productive capacity and competitive position of your neighbour's business start to suffer, and their business starts to make considerably less money. But your neighbour has to keep reinvesting in the business, otherwise it will stop working altogether. However, this doesn't mean that your neighbour's spending, or GDP will necessarily fall. No, indeed. There is one thing that neighbours all over the world have used to spend more than they earn: debt. Debt pleases policymakers, but borrow-to-consume-today behaviour means that those who are lending you the money and think that they are investing are, in fact not. Sure, you owe them money, but you are not using the money productively so that you can pay them back. You can only pay them back by taking on more debt from someone else. This behaviour has become rampant in developed economies as individuals and governments increasingly adopt the short-term, something-for-nothing, entitled mindset. And they are cheered on by central banks, because, hey, it's good for GDP!

Debt in the Driver's Seat

Because policymakers believe that spending is what drives an economy forward, rather than saving and investment, they extract capital from the productive side of the economy and transfer it to those who will consume it. But every time they do this, the productive side of the economy has less capital than it would otherwise have had with which to produce stuff. Yet the amazing thing about free markets and entrepreneurs is that because of their incredible productive efforts, so far, actions by policymakers have only been able to slow the productive growth of the economy, not eliminate it. However, as productivity growth continues to slow, the danger is that we eventually slip into a structural reverse situation – not a healing recession but, rather, a devastating long-term decline in productivity.

For years, debt has been slowly replacing productivity as the driver of GDP (final spending). In the case of your neighbour, once they get to the point where they can't reduce the amount that they reinvest in their business, they can still keep their spending going by borrowing money. Of course, if you are aware that your neighbour's annual growth in spending is occurring because they're taking on increasing amounts of debt, then you would start to question the sustainability of their GDP. You would assume that eventually they wouldn't be able to borrow any more money – because whoever is lending to them would start to worry that they wouldn't be able to pay them back.

As you know, when you borrow money (e.g. car loans, credit cards), you're expected to pay it back, and you usually do that on a monthly basis. The more your neighbour borrows, the more their monthly debt repayments will rise, until, eventually, they have to borrow more money simply to pay off their previous borrowings. Your neighbour has become a 'zombie'. That term is used to describe companies that have so much debt that their total operating profit is not even enough to cover the annual interest expense on their debt. Zombie companies have to borrow more money to help pay their interest expense. When they see your zombie neighbour reducing their GDP, policymakers will start to panic, because they've convinced themselves that spending is the fount of all economic prosperity and that if your neighbour can't continue increasing their spending each year, then the economy will be in big trouble. Here's how that might play out.

Central Banks to the Rescue

Say your neighbour earns $3,000 per month after taxes (i.e. disposable income). After paying for all their essentials such as rent/mortgage, utilities and food, they have $1,062 left over (i.e. discretionary income: money left after paying for necessities and which they can dispose of as they wish without affecting their basic living standards). They could decide to save that discretionary income (but policymakers wouldn't like that because of their conviction that consumption, not saving/investment, is what leads to a productive economy), or they could spend it on consumption goods (policymakers love that: your neighbour doing their patriotic duty to help the economy), or they could do a combination of the two. On the other hand, $1,062 is just enough money to service a five-year variable rate loan of $50,000 at an interest rate of 10%. (If they were to borrow $50,000, the bank would require them to pay it back over five years at a rate of $1,062 per month.)

Your neighbour decides to borrow $50,000 and use it to renovate their kitchen, build a pool in the backyard, and fly the family to Florida to treat them to a luxury vacation at Disney World. Central banks would like this a lot, as they're going to make a much more significant and immediate contribution to GDP by spending $50,000 instead of spending their measly monthly discretionary income of $1,062. The home renovator, pool company and Disney are all happy; their income has gone up because your neighbour borrowed money from the bank and spent it. And, as many other people are doing the same thing, these companies are all able to report to their investors that they expect their sales to continue to grow. And as demand continues to increase, these companies will all plan to raise their prices.

However, once your neighbour has spent all of the borrowed money, their contribution to GDP declines significantly, because now all of their discretionary income is being used to service the debt. Central bankers don't like this: therefore, when they see your neighbour's GDP starting to decline, they decide to lower interest rates so your neighbour can afford to borrow even more money and spend it and, thus, continue to do their part to help drive the economy forward. By dropping the interest rate from 10% to 5%, their discretionary income of $1,062 would be able to service an additional $9,000 of debt, so now they can borrow some more money. They use that $9,000 to refurnish their basement with luxury Scandinavian recliners and a hundred-inch 4k television – which is good news for the furniture and appliance stores. Now they owe the bank $59,000, and then, again, their spending slows because they can't borrow any more money. So, the central banks lower the interest rate again, dropping it all the way down to 1%.

The lower monthly interest expense enables your neighbour to borrow roughly another $6,000 which they dutifully spend on a hot tub jacuzzi and a swim-up bar for their pool. Again, the central banks have helped put your neighbour in a position to boost the economy. Now they owe $65,000 to the bank. But because interest rates are already about as low as they can get, the central banks can't lower them any further to enable your neighbour to service more debt.[3]

Now, in the real world, banks would not lend your neighbour more money if they knew all of their discretionary income was being used to service existing debt. As you might expect, they would be concerned that they wouldn't be able to pay the money back. But, also, in the real world, if financial institutions won't lend more money to people or companies who already have more debt than they can ever repay, governments and central banks will step in and do it for them or give people money outright. The difference, of course, is that policymakers don't have any skin in the game, and, thus, they have nothing to lose; for you, a taxpayer and saver, the skin they use is yours. Even worse, policymakers are starting to convince themselves that no one's skin is involved.

Slack

When you have millions of people in an economy spending more than they earn, it sends misleading signals to home renovation companies, pool companies, electronics and furniture stores, and resorts like Disney. With their businesses booming, they start hiring more employees and investing more in their businesses. However, this investment in people and equipment is not to improve productivity – it is to expand capacity.[4] When people get to the point where they can't service any more debt, their spending starts to decline, and then all of those businesses will have far more capacity than they need. Central banks call this excess capacity *slack* (i.e. there is all of this excess productive capacity in the economy that's not being used). Those companies may have to start laying off some of their employees. But, as crazy as it might sound, central banks don't believe that the problem is due to companies overexpanding in response to an unsustainable debt-fueled spending spree. They believe it's because there are too many people out there who refuse to spend their savings or who refuse to borrow money and use it to purchase things. In the eyes of policymakers, these people are too stupid, scared, or selfish to spend at the level required to use up the excess capacity that has built up in the economy. Thus, governments (through taxation and debt) and central banks (through printing money) will take your capital and give it to someone else who will spend it to match that excess capacity.

Most GDP is made up of consumer and government spending (85% in 2023), and virtually all of that spending is consumption rather than investment. And all spending is, ultimately, financed by saving and investment that produces capital. When someone produces capital, they can either spend it themselves or lend it for someone else to spend. When GDP rises, it doesn't tell how the spending is being financed: whether by those who created their own capital and can continue to consume or by those who have only been able to consume by taking on more and more debt and are close to reaching their debt ceilings. Thus, it should be obvious that GDP is primarily a symptom of what is happening in an economy, rather than a measure of its cause. Focusing on the symptom won't tell you if the increased spending is due to increased savings, higher investment, and productivity (really good), or less savings, declining investment and more debt (really bad).

Capital Consumption

To recap, all consumption is, ultimately, a result of productive investment; it cannot be otherwise. Your neighbour who borrows to consume and, thus, drives GDP higher is able to do so because of productive investment by someone else that has been transferred to them. The result of such transfers is that more capital in the economy is consumed and less is invested to produce more capital in the future that could then be consumed.

Note that from a *world* perspective, the globe cannot consume more than it produces. Within our world, there are those who consume more than they produce and those who produce more than they consume. Those consuming more than they produce either borrow from savers or are given the money by governments who take it from savers through taxation, borrowing, or printing money. To the extent that governments redistribute wealth through taxation to those in need, I think most would agree that not only is this acceptable but it's also a very good thing (within reason, of course). However, if governments fund consumption by borrowing[5] or printing money such that those who ultimately foot the bill don't realise they're doing so and, thus, don't have any say in the matter, then that is an invasion of property rights. Not only that, but extracting capital from savers and the next generation and giving it to consumers to spend today results in less capital being invested which could then fund more consumption in the future by those who produced it (i.e. savers and the next generation). Thus, the world's ability to continuously increase its consumption steadily declines; that is, the growth in the productive capacity of the global economy is less than it otherwise would have been because more capital is being consumed rather than invested to produce more stuff.

In the United States, if one looks at the 10-year moving average of productivity growth (a moving average helps to smooth the results, as they can be choppy from year to year), it averaged around 2.8% from 1957 until 1971. But the inflationary policies of the late 1960s and 1970s caused it to fall such that, by 1979, the 10-year moving average of productivity growth fell below 2% for the first time. Productivity growth started to rise again in the late 1990s with the advent of the internet, but it collapsed again due to the financialisation of the economy and a central bank policy of deliberately creating a wealth effect to attempt to drive the economy forward. Going off the gold standard in 1971 enabled the United States to continue with their inflationary policies, and I don't believe that it was merely a coincidence that productivity growth started to decline around the same time that they adopted a softer fiat money standard. This change enabled governments to borrow more money and central banks to print money and extract even more wealth from savers and investors and redistribute it to those who consumed more than they produced, thus driving that GDP number higher.

Government's Role Should Be Limited

Policymakers should limit their focus to national defense, personal security, the rule of law, and redistributing wealth to those in need. And they can play a role in coordinating taxpayer dollars to provide things like healthcare, education and building infrastructure.[6] In addition, governments need to help establish the conditions that allow people to do great and productive things. However, many policymakers aren't satisfied with those limited roles. First, the benefits of establishing the optimal conditions for productive investment are not immediate; instead, they can accrue slowly, over years. It's quite possible that the policymakers who establish the conditions for long-term prosperity won't be in power when that prosperity arrives. Secondly, for the most part, it requires policymakers to simply get out of the way. If they were to do that, they wouldn't get much credit for all of the great things that eventually happened in the economy. Even worse, from their perspective, it might be the next government who takes all the credit for all those good things when they happen. Of course, if policymakers were to do the right thing, then the credit for all of the great things happening in the economy would go where it rightly belonged: those producing stuff and doing all the work.

Another thing that causes policymakers to act with a short-term focus is that they've convinced the population that they know what to do to fix an economy. Therefore, when GDP starts to slow, everyone expects the policymakers to do something; and if they don't, and the economy slips into a recession, the policymakers will get blamed for not doing anything to stop it. This despite the fact that a recession is the natural healing process that realigns the malinvestment[7] that previously took place in the economy.

So you can see why governments are very keen to believe economic theories that make them look like heroes by borrowing money and spending it (which the next generation pays for); or by printing money and driving stock markets and housing markets higher (which savers and the next generation pays for). We're all susceptible to believing in anything that gives us the opportunity to take the easy way out or get something for nothing. Thus, when certain policymakers tell us that, yes, we are special, and that we deserve more than we produce, then it's far too easy to jump on board the free-lunch, fairy-tale bandwagon. But nothing comes from nothing, and even though policymakers may create the illusion that such a thing is possible, it always occurs at someone else's expense.

Imagine you're trying to lose weight, and a central banker advises you that to lose weight, you actually need to eat *more* cheeseburgers. That it's all about consumption. Who wouldn't want to hear that? I sure would. Of course, my immediate satisfaction from eating more cheeseburgers will lead to disappointment when I start packing on the pounds. But it's even more alluring for governments who spend and encourage debt-fuelled consumption because the immediate consequences or their actions actually look like they're working: GDP starts rising and more people are hired to deal with the higher spending, and, thus, unemployment goes down. They point to these measures as sure-fire signs that they've fixed the economy – mission accomplished! – but, of course, that rate of final spending is not sustainable because more capital is being consumed than invested. Eventually the spending starts to slow again, because it's not supported by saving/investment/productivity, which then requires policymakers to borrow and print even more money. And so on and so on.

According to the International Institute of Finance (IIF), total global debt reached a record of $250 trillion in 2019. And, remember, that this was after the longest economic expansion in the United States since the Second World War. That is, despite not experiencing a recession for twelve years, government finances were in the worst shape ever. The following figures show how debt has increased in the US as a per centage of GDP, according to the St. Louis Federal Reserve:

- 1979: 31%
- 1989: 51%
- 1999: 58%
- 2009: 84%
- 2019: 106%
- 2023: 122%[8]

GDP has increasingly been driven higher by debt-fuelled spending. This is the consequence of the short-term mentality that focuses on final spending today rather than taking a longer-term view and focusing on investment, which would increase final spending even more in the future, and in a more sustainable manner. Debt grew to such a monumental level only because central banks enabled and encouraged it by driving interest rates to zero and by printing money out of thin air in to purchase government debt. The main interest rate that the US Federal Reserve uses to influence ~~stock markets~~ economic activity is the federal funds target rate. The following history of that rate will help put into context how far interest rates have fallen from their peak over the last forty years:

- June 1981: 19.1%
- June 1991: 5.9%
- June 2001: 3.8%
- June 2011: 0.09%
- June 2021: 0.08%

I have another analogy that I have used in the past, which helps to caution against focusing on GDP.

Another GDP Analogy

Imagine that the head of the US Federal Reserve in Washington, D.C., has decided to ride a horse across the United States. He had received an alarming letter from the head of the San Francisco Federal Reserve. She said that people in California had started consuming less and, instead, they had been recklessly saving and investing more of their money with the result that GDP had started to slow. Each time the Federal Reserve lowered interest rates, people would initially borrow more money and spend it, but after the initial burst, the spending would slow again. The Federal Reserve kept lowering interest rates; however, each time they did it, they got less and less bang for their buck (the amount of debt that was being taken on was resulting in less and less economic growth). This was happening because, increasingly, the debt was not being invested to produce more stuff; instead, it was being consumed. Now, interest rates were zero[9], and they were not able to lower them any further. Of course, the government was also doing its part by taxing savers and borrowing money on the backs of the next generation to keep spending growing, but it was getting to the point where the savers would likely rise up in protest if the government consumed any more of their savings by increasing taxation. And it was getting hard to convince people to lend more money to the government when they weren't be rewarded for doing so (zero interest rates). Therefore, the San Francisco Federal Reserve *had had no choice* but to extract wealth from savers by printing money and using that capital to create a wealth effect by driving stock markets higher. However, while the money-printing had initially resulted in higher stock prices, once she slowed down the printing presses, stocks would start to fall again, requiring her to print even more money. Bottom line was that she was running out of ink. Her letter had ended with the foreboding message that 'Only ink can save us now.'

The head of the U.S. Federal Reserve tells her not to worry. He will personally replenish her ink *reserves*. He announces to the world that he expects to reach San Francisco in about three months. He has calculated based on a horse walking at around four miles per hour. As San Francisco is around 2,800 miles from Washington, D.C., if he rides eight hours a day, it should take him around ninety days to cross the country. (Note that walking cross-country at four miles per hour is an analogy for GDP growth.)

And so, off sets our courageous hero to great fanfare and thank yous from the cheering and adoring crowds. During the first month, news reporters keeping tabs on the central banker's progress report back that he is, indeed, moving at a steady pace of four miles per hour and that salvation for California is on its way. However, starting in the second month, as the horse reaches the Midwestern states of Missouri and Kansas, the temperature starts to rise. Naturally, as a result, the horse starts to fatigue and slows its pace to three miles per hour. Of course, this is a sensible and *natural* thing for the horse to do to help ensure that it can actually keep moving forward rather than overheating and collapsing from exhaustion. And, of course, once it reaches the mountain states of Colorado and Utah, temperatures will cool again, allowing it to resume its pace of four miles per hour.[10] Unfortunately, this means the San Francisco central banker will have to wait a little longer than expected for the economy-saving ink.

News reporters write about this distressing news and politicians start to worry. Of course, the central banker assures everyone that he knows what he's doing. He shows them his complicated financial models that *prove* that the horse should be walking at four miles per hour, not three, even though the temperature has gone up. He simply assumes that the horse is too stupid to know any better and that all it will take is a few swift kicks to quickly bring the horse back to its senses. As you might expect, at first, the horse responds to the spurs digging into its sides and resumes its pace of four miles per hour. Everyone breathes a sigh of relief and congratulates the central banker for getting the horse moving forward again at the appropriate pace.

However, before long, the horse slows down again, but not only that, because it was being forced to walk at an unsustainable pace in the heat, it now slows down to only two miles per hour. Reporters now ask the central banker why this is happening after he had assured them that he knew how to get the horse back up to four miles per hour. At first, he simply states that the reason the horse slowed is that he hadn't kicked it hard enough. It seems that the *neutral rate* of digging his spurs into the horse's sides to get it to resume its pace has gone up.[11] He resumes digging his spurs into the horse's sides until it finally responds.

This pattern repeats – the horse initially speeding up in response to central banker's *spurious* economic doctrine only to then slow once again to an even slower speed. Each time it requires even more vigorous spurring to get the horse back up to speed. When asked why the neutral rate of spurring keeps rising, the head of the U.S. Federal Reserve says that it's the result of equine secular stagnation brought about in part via demographics: the horse is ageing. It never dawns on him that it's because the horse is being forced to walk at a pace faster than its body is telling it is sustainable. Eventually, the horse gets to a point where it has been kicked so often that it simply stops responding.

My Way or the Highway

The economy is a vast and complicated intricate network of billions of transactions happening daily, with billions of people making risk–reward decisions about what to do with their hard-earned capital. People's preferences change; they make mistakes, innovations occur, people retire. And, left alone, it all works incredibly well to relentlessly drive the economy forward. However, its speed will not always be constant, and, indeed, if the economy has been artificially driven forward by central bankers, there may have been times when it may have even needed to go backwards. For instance, in the analogy, say the central banker approaches a deep, wide river with strong currents. The wise thing to do would be to backtrack and find a narrower and shallower spot to cross. But today's central bankers would force the horse into the rushing water to keep it moving forward, which, of course, would risk sinking the economy. And even if the horse did make it to the other side, it would likely collapse from exhaustion on the opposite bank.

Fortunately, the global economy has not yet been kicked to the point of complete exhaustion – but it's getting perilously close. However, central bankers' attempts to drive GDP forward at all costs have so far resulted in monumental levels of global debt, declining productivity growth and obscene levels of wealth disparity. And while this is all bad enough, if we don't change course soon, things will get considerably worse – and the consequences will be catastrophic for all of us.

ENDNOTES

[1] https://www.imf.org/external/datamapper/exp@FPP/USA
[2] This is known as the streetlight effect. People often look only at the most obvious symptoms for an underlying cause because those symptoms are the easiest to identify or measure – even though those symptoms may have nothing, or very little, to do with what's going on. The story usually cited for this is that one night you see a person on the street looking for something, and they are directly under a streetlight. You ask them what they are looking for, and they tell you they're looking for their car keys, which they lost somewhere around the corner. You ask them why they're not looking for them where they lost them, and they say, 'Because the light's better here.'
[3] Interest rates can actually be driven into negative territory by central banks, but that is even more damaging for the productive capacity of an economy.
[4] Note that companies can also increase productive capacity through investments in productivity, but this tends to happen more slowly over time rather than as a response to a sudden jump in demand.
[5] Government borrowing during times of war or limited borrowing for investment purposes are exceptions.
[6] Some feel that these latter services should be the responsibility of the private sector. There are pros and cons to this view.
[7] Malinvestment that occurs as a result of driving interest rates below their natural level and rapidly increasing the money supply.
[8] Note that some of the US government debt is held by government agencies. Netting that out gives you debt in 2023 held by the public as a percentage of GDP of around 97%. However, to the extent that the debt held by government agencies is meant to fund things like Social Security, after netting out that debt, the now unfunded liabilities should be added back to the government's debt pile.
[9] The US Federal Reserve doesn't like to say 'zero'; they always call it the *zero lower bound* (even though other central banks have lowered interest rates below zero), as that sounds a lot more impressive.
[10] Of course, traversing mountain terrain would again slow its progress leading to even more frustration for the central banker, but let's put that aside for a moment.
[11] See Chapter 9 (Neutral Interest Rates).

CHAPTER 6
GDP PART 2

AGAIN, A REMINDER: in my view there is nothing wrong with – and, in fact, I am very much in favour of – the government taking our money to fund welfare programs for those who truly need it, whether temporarily or permanently. But these programmes should be funded through taxation so it's clear exactly how much of your wealth is being taken from you, and so that it's coming from this generation and not the next.[1] And if the government is investing in things such as infrastructure, that's not as bad as just handing out your capital to people or companies that don't need it. Spending on infrastructure facilitates improved productivity in the economy. Of course, that infrastructure investment often ends up being way over budget and takes far longer than first announced. And could be done far more efficiently by the private sector. But still, if government limited their spending to those sorts of things and activities such as defending the country, protecting citizens from each other and enforcing contract law, then the government would contribute far more effectively to the productive capacity of the economy.

Micromanaging

My beef is with governments and central banks trying to *manage* the economy by taking your money and giving it to others to consume, all to achieve the level of final spending that they believe is right for the economy. Perhaps it's because policymakers feel the need to convince themselves that they know what to do and justify their existence and take credit for what is going on in the economy. They'll point to examples of how unfettered capitalism brought the world to its knees, citing the Great Depression and the Global Financial Crisis and how governments and central banks were there to protect the world from the reckless behaviour of capitalists. Yet, both of those economic disasters were caused by governments and central banks creating the very conditions that encouraged such reckless behaviour to occur.

Bad Incentives

By not cracking down when some of the rules of engagement were clearly being broken[2]; by reducing regulations that had been put in place to protect against the consequences of rampant speculation spilling over into the broader economy[3]; by reducing interest rates to allow for monumental debt accumulation by governments, corporations and individuals so that they could keep growing their spending[4]; and by increasing the money supply to drive asset prices higher to create a wealth effect[5], policymakers incentivised bad behaviour by players in the market system. And as we will see, when this bad behaviour came home to roost, policymakers bailed out the bad behaviour that their short-term, GDP-focused, consumption-targeted actions had engendered in the first place. This has set the world on a path toward economic stagnation.

There was plenty of poor and reckless behaviour by corporations and individuals that deserved to be punished through bankruptcy and/or jail time (Note that an unhampered capitalist system wouldn't provide the policies and conditions to encourage such behaviour on a mass scale in the first plus). However, rather than enforce the rules, the rules are often changed and instead the bail-out mentality takes over. This is good for those getting bailed-out but terrible for everyone else and especially for the long-term productive capacity of the economy.

Unfortunately, allowing businesses or individuals to fail can result in a recession. However, a recession doesn't mean that an economy stops; it means that people are spending less than they previously were, as resources within the economy are rearranged to better account for the desires of the consumer. Disinvestment is required in some industries, more investment in others. This is how slack should be taken up in the economy – not by redistributing wealth so that consumers can spend other people's money to keep overexpanded industries in business.

Capital can be misallocated in two ways. First, through entrepreneurial errors – which is a good thing. We have a profit and loss system, and entrepreneurs discover through trial and error how best to satisfy customer wants – and how to do that in the most efficient manner. When there is slack in the economy, it means that entrepreneurs have miscalculated and there needs to be a rearrangement of capital before sustainable consumption (i.e. consumption funded through the creation of capital) can continue at the previous pace. The second way capital is misallocated is through policymakers intervening in the workings of the economy. Essentially, they attempt to prevent the economy from rearranging itself to the new reality and instead reinforce the entrepreneurial errors by allocating taxpayer dollars to take up the slack. Thus, consumption is not funded by the creation of capital but by its redistribution through taxation or the printing of money. Simply transferring the capital from savers (those who don't want to purchase the excess things that are being produced) to those who will purchase those things serves only to perpetuate the imbalances.

Want vs. Demand

Companies take their cues from consumers as they try to predict demand in the future. This is very different from saying that demand drives an economy. Consumers are in a position to demand goods and services because they previously produced goods and services of their own or somehow obtained capital from someone else who did. Therefore, it is saving and investment that ultimately drives demand (no saving and investment, no demand). To make it clearer, remember: *want* is not *demand*. For instance, most males between twenty and thirty years of age would probably love to own a Ferrari. However, the demand from that age group is very low because few of them have produced enough stuff to give them the wherewithal to demand one.

Shop 'Til You Drop

However, policymakers are still convinced that they need to take actions that help stimulate demand and get people to spend more money. But people hardly need to be encouraged into spending more money. The problem we have is the exact opposite: people need to be encouraged to save and invest more. *That* is what will boost the future productivity of the economy. However, the short-term, immediate gratification attitude that has been with us for so many years seems to be getting worse. And now we have come up with fun acronyms such as FOMO (fear of missing out) or YOLO (you only live once), that seemingly justify the reckless behaviour:

- Are you sure you want to take on so much debt to buy that expensive car?
- YOLO.[6]

Tariffs

One method that policymakers use to boost GDP is to impose tariffs on foreign goods. A tariff is essentially a tax placed on foreign goods coming into the country. The idea is that if US consumers have to pay more for foreign goods, they'll be more inclined to buy the goods of US producers; and, thus, this will help grow GDP[7].

While there can be a number of knock-on effects from imposing tariffs, in my opinion they are generally a net negative. For instance, say your bike company sells bikes for $500 apiece. An Italian producer makes bikes of similar quality but more efficiently than you, and they sell them for $400. All of a sudden, your sales start to decline as the sovereign consumer seeks out the best customer value proposition (deal), and it's not yours.

You lay off some of your employees and complain to your local politician that if you continue losing sales, you'll have to lay off more employees. Those out-of-work ex-employees will then have less money to spend, which is not good for GDP. So, the government imposes a 50 per cent tariff on the importation of Italian bikes; the government adds a tax that increases their price by $200 ($400 × 50% = $200). Now it will cost $600 to buy an Italian bike.

Of course, your sales start to rise again, and you re-hire the employees you had previously laid off. Not only that, but the US government gets to collect $200 in tax for every Italian bike sold in the United States – even though the tax revenue would likely be minimal, as far fewer people would be purchasing Italian bikes.[8] On the surface, it seems as if this is good for the United States. It comes at the expense of a few Italian bike manufacturers, but who cares about them? But, of course, the other victims in all of this are US consumers, who now have to pay $100 more for a bike than they would otherwise have had to. That's $100 that the US consumer could have spent on other goods or saved and invested, thus contributing to the productive capacity of the economy.

Another situation could be that some Italian manufacturers are producing bikes that are far superior to yours or any other bike made in the US and, even though they cost more than yours, consumers are willing to pay for them. Tariffs can be slapped on these products, too, forcing consumers to pay more – even if there is no US-made bike of similar quality.

A recent example of this occurred in 2019 when the US put a 25 per cent tariff on many European wines including most from France and Spain. The resulting higher costs that US consumers had to pay for French and Spanish wines meant wine imports from those countries fell significantly in 2020. Not good for their GDP.[9] Policymakers just assume that if you put tariffs on French wine, Americans will simply switch to American wine. That's good for sales and employment in the US wine industry. But it's not good for those consumers who prefer to drink Bordeaux or Châteauneuf-du-Pape rather than a Californian Cabernet Sauvignon or Pinot Noir. Some of the best wines in the world are produced in California and other US states, and they don't need *protection*. Lower-quality wines would benefit from tariffs, but that would mean the government was forcing Americans to drink wine of a lower quality than they desire.

Tit For Tat

In response to one government placing tariffs on the importation of another country's goods into their country, the government of the affected country will typically retaliate by placing tariffs of their own for goods going in the other direction. This is what happened in the 1930s after the US government-imposed tariffs on imports via the Smoot-Hawley Tariff of 1930. Other countries responded with their own tariffs on US goods. And global trade came to a standstill. Many people blame this Act for precipitating and prolonging the Great Depression of the 1930s.

Consumers should be given the choice to buy whatever products they want regardless of whether those products are produced in the United States, or Italy – or any other country, for that matter.[10] Tariffs protect local jobs in the short term but harm the economy in the long term; again, the short-term mindset combined with *that which isn't seen* (*Bastiat*), makes tariffs very popular with policymakers. Tariffs protect local manufacturers who either produce inferior products or charge consumers higher prices for things others can make more cheaply.[11]

As you can imagine, tariffs are also a disincentive for local manufacturers to reinvest in their businesses to make better products at lower cost, because a large part of the competition has effectively been eliminated by the government. In the case of bike tariffs, the Italian makers might be encouraged to reinvest even more in their businesses to manufacture the same quality bike at an even lower price. But then the government would simply increase the tariff again to ensure local bike manufacturers remained 'competitive'. Tariffs disincentivize investment in the country which imposes them and incentivises investment in the countries that are targeted by them.[12]

No Tariffs

If the government didn't step in to protect your bike business by slapping a 50 per cent tariff on the evil Italians, then one of several things would have happened. Your sales would have continued to decline, and, eventually, you would have gone out of business, because consumers would rather have spent their money on better-made bikes. Or perhaps your sales might have simply declined and stabilised at a lower level, which would have necessitated your letting go some of your staff. Or, finally, you might have chosen to reinvest in your business to make better bikes to compete with those cool bikes arriving from Italy. Of course, if you were successful, the final scenario would have led to higher sales for your business and greater employment, and your customers would have benefited from having been able to purchase either higher-quality bikes or similar-quality bikes at a lower price.

This is how capitalism works. Again, the sovereign consumer ultimately decides what products to purchase, and at what prices, and, in this way, they decide the fates of businesses. However, a business can influence the consumer by providing a great and/or improving customer value proposition. In this way, if a capitalist system operates unhampered by government policies such as tariffs[13], the consumer wins through more and better choices at lower prices (i.e. good deflation). And, of course, the same can be said for cheese, cars, clothing and any other economic good.

One thing about good deflation that results from productivity improvements and competition is that it doesn't make debt outstanding prohibitively more expensive – unlike the 50 per cent deflation we saw earlier that was caused by a drop in the money supply (when the billionaire burnt his money). First, if prices are falling due to productivity improvements and competition, that will happen very slowly. Secondly, it doesn't mean that the wages of workers are falling or that company profits are falling. Therefore, both workers and companies would be able to continue servicing any outstanding debts that they might have. Also, in a world of good deflation, interest rates on debt would be lower because they would no longer need to account for inflation or debasement of the money that has been lent.[14]

Absolute Advantage

Countries have differing natural resources, weather and histories. Therefore, they tend to specialise in certain areas: think Germany and beer, France and wine, Scotland and Scotch whisky (quite the booze theme here).[15] We all benefit from countries specialising in what they do best when we trade with those countries. Why shouldn't we benefit if other countries can produce certain things better or cheaper than we can (this is known as *absolute* advantage). Our country will be better at producing in other select industries, and we should focus on producing those things.

For instance, assume that in the desert island economy, you and Shirley each spend half a day catching fish and half a day collecting coconuts. Shirley's production at the end of the day is ten fish and fifteen coconuts; your's is twelve and ten. Thus, total production would look like this:

	Fish	Coconuts	Total Goods
Shirley	10	15	25
You	12	10	22
Total Island Economy	22	25	47

However, you would both be better off if you each spent the whole day focused on your absolute advantage (what you do best) and then traded with each other. Shirley can now collect twice as many coconuts. And you can double your catch of fish. That scenarios would look like this:

	Fish	Coconuts	Total Goods
Shirley	0	30	30
You	24	0	24
Total Island Economy	24	30	54

Thus, by focusing on your respective absolute advantages, you and Shirley are able to increase the productive capacity of the island economy from forty-seven to fifty-four units (total fish goes up by 2 and coconuts by 5).

You and Shirley then trade with each other and agree on a fair exchange ratio of fish for coconuts. Perhaps you decide on a ratio of 1.25 coconuts for one fish. Each of you could now consume the following:

	Fish	Coconuts	Total Goods
Shirley	12	15	27
You	12	15	27
Total Island Economy	24	30	54

Shirley started off consuming ten fish and fifteen coconuts. But now, by focusing on her absolute advantage and then trading with you, she maintains her coconut consumption but can consumes two more fish. Meanwhile, you also maintain your fish consumption (twelve) but increase your coconut consumption by five.

Comparative Advantage

Now, it's quite possible that Shirley is better than you at catching fish *and* collecting coconuts. The amazing thing about this situation is that it would still be in both your best interests to focus on one thing and then trade, but it only works if Shirley focuses on her *comparative* advantage.[16] Although Shirley has an advantage over you at both fishing and collecting coconuts, her advantage in fishing might be greater than her advantage in collecting coconuts. If Shirley were to focus on fishing and you collected coconuts and then you exchanged with each other, you'd both be better off.[17]

Note that in terms of trade, there may be certain exceptions where, due to concerns about national security, countries will always want to have certain things produced in their own country even if others could produce them more efficiently. Also, some disapprove of letting too much of what they need being produced in other countries, as that can mean job losses at home for the affected industries. And, to be sure, many people have been negatively impacted by this over the years. For example, back in the 1970s and 1980s, much of the UK's coal production and US steel production disappeared and the supply of those items went to countries that could produce them at a much lower cost. This was particularly difficult for the coal miners and steel workers who lost their jobs. And while it's easier for younger workers to go back to school or retrain for other industries, it's not quite as simple for older workers. In those cases, governments can help those affected with taxpayer dollars, while taxpayers benefit from cheaper coal and steel. The alternative is to keep those jobs at home with the rest of society having to pay for it through higher prices than they would otherwise be paying.

You Can't Spend Your Way to Prosperity

Here's another way to think about why relying on the symptom of GDP to gauge the health of the economy is a bad idea. How can final spending that is consumed rather than invested cause overall wealth to grow? Do you find that spending and consuming more money now increases the amount of money you have to spend the following year? I'm guessing you probably figured out long ago that spending more of your money today results in you having less of it tomorrow, not more. It's common-sense economics. It's exactly the same for an economy, despite the efforts of some people to convince you otherwise.

Of course, it would be great if we could consume our way to riches; spending money is a lot more fun than saving and carefully investing it, or working for it. However, policymakers will tell you that the more money you spend, the more income you provide to other people, as if it's somehow your duty to spend your hard-earned income on products and services you don't want to buy so that someone else has an income. And if you refuse to spend your savings, policymakers will take it from you in one form or other and give it to someone else who will.[18] Regardless, they will then tell you not to worry, as the benefits of others spending your capital will eventually trickle down to you.

It won't.

The way policymakers describe it, we can, supposedly, all happily spend our way to Nirvana.

We can't.

Seed Corn

An analogy that is often used by economists is a farmer who has seed corn.[19] The farmer can do a few things with the corn. First, they might decide to plant all of their seed corn; however, if they did that, they'd starve before they had the chance to enjoy any of the next year's abundant harvest. Secondly, they could decide to consume it all. This would be a lot of fun in the short term, especially if they're planning to consume some of it in the form of bourbon.[20] However, if they did this instead of planting it, they wouldn't have any corn (or bourbon) next year. Thirdly, the farmer could, and likely would, decide to consume some of the seed corn and plant the rest to ensure they have enough corn again the following year to consume and replant, thus striking an optimal balance between consumption and savings/investment (and maybe a bit for bourbon).

Importantly, a ratio of consumption to savings/investment that is optimal for one farmer may not be so optimal for another. While all of us prefer consumption today rather than at some point in the future, the degree of that time preference varies from person to person. A farmer with a high time preference has a high preference for consuming things earlier and would, thus, plant less corn compared to a farmer with a low time preference. Obviously, how much they consume and invest (plant) is a personal decision, and no one has a right to dictate that ratio or chastise a farmer for their preference. However, policymakers look down on savers and applaud consumption because saving doesn't help boost today's GDP number.

Regardless, it stands to reason that the more corn a farmer saves and plants (i.e. the more consumption that the farmer is willing to forgo today), the more the farmer will have next year. This is the essence of the consumption vs. investment decision. The more you consume and the less you save/invest today, the less you can consume in the future.

Unfortunately, the more you save/invest, the more the government will take from you. In the case of the farmer who consumes less corn and plants it instead, the following year, the government will take more corn in the form of taxation. Each year the farmer plants and harvests more corn, the government will take more. And note that if the government hadn't taken so much corn from the farmer, even more corn could have been produced in following years.

In an ideal world, the corn taken from the farmer would be used to help pay for services such as the army, police, courts, infrastructure and welfare programmes for those truly in need. Governments can also tax to help fund medical expenses and retirement benefits such as social security.

Not Satisfied

However, governments are rarely satisfied with these important, but limited, roles. Instead, they take more of the farmers' corn to stimulate consumption by others. These other people are not hungry, but every time they consume, it boosts the GDP number, which the government will use to show that it is doing a good job managing the economy. As governments haven't yet figured out how to print corn, they will simply increase the tax on the productive farmer and take more and more of their corn such that the farmer would have less and less to plant every year. And then each year there would be less and less corn for the government to tax away from the productive farmer.

Consider the scenario where one farmer saves/invests/plants a lot of their corn for future consumption and then sells a bunch of it to other people, and a second farmer consumes all of their corn today and saves/invests/plants nothing. (I guess if they're not planting anything, then they are not really a farmer anymore, but bear with me.) The next year, the second farmer is in big trouble because they don't have any corn, so they go to the government begging for help. As the government doesn't produce anything and, therefore, doesn't have anything of its own to give, it goes to the first farmer and takes some of their corn to give to the second farmer to consume. This makes the government very popular with the second farmer. Now the first farmer has less corn to save/invest/plant, and, thus, there is even less corn harvested in the third year. But a big problem now is that, by the third year, the second farmer has become permanently reliant on the government redistributing corn to them from the first farmer, and so there is no incentive for the second farmer to save/invest/plant any corn at all. But as the first farmer had less corn to save/invest/plant in the second year, less corn is produced, and so, with part of that reduced harvest again being redistributed to the second farmer in the third year, there is even less corn for the first farmer to save/invest/plant and, thus, harvest in the fourth year.

Things Should Be a Lot Better

This is what happens when you constantly siphon capital from those who would put it to productive use and give it to those who only consume. Less stuff is produced than there otherwise would have been. This is not a free market and is what we have been moving towards.

The ingenuity, entrepreneurial spirit and work ethic of most people are so strong that the economies of free-market societies have been growing at healthy rates ever since they adopted that system. This is the best system we know of to transform these great human traits into productivity growth that benefits everyone. And despite central banks distorting this system in favour of asset prices (and asset holders); and despite governments increasingly channelling capital from producers to consumers, developed economies still continue to grow. They're just not growing nearly as fast as they used to, or should be. And those who are doing the producing have to work that much harder than they would otherwise need to if central banks and politicians were not increasingly part of the equation. Perhaps we would be down to a three-day working week by now.[21] The problem with taking more and more from producers of capital and giving it to those who just consume it is that both parties are disincentivised from working. The producers see less benefit in working, and the consumers no longer have to.

We All Lose

With fewer people working, a lot less capital is created. This leads to less housing, less healthcare, less education, more conflict and less human flourishing. And there is less to redistribute to those who truly need it. I know this sounds obvious; that's because it is. Of course, policymakers refuse to admit that their efforts have in any way led to the slowing productivity growth, gargantuan debt load and obscene wealth disparity. Instead, when things don't turn out the way they said they would if they stimulated demand, they conjure up excuses, citing things they claim have come out of left field. They use sophisticated words to give their excuses credibility, such as global secular stagnation, or global savings glut. Sometimes they claim that their demand stimulus didn't work because they didn't do enough of it. As we get into the chapters on the housing and stock markets, you'll get a better understanding of why productivity growth has been slowing for decades and how central banks are primarily responsible for growing wealth disparity.

> *There is no opinion, however absurd, which men will not readily embrace as soon as they can be brought to the conviction that it is generally adopted.*
>
> – Arthur Schopenhauer

Wilful Blindness

Once enough people believe something to be true, it takes on a force of its own and is readily adopted by the populace, despite the fact that whatever is being put forward may be completely bogus. This is especially true if those spreading the fallacious ideas are authoritative figures, for example, central bankers who use sophisticated terminology that most people don't understand. It's related to *argumentum ad verecundiam* (appeal to authority). This is powerful stuff. In fact, simply reading that phrase makes you immediately want to believe anything that comes next. Now imagine that you are told that a particular economic doctrine espoused by well-known authority figures that is supposed to be good for the overall economy will just happen to also drive the price of your house and investment portfolio significantly higher. Well, it's game, set and match: the policymakers have won you over to their way of thinking, at least for a while. But over time, people start to understand that something doesn't add up. Yes, I did benefit from the government sending me a stimulus cheque, and I did benefit because central banks reduced interest rates to zero and printed money, thus driving higher the value of my house and my stock portfolio. Yet, why do I seem to be working harder than ever before and not getting anywhere. Or why can't I find a decent job? Why do I have so much debt, and how will I ever pay it off? Why do the rich seem to get increasingly richer? Why is it that most of the next generation cannot even dare to dream about owning a home one day?

This is all happening because of the mistaken belief that consumption is responsible for all economic prosperity – that consumption leads to all that's good in this world.

Gross Output

Of course, final spending is not all the spending that takes place in an economy, just as the people employed in making final sales are not all of the people employed in an economy. There is also the *intermediate* spending that takes place between businesses as products move along the supply chain towards the final good. There is another, much more comprehensive measure of what is going on in an economy that captures this intermediate spending: gross output. This measure has been championed by Mark Skousen for many years.[22] However, only in recent years has the government (Bureau of Economic Analysis) begun to report gross output alongside GDP.

For the year 2023, US GDP and its breakdown were as follows (all numbers in billions):

GDP: $27,361[23]

- Personal consumption expenditure: $18,571
- Gross private domestic investment: $4,844
- Government consumption expenditure and gross investment: $4,745
- Net exports: -$799

Total gross output was $47,837 billion[24] and GDP is included in that number. Subtracting GDP from gross output gives the value of intermediate spending: $20,476 billion. Thus, if we add the final investment from the GDP number of $4,844 billion to the intermediate investment of $20,476 billion, we get total business spending of $25,320 billion.

Investment Drives the Economy
Thus, total business spending in 2023 was 53% of the total gross output of the US economy.

Here are all the contributions to the total gross output:

- Business spending/investment: 53%
- Consumption: 39%
- Government: 10%
- Net exports: -2%

Note that government spending is actually a much higher per centage of the spending in the economy than 10%, as GDP and gross output do not include the money government spends on things such as Social Security and Medicare. According to the IMF, by 2015, total US government spending as a per centage of GDP was 35.2%.[25] In the 1950s, this number was less than 20%; thus, the much stronger economic growth back then.

Some criticise gross output because it suffers from double counting. But as Mark Skousen says, the double counting is necessary because the nature of a product changes as it moves through the production process. Gross output gives one a much better sense of what is leading to the final value being created, that is, how much business spending and, thus, employment is happening further up the supply chain. Skousen likens this to analysing the health of a corporation. For instance, you wouldn't simply look at the gross profit to assess whether or not the company was in good shape; you'd also want to know how sales are doing.

In summary, the capital used for final spending can be obtained in two ways. It can be obtained through work, savings and productive investment, or it can be obtained by having it transferred from someone else (e.g. via charity, borrowing, theft, taxation or money printing). And as we've also seen, if final spending is a result of productive investment, then it will be sustainable and even grow. However, if consumption is increasingly a result of capital simply being redistributed from the productive side of the economy, then that higher consumption comes at the cost of less stuff being produced in the future. Savings, investment and productivity are the 'seed corn' of all consumption. Therefore, it stands to reason that the less capital that is available for those things, the slower the economy will grow.

We will soon take a deeper dive into some of the methods that policymakers have used to keep that GDP number growing at all times and all costs. But before we do that, it's time to talk about capital.

ENDNOTES

[1] Any kind of government welfare programme, including Social Security and Medicare should be self-funding and not a pyramid scheme that requires an ever-growing population of next generations to fund the previous ones. (See the chapters on government).
[2] An example being NINJA loans during the Global Financial Crisis: no income, no job, no assets.
[3] For example, the Glass-Steagall Act.
[4] Policymakers believe that as long as all of that debt-fuelled consumption doesn't lead to inflation, then it's a very good thing. It's not.
[5] The finance industry likes to describe lowering interest rates and printing money as *easing financial conditions*.
[6] Another popular term is *doom spending*.
[7] Net imports detract from GDP; net exports increase it.
[8] Sometimes a government will subsidise its local manufacturers if their products are being subjected to tariffs by another country.
[9] COVID may have also impacted these numbers.
[10] Assuming, of course, those countries aren't using child or slave labor, and/or are meeting reasonable environmental standards.
[11] A case can be made for imposing tariffs on goods from other countries that are benefiting from government subsidies. On the other hand, others would say that if other countries are willing to subsidise production, which effectively means their taxpayers are paying to lower the prices that we pay for their goods, then why shouldn't we let them do so? However, that might impact employment in those industries in our country. That discussion is beyond the scope of this book.

12. On the other hand, there are instances where imposing tariffs can encourage foreign manufacturers to build a plant in the country imposing the tariffs which would lead to greater investment in that country.
13. It should be noted that a *hampered* capitalist system is, by definition, not capitalism.
14. If we did get to a point where productivity growth was so significant that it resulted in a contraction over time in wages in nominal terms, but it was still rising in real terms (adjusted for deflation), then it would likely happen very slowly, making debt service manageable.
15. I got these examples from Thomas Sowell's great book *Social Justice Fallacies*. Published by Basic Books: 2023.
16. Also known as the Ricardian Law of Comparative Advantage after nineteenth-century British classical economist David Ricardo. However, American economist Murray Rothbard believes that Ricardo's fellow classical economist James Mill was the one who first recognised this law.
17. The math starts to get a little complex, but you can find examples of the benefits of comparative advantage by searching on the internet.
18. This is somewhat related to the 'the euthanasia of the rentier', as proposed by John Maynard Keynes. In his mind, better to take interest rates to zero and thus eliminate the ability of savers to earn a return on their capital. Perhaps it was due to his short-term approach (In the long run, we're all dead). In other words, better to get people to spend/consume and use up the slack in the economy than allow market derived interest rates to best allocate scarce resources which will allow for the greatest production of capital in the future.
19. I always wondered why they called it 'seed corn' rather than 'corn seed'. Seed potatoes is another one. On looking it up, I think it might be because the seed is the vegetable itself, rather than the seed being inside or part of the vegetable, that is, to grow corn or potatoes, you plant an actual kernel of corn or a potato. But I'm still not sure. However, I did discover another definition for seed corn: a type of corn you get on the bottom of your foot. (The learning never stops.)
20. It actually takes a couple of years to turn corn into bourbon, so the party would have to wait.
21. Some companies are experimenting with a four-day work week – despite, not because of, policymaker actions.
22. See Mark Skousen's website www.grossoutput.com, as well as his book *The Power of Economic Thinking*, pp. 175–178. Foundation for Economic Education: 2002.
23. https://www.bea.gov/sites/default/files/2024-03/gdp4q23-3rd.pdf
24. https://www.bea.gov/sites/default/files/2024-03/gdp4q23-3rd.pdf
25. https://www.imf.org/external/datamapper/exp@FPP/USA

CHAPTER 7

CAPITAL

Definition

There are various definitions of the word 'capital'. I like to think of capital as anything that you produce – a good or a service – that other people value. To get their hands on your capital, these other people also need to produce some form of capital that others will value so they will have something to offer you in exchange. Let's go back to the bike company example. Assume for a minute that we're in a direct exchange barter economy with no money. The bikes that you make are your capital, and this capital gives you purchasing power that you can either spend or save. You might decide to exchange some of your bikes for consumer goods such as clothes or food. This is known as capital consumption; your capital (bike) has gone. On the other hand, you could save your capital (i.e. capital accumulation) and then use it to purchase capital goods. For instance, if you saved a hundred bikes, you could exchange them for more equipment that you could use to make even more bikes (grow your capital).

Exchanging Capital

As we saw earlier, a barter economy (direct exchange of goods) of any size cannot function very efficiently; instead, we have a system of indirect exchange in which money is used as the medium of exchange. Instead of exchanging or saving your bikes (capital) directly, you sell your bikes to your customers, and they give you money in exchange for the bikes. Your customers created their own capital (shoes, bread, whatever) and exchanged it for money. Now your capital is in the form of money instead of bikes; the value of the money represents the value of the bikes you created. Your willingness and ability to build bikes that people wanted to buy gave you the wherewithal to go out and purchase other things. The bikes are your means of payment; the money is simply the method of transmitting your means of payment.

This is where the trouble starts, because as soon as you store your capital up in the form of money, it becomes vulnerable to others taking it from you without your permission and giving it to someone else.

As we saw earlier, when the supply of money increases, the money price of capital rises (inflation), or it doesn't fall as much as it should (good deflation). We also saw that the production of goods and services (capital) is what increases the wealth of an economy, which can only happen when people decide to save their capital and invest it and, thus, contribute to the production of yet more capital.

Money Is Not Capital

Money and capital are not the same thing.

An important distinction between money and capital is that capital, in whatever form, eventually gets used up or consumed, while money does not. If you create capital and exchange it with someone else, they will consume that capital either immediately or slowly over time. For instance, if you build a bike and sell it to someone else, they will use up that bike over a number of years. However, the money you receive in return for the bike does not get used up. You will use it to purchase capital from someone else. Then that person will use that same money to buy capital from another person, and so on.

Money has value only if capital is effectively stored up in that money. People will willingly store their capital in money only if that money is a widely accepted medium of exchange, that is, if a large number of people are willing to use it to exchange their capital. And it should be obvious by now that printing more money does not increase the wealth of an economy, because no matter how much money is printed, it does not increase the amount of capital being produced; all it does is increase the prices of all of that capital. The price of capital goes up not because the capital became more valuable all of a sudden but because the money in the system became less valuable. And that's because the more money that's printed, the less capital is stored up in each unit of money (i.e. the capital gets diluted).

As asked earlier, if you were on a desert island, would you rather have money or capital (axe, food, fishing net, clothing)? Most people who found themselves on a desert island would immediately go about finding and creating capital, for example, building some form of shelter and finding food and water. A central banker who washed up on shore wouldn't have the foggiest clue about creating capital other than building a machine to help them print money. But as their final product of money cannot be consumed in any way, and if there is no one on the island to exchange with anyway, the central banker would soon perish. If there was someone else on the island, that other person would be unlikely to exchange some of their capital for the central banker's money. This is because the money would not be representative of any capital that the central banker had created; it would have no capital stored up in it because the central banker had done nothing to earn that money and had acquired it while contributing precisely zero to the island economy.

It's the same today. When central banks print money to buy government debt, which the government then uses for spending or handing out cheques, the government has made no contribution to society and, therefore, did not earn that money. Thus, that unearned money obtains value only by extracting capital from everyone else's money.

Consuming Your Capital

Another way to think about it is to consider what happens when you go out to a restaurant and use money to buy yourself a meal. You had earlier made a bike and sold it to somebody in exchange for money. The capital of the bike you made is now stored up in that money. You go to the restaurant, where you order a meal and eat it. Effectively, what you have consumed was the capital that you had temporarily stored up in money (the bike that you had previously built and then sold). Once you've finished your meal, it is gone and cannot be eaten again. Meanwhile, the restaurant provided you with its capital in the form of a meal, as well as the service and ambience that came with that meal. You exchanged your capital for the restaurant's capital, which you then consumed. The restaurant now has the value of the capital that it provided (meal, ambience and service) stored up in the money you exchanged in return for your meal. Your capital has been consumed, but the restaurant now has your money and they are using it as a temporary store for their capital.

The same thing goes for most of the other diners in the restaurant. They are able to consume capital (meal, service, ambience) produced by the restaurant because they themselves have previously produced capital in some form, then they sold it and now have their capital stored up in their money. One table might have a nurse and teacher, another a construction worker and a software engineer, another a pilot and a customs agent, and another an insurance agent and a security guard. All of them have created their own capital by providing a useful product or service valued by other people in the economy. Those other people were willing to use their money to acquire those goods and services and their money had been obtained by exchanging with someone else the capital that they had previously produced.

When the market system is working properly, people have capital only because they first created it and then exchanged it for someone else's capital – and the exchange took place in the form of money. Everyone benefits from their and everyone else's productive efforts.

Obtaining Capital

However, in our restaurant example, there will likely be a few people dining there who did not create any capital, yet they still have capital with which to pay for their meal. That's because their capital was produced by someone else (for example, you). Unfortunately, people are increasingly able to get their hands on capital without first producing any themselves, and they do so because it's a lot easier that way. The more that people focus on getting capital from others (even fairly) rather than creating it themselves, the less productive the economy becomes. This is getting to be a real problem. The market system has morphed into something quite different from what it used to be. Increasingly, people are relying on capital being redistributed in the system rather than trying to create it. Not only that, but some people have become extremely wealthy from this capital redistribution, which, of course, has come at the expense of everyone else.

People can obtain capital from you and others without offering any of their own capital in return. This is done in several ways – some through coercion; some with your consent; some through luck; some through violence; and some without your knowledge.

Here are some ways people can obtain capital without creating it:

- The government taxes you and hands your capital to others. (You don't really have any choice here, unless you'd rather go to jail.)
- The government borrows your money and hands it out to others.
- Inheriting money.
- Winning money at the casino, or any other form of gambling.
- Owners of assets such as houses and stocks benefiting from zero interest rates which drives the value of those assets higher.

- Your capital is stolen from you at gunpoint, or you are the victim of a scam.
- Central banks printing money.

Whether fair or unfair, in most of these instances where people obtain capital without producing any of their own, their gain has come at someone else's expense; the exceptions being inheritance or when someone lends money to the government and expects to have it repaid.[1]

Extracting Capital by Printing Money

Let's take a quick look at the unfair example of extracting capital by printing money. Let's say that it takes you one day to make a bike, and you can sell it for $500. You deposit that $500 in your bank account as you plan on using it to buy a $500 suit. It takes the tailor one day to make the suit.[2] But before you can buy the suit, the central bank doubles the money supply, which, all else being equal, doubles the prices of all goods and services in the economy.[3]

So now the price of your bikes rise to $1,000, as does the price of the tailor's suit. However, clearly, the value of your bike has not doubled; only its money price has. It still takes you a day to produce a bike and you can still exchange one bike for a suit because it also still takes the tailor a day to make a suit. The amount of time you need to work to buy a suit has not changed. However, the $500 that you had previously earned by selling a bike is no longer enough to buy a suit. With the central bank doubling the money supply, that $500 will now buy you half a suit. And because your bikes are still worth as much as suits, your $500 of money will have only half a bike stored up in it.

By simply printing money, the central bank was able to effectively transfer half a bike's value out of your $500 and give it to someone else.

Bread Analogy: Stealing Your Dough

Some have used the analogy of slicing a loaf of bread to demonstrate that printing money does not add value to society. A central banker might believe – or at least convince others – that if you had a loaf of bread and cut it into thinner and thinner slices (money) that you would somehow have more bread (capital), because you would then have a lot more slices of bread. But, of course, the thinner the slices, the less bread there is in each slice (the capital in each slice gets diluted). The supply of slices of bread has gone up, but there is still only one loaf.

Another way to think about it: you're about to slice the loaf into twenty slices, and your friend has agreed to swap one of their eggs for ten of those slices. But before you do the exchange, you slice each of the twenty slices in two; now you have forty slices. Your friend, unless they're an idiot, is not going to still accept only ten slices of bread for their egg. As the slices are now half as thick, ten slices will give them half the value of bread (capital) they were expecting. They will likely do one of two things: demand twenty slices or offer you half an egg for ten slices.

In the example of the central bank doubling the money supply, that would be like having twenty slices of bread in your bank account, and, overnight, a central banker sneaks into your bank and splits each of the slices in two, then takes twenty of the thinner pieces and gives them to someone else. Your bank statement will still say that you have twenty slices of bread, but each slice now contains half as much bread. Now, if you wanted to use your bread to buy something, it would cost you twice as many slices. Policymakers call these price rises inflation, and they treat it as if it comes out of nowhere, or that it was caused by supply shocks or greedy companies. They say that everyone is harmed by it, but that's not true. It's a deliberate transfer of *your* capital to someone else without your permission i.e. for each person that is hurt by an increase of the money supply (inflation) someone else benefits. Your capital was transferred to someone else, and they received it without offering their own capital in return. Their proverbial free lunch was paid for by you.

Maybe one last thing to say about the slices of bread analogy. As central bankers slice your bread (i.e. your capital) into thinner and thinner pieces and take a few each time, you might not notice that some of your bread is missing. The central bankers may then congratulate themselves that they have successfully taken some of your slices of bread (i.e. without resistance) and given them to someone who really needed it, or used it to drive stock markets or house prices higher. However, redistributing wealth within society is the responsibility of elected officials, who do so through taxation, which is at least clear (although extremely excessive in many instances and getting worse). Citizens can then vote for the party they believe will tax them most fairly and disburse their capital most responsibly. In contrast, people don't get a chance to vote for central bankers, because they are appointed rather than elected.

The redistribution of wealth that occurs when central banks increase the money supply is hidden and dishonest.

The Great Shell Game

If your capital was left in the form of a good or service, then it would be much more difficult for central banks to take it from you. They could still do it, but they'd have to instruct the police to take it from you at gunpoint or threaten you with jail time for not handing over your capital. However, central banks can easily part you and your capital when it is in the form of money, and they don't have to come to your home or go to your bank to do it. With a few keystrokes in their office, they can electronically increase the supply of money in the system and, thus, take your wealth from you. Let's go to our island economy and use another analogy to explain how this happens.

As a reminder, there are three people in our island economy. You catch three fish per day; Shirley picks three coconuts; and Jane collects three litres of water. Each of you obtains capital each day, and you exchange your capital with each other; each of you consumes one fish, one coconut and one litre of water per day. The market prices for everyone's capital are thus:

- 1 fish = 1 coconut
- 1 fish = 1 litre of water.
- 1 coconut = 1 litre of water

Everybody is getting along fine by producing and then exchanging capital according to their needs. But one day, a raft washes up on shore. On it is a central banker. The banker witnesses this market exchange economy and wants in on the action. But he doesn't have any capital with which to make exchanges with the others. In his previous life, he had never actually produced anything and, thus, had never acquired any skills with which to create capital.[4] All he did was *lubricate* the exchange mechanism through the creation of money. The central banker decides to put in place the only thing he knows, to justify his existence and partake in the island's economy.

He wanders around the island, searching the shallow tidal pools for rare and distinct seashells. Eventually, he finds a hidden trove of ornate seashells which can be found nowhere else. Once he has collected 120 of them, he goes to the other residents and convinces each of them about the beauty and rarity of the shells. In so doing, his shells become capital; they have become valued by the other island residents. The others agree to exchange some of their goods for the central banker's shells. However, up until now each resident was producing just enough capital to satisfy their daily consumption needs: each person consuming one fish, one coconut and one litre of water. To have enough capital to maintain their daily consumption *and* buy shells, each resident now needs to produce more capital. They now have to work longer and forgo some leisure time to catch more fish, collect more coconuts, or fetch more water if they want to have some fancy seashells.

So, previously, the total production on the island was as follows:

Fish: 3
Coconuts: 3
Fresh water (litres): 3

However, with each island resident now working longer because they want to purchase the central banker's shells, production increases to:

Fish: 4
Coconuts: 4
Fresh water (litres): 4

There is now more production in the economy. Each of the residents has to work a couple of hours extra so they can buy a shell.

Too Much of a Good Thing

The law of diminishing marginal returns applies here. For each shell you buy from the central banker, the less you are inclined to buy another. You may have been excited about your first few shells purchased, but once you have accumulated a certain number, you will start to think that you have enough and won't want to buy any more. Perhaps you'd rather have back the leisure time you were previously enjoying before you decided to work longer hours so you could buy the shells.

Let's assume fish, coconuts and water are being exchanged for five shells.

1 fish   = 5 shells
1 coconut   = 5 shells
1 litre of water = 5 shells

After just three transactions each person would have fifteen shells, and at this point, everyone might decide that they have enough shells and no longer wish to exchange any more of their goods with the central banker. But the central banker is not in danger of starving; he's not finished yet, because he has a plan. He convinces the hardworking island residents that, rather than continuing with the current barter system (direct exchange) they should all start using their shells as money (indirect exchange), because that will facilitate trade. It takes some time, but he is able to convince them of the myriad benefits of money: medium of exchange, unit of account, store of value.

And he points out that each of them is starting from the same place as they each have fifteen shells. He also tells them that he only has fifteen shells even though he has a lot more than that hidden behind the bushes.

Now you don't have to tote your fish around to exchange them for other goods. Also, perhaps the coconut Shirley is selling this morning is a little smaller than usual, and, rather than trying to catch a smaller fish to make it a fair trade, you can simply pay her four shells instead of five. You also have the benefit of deciding when you want to fish. Perhaps you would like to have a coconut before you go fishing. You can simply give Shirley five shells and go fishing later in the day.

Of course, if you stopped fishing, you would quickly run out of shells to buy coconuts and fresh water. Therefore, to maintain their collection of shells, each resident must continue to produce something that someone else on the island values enough to purchase with their shells. The shells that each person has is representative of the fish or coconuts or fresh water produced on the island.

The Sting

Now we have our new monetary system on the island, let's see how things might work. On the first day, you start off with fifteen shells. You catch four fish and sell three of them (one each to Shirley, Jane and the central banker), and you eat one yourself. You have received a total of fifteen shells. So now you have thirty shells. But you use ten shells to buy a coconut and fresh water. At the end of the day, you are left with twenty shells. Likewise, Shirley starts with fifteen shells. She collects four coconuts and sells three to the others. Thus, she also receives fifteen shells in payment. She spends ten shells on fish and water, to end the day with twenty shells. Finally, Jane collects four litres of water and sells three of them; thus, she is paid fifteen shells. Then she spends ten shells on fish and coconuts, to end the day with twenty shells. But what about the central banker? Like everyone else, he starts the day with fifteen shells to spend. He spends it all on fish, coconuts and water. But because he didn't produce anything he didn't have anything he could sell to the others in exchange for shells. Therefore, at the end of the day he has no shells.

However, now that the central banker has the island residents using shells in a monetary system, he has them right where he wants them. He can start extracting capital from the other residents without offering anything in return. He hasn't told them about the extra stash of shells he has behind the bushes. Therefore, despite the fact that he is not producing any capital, he always seems to have the shells to buy capital from you, Shirley and Jane.

Shell-Shocked

Over time, the three of you start to get the feeling that something's not quite right with the economy. First, you never see the central banker producing anything, yet he's always got shells to spend. Secondly, because the residents are limited by how much capital they can provide in a day and the central banker's shell supply seems limitless, the prices of all of those goods started to rise. You, Shirley and Jane have found that you are having to work longer and harder to buy the same amount of stuff. And that's because someone on the island is getting their hands on shells without having to produce any capital.

A Disingenuous Response

Central bankers may admit that the value of money erodes over time as they print more of it, but then they'll tell you that all you have to do is put your money to work by depositing it in the bank to earn interest on your money.

For instance, assume that the central bank is increasing the money supply by 3%[5] and, thus, extracting 3% of your capital from your money. A central banker will tell you that you can offset that 3% loss by depositing your savings in the bank and earning 3% interest – therefore, no loss of capital. But that interest you earn on your savings is a *reward* for forgoing consumption. At the end of the year, your capital should not be the same; rather, it should be 3% higher. But it's not higher, because by increasing the money supply by 3%, the central banker took from you the capital that you would have fairly earned.

This is a little like saying, 'Sure, I stole 3% of your money, but all you need to do is work a bit more overtime and you'll be able to offset the loss.' In both ways, you end up with less capital than you should. In the central bank's case, they gave it to someone else by printing money. Not only that, but for the last fifteen years, you have earned far less in your bank account than the central banks took from you with their money-printing. That was because interest rates were manipulated far below their natural rate.

That is the subject to which we now turn.

ENDNOTES

[1] Note that even in this case, because governments print money to diminish the value of the debt they owe, the capital transfer, in part, comes at the lender's expense.
[2] It's not necessary that goods of the same price require the same amount of time to be produced, but I'm assuming that to be the case here to make things clearer.
[3] As mentioned earlier, not all prices adjust immediately to new money being injected into the economy (due to the Cantillon effect), but we'll assume that here to make the point.
[4] Many of us are in the same boat, as pretty much anyone who works in finance or government are merely facilitators of capital creation. Very important, but it wouldn't help us much on a deserted island. On the other hand, a brain surgeon might also be in trouble.
[5] Note that the money supply typically increases much faster than 3%. In the United States the monetary base has grown at an annual rate of 7.6% since 1959. St. Louis Federal Reserve.
[6] Note that it's not quite 3%. With a 3% increase in the money supply, 2.9% of your capital is transferred to someone else; 50% increase in the money supply one third of your capital and 100% increase in the money supply 50% of your capital.

CHAPTER 8

THE NATURAL RATE OF INTEREST

Why Are There Interest Rates?

Have you ever wondered what interest rates are and why they exist? Why does your bank pay you interest on your saving (granted they haven't paid you much for many years), and why do you have to pay interest when you borrow money? Believe it or not, the interest rate is perhaps the most important price in our economy. Left alone, this price contributes to the most productive economic activity and the fairest distribution of the wealth produced by the economy. However, this price has not been left alone, which I believe is the main cause of today's unfairness. It's necessary to discuss why interest rates exist; what determines the *rate* of interest; and then, why central banks distort it.

An interest rate exists as a result of two people being on the opposite ends of a situation in which one has money, they are willing to lend and the other would like to borrow that money. Therefore, once a loan is made and money is borrowed, we have both interest income and interest expense, which are, of course, two sides of the same coin. For instance, if you lend $10,000 to Ken for one year at a rate of 10%, then you would earn $1,000 of interest income ($10,000 × 10% = $1,000). Ken paid an interest expense of $1,000 to you. I know this relationship is fairly obvious, but as you'll soon see, it often gets conveniently forgotten or ignored.

But that still doesn't explain why there is such a thing as a rate of interest. Why should Ken pay you $1,000 in interest just because you lent him $10,000. Why can't he just borrow $10,000 from you and then pay you back the same amount a year later? Well, there are a number of reasons why you should be paid interest, and it all starts with what's called the *natural* rate of interest – not to be confused with the *neutral* rate of interest (which I'll explain in the next chapter).

Natural Rate of Interest

There are differences of opinion about why the natural rate of interest exists. I will focus on the theory that, I believe, makes the most sense: time preference. It is also referred to as the time value of money[1], which simply means that, all else being equal, we prefer the enjoyment of consuming earlier rather than later. Ludwig von Mises said that it has to be this way, because if consumption were always preferred later rather than earlier, then nothing would ever get consumed.[2] For instance, if you preferred a cheeseburger later rather than sooner, you might put off eating one for a few hours. But once a few hours had passed, you might still prefer to delay eating it again. A good way to lose weight, I suppose – but nonsensical, obviously.

Anyway, assume that just as you're about to bite into a cheeseburger, Ken asks you if he can have it instead. When he's finished eating it, he'll go out and buy you another one in an hour or two. If you're like me, you'd probably tell Ken to get lost, unless of course, he was a family member or close friend (but even then...). The way to think about it is that there's nothing in it for you to delay the consumption of your cheeseburger for a couple of hours. However, Ken might offer to buy you two cheeseburgers later in return for letting him eat your cheeseburger now. If you agree to these terms, then you are effectively lending Ken your cheeseburger for a couple of hours and, in return, earning interest income of 100% – in the form of an extra cheeseburger.

In the above example, where you lend $10,000 to Ken for a year, you are rewarded with $1,000 of interest income for delaying your consumption of that $10,000. Perhaps you wanted to buy a new TV or do some renovations in your basement. That is all considered consumption spending. So, you put off for a year buying some things that you would like to have today and, instead, lend your $10,000 to Ken in return for some interest income. The result is that you will have even more money to spend a year later: $10,000 of the repaid loan plus $1,000 of interest income.

Let's look at it from the perspective of ordering a pizza. If you decide to order a pizza, you will typically want it as soon as possible. If the pizza place tells you they can deliver a pizza within thirty minutes for $15 or in two hours for $12, you might consider that saving $3 is not enough to compensate you for not having your pizza delivered within half an hour. However, if they said you could have the pizza for $10, thus saving you $5, you might be encouraged to delay your pizza consumption for a couple of hours.

Obviously, the degree to which people are willing to forgo their pizza consumption and how much of a discount they would require will vary from person to person. For instance, some people may be willing to delay their pizza consumption for as little as $1. For others, you could offer the pizza for free in two hours' time and they would still choose to pay full price to have it now.

Time Preference in Action

People with a very high time preference typically save less and spend more today. For instance, if Ken earns $50,000 a year and immediately spends it all as it comes in, he will likely continue spending $50,000 a year as long as that is how much he is paid. If you had a lower time preference than Ken, you would save more and spend less today, but your savings would enable you to spend considerably more in the future. For instance, if you earn the same amount as Ken and you save $25,000 each year, earning 10% on your savings while Ken spends all of his money, by year 10, you will be spending as much each year as Ken, but you'll also have $275,000 sitting in your bank account (I've excluded taxes to make the example clearer). By year 20, your annual spending increases to $75,000 and you have a cool half-million dollars in savings sitting in the bank.

And of course, as time goes on, both your annual spending and savings will increase, while Ken with his YOLO lifestyle will still be spending only $50,000 a year and have no savings. Don't you love how this stuff works?

Year	Salary	Interest Income	Total Income	Savings	Cumulative Savings	Spending
0	$50,000	0	$50,000	$25,000	$25,000	$25,000
1	$50,000	$2,500	$52,500	$25,000	$50,000	$27,500
2	$50,000	$5,000	$55,000	$25,000	$75,000	$30,000
3	$50,000	$7,500	$57,500	$25,000	$100,000	$32,500
4	$50,000	$10,000	$60,000	$25,000	$125,000	$35,000
5	$50,000	$12,500	$62,500	$25,000	$150,000	$37,500
6	$50,000	$15,000	$65,000	$25,000	$175,000	$40,000
7	$50,000	$17,500	$67,500	$25,000	$200,000	$42,500
8	$50,000	$20,000	$70,000	$25,000	$225,000	$45,000
9	$50,000	$22,500	$72,500	$25,000	$250,000	$47,500

Year	Salary	Interest Income	Total Income	Savings	Cumulative Savings	Spending
10	$50,000	$25,000	$75,000	$25,000	$275,000	$50,000
11	$50,000	$27,500	$77,500	$25,000	$300,000	$52,500
12	$50,000	$30,000	$80,000	$25,000	$325,000	$55,000
13	$50,000	$32,500	$82,500	$25,000	$350,000	$57,500
14	$50,000	$35,000	$85,000	$25,000	$375,000	$60,000
15	$50,000	$37,500	$87,500	$25,000	$400,000	$62,500
16	$50,000	$40,000	$90,000	$25,000	$425,000	$65,000
17	$50,000	$42,500	$92,500	$25,000	$450,000	$67,500
18	$50,000	$45,000	$95,000	$25,000	$475,000	$70,000
19	$50,000	$47,500	$97,500	$25,000	$500,000	$72,500
20	$50,000	$50,000	$100,000	$25,000	$525,000	$75,000

Because of your low time preference, you were able to delay some of your consumption and instead save some of your money, which led to the creation of more real resources in the economy by those who borrowed your savings. The real resources the borrowers created gives them the wherewithal to pay you back more than you lent them. As you can imagine, the more people in society with a lower time preference, the more money will be saved and stuff produced. And as we have seen, stuff produced is your means of payment, which enables you to purchase things. Thus, the lower the time preference, the more savings there are, which means more capital is invested, resulting in more stuff being produced, which then enables more spending. But the higher level of spending is only possible because savings happened first.

Determining the Natural Rate of Interest

So that is how time preference affects people's spending and saving decisions. But how does it impact the natural rate of interest? When more people in society have a high time preference, that is, they prefer to spend and consume now rather than save, then there are fewer savings available for companies, or governments to borrow. And as we know from the rules of supply and demand, when the supply of something is reduced, all else being equal, the price of that good goes up. Money is no different. A high-time-preference society that is spending a lot and saving little will see a higher borrowing cost for those entities wishing to borrow the limited amount of savings available – which means interest rates will be higher. Conversely, if a society's time preference is low, meaning more people are saving than spending, then all else being equal, because the supply of savings has gone up, the cost of borrowing those savings goes down and, thus, interest rates will fall. As you might expect, a society's average time preferences doesn't change much over time; thus, the natural rate of interest doesn't move around very much.

Another theory on how the natural rate of interest is determined is covered by the liquidity theory.[3] In short, this theory says that people typically desire immediate access to their money, and, to entice them to lend it to someone else and, thus, not have access to it for a period of time, they need to be rewarded. And that reward is interest income.[4]

The actual rate of interest, as determined by the natural phenomenon of time or liquidity preferences, has been debated for decades, but one number I have often seen being suggested is that it is approximately 3%. However, ever since the Global Financial Crisis of 2008, policymakers would have you believe that this natural rate of interest had been grinding lower for many years and, thus, they were left with no option but to push interest rates lower. But it should be obvious that if the natural rate were lower, you wouldn't need central banks to manipulate it down, as it would fall on its own naturally. What central banks attempt to lower is the neutral rate (discussed in the next chapter) – a very different thing from the natural rate.

Policymakers will also tell you that the natural rate of interest is unobservable and is, thus, impossible to determine with any accuracy. However, the only reason it's unobservable is because central banks won't let it be determined by market players. Instead, the interest rate is distorted (usually by being pushed lower) from its natural level. If it weren't being distorted, it would be visible to all, as it is determined not by a central banker but by millions of people each with their own time preference and skin in the game.

The natural rate has likely moved within a narrow range for decades, or even centuries, as it is driven by sociological factors that influence people's decisions with respect to spending and saving. Of course, policymakers don't like the idea of a natural rate because it may not coincide with the level of spending they deem appropriate for the economy. If interest rates are too high, people won't borrow and spend as much. But as you have seen, encouraging more spending today comes at the expense of more spending tomorrow. That is what happens when central banks drive the interest rates below the natural rate.

> *Policymakers can deny your right to receive the natural rate, but they can't eliminate its existence.*
> – Ludwig von Mises

I believe that by not allowing the natural rate of interest to be expressed and, thus, not allowing savers to earn what they deserve, and, instead, enabling borrowers to pay less than they should have, policymakers set in motion a very unnatural chain of events that has left us with our current perilous state of affairs.

Adding to the Natural Rate of Interest

Okay, so far, we have the natural rate of interest – but the market rate of interest will be higher than that. There are two natural reasons for this – time and risk – as well as an unnatural reason: inflation.

Time

In the above example, you were lending Ken $10,000 for a year at an interest rate of 10%. But suppose Ken said to you that he needed to borrow the money for five years instead of one. Instead of earning $1,000 in interest income with a one-year loan, you would earn $5,000 of interest income over five years. That sounds pretty good. However, you're a little uncomfortable lending your money for five years because you might want to spend it some time over the next five years. Or you might be worried that some unexpected expenditures might arise over the next five years, for example, home or car repairs. And so, you might instead decide to make five one-year loans to Ken. To compensate you for taking the risk of lending the money for a longer period of time, you will ask Ken to pay you a higher rate of interest.

Most of the time, the longer the term (number of years) of the loan, the higher the interest rate to compensate the lender for the greater amount of uncertainty they are taking on and for not having access to their capital for a longer period of time. In the finance world, this is called the *term structure* of interest rates, which simply shows you how much higher interest rates are for loans of longer durations. For example, a three-year loan would have a higher interest rate than a one-year loan; a five-year interest rate would be higher than a three-year rate; and a ten-year rate would be higher than a five-year rate. Very short-term loans for three months would have the lowest interest rates as three months is not a long time to forgo your spending, and there is less of a chance of something going wrong over three months.[5]

Risk

Another reason that market interest rates are higher than the natural rate is risk. For instance, if you were lending Ken $10,000 for a year and you knew that Ken had a good job and was trustworthy, you might be very comfortable lending him the money at 10% and not worry that he wouldn't pay you back the money. On the other hand, if Ken had been out of work for some time and/or you knew him to be living a rather reckless YOLO lifestyle, you may seriously question Ken's ability, or willingness, to pay you back. In this case, you may decide to not lend Ken any money at all, or lend to him but at a much higher interest rate to compensate for the higher risk of not getting all or any of your money back. Instead of 10% interest, you might charge him 20%. Obviously, the higher the risk, the higher the interest rate – and vice versa. For instance, when you lend money to the government, you earn the lowest rate of interest because government debt has the lowest risk of default. If necessary, they can always raise your taxes to repay the money you lent them.[6]

When lending money to companies, those considered to be the best at putting that money to productive use and that have the strongest balance sheet (i.e. little debt) will pay the lowest interest rates, as there is a greater chance that they will be able to pay the money back. By successfully investing that money, the company will be able to produce more real resources; and the production of real resources gives the company the means of payment with which to repay the loan. Basket-case companies that are not able to make a profit are not putting capital to productive use and, thus, they are, in effect, consuming capital rather than creating it. These companies risk not having the means of payments to pay back a lender; thus, a lender will necessarily demand of them a higher rate of interest to compensate for the higher risk of not being paid back. The higher rate of interest may make borrowing by these companies so prohibitive that they can no longer operate, which is a good thing, as it means that they stop destroying capital and reducing the productive capacity of the economy.

An Example
Let's quickly look at both scenarios: productive and basket case.

Let's say that your bike company is very successful because of your passion for cycling and your extreme focus on the customer. This drives you to constantly reinvest in your business to make better and better bikes and provide better and better customer service. As a result, people are willing to lend you more money at attractive rates, which enables you to expand your business yet further and hire more employees. Your business grows as you create more and more real resources, contributing to the productive capacity of the economy.

On the other hand, let's say you don't really have a passion for cycling and don't care much about the customer. (Perhaps you inherited the company). Your main focus is on having fun. So instead of reinvesting in the company, you spend all of the profits and go on extended holidays. Over time, the quality of your bikes and customer service start to suffer and, so, fewer people are buying your bikes. You increase the prices of your bikes in an attempt to offset the fact that you are selling fewer of them, but this serves only to diminish the customer value proposition even more. Your sales fall further. You are now in a situation where you can't charge enough for your bikes to cover your costs, which means you're losing money and consuming capital rather than producing it. You've become a net negative on society from a productivity perspective. In this case, you would need to borrow money to cover your losses, but lenders would be reluctant to lend to you because, based on the lack of profitability of your company, they would fear you wouldn't be able to pay them back. However, they may be enticed to lend you money if you offer to pay them a higher interest rate and convince them that you are taking remedial steps to fix your business.

Irony: The Lowest Rates Are Paid by the Least Productive
As mentioned previously, governments pay the lowest interest rates because their risk of defaulting on a loan is the lowest. However, this risk is not the lowest because they put the capital borrowed to the most productive use; in fact, quite the opposite is true. Most money lent to governments is consumed rather than invested. The production of real resources isn't what gives governments the wherewithal to pay back loans. Instead, the means of payment is achieved by a government taxing its citizenry, borrowing more

money to pay off previous debts, or printing money. And as government debt continuously rises and most government spending is consumption-related, more and more capital is being taken from the productive side of the economy, meaning there is less investment than there would otherwise have been.

Therefore, the larger the proportion of an economy is taken up by government, the more that economy's productive capacity is diminished. Later, I'll discuss how demand went through the roof for government bonds, and how that demand was not from savers/investors but, rather, central banks who were printing money to buy the bonds and, thus, driving interest rates to absurdly low levels.

Interest Rates Naturally Determined

So far, we have discussed three things that determine interest rates:

1. Natural rate as determined by time preference
2. The length of time the money will be borrowed
3. The risk level of the borrower

The interest rate that Ken has to pay might be a combination of the following:

- Natural rate: 3%
- Time (1 year): 3%
- Ken's risk: 4%
- Total: 10%

For a five-year loan, the time component would be higher. It might look like this:

- Natural rate: 3%
- Time (5 years): 5%
- Ken's risk: 4%
- Total: 12%

If Ken were a deadbeat, a five-year loan would see the risk component rise:

- Natural rate: 3%
- Time (5 years): 8%
- Ken's risk: 7%
- Total: 18%

The Unnatural One

Unfortunately, there is another factor impacting interest rates that is wholly unnatural: inflation. As you know, inflation steals capital from your wages and any money you happen to be holding and transfers it to someone else. If you lent $10,000 to Ken for a year at an interest rate of 10%, but inflation was 15%, by the time Ken paid you back your money plus interest ($11,000), it would be worth less than the $10,000 you had originally lent him.

Suppose you are planning to buy a high-end entertainment system for your basement costing $10,000. Because you have a low time preference, you are willing to wait a year to make the purchase and instead earn $1,000 of interest income by lending your money to Ken. However, because inflation is 15%, you know that in a year's time, the cost of the entertainment system will rise 15% from $10,000 to $11,500. Thus, you will only have $11,000 when he repays the loan, leaving you $500 short. So, instead, you could do one of two things. You could buy the entertainment system now before inflation drives the price higher, or you could require Ken to pay you a rate of interest that would compensate you for the rate of inflation theft.

For example, a loan to Ken that accounts for 15% inflation:

- Natural rate: 3%
- Time (1 year): 3%
- Ken's risk: 4%
- Inflation: 15%
- Total: 25%

The Economy's Natural Regulator

Interest rates regulate the lending and borrowing of capital in the most efficient manner. Because those rates are determined by people with skin in the game and according to their own time preferences on both sides of the transaction – lender and borrower – it leads to the most efficient allocation of capital, which, in turn, leads to the greatest productive capacity of the economy. Mess with those rates in any way, and it will lead to inefficient or suboptimal allocation of capital, which, over time, will erode the economy's productive capabilities. In my opinion, the distortion of interest rates by central banks is the one of the main reasons why the productivity growth of developed economies has been grinding lower for decades. Not unrelated to distorted interest rates is the rising per centage of the economy taken up by two necessary entities that don't produce real resources: government and Wall Street. We'll touch more on both a little later, but first it's necessary to discuss neutral interest rates.

ENDNOTES

[1] See William Chancellor's excellent book on this subject, *The Price of Time*. He goes into great detail about how interest represents the time value of money.
[2] Human Action. Chapter 18, Action in the Passing of Time.
[3] This theory is associated with John Maynard Keynes.
[4] A good audio by Lucas Engelhardt that compares the two theories can be found here: https://mises.org/library/attempt-reconciliation-time-preference-theory-interest-and-liquidity-preference-theory
[5] There are brief periods of time when the rate of interest on a longer-dated bond can be lower than a shorter-dated bond. This is known as an inverted yield curve. In the past, its uninverting has often been quickly followed by a recession.
[6] Governments can also borrow more to pay you back. They can also print money to pay you back, but, of course, that diminishes the value of the money they are repaying you.

CHAPTER 9
THE NEUTRAL RATE OF INTEREST

Symptoms

Interest rates determined by free-choosing market forces (time preferences, loan duration, risk and inflation expectations) with skin in the game result in the most efficient allocation of scarce resources and, thus, the greatest productive capacity of an economy. Why, then, do central banks constantly distort interest rates to much lower levels which, by definition, must result in lower productive capacity?

Economies go in cycles. They can grow for years but then they can experience slowdowns – recessions. There are different theories about what causes recessions, but many believe that central banks are the main cause and that they are then forced to rescue the economy from calamities of their own making.[1] And while I believe there is a great deal of truth in this, as I've said, it's obviously not the intention of central banks to cause recessions. However, the negative impact on the economy created by central banks is real and, I believe, the result of a mix of short-termism and focusing on the wrong barometer of economic strength, which then leads them to adjust the neutral rate of interest. This results in the symptom of economic strength (spending) oscillating between expansion (growing economy) and contraction (recession), while the fundamental drivers of a healthy economy continue to deteriorate over time.

Defined

But first, let's look at the definition of the neutral rate of interest from the Federal Reserve Bank of Dallas:

> The neutral rate is the theoretical federal funds rate at which the stance of Federal Reserve monetary policy is neither accommodative nor restrictive. It is the short-term real interest rate consistent with the economy maintaining full employment with associated price stability.[2]

In the past, I have heard a number of policymakers and economists say that central banks were targeting the correct natural rate of interest. However, more recently, they have been consistent in calling the central bank's manipulated rate the neutral rate. Perhaps people have finally recognised the absurdity of calling something 'natural' when it had to be continually *unnaturally* manipulated by central banks down to a lower level.

Regardless, on reading the above definition, you may feel that the neutral rate makes a lot of sense. Who wouldn't want full employment? And price stability certainly sounds a lot better than persistent inflation. However, the problem starts with what central banks believe leads to full employment, and their haste in trying to achieve it. The problem is then compounded by attempting to maintain stable prices rather than allowing consumers to benefit from the gradually declining prices that naturally result from an economy not burdened with interest rate manipulation.

GDP Focus
Remember that policymakers tend to look at gross domestic product (GDP) – all final spending – to determine whether or not the economy is in good shape. And as consumers make up around 70% of all final spending, they are mistakenly deemed to be the engines of economic growth.

Race to the Bottom
One curious thing about the central banks' neutral rate of interest – which is supposed to lead to the most spending without resulting in inflation – is that the rate has been declining for many years; central banks have to continually lower the interest rate to ensure spending keeps growing. They trot out all kinds of possible reasons for why this might be, for example, the aforementioned global secular stagnation. However, the reason the neutral rate of interest has been falling for many years is because debt and an increasing money supply have been replacing the production of stuff as the means of payment. Rather than spending being a symptom of the economy's productive capacity, it has increasingly been a symptom of debt and newly printed money. Consumers have been borrowing to maintain their consumption lifestyles – and central banks are not only enabling but also encouraging this sort of behaviour. Central banks have also enabled reckless government spending and significant fiscal deficits by printing money, which the government effectively borrows.

Push Me Pull You

So how does all of this result in GDP (final spending) eventually going into reverse and resulting in a recession?

When people are borrowing money to maintain their levels of consumption, they eventually get to the point where they can't service any more debt, and so they reduce their spending. To get people to continue their spending, central banks need to make it easier for consumers to take on more debt. They do this by lowering interest rates below the level determined by market forces. This neutral rate makes borrowing more affordable; thus, spending picks up, but because that rate is set at a level below the market-determined natural rate, it results in lower productivity growth. Not as much stuff is produced as there otherwise would have been. And because spending has resumed with not as much stuff being produced, the prices of that stuff go up (inflation).

Central banks respond by raising interest rates to ensure that inflation doesn't get out of control, which makes borrowing more expensive and thus spending slows or goes in reverse, resulting in a recession, which, in turn, causes inflation to fall.

Central banks, on witnessing GDP starting to slow (or go in reverse), and with inflation under control, decide it's safe to once again lower interest rates so people can, once more, borrow more money and spend. However, because there is already so much more debt in the economy, central banks find that they need to lower interest rates even more than they did last time to achieve further growth in spending. Therefore, they determine that the neutral rate of interest must have fallen. They lower rates even further from the natural rate, and the economy's productive capacity suffers even more.

Wash, rinse, and repeat.

While interest rates have been falling since the early 1980s, initially, it was because the head of the US central bank, Paul Volcker, was successful in slaying the inflation of the late 1970s. The real distortions started around 2002 in the wake of the dot-com crash.

Absurdity

Not long ago, interest rates got down to absurdly low levels. Remember in the previous chapter we talked about how if there is high demand to purchase the debt (bonds) of an entity, then the rate of interest that entity will be required to pay will be low? Well, demand for government debt has been so strong since the Global Financial Crisis of 2007–2009 (GFC) that the interest rate that governments had to pay in order to borrow money was driven down to absurdly low levels. However, much of this demand for government debt was not a natural phenomenon but was a result of central banks printing money to buy it. With record low interest rates for many years after the GFC, people were lending money to governments free of charge. Even worse, at one point, over $18 trillion of debt worldwide had a *negative* interest rate, that is, people were actually paying governments for the honour of lending them their money. The governments were being paid to borrow, and if you were the lender, you had to pay *them* interest for the pleasure of lending them your capital.

So, the rate of interest was not reflecting time preference, loan duration, risk, or inflation – all of which should be positive. This unnatural situation was not achieved by an explosion of private investors wishing to lend to governments but by central banks around the world effectively printing trillions of dollars to buy the governments' debt. And as we saw earlier, when money is printed, it obtains value only by extracting capital that you have stored up in the money in your bank account. Thus, you had an indiscriminate borrower (a government) getting money from a price-indiscriminate lender, and neither of them had any skin in the game, as it wasn't their money. And governments don't worry about accessing the capital to back the borrowed money because if they can't raise enough taxes or borrow enough in the future to repay the loans, central banks will simply access the capital (yours) by printing money.

The Short Run Is Someone Else's Long Run

I'm not sure if policymakers would agree that a natural rate of interest leads to greater economic productivity than a neutral rate. But even if they did, in their mind, the natural rate would take far too long to encourage more consumer spending. Related to this is a quote by economist John Maynard Keynes, who wrote 'In the long run we are all dead' (meaning that doing the right thing takes too long). Of course, over time, the long run of someone today becomes the next generation's short run. Increasingly, and in many ways, the next generation is dealing with the consequences of the previous generation not having done the right thing. Policymakers convinced themselves that something would eventually come out of left field to save the day. They believed that by not dealing with the fundamental problems and, instead, increasing the money supply to encourage spending and inflate asset prices, the benefits of all of this would somehow trickle down to everyone, and the economy would inevitably reach escape velocity from which the next generation would, no doubt, benefit. Unfortunately, this has not happened, because it was all based on fallacious economic doctrine. It doesn't work in practice or theory.

My belief is that policymakers don't believe the natural rate is best for the economy, and, instead, they have convinced themselves that the neutral rate should be the focus, because such a view justifies their actions in making the painful symptoms go away immediately, and, thus, they can take credit for this happening. Lowering interest rates to the neutral rate has an immediate impact on spending. And, as most people have been conditioned to expect the government to do something when the economy slows, central banks are quick to oblige by lowering interest rates.

Functioning Alcoholic

Some have likened this behaviour to that of an alcoholic who is suffering from withdrawal symptoms. The person is under considerable stress and unable to function until they get another shot of the good stuff. Once they get their fix, they are no longer suffering, but they are likely not what one would call fully productive. Some alcoholics are completely unable to work, while others are considered functioning alcoholics who, while functional, are likely not fully functional. I drink alcohol, and if I have too much, it affects the quality of my sleep, and how long I sleep, and I will feel a bit tired the next day. I'm still functioning, but not as well as I could be. I suspect that this is the state of a functioning alcoholic, that over time this slowly becomes the new normal.

That is how I view our economy today – as a functioning alcoholic. The economy needs never-ending shots of stimulus to keep it moving forward. This stimulus comes from central banks in the form of ever-lower interest rates and ever-higher levels of printed money. But the constant distortion of interest rates leads to constantly diminishing productivity growth, monumental debt levels, and absurd levels of wealth inequality. Ever-increasing levels of alcohol coursing through the arteries of the economy appear to give an immediate boost to the economy as evidenced by more spending, higher house prices and higher stock markets. But the alcohol gives only a temporary boost to the symptoms of a strong economy (spending and asset prices), and it harms the underlying fundamentals (productivity growth that results from saving and investment). And while productivity growth has been grinding lower for many years as a result of these policies, the amount of alcohol in the system is becoming toxic, leading to things potentially far worse than hampered productivity.

Robbed

Remember earlier I mentioned the obvious relationship of one entity's interest expense being another's interest income? Well continually driving interest rates lower to the neutral rate over time has benefited some but punished others. Two of the main beneficiaries have been governments and corporations, because they paid a lower interest expense on the money that they borrowed.[4] A study by consulting firm McKinsey[5] found that between 2007 and 2012, governments and corporations in the US, the eurozone and the UK saved almost $1.4 trillion in total interest expense due to ultra-low interest rates. However, if interest expense is someone else's interest income that means the lenders to those entities, such as households and pension plans, earned almost $1.4 trillion less than they would have if central banks hadn't driven interest rates down to those ultra-low levels. And that was only as of 2012. With interest rates even going negative since then, you can imagine how much more capital since then has been unfairly transferred from savers to governments and corporations. It measures in the trillions of dollars.

No More Cash

But as bad as all of this has been, it could get considerably worse. Over the last several years, some policymakers have been trying to make the case for eliminating physical cash entirely so that all of our money will be in electronic form. This campaign is known as the *war on cash*. They trot out what I believe to be disingenuous reasons for why they want to eliminate cash (for example, 'cash is used by organised crime'). Of course, organised crime no longer needs cash to flourish. In my opinion, the reason governments want to get rid of cash is that they want the option of taking interest rates deep into negative territory to force you to spend your savings.

Here's how it would work. Assume the economy continues to slow despite the fact that governments have lowered interest rates to zero. Of course, it's because they lowered rates to zero that economic productivity has ground to a halt. However, policymakers believe that spending, rather than saving and investment, is what drives economic growth, and so they need a way to get you to spend your money. Perhaps you are saving it for your retirement, and, even though rates are down to zero, you'd still rather keep your money safely in the bank for future spending.

What would happen if central banks took interest rates deep into negative territory, say, -5%. In this case, you would have to pay the bank 5% of your savings every year for the pleasure of letting the bank earn money by putting your savings at risk by lending it to other people. Of course, you wouldn't be too happy about this, so you would withdraw all of your money from the bank to avoid paying 5% every year. Perhaps you store your money in a safe to thwart the policymakers' efforts to get you to spend your money. And that's why they want to eliminate cash.

Thus, if policymakers are successful in eliminating cash and they then reduce interest rates to -5%, these would be your options:

1. Leave your savings in the bank and pay 5% every year.
2. Spend your money on consumer goods.
3. Put your money at risk by investing it in overpriced assets such as stock markets[6] or houses, and contribute to the fallacious wealth effect economic doctrine.

The elimination of cash would be terrible for you and the economy.[7]

To summarise the two interest rate chapters:

Natural interest rates: Good
- Greater economic prosperity
- Less wealth disparity
- Less debt

Neutral interest rates: Bad
- Less economic prosperity
- More wealth disparity
- More debt

The amazing thing is that despite central banks driving the neutral rate of interest further and further from the natural rate – which results in lower productivity growth and a wealth transfer that measures in trillions of dollars from workers/savers to governments and corporations – the system still manages to function. Of course, this is down to the amazing entrepreneurial spirit and work ethic of millions of people who keep this thing ticking over. However, as productivity growth grinds lower and lower and debt loads grow higher and higher and more wealth is redistributed, people are getting closer to the breaking point as it gets tougher and tougher to make ends meet. At the same time, the top one per cent are doing better than ever. A little later, we'll look at the mechanisms used to transfer this wealth, but first it's time to spend a little bit of time talking about government.

ENDNOTES

[1] Following are my interpretations of what some people believe might cause recessions.

One theory is that as central banks attempt to make the economy grow at a faster rate by driving interest rates below that which would be dictated by market forces (natural rate, time and risk). Companies respond by increasing their borrowing and investing more in longer-term capital projects that can take many years to complete. However, remember that natural interest rates don't change much over time and would only go lower if, on the whole, society's time preference reduces, meaning more people save than consume. (And if this was the case, there would be more real resources in the economy that could be put to use by companies in longer-dated projects. On the other hand, when interest rates are being driven lower *unnaturally* by central banks, those lower rates are not accompanied by higher savings. Resources are still being consumed rather than saved, and companies eventually run out of enough resources to finish their longer-dated projects.

Another theory is that a recession is a result of central banks distorting interest rates below their natural rate and, thus, making it easier for companies and consumers to borrow money and increase their spending. This results in an unsustainable spending boom, which, in turn, leads to inflation. This happens because the spending is being funded not by more stuff being produced but by more money being created through lower-interest loans. More money being created without an accompanying increase in goods and services drives up prices (without the money supply going up, people would only be able to fund their purchases with the stuff they produce, and so prices wouldn't rise). When the central banks then raise interest rates to dampen the inflation caused by too much money in the system, that makes debt more difficult to service and new loans more expensive, resulting in an economic slowdown which solves the inflation problem.

But note that the United States suffered from recessions long before the Federal Reserve (central bank) was established in 1913, so if there was no central bank around back then to manipulate the interest rate below its natural rate, what caused those earlier recessions? Some believe it was a result of the fractional reserve banking system, which creates deposits out of thin air every time a bank makes a loan. The increasing money supply lowers interest rates and causes a boom of investment, which would then follow the same pattern as outlined above.

Still others claim that recessions in the years before central banks had nothing to do with fractional reserve banking; instead, recessions were a result of government interference with the market in terms of policy/regulation or changes in the money system.

Another theory is that economic prosperity is a result of animal spirits and that recessions are a result of those spirits going into reverse. They view an animal spirit–driven economic boom as the normal course of events and the bust as an unnatural occurrence that needs to be corrected. Central banks see it as their job to reignite those animal spirits and get people borrowing and spending again. While speculative manias do occur, I don't believe they can cause widespread economic downturns unless they're sustained by a continuing increase in the money supply, aided and abetted by interest rates being manipulated below their natural rate.

[2] *Federal Reserve Bank of Dallas - The Neutral Rate of Interest.* 24 October 2018.
[3] Of course, policymakers look at a whole host of data to keep tabs on the economy, including the very important unemployment rate. But the focus on GDP, or final spending, is generally used to determine whether the economy is growing or in a recession.
[4] Note that consumers would also have benefited from lower interest rates on their mortgages, but all that served to do was create a housing affordability crisis by twice driving housing prices through the roof.
[5] *QE and ultra-low interest rates: Distributional effects and risks.* McKinsey. November 2013.
[6] Note that stock markets are not always expensive – although they have been for a very long time. When stock prices fairly reflect the productive capacity of the underlying businesses, then it can be very prudent to invest in them, but that should be a choice people make rather than being coerced to do so.
[7] If we got to a place where the natural rate of interest was allowed to prevail and policymakers no longer believed that they had the right to dictate to you what you should be doing with your savings, then the elimination of cash would not be so catastrophic.

CHAPTER 10
GOVERNMENT PART 1

Note that what I have to say in the next two chapters refers mainly to the asset price–distorting decisions of policymakers who believe that reckless spending and debts don't matter (i.e. the *something-for-nothing* crowd). This is not meant to be in any way critical of the many hard-working public employees (police, customs agents, teachers, nurses, park rangers) who all make crucial contributions in facilitating economic activity (just like the finance industry does). Nor is it targeted at politicians who are truly committed to making a difference.

Obtaining Capital

You obtain capital by earning it through work or investment. You can then use can save that capital or use it to purchase things. However, even if someone didn't contribute to the productive capacity of the economy, they could still purchase something if they were somehow able to get their hands on the capital that you produced. They could do this in several ways. For instance, you could simply decide to give your capital to them as a gift/charity. Or you may decide to lend them your capital. However, they might not like this latter option, as they would eventually have to pay you back your capital. Therefore, they may decide to take matters into their own hands and steal your capital from you. Of course, by doing this, they run the risk of getting caught and possibly going to jail, so people who don't produce anything typically rely on someone else to act as an agent in transferring your capital from you to them and with no obligation to ever pay you back. That agent, of course, is the government.

The first and most obvious way that government transfers your productive efforts to others is through taxation: the government takes one-third to half of the capital that you produce and redistributes it to others. The second and less obvious method by which the government redistributes your productive efforts to others is by increasing the money supply. The newly minted money extracts some of your capital that you have temporarily stored up in money. There is another policymaker-driven capital transfer that happens when they drive asset prices higher, but we'll look closer at that in the chapter on the wealth effect.

Someone Always Pays

In 1983, then French president Francois Mitterrand reduced the retirement age in France from 65 to 60. In the short-to-medium term, he looked like not only a compassionate hero but also an economic genius. Not only was he viewed as a nice guy because he wanted everyone to retire at a younger age, but there was also no impact to the economy from having to pay people their retirement benefits five years earlier. France simply borrowed the money they didn't have to pay the benefits. Of course, someone always has to foot the bill, and, as usual, that responsibility has largely fallen on the next generation. Again, a very simple way to think about it is that if you receive more from the system than you put in, then someone else is paying for it – whether knowingly or unknowingly, voluntarily or involuntarily. There's simply no way around it. In this and the following chapter, I'll talk not only about the importance of government but also what I believe are some misconceptions.

Earlier, we saw that the island economy didn't need an increase in population for the economy to grow. Instead, it grew through savings and investment. I believe that some policymakers encourage population growth because that will paper over fundamental flaws in their economic policies – policies that foster shorter-term spending growth at the long-term expense of economic productivity.

First, by encouraging spending at the expense of saving and investment, policymakers initially get that GDP number rising higher, thus making the economy look stronger than it is. But eventually, the economy starts to falter due to the lack of investment. Rather than encouraging saving and investment, which would, at first, have a negative impact on the GDP number but give it a boost longer term, some policymakers will increase population growth through immigration. Of course, the per-capita GDP number will still not be great, but policymakers will point to the overall GDP number, which will be rising simply because there are more people in the country – even if those people are spending less per person.

Secondly, many countries have state pension plans through which the beneficiaries are paid more than they have contributed. These plans work only if the population continues to rise and, thus, the government can steadily tax more and more people to pay those taking out more than they put in (that's the definition of a pyramid scheme).

Thirdly, too many policymakers believe rising house prices are good for the economy.

They are decidedly not.

That hasn't stopped some policymakers from allowing levels of immigration into their countries that far exceed their abilities to expand their infrastructure or increase their housing stock.

During the COVID crisis, I was talking to my retired mother who lives in Florida. She had just received a $600 cheque from the government. Her income was completely unimpacted by the crisis, because her income was made up of retirement benefits. Of course, she was very happy about receiving the cheque. Who wouldn't be? Party pooper that I am, I asked her if she realised that someone else actually has to pay for that $600 she received. Her response was typical of so many people: 'No one has to pay for it, it comes from the government.' I then asked her where the government gets the money to hand out to people. She quickly realised that it was 'from the people'. For me, it was a perfect reminder of how much easier and convenient it is to not think about where all the government's free stuff comes from. But, also, that it doesn't take much effort for people to realise or understand what's truly going on.

All Government Spending Is Funded by the Private Sector

This chapter will touch on only a few aspects of government spending, also known as fiscal policy. It's important, as I believe there are some similarities in attitudes and understanding between central banks printing money and governments spending trillions of dollars – for some reason, many people think it's free and doesn't cost them anything. It's the people and corporations – and corporations are made up of people – who pay for everything. Whether it's governments spending or central banks printing money, all the value of that spending and printing is created by individuals and corporations who create stuff, keep some of it for themselves, and then have the rest taken from them by governments through taxation and by central banks through money-printing. It really is that straightforward, despite policymakers' attempts to convince you that borrowing money at zero interest rates is free, or that printing money has zero cost to society as long as it doesn't lead to hyperinflation.

A Question of Degree
Now before I get into it, I will say right from the outset that I am not against government. In fact, I am very much for it. And there are many great public servants and smart government employees who work extremely hard and contribute considerably to society. However, there are pros and cons regarding the different levels of government involvement in the economy. A typical classification for the varying levels of government involvement in the economy is 'left' and 'right' – 'left' being more involved and 'right' being less involved.

I live in Canada, which I think is the greatest country in the world. (Hopefully, wherever you live, you are fortunate enough to feel that your country is also the greatest in the world.) Until recently, we had, I believe, a good balance between a free-market economy and welfare benefits that helped those temporarily or permanently in need. It's important not to dissuade those receiving benefits from looking for ways to improve their own lives and the lives of their loved ones.[1] At the same time, those doing all the work should not be discouraged from doing so by excessive taxation. Unfortunately, like many countries, Canada has started to go down the something-for-nothing, free-lunch, virtue-signalling path, and to do so with taxpayers' capital. It seems both sides, right and left, have shifted further to the left, with government spending and debt constantly rising no matter which party is in power.

Motives
For most of us, it always feels good to know that we're doing our part, particularly if we're helping other people. However, the COVID government benefits, in my opinion, were more about trying to ensure the GDP number maintained a certain level than helping people in need; although related, the motives behind each are very different (that's why they were called *stimulus* cheques and not *financial aid* cheques).[2] Those benefits also made politicians very popular with a lot of people.

Incentives
According to a report by the Congressional Budget Office on 4 June 2020, 'Roughly five of every six recipients would receive benefits that exceeded the weekly amounts they could expect to earn from work during those six

months.' Not only is this a disincentive to be a productive part of society, but it also hardly seems fair to fund those benefits by taxing those who are working and, in many cases, actually making less than those sitting at home. Of course, one can hardly blame those receiving the benefits.

However, helping those in need while not providing a disincentive to them getting back on their feet is a tricky balance to strike, but I think we had done a relatively good job here in Canada. Having said that, I also admire parts of the United States model, which is further to the right:[3] The US is an incredibly entrepreneurial and innovative economy with an amazing can-do spirit that benefits the whole world.

Those on the right are often viewed as selfish and callous people who only look out for number one, with little or no compassion for others; those on the left are frequently considered envious and suffering from hero syndrome, that is, they can't stand the fact that other people are successful, so they want to take their wealth from them and look good by giving it to others. Personally, I don't believe that most of those on the right are against helping the little guy, and I don't believe that most of those on the left are envious of those who are successful. Left and right share many values, but, again, it's a question of degree or how much.

Equality

However, regardless of one's leaning, left or right, I believe that there are some misperceptions from which both suffer. On the right, people talk about equality in terms of equal opportunity. This is a great idea; however, the reality is that opportunity is rarely, if ever, equal, and it varies significantly from country to country. Although great strides have been made over the years, the reality is that many people still never stand a real chance of *making it*. Having real equality in terms of opportunity is something I believe that both sides would champion, as the more people who are successful, the greater the wealth of society, and the more we all benefit. On the left, people talk about equality in terms of equal, or less-unequal, wealth. And while one can understand why some people feel this would be a better state of world affairs, it's misguided and cannot be achieved without crushing the human spirit and, ultimately, reducing wealth for everyone.

How we improve opportunity for everyone is a vitally important subject, and there are many who work tirelessly at moving the world closer to such a state. Not only is it important from a moral perspective, but ultimately, we would also all benefit from a happier and safer society, with many more people in a position to contribute to making the world a better place. Having said that, I'm also very much a believer in people's right to decide what they want to do, no matter what it is, as long as they do no harm to others.

Whether you lean left or right, I believe it's crucial to have a good understanding of the impact that less or more government has on the productive capacity of the economy.

Go-Between

The government is not a productive entity, a fact that is obvious to many, but not all. For the most part, government acts as a go-between. It takes capital from people and organisations that add value to society and then spends that money or gives it to others. Therefore, any time a politician makes grandiose statements about how much money they're going to spend and how many benefits they will bestow, what they're effectively saying is, 'This is how much money I'm going to take from those who are working to spend or give to others.'

Some politicians like to think that the more they spend and give away, the more generous they are. But you can't be considered generous unless it's your own money that you're giving away. Governments and central banks are, somehow, considered to be great benevolent entities that have endless wealth to bestow upon the citizenry. The truth is that these entities create no wealth and the wealth they do dole out was created by others (you and all of the other taxpayers).

As you can imagine, taking people's hard-earned wealth from them (no matter which method is used) and then redistributing it to others and consuming it should be considered a huge responsibility. If you're taking people's money from them, you would want to ensure that you're only taking as much as others really need; that the government services that the collected money pays for are provided in the most efficient manner; and that government salaries and pension benefits are fair (i.e. similar to what could be obtained in the private sector).

Looking at June 2024 data from the US Bureau of Labor Statistics (BLS), the average wage/salary of a private industry worker in the US was $30.90 per hour, which compares to $37.80 for state and local government workers.

So, government workers are making 22% more than those in the private sector. But the difference is much starker when benefits are included. Total per-hour compensation including benefits is as follows:[4]

- Government employee: $61.37
- Private industry employee: $43.94

While government workers, on average, make 40% more than those in the private sector, some feel that government employees should actually earn less than those in private industry because they have better job security. My view is that government workers should enjoy the same salaries and pension benefit opportunities as those in the private sector, and they should have the same job security.[5]

Who Decides?

As you might expect, people's views differ significantly regarding how much government should be involved in our day-to-day lives. While some don't trust governments at all, others don't trust big business – and many don't trust either. I think that a good dose of scepticism about both is healthy and necessary, because, in each case, you're ultimately dealing with people and, thus, human nature. Not to say that human nature is evil, but we're all susceptible to self-delusion, particularly when it comes to what we believe our true contributions are and thus what we think we deserve in compensation. The private sector has a check on this: the consumer. The consumer decides if the goods and services you provide are worth paying for.[6]

The private sector also has the measuring stick of profit, the lack of which indicates that customers aren't willing to pay enough for the product or service to cover the company's costs. This usually speaks to the sustainability – or, rather, the lack thereof – of the company's business model. Perhaps the product or service is inferior to its competitors and, so, not enough customers are willing to pay for it. Or perhaps it's very good but the company is not able to charge enough to cover its costs. And there are scenarios where customers value a product or service that loses money, and investors are willing to continue funding losses in the belief that the company will one day become profitable.

These two things – a check provided by consumers determining if a service is worth paying for and the measuring stick of profit – are both absent from services being provided by governments. The reason they are absent is because a service being provided by government is typically a monopoly situation where private companies are not allowed to compete. Likewise, they have no real way of deciding how much that service is worth because people don't pay for government services directly; rather, they pay indirectly through governments taxing, printing money and borrowing money. And if the cost of providing the service goes up, the government simply increases your taxes.

Deficits

More often than not, a government spends more than it collects in taxes; this is called deficit spending. For instance, in the US in 2023, we have the following:[7]

- Government revenue (taxes): $4.441 trillion
- Government spending: $6.131 trillion
- Government deficit: $1.690 trillion

In other words, in 2023, the US government spent $1.69 trillion more than it collected in taxes. The two obvious ways to deal with this shortfall would be to increase taxation or reduce spending. However, both are unpopular with voters. If the government increases taxation, then they increase the amount of your productive efforts that they take from you in order to balance their budget, so you're not happy. If they cut spending, the recipients of that spending are not happy. Therefore, governments often do neither and, instead, borrow to fund their spending above the level of the wealth that they collect from you.

Governments like to borrow money to fund their excess spending because when they do that, they rarely get any complaints from their voters This is because people don't see any immediate impact on their personal finances. Everyone seems to be better off; more people or industries are receiving money from the government, and no one has to pay more taxes to fund it. However, as you know, nothing is free, and whatever wealth you receive that you didn't create yourself was provided by someone else. So, when a government borrows money, it borrows from those who have created wealth and stored it up in the form of money. The government takes that money/

wealth and spends it on whatever programme it deems appropriate or on various social benefits. However, the wealth that was borrowed eventually needs to be paid back; otherwise, the government will gain a poor reputation and no one will lend them money anymore, or lenders will demand to be paid a very high rate of interest.[8]

Borrowing From the Future

Here's how it works. The government issues a bond, which means that they borrow money and issue the lender with a certificate explaining how much interest the government will pay on the borrowed money and when they will pay it back. Let's say it was a ten-year bond and that the government borrowed $50 billion. That was $50 billion of productive efforts by people in society who decided to not consume the results of their productive efforts and who, instead, wanted to save it for future consumption; perhaps to spend once they retire. That $50 billion in productive efforts saved as money is then consumed (spent) today by the government. Ten years later, the money needs to be paid back. But, remember, the government consumed the capital and did not invest it. So, the government doesn't have the resources to pay back the loan and so must obtain that $50 billion from the productive efforts of people ten years after issuing the bond. That is, they must tax people in ten years to pay for the *government* benefits that people consumed today. This is how wealth is transferred from the next generation to the one that precedes it. It's effectively a pyramid scheme; those first into the scheme benefit at the expense of latecomers.

Making the duration of the loan an extreme length of time will help explain what is happening. Assume you are very wealthy and you lend the government $1 billion for fifty years and that you will live long enough to have your money eventually paid back to you. The money that the government borrowed from you is consumed immediately by the government handing out cheques to people and paying government workers. But by the time the bonds need to be repaid fifty years later, many or most of those who benefited from that government spending will have passed on. Many of these people will have taken more from the system than they had contributed, which, of course, means that someone else will be needed to put more into the system than they take out. And that person won't be you, because you will be paid back the loan.

Who, then, must put into the system more than they take out? Where will the government get the money to pay you back? The burden will fall largely on the next generation, because they're the only ones from whom the government will be able to extract capital. And, as you know, the extraction could occur in one of three ways. First, they could increase the tax rate on people who will be working fifty years from now, most of whom won't have even been alive when the money you lent the government was consumed by others. Secondly, the government could borrow more money to pay you back. This is what governments have been doing for years, as it meets with little resistance from the populace. However, the amount of interest expense the government (taxpayers) pays on the growing debt pile increases each year. At time of writing, the annual interest expense on federal government debt in the US is steadily moving closer to $1 trillion, and it won't stop there. (Imagine how large the interest expense will be on government debt in fifty years if we don't mend our ways.) Thirdly, the government could print money, which would extract capital from the savings and earnings of workers while at the same time diminishing the value of the money with which they would eventually pay you back. The future generation will be screwed no matter which method the government chooses.

Team Effort

How careful has the United States government been with the wealth they have been taking from the citizenry? By 31 December 2019, before the onset of the global COVID-19 pandemic, total federal debt in the United States had ballooned to $23.2 trillion from $9.2 trillion on 31 December 2007 – a growth rate of 8% per annum over twelve years. This rate of growth in public debt far outstripped the growth of the US economy. This is demonstrated by looking at the total debt as a per centage of GDP. Back in 2007, it was 63%; by the end of 2019, it had reached 107%. (Again, a real team effort; debt has exploded higher no matter which party has been in power.)

Increasingly, it has been debt rather than investment and productivity that has supported GDP. Thus, not only is the level of debt to GDP much higher than it was twelve years ago, but the quality of the GDP is also much lower. As much of the debt was accumulated to support consumption rather than investment, the economy is not in a position to produce the wealth that is required to pay the debt back.

So it won't.

Deficits Matter

A lot of economists and policymakers defend government debt and deficit spending by claiming that the finances of a government are in no way similar to that of an individual or household and that, therefore, government debt and deficits don't matter. They claim that this is true for any government that controls its own money supply. However, the basic principle behind the finances of an individual or household and a government is exactly the same. But there is one significant difference, and now that you have a clear grasp on the concept of money, you probably have a pretty good idea as to what that difference is and how most of us bear the significant and ongoing consequences of that difference.

Let's start by thinking about things from the perspective of a lender making a loan to a family or individual. If a bank were to lend you money so that you could spend more than you're currently earning, the bank would still expect to eventually be paid back the full *value* of the loan.

You'll notice above that I emphasised the word 'value'. Now that you understand the concept of money and you know that governments continually increase the money supply, you also understand that the value of money is continually falling. Value does not mean the same thing as money. Money has value, but that value is constantly being eroded by governments through central banks that continually print money and increase the money supply. That's why when a bank lends you money, it estimates how much money the central bank will print (inflation) over the life of the loan and thus how much value will be extracted from the money that you will eventually pay back. The banks will compensate for all of this by adjusting the interest that they charge you on the loan.

To have confidence that you'll be able to pay the loan back, the bank will want to know all sorts of information about you: *Do you have a job? How long have you been working there? How much do you make? What are your savings and other assets? How much debt do you already owe to other banks?* The bank may even want to know things about your personal character (e.g., *Do you have a criminal record?*). All of this information is collected by the bank to determine the probability of your eventually paying back the full value of the loan plus interest.

Now let's assume you are lending money to a government. Just as with a loan to a family or individual, you expect to eventually be paid back the full value of the loan plus interest. Therefore, you will make an assessment of the likelihood of being paid back the full value by the government.

Before loaning the money, you will be interested to know how much debt the government already owes to other lenders; how much the government is already taxing its people and corporations; and how productive the economy is. This will give you a rough idea as to whether or not the government will be able to raise the necessary taxes to pay back the loan or whether future lenders will continue to be willing to lend the government money. Therefore, the amount of the government's debt and deficits matter a lot.

Backdoor Tax

However, as mentioned above, there is a third method by which a government can raise funds to repay a loan: printing money. This is why some economists and politicians believe that deficits don't matter: governments can simply print whatever they need. But the money that a government prints is made from worthless pieces of paper (or digital numbers) and only achieves its value by extracting capital from the money already in existence – the stuff in your bank account. When a government prints money to repay its debts your money savings decline in value. Of course, if you lent money to the government you would assume a certain amount of future money printing and factor that in to the interest rate you must receive from the government. However, there are two things worth considering. First, for many years governments were not nearly compensating enough for the expected rate of future inflation and in some cases government bonds were issued paying zero interest rates.[9] Second, if our current path continues, the rate of money supply growth could be significantly higher than expected thus diminishing the value the money that's eventually repaid to you by the government.

There are, of course, limits to how much money a government can print. First, if it prints too much money, that could lead to hyperinflation, which would destroy the economy. Secondly, people will eventually figure out that all of the value of printed money comes from their savings and wages. Therefore, a more correct statement than saying that deficits don't matter because governments can print as much money as they need to pay off their debts would be that deficits don't matter – until the explosion of printed money destroys the economy. Or government deficits don't matter – until the populace wakes up to the fact that the money the government prints to fund its deficit spending extracts capital from the rest of society (i.e., it's a hidden tax).

A government is not like a family because a family is not legally allowed to extract capital from their neighbours by printing their own money; only governments can do that. In a nutshell, some people believe that deficits don't matter, because, through the printing of money, the government can take your capital from you without your permission. I think most would agree that this is not okay.

Debt Tsunami

The world's balance sheet is in a terrible mess, and it seems to be deteriorating at an accelerating rate. There is a record amount of debt outstanding, and much of it is, or will be, addressed through an intergenerational transfer of wealth. Government debts don't need to go to zero as long as governments borrow only for *investment* in things like infrastructure, that is, as long as they're actually investing and creating capital rather than consuming it. This sort of investment facilitates productivity growth in an economy. However, most investing should be done in the far more efficient private sector by market players with skin in the game.

The debt pile needs to come down, but it shouldn't be done by simply raising taxes. Rather, it should happen through government reducing spending and government itself shrinking as a percentage of the overall economy. This would result in two things: a reduction in debt and an acceleration of productivity growth in the economy, which will help to shrink the debt as a percentage of the economy. Of course, policymakers are not in favour of reducing spending or shrinking, and that is why many of them recommend printing money to pay back the debt. Printing money takes capital from you just as surely as taxation, but the people will kick up much less of a fuss, as capital extraction through the printing of money is hidden and indirect.

Remember that when a government borrows money and then spends it, it's not the government that has to pay the money back. It's you! Not only does the government take a significant percentage of your productive efforts away from you in the form of taxation, but they also borrow even more money and will present you and your kids with the bill at a later date. They'll tell you it's for your own good. And while some people will benefit from this wealth transfer, by definition, many won't.

Controlling your own printing press is deemed by some to be all that is needed for a country to freely spend as much money as it wants, as long as it doesn't lead to high inflation. I've even heard some policymakers claim that the Federal Reserve could print an infinite amount of money. What does that number look like, exactly? Would they simply put the infinity symbol (∞) on the account at the Fed?

Assuming they were able to inject an infinite amount of money into the economy, that would immediately destroy it. It's like a central banker saying that they can jump off a cliff. Well, that's true, but once they hit the ground, they'd be dead. So why make such a statement? Forget infinity for a second. Assume that the Federal Reserve printed $100 trillion and injected it into the economy. The wealth stored up in your savings you earned over your lifetime would be wiped out as the prices of just about everything you need to buy to enjoy your life would soar. In addition, if you were on a stable pension income, your weekly pay cheque would buy only a fraction of what it had bought previously. The same would be true if you were earning a steady wage – unless you were able to convince your boss to rapidly increase your pay to keep pace with rising prices. Technically, the central bankers could, indeed, print as much money as they want, but, ultimately, it destroys the economy. We'd all be much better off if, instead, they jumped off a cliff. (And yes, that was a joke.)

Default

There is one other thing that differentiates a government from a family or person when it comes to repaying borrowed money: the government can simply decide to default on the loan (i.e. not repay it). Of course, that would ruin the country's credit rating, and people or other countries would stop lending to that country, at least for a while. However, no one would suffer any penalties or jail time. But if you decided not to honour your debt or pay your taxes, there would be severe consequences.

But It's Free

You hear this free money thing a lot from people who attempt to justify why government debts don't matter and, thus, why they should borrow more and more money and spend it when interest rates are very low, because it's free. And the interest rates were only low because central banks were printing trillions of dollars to drive interest rates down, and in so doing, they were extracting trillions of dollars of capital from the citizenry. Some people even claim that it would be irresponsible for governments *not* to borrow and spend when interest rates are so low. I know it should be obvious, but when you borrow money, even at a very low interest rate, that money is not free. It would only be free if you didn't have to pay it back.[10] It would be like saying that if you went to the bank and borrowed $20,000; and the bank didn't charge you any interest on the loan; and you used that money to buy a new car, the car would be free. This is another one of those examples where some policymakers or economists will attempt to convince you that you can get something for nothing.

You can avoid falling victim to this sort of delusion by simply reminding yourself of the cold, hard fact that, apart from things such as sunlight, air and water, nothing comes from nothing. If you receive money for free (not a low-interest loan, but are actually given money) or some economic good at no charge, then that is a transfer of wealth from someone else to you. That transfer may have been voluntary; for example, it might have been a gift. But, more often than not, that transfer is affected through taxation, which, of course, is not voluntary; people would rather pay their taxes than go to jail. However, many of us are more than happy to pay our fair share of taxes to pay for required government services and help those in need.

Some would argue that many government services would be a lot less costly if they were provided by private companies with skin in the game. As well, many believe that we could much more efficiently help those in need without having to use the expensive and inefficient government middleman. Maybe. Regardless of your leaning, at least, with the redistribution of wealth through taxation, it is out in the open and we all know what it is.

Less Bang for Debt Buck

With interest rates having been relentlessly driven down by the Federal Reserve for forty years, governments have taken on a monumental amount of debt for which future generations will be on the hook. Federal debt held by the public in the United States alone has ballooned from $317 billion in 1971 to over $25 trillion by mid-2023.[11] This amounts to over $76,000 of debt per person – every man, woman and child in the country – compared to around $1,500 back in 1971. For a family of five, that's around $380,000.

Over the same time, nominal GDP per capita grew from $5,609 to $81,624.[12] This means that, for the 52-year period from 1971 to 2023, total debt per capita in the United States grew 50x. In contrast, total GDP per capita grew by only 15x. This does not include personal debt. Adjusting for inflation, real GDP per capita grew only 2.5x, or 1.8% per year since 1971. Bottom line is that it takes increasing amounts of debt to keep spending growing. It's not sustainable, and something's gotta to give.

The US federal government debt is over $25 trillion. This means that the government's creditors have the equivalent amount in assets. That is, the taxpayers owe them $25 trillion. However, those assets are an illusion, as they are only worth a fraction of what their holders think they are for the very simple reason that it's impossible to pay those loans back in *real* terms. The only way the government can pay the money back is by using devalued dollars, which means that by the time the asset holders get their money back, it will buy only a fraction of what it could have when they originally lent the money to the government.

Colossal levels of debt and printing money detract from the productive capacity of an economy. The result is that, over time, the government will have an ever-shrinking pile of wealth to redistribute. Of course, this is not good for those who rely on things like unemployment insurance, welfare benefits, healthcare spending and public pension plans – which means that something must change.

ENDNOTES

[1] Simply by providing products and/or services that others are willing to pay you for, you can't help but make the world a better place.
[2] Although there were indeed income thresholds that determined whether or not you were eligible to receive a cheque and help stimulate the economy.
[3] By 'further to the right', I mean from a fiscal perspective rather than social.
[4] US Bureau of Labor Statistics. *Employer Cost for Employee Compensation*. 10 September 2024. https://www.bls.gov/news.release/ecec.nr0.htm?utm_source=substack&utm_medium=email
[5] Some believe that, on average, government workers have higher levels of education than those in the private sector and, thus, they deserve to be paid more. However, pay should be based on output/productivity and not education.
[6] Once companies are paid, you do have the issue of senior executives usually taking far more compensation than is warranted by their contributions. I deal with that in the chapters on stock markets.
[7] Congressional Budget Office.

[8] Discrediting this statement is the one-hundred-year bond that was issued by the serial defaulter Argentina in 2017. It was lapped up by investors who believed that this time was different, that this time Argentina wouldn't default on its promise to pay the money back. However, those investors didn't need to wait long to discover that a leopard never changes its spots. True to form, the Argentine government did default on its hundred-year bond, only three years after it was issued. Give it time, and they'll come out with another hundred-year bond issue; there are always enough gullible investors out there willing to delude themselves and risk their clients' capital for a little extra yield. Note that since writing this, Argentina has new leadership with the intention of getting the country's fiscal house in order.

[9] In 2019, the German government issued €869 million in 30-year bonds that had a negative yield.

[10] Note that for a certain percentage of the population, money is actually free. Free money given to those in need, paid for through taxation of income-earners – is something that most of us would agree is a good thing. However, free money given to the top one percent by printing it and, effectively, stealing it from the hard-earned savings/capital, or purchasing power, of the middle class is completely unacceptable.

[11] By early 2024 this had already grown to $27 trillion.

[12] Federal Reserve Bank of St. Louis.

CHAPTER 11
GOVERNMENT PART 2

No Skin in the Game

So why is it that governments of all kinds seem to spend so freely and take on so much debt? There are a number of reasons, one being that those in government who are making the decisions have no skin of their own in the game. The skin is *yours*. If you don't have your own skin in the game, you're never as careful, and you never work as hard. This is not a criticism; it is merely a fact of human nature, and it's true inside and outside government. Think of how careful you are with your own car compared to a rental.[1] But it's even worse than you think. Not only is the skin not the government's, but, in large part, they've also been convinced by others that it's no one's skin.

> *It is hard to imagine a more stupid or dangerous way of making decisions than by putting those decisions in the hands of people who pay no price for being wrong.*
>
> – Thomas Sowell[2]

Politicians are told that as long as you print your own money, then deficits don't matter; and debt doesn't matter, either, because you can just print money to pay off the debt. It's all part of the something-for-nothing, short-term, delusional way of thinking that runs riot in today's world, and, of course, we're all susceptible of falling for it. Prime evidence of this is a statement made by the Canadian government during the COVID pandemic: 'We took on debt so Canadians wouldn't have to.' Who do they think is on the hook to pay back that debt? I assume the Members of Parliament are not volunteering to pay it back themselves. It would be like your teenager racking up thousands of dollars on your credit card and then telling you that they took on that debt so you wouldn't have to.

It's really quite astonishing, but, sadly, our government is by no means unique in their seeming willingness to convince themselves that they can conjure up real wealth out of thin air and heroically bestow it upon a gracious and applauding group of beneficiaries. Those receiving the money then duly fulfil their patriotic duty by spending it as fast as they can; putting it into stock markets to drive the prices of those stocks higher; or creating a housing bubble – all these things giving the illusion that the economy is in great shape simply because GDP, stock markets and housing prices are all soaring.

Tautologies

Sometimes people will throw a tautology at you – a statement that is always true. Once you've acknowledged it, they will then go on to make false or misleading statements that seem to justify the government printing money or running large deficits. One of my favourites is people saying that there can only be *net investment* in the private sector if the government runs a deficit by borrowing money and spending it. Or put another way, *Thank goodness the government is spending more than it collects in taxes, otherwise there wouldn't be any net investment in the private sector. And let's hope the government runs even larger deficits, so we can have even more private sector net investment.* On first reading that, you might start to think that not only do deficits not matter, but, in fact, they are also a very good thing. However, the truth is, it's all complete nonsense.

Trickery

The trick is getting you to believe that net investment in the private sector is a good thing.

It most decidedly is not.

Investment in the private sector is a good thing; net investment isn't. In fact, net investment is not investment; it is consumption at the expense of investment. The best net investment number for the private sector would be zero. Let's walk through it.

If the level of net investment in the private sector were zero, it wouldn't mean there was no investment going on. For instance, if you lent $50,000 to a company so it could expand its production, there would be a positive investment in the private sector of $50,000. However, the company borrowed that money from you so there is also a negative $50,000 investment (i.e. the company owes you $50,000). When you add your positive $50,000 investment to the negative $50,000 the company borrowed from you, the result is, of course, zero. The situation in the private sector would look like this:

Your loan to the company	+$50,000
The company's liability to you	-$50,000
Net lending in the private sector	$0

All investment within the private sector (i.e. private investors allocating capital to private companies) results in a private sector net investment of zero. This is because every private sector investment has a corresponding private sector liability.

So, what does it mean if the private sector is in a positive net investment position. Well, first off, it is not really investment. All it means is that, instead of money being lent within the private sector to invest and create more capital, private sector lenders have lent that money to the government, which consumes that capital. For instance, if you lent the government $50,000, like in the above example, you would be increasing investment in the private sector by $50,000 i.e. you have a $50,000 investment. However, there is no off-setting negative $50,000 liability in the private sector to take the private sector net investment number down to zero. Instead, you lent your money to the public sector (government). The situation in the private sector would now look like this:

Your loan to the company	+$50,000
Private sector liability	$0
Net investment in the private sector	+$50,000

However, that doesn't mean there is no liability offsetting your investment. The liability is with the government, as the government owes you money, not the private sector. And, therefore, government liabilities or deficits must equal net investment in the private sector:

Your loan to the government: +$50,000
Government deficit spending: -$50,000

And here's the kicker: net investment in the private sector is not really investment. The money has been lent to the government and most government spending is consumption rather than investment. So, the government takes your $50,000 loan and pays government workers, spends it on projects, or gives it to people in the private sector to consume.

Another way in which this is all nonsense is that these people will try to get you to view government deficits as private sector savings. If the government owes $30 trillion, then the private sector has savings of $30 trillion. But this is not true, because the government is not a productive entity. If the government had put that money to productive use and was able to use the proceeds to pay back the $30 trillion, then in that case, the private sector would have savings. However, this is not what the government does with that $30 trillion; instead, they spend it. Then they don't have it anymore. So, the only way the government can pay back the $30 trillion to the private sector is by first taking $30 trillion from that very same private sector. And they will do so through taxation, more borrowing, printing money, or a combination of any two or all three of those methods. All three methods transfer capital from the private sector to the government so it can repay the loan. In short, when there is net investment in the private sector, it simply means that there is a future liability that the private sector owes to itself and, of course, it equals the total amount of government debt.

If the private sector has lent $30 trillion to the government, here's how you can think about it from an accounting perspective:

> Present private sector assets (loans to the government): $30 trillion
> Future private sector liabilities (how the government
>   will repay the loan):   -$30 trillion
> Net private sector assets: ZERO

So, you can see how by just throwing a term out there like 'net investment', proponents of *deficits don't matter* trick you into believing that government is somehow responsible for investment in the private sector – while the truth is the exact opposite. Any time there is net investment, it means that there is that much less investment in the private sector, not more. Not only that, but it also means more capital is being consumed by government and whoever it is they send the money to. So, the larger the net investment number in the private sector, the less capital that's being invested and the more that's being consumed.[3]

Another implication made by those who say that without government deficits there could be no net investment in the private sector is that those private sector assets could not exist without government deficit spending. Again, this is nonsense. The private sector asset existed first and then the private sector decided to lend that pre-existing asset to the government so the government could spend it and create a deficit. It's private sector lending to the government that creates deficits. Public sector deficits do not create private sector assets.

The best net investment number in the private sector would be zero, because that would mean much more capital would be available for investment in the private sector rather than consumed by government. If that number were zero, trillions of dollars could be invested instead of consumed. One can dream.

The Blob

The larger government becomes, the greater its drag on the productive capacity of the economy. This is because more and more capital is extracted from taxpayers, and less and less capital is available for saving and investment in the private sector. And it's not just workers in the private sector who are harmed with out-of-control growth in government; government employees are also at risk of eventually having their pension benefits cut because they simply won't be affordable. Any retired or soon-to-be-retired government workers should worry when they see government payrolls soaring, because at some point their pensions will be shared with the new government workers (i.e. their pensions will be reduced).

Withholding Tax

Of course, politicians who spend all kinds of money become very popular with the part of society that receives the benefits. And because of the way we're taxed, there seem to be fewer consequences for politicians who take more and more wealth from the productive side of the economy. I think this is partly due to the fact that most of the tax we ultimately pay is deducted at source. Our employers withhold the tax and send it to the government. Thus, we never actually get our hands on the full results of our productive efforts. And because we never get our hands on it, we don't have that feeling of government taking it away from us. It's almost as if we feel it was never ours to begin with, and so we don't get as frustrated as we might that such a large part of our wealth is being taken from us.

To a degree, we have all become desensitised, and some more than others. Our pay cheque will tell us what our total, or *gross*, pay was, then it will itemise the different taxes that have been deducted at source and remitted to the government. What we are left with is our *net* pay – the amount that gets deposited into our bank account. Because of this system of deducting taxes from source, we have become conditioned into thinking that it's just the natural order of things that we get to keep only half or two-thirds of what we've earned. But I think it goes even further than that. Because we get our hands on only half or two-thirds of what we earn, we start to think that half or a third is all that we really produced and, thus, have to exchange with others. However, the truth is that our real contribution was our gross pay. Our gross pay is what our company or our customers were willing to pay to us for whatever our contributions, efforts or value propositions were.

This method of deducting taxes at source also has the effect of making it emotionally easier for politicians to take our money from us. It also helps many of them to convince themselves that *they* are the benevolent benefactors bestowing benefits on the populace. Don't get me wrong, I believe there are many politicians who really want to make a difference. And who doesn't like it when people thank them for helping them out? However, if you're helping people with other people's money, then you have no right to take credit for it, whether emotional or reputational. You've probably experienced this when a group of you collected money for a friend or colleague who had experienced some sort of financial or personal setback, and then someone in the group who had contributed nothing or very little tried to take all of the credit by insisting on being the one to hand over the cheque. We all know how annoying that is.

Governments often play the role of hero with other people's money. They collect taxes from a faceless entity called the working population, which makes it very easy for the government to spend that money, and somehow they believe that they are the ones responsible for the wealth that has been created. How many times have you heard politicians say how much *they* are going to spend and how much *they* will give.

We Owe it to Ourselves

Some actually believe there is no cost to governments borrowing money as long as *we owe it to ourselves*. If the US government borrows from US citizens, then for every dollar of debt that the US government has, its citizens have an equal amount in the form of an asset. As demonstrated in the above example, where you lent $50,000 to the government, add your positive $50,000 to the government's negative $50,000 deficit, and it comes to zero.

Thus, you can see that if the US Government borrowed only from US citizens, then no matter how many trillions of dollars the government were to borrow, the country as a whole would have assets that offset those liabilities. The net effect on the balance sheet of the country would be zero. And because the net effect is zero, some mistakenly believe we have nothing to worry about.

We do.

First, as we saw above, your asset of $50,000 is not backed by a government investment of $50,000. Instead, the $50,000 you lent the government was consumed. The government can only pay you back by, in one form or another, taking another $50,000 from the private sector. There is no corresponding asset to back the loan you made to the government. And the more the government borrows, the more that there are no assets to back all of those loans. From an accounting perspective, it looks as if the private sector has all of these savings owed to it by the government, but, in reality, it has zero.

We Don't Owe it all to Ourselves

Of course, not all of the debt the US government borrows is from Americans; much of it is owed to foreigners. The US government balance sheet is in a deficit position with respect to the rest of the world. It has borrowed money from other countries to spend or pay benefits to American citizens, and that money will eventually have to be paid back. And the next generation will largely have to pay off the debts of this generation, just as this generation is paying off the debts of the previous one. The US government's borrowing from foreigners flies in the face of those who say that government debt doesn't matter because we owe it to ourselves, even though that statement is also nonsense. I suppose they could say something like 'We owe it *largely* to ourselves.' They might even to go the extreme of saying that, from a global perspective, debt doesn't matter because the world owes it to itself.

Debt: A Redistribution of Wealth

Regardless, whether a country owes its debt to itself or someone else really makes no difference if the ones who have borrowed the money can't repay it. Let's look at a very simple example. Rather than a country, or the world, I'll use the example of a neighbourhood. Assume that your neighbourhood consists of you and one other person, your neighbour. Your neighbour loses his job and comes to you with a brilliant business proposal. But to get the business up and running, he needs some capital and asks to borrow $10,000 from you, which he promises to pay back in a year. Although he's your neighbour, business is business, so you require him to pay you interest on the money you are lending him. And although the business plan sounds very exciting, it's still a new and unproven business model. Therefore, you require him to pay you a high rate of interest, let's say 10%.

However, things don't work out as planned. Your neighbour had invested $8,000 of the money you had lent him, but after a few months, the business had turned out to be a failure, and it is now bankrupt. He still has $2,000 left of the money he owes you, but he doesn't have to pay the money back for several months. Feeling down and needing a pick-me-up, he decides to use the remaining $2,000 to book an all-inclusive Caribbean trip to Club Delusion. YOLO. He convinces himself that something will come along later that will enable him to somehow pay you back the $10,000. In this scenario, those who say debt doesn't matter would say that this is not a problem, because the neighbourhood owes the money to itself. The neighbourhood has a $10,000 liability (the money your neighbour owes you), and a $10,000 asset (the loan you made to your neighbour). But guess what? You're not getting your money back. There has been a redistribution of wealth within your neighbourhood, from you to your neighbour.

So much of the value of the debt that is outstanding today will never be repaid, because it can't be. The maths simply doesn't work. What is happening is that wealth is being redistributed on an absolutely monumental scale within the system. However, with the ability of policymakers to print money, you can imagine that the debt will be paid back in money terms, but the value of that money will be a fraction of what it was when the lenders originally made the loan. For instance, assume your neighbour prints $10,000 plus interest in order to pay you back the loan you made to him. And assume that there was only $10,000 in the system to begin with. Your neighbour has just doubled the money supply, so now everything doubles in price. Now, the $10,000 of money that your neighbour repays you can only buy half as much stuff as it could when you originally made the loan.

Another way of thinking about it is that, rather than borrow the money from you in the first place, your neighbour could have simply printed $10,000 and used that to try to get their business going – and then go on an all-inclusive trip once the business failed. The impact on you would have been exactly the same; the $10,000 that you didn't lend to your neighbour would have had its purchasing power cut in half because of the newly printed money.

This is what happens when money is printed out of thin air and spent. It happens not only when counterfeiters print money illegally but also when central banks do it legally. Any time someone gets money without that money being a result of first producing capital and then exchanging it for the medium of exchange, then that person gets to consume something at the expense of someone else.

Gross

If we had a system whereby people received all of their gross income and had to write a cheque to the government to fund their fair share of government spending, then I believe governments would be a lot more careful about what they do with that money. They would have to outline *clearly* what the government expenses are and why, and who really needs the money, and then go to the citizenry and ask them to write the government a cheque. It's similar to the way property taxes are paid. Once a year, you get a bill outlining all of the government services for which you are helping to pay. I know that this sort of system would be much more cumbersome than the current one, and governments would likely have to chase down tax-dodgers, so it's probably not feasible. But, prior to 1943, this was the way income tax was collected. Then the government came up with the idea of having employers collect the taxes for them in advance.

A Matter of Trust

Taxes collected by governments fund all kinds of programmes; some are important, some aren't. But government bears a great responsibility for how it doles out that tax revenue. People need to trust that the considerable amount of their productive efforts that are taken from them by the government will go to services that society truly requires or to people who truly need it. One recent example is unemployment insurance in the US and here in Canada. When people are unemployed, our system provides for them via temporary unemployment insurance. Of course, 'the system' is simply you or anyone else who is still working being taxed to fund those benefits. Most people would agree that unemployment benefits are a good thing to have in society. It's sort of an insurance programme that we all pay into, knowing that one day we might need to make a claim on that insurance. However, if the unemployment insurance benefits are too generous, they can dissuade people from looking for work. As mentioned earlier, during the COVID pandemic, the government boosted unemployment benefits to such a level that many people could actually make more money sitting at home than they could going to work and contributing to society.

> ... *any country can have heavy unemployment if it is willing and able to pay for it.*[4]
>
> – Benjamin M Anderson

As a community, we agree to have some of our money taken from us and given to those out of work and I think we do so for two reasons. First, we like to help those who have fallen on hard times. And I don't believe that we do this because we know that one day we could be the one who needs help. Of course, it is true that we could one day be unemployed, but even if we were confident that that would never happen to us, we're still more than happy to help those in need. It's the humanitarian thing to do and it feels good (at least for most of us). The second reason we agree to have our money taken from us and given to others is that we know that, given a chance, people can get back on their feet and retrain or re-educate themselves and then re-enter the workforce and continue making their own contributions to society.

However, importantly, we don't want to give so much money to someone that they are no longer incentivised to go out and find a job. Of course, not everyone would rather just sit around but I don't look down on people who would rather enjoy more leisure time than go to work. I know that if I were younger and in their shoes, I'd be tempted to do the same thing, that is, rather than work forty hours a week, stay home and make almost the same amount of money – or more. Mainly because when I was young, I didn't understand where the money was truly coming from – I wouldn't have put two and two together to see that I would have been benefiting at someone else's expense. When I was in my twenties, I had a real thirst for knowledge (history, geography, philosophy, nature) and I spent a lot of time reading books. However, that didn't pay the bills. But if I was able to collect a monthly cheque that was extracted from my neighbours, it would have been very tempting for me to not look for work and instead sit at home and read a lot more books. And obviously what makes this easy to do is that I don't have to take money from my neighbours, family or friends, the government does it for me by taxing them. A cheque magically arrives in the mail, or my bank account has money deposited into it from the benevolent government.

Unemployment benefits are important, but we should strive to get people off them as soon as is humanly possible – for the good of both the recipients and us.

It is human nature that the more you are taxed, the less incentivised you are to work. The more benefits you receive from the government, exactly the same outcome: the less incentivised you are to work. Unfortunately, suffering-both physical and mental-will always exist. However, our economic prosperity provides the means to support those truly in need. But the more generous we are with people who don't really need the assistance, the less capital there will be for those who really do.

Governments temporarily helping those in need with taxpayer dollars contribute to a stronger economy over time. However, the motive behind driving GDP forward is political and short-term in nature, and the only quick way to influence GDP is through spending (because investment takes too long), which, over the longer term, weakens the economy.

Saved Money is Spent

It's very easy for people to assume that governments can just tax more without there being any impact on the economy, because of the belief that there is lots of excess money out there being hoarded by greedy people (savings) or corporations (retained earnings). However, savings and retained earnings don't sit there idly. They are invested and, thus, they boost the productive capacity of the economy. And note that investment is also capital that is spent, but it is often spent on production processes that are further up the production chain (intermediate goods), and much of that spending doesn't get captured in GDP until a final product is sold.

Who Pays?
Roughly three-quarters of tax revenue in the United States comes from individuals, either directly, through payroll taxes, or through excise taxes (taxes you pay when you buy things like beer – you know, the fun stuff). Thus, only about a quarter of the tax revenue come from corporations (also made up of people). Of the individuals who, collectively, pay three-quarters of the taxes, the wealthy pay the most, but the part of society on which taxes have the biggest impact is the middle class. They may pay a lower tax rate than wealthier people, but more of the income of a middle-class family goes to the necessities of life such as rent/mortgage, food, clothing and education.

For instance, someone making ten million dollars per year may have a much higher tax rate and pay much more in taxes, but their lives are much less impacted than someone making $80,000. I'll just make some numbers up so you can see what I mean. Assume someone making $80,000 has a tax rate of 25%, which is only half the rate paid by someone making $10,000,000. The person making $80,000 pays $20,000 in taxes ($80,000 × 25% = $20,000), while the person making $10,000,000 pays $5,000,000. The person making $80,000 has $60,000 left over with which to pay the bills, for example, the mortgage, utilities, car, education and healthcare. Once all of that has been paid for, the person/family probably won't have that much left over. Meanwhile, the person making $10,000,000 would have $5,000,000 after taxes and a lot more left over once they've paid for the necessities of life. (They probably don't even have a mortgage.) Of course, the wealthy are able to afford better accountants who can help them find ways in which they can reduce their tax bill through offshore tax havens and the like, but the wealthy still pay the largest share of tax revenue.

Progressive Taxation
Progressive taxation is the term for a system whereby you pay a higher tax rate when you earn more money. As we saw above, the more you make, the higher the average tax rate you pay; the rationale being that it will have less of an impact on your day-to-day life. In some ways it seems intuitive that if you make a lot of money then you should pay more taxes, not only in absolute terms (i.e. the number of dollars), but also as a per centage of your income. A person making $10,000,000 and paying a 25% tax rate pays a lot more in taxes ($2,500,000) than someone taxed at the same 25% but making only

$80,000 ($20,000 in taxes). A progressive tax rate means that the average percentage of your income that is taxed also goes up. If the $10,000,000 is taxed at 50%, the tax take will be $5,000,000.

Of course, one could make the argument that just because you can afford to pay more in taxation, it doesn't mean that you should. This view is related to property rights, which are extremely important for an economy to thrive. No property rights, no economy – or, at least, not much of one. Generally, if you have a lot of wealth because you have created more capital than most – capital that others desired and for which they freely exchanged their own capital – then why should someone then have the right to take more of it from you just because you have been so successful? Your wealth has not come at the expense of others. This view would suggest that the fair share of taxation that you pay should equate roughly to the services that you receive from the government. If you happen to be ten times more productive than someone else, why does that give the government the right to take considerably more than ten times from you than what they would take from a someone who produces less?

For instance, let's go back to our island economy where you catch fish, Shirley picks coconuts and Jane collects water. Assume that a fourth person, Grant, arrives on the island. Grant tells the three of you that he will provide government services such as protecting you from wild animals and building paths through the woods that all three of you could use. In return, you each are required to pay Grant for his services; you pay one fish per day, Shirley pays one coconut and Jane hands over a litre of water. You all agree that those services are worth paying for, but it also means that each of you has to work a little longer each day to catch one extra fish, pick one extra coconut and collect an extra litre of water. Thus, the fish, coconut and water you pay to Grant are the taxes you all pay for the government services he is providing. As each of you are collecting four items and giving one to Grant, your tax rate is 25%.

So far, so good. But say you decided to save some of your coconuts and water to invest the time required to build a net so that you can catch more fish. Now you are catching a hundred fish per day. When you hand your one fish over to Grant, he tells you that it isn't enough. He wants more fish because now you are catching more. You tell him it's not fair that you should have to hand over 25% of the fish you catch, because you would be paying twenty-five times more for his government services than Shirley or Jane. You point out that it's not as though you all of a sudden started using twenty-five times more of his government services.

However, it's actually worse than you think, because Grant tells you that to continue benefiting from his services, you need to pay a progressive tax. Because you produce more stuff than the others, the per centage of what you produce that goes to Grant will now be 50%. Fifty fish per day.

There are a few things to note here. First, the more productive you are, the more taxes you pay – and they increase at an accelerating rate. There is more stuff for Grant to tax – a hundred fish instead of four, and then he also increases the tax rate from 25% to 50%. Secondly, you are paying significantly more despite the fact that you are not using any more government services – and there is no increase the level of services provided, . Thus, the government increases its take without making any further contributions to society. Thirdly, if you then take the time to build a boat and become even more productive, Grant will take even more of your fish, in both absolute and per centage terms; perhaps your tax rate will go up to 75%.[5]

Progressive taxes dissuade saving and investment in that entrepreneurs see that the more successful they are, the more that will be taken from them in taxes. An extreme example was the United Kingdom in 1974, the highest rate on earned income was 83%.[6] That rate applied to people making over £20,000, which equated to around £181,000 in 2023 money. In addition, investment income suffered from a surcharge such that it was taxed at 98%.[7] Today, in California the top marginal tax rate (federal and state) is around 50% compared to 37% in Texas which doesn't have any state income tax. I live in the Toronto area and our top marginal tax rate is over 50%. And note that your after-tax take home income is taxed further through things such as sales taxes and property taxes.

Another way of thinking how a progressive tax is an invasion of property rights is to imagine if there were progressive pricing, based on your income, for the things you bought. For instance, if you went to the movies, should you pay twice as much as someone who makes half as much as you – or pay half as much as someone who makes twice as much as you?

One thing that makes progressive taxation seem fair to some people is that there is a belief that many of the people who are making so much money simply haven't earned most of it. Increasingly, this view is accurate, but I believe the answer is to stop providing opportunities for people to obtain capital at the expense of others rather than taking most of the productive efforts away from those who are truly creating value in society.

In some European countries, if you get a speeding ticket, the amount you have to pay depends on your income. This truly is absurd. How can there be different penalties for different people for breaking the same law? Traffic laws are put in place to make drivers safe from each other. If two people are both driving over the speed limit, it's not that one is more dangerous if they make more money. If authorities wish to use a deterrent for repeat offenders, then there are various systems of demerit points that can be implemented i.e. once a driver reaches a certain number of demerit points, then they lose their licence and thus the roads become safer, with even rich offenders no longer being a menace to society (at least not on the road). I know it's not exactly the same, but it would be kind of like giving a twenty-year-old convicted of armed robbery a lengthier prison sentence than a fifty-year-old convicted of the same crime simply because the younger person likely has more years to live (and, therefore, they have more time to give than the fifty-year-old). And that, somehow, a younger person will not be as deterred from the threat of prison because they have that many more years to live. Of course, another absurdity exists in society for some people who commit crimes. Those with the most money are able to hire the best lawyers and will often receive reduced sentences or get off with a warning, while those without the financial means face the full force of the law. Again, effectively, different penalties for people breaking the same law. At the end of the day, we should all be equal before the law, but unfortunately that's not always the case.

Making it Clear

Helping those in need or who are less fortunate is a great thing, but that should be done voluntarily (charity) or through fiscal policy (taxation). Governments should clearly outline how much of your money they will take away to give to someone else who truly needs it. There are statistics that detail how many people in the country are receiving *government* support. This is a misrepresentation of what is going on, and that is part of the problem.

The government does not support anyone. Because the government doesn't produce anything.

All the government can do is transfer capital from one part of society to another. Taxpayers are the ones providing the support, not the government. We should eliminate terms like *government benefits* or *government subsidies* and instead call them what they truly are: *taxpayer benefits and taxpayer subsidies.*

Regardless, you might feel that the government is taking too much from you and giving too much to someone else. Or you might want the government to collect even more in taxes, preferably from someone else. Or you might be a socialist wanting to confiscate most people's wealth to redistribute it to the less fortunate. Regardless of your political views, with taxation, how your money is being confiscated from you is clearly outlined (more or less), and we all have the opportunity to voice our opinions to try to effect change if we deem the level of taxation and/or spending to be inappropriate. However, if governments are spending more than they collect in taxes, it gives even more people the opportunity to consume more than they produce. And while this is very popular with those receiving the extra benefits, the government can only spend more than it collects in taxes by either borrowing or printing money – and that capital also comes from taxpayers. One simple rule to remember is that the more the government spends, the more that is taken from the citizenry. And it matters not which way the government gets its hands on the capital. It's just that some ways of getting it are a little more obvious than others.

Of course, if the only methods of obtaining capital from the citizenry were through taxation and borrowing more, then government debt and deficits would be much lower today. First, if the government kept increasing taxes, then tax rates would soar and the public would not stand for it. Secondly, if the government borrowed more, interest rates would soar, as lenders began to fear that the government would not be able to raise the required taxes to repay the debt.

The Path of Least Resistance

The third method of obtaining capital from the citizenry, printing money, is the least painful for governments because it's the method that meets with the least resistance. It meets with the least resistance because people can't directly see their capital being confiscated. But, rest assured, it's being confiscated just as surely as it would have been through higher taxation. For the last fifteen years, central banks around the world have been printing money hand over fist and using it to buy government bonds. Thus, the central banks own a significant amount of government bonds, which represents the money borrowed by governments.

For instance, the Bank of Japan owns approximately half of that country's government debt. It purchased that debt by printing money, which extracted capital from the money holdings of its citizenry. In my opinion, this stealthy confiscation of capital is immoral and an invasion of property rights. It enables governments to extract far more capital from their citizenry than they would ever agree to or vote for. It results in significantly more capital being consumed than invested in society and results in declining productivity growth and far less wealth in this world than there otherwise would be. Even worse, it has resulted in obscene levels of wealth disparity. Finally, printing money leads to higher prices, which is the subject we turn to in the next chapter.

ENDNOTES

[1] Note that this doesn't apply to everyone, as there are some out there who are more careful with other people's money than their own.
[2] Thomas Sowell is a great economist and an even greater communicator. I highly recommend reading any of his many books.
[3] See Bob Murphy for more discussion on this subject.
[4] *Economics and the Public Welfare*, p. 171.
[5] Note that the way a progressive tax works is that the rate increases only for the additional money you make. For instance, you might pay 20% federal tax on your first $100,000, 25% on the next $100,000 of income and so on.
[6] Eduqas, Part of WJEC. https://resource.download.wjec.co.uk/vtc/2015-16/15-16_20/unit7/TaxRates73-90_resource.pdf
[7] *Wikipedia*. History of Taxation in the United Kingdom.

CHAPTER 12
INFLATION: WHAT CAUSES IT?

Resignation

Inflation has become such an accepted fact of life for most people that they expect the prices of almost everything to rise over time. They have resigned themselves to the fact that this is just the way things are and that it's some sort of unavoidable, natural phenomenon. And people feel this way because it is all they have known – and what their parents have known. Indeed, it seems that most policymakers have convinced themselves that not only is inflation a fact of life, but that it's also actually a good thing. And as long as inflation doesn't get out of control, rising prices are needed for an economy to grow.

Nothing could be further from the truth.

In fact, as discussed earlier, the natural order of things is the exact opposite. In general, prices should be slowly but steadily falling over time.

In this chapter, I'll attempt to explain what inflation is and then discuss why policymakers desire it.

Muddying the Waters

The concept of an increase in the money supply leading to higher inflation was accepted as common sense by great thinkers from the philosopher David Hume to the aforementioned classical economist David Ricardo. As we have seen, the term 'inflation' used to mean an increase in the money supply, which, all else being equal, would then result in an increase in the prices of goods and services. Conversely, a decrease in the money supply was known as 'deflation', which, all else being equal, would result in a decrease in the prices of stuff.

However, today, inflation and deflation are generally considered to be a rise and fall, respectively, in the prices of consumer goods and services such as cars, phones, food, and air travel. The change in the definitions of the words 'inflation' and 'deflation' was not some innocuous happenstance. Rather, it served to muddy the waters in terms of understanding the cause of rising prices. The change in definition means that today, the word 'inflation' denotes a symptom (rising consumer prices) rather than the cause (increasing money supply). And, like anything, if you focus only on the symptoms, it can be tricky trying to figure out the underlying cause.

Regardless, although inflation and deflation should refer to changes in the money supply, due to convention, I'll also use it to describe changes in the prices of stuff. But I believe things will remain clear as we progress.[1]

Inflation/Deflation Scenarios

With the old definition, things were very clear (too clear for some) with respect to cause and effect. If the amount of money in the system was inflating at a rate faster than goods were being produced, then the prices of those goods would necessarily go up – because there was more money than goods. And, conversely, if the amount of money in the system was deflating, the prices of goods would fall – because there was less money than goods. It was all very intuitive.

Here are several scenarios relating to changes in the amount of money and stuff being produced and the impact those changes can have on the prices of that stuff.

Scenario 1:
- Supply of money is inflating.
- Supply of stuff is deflating.
  - Result: More money chasing less stuff, resulting in the prices of stuff rising rapidly.
  - Example: The amount of money in the economy is growing rapidly and each year, fewer bikes are produced. The result is far more money per bike in the economy; thus, the prices of bikes rise rapidly each year.

Scenario 2:
- Supply of money is inflating.
- Supply of stuff also inflating but at a slower rate than money.
  - Result: More money chasing not as much more stuff, resulting in the prices of stuff rising, but not as rapidly as in Scenario 1.
  - Example: The amount of money in the economy is growing rapidly. Each year, the number of bikes produced also increases, but at a slower rate than the growth of the money supply. The result

is, again, more money per bike each year. Thus, prices of bikes still go up each year, but the increase is not as much as in Scenario 1.

Scenario 3:
- Supply of money is inflating.
- Supply of stuff is also inflating but more rapidly than money.
  - Result: More money but even more stuff, resulting in the prices of stuff falling.
  - Example: The amount of money in the economy is growing each year, but bikes are being produced at an even faster rate. The result: each year, there is slightly less money per bike in the economy. Thus, each year, the prices of bikes fall.

Scenario 4:
- Supply of money is deflating.
- Supply of stuff is inflating.
  - Result: Less money chasing more stuff, resulting in a rapid decline in the prices of stuff.
  - Example: The amount of money in the economy falls each year, while bike production grows. Result: Far less money per bike each year. Thus, the prices of bikes fall rapidly.

Scenario 5:
- Supply of money is deflating.
- Supply of stuff is also deflating, but not as fast as money.
  - Result: Less money chasing 'not as much' less stuff, resulting in a slow decline in the prices.
  - Example: The amount of money in the economy falls each year. The production of bikes also falls each year but not as rapidly as the supply of money. Each year, there is less money per bike in the system and so the prices of bikes fall slowly over time.

Scenario 6:
- Supply of money is deflating.
- Supply of stuff is also deflating, at a rate faster than money
  - Result: Less money chasing even less stuff, resulting in an increase in prices.
  - Example: The amount of money in the economy falls each year,

but bike production falls at an even faster rate. The result: each year there is more money per bike in the system and so the prices of bikes rise each year.

There are other scenarios, but I think you get the idea. But note that there can be two main causes of a sustained increase in price inflation: either the money supply grows faster than the supply of goods or the supply of goods falls faster than the supply of money.

What we have been experiencing for decades is Scenario 2, where the amount of stuff being produced in the economy increases each year but the supply of money increases even faster. This has resulted in a steady rise in the prices of goods and services over time, and it has become known as inflation.

Good Deflation

However, it was not always this way. For most of the 1800s in the United States, Scenario 3 was the norm. There was an increase in the supply of money, and that increase was very slow because it was based on the amount of gold in the economy. Thus, the growth of the money supply was restricted by how much gold was mined and minted into new money. There were also periods during that century when there were tremendous increases in the amount of stuff being produced; thus, for many years there were steady declines in the prices of stuff. Note also that during this period, the United States experienced rapid population growth, yet the slow but steady growth of the money supply was still enough to make the US the greatest economic power in the world. Its booming population did not require a booming money supply.

With money being based on gold, discoveries of new gold deposits somewhere in the world would result in faster increases in the money supply and, thus, consumer price inflation. However, these discoveries were rare, and their impacts were small. For instance, according to Lawrence H. White, the largest gold supply shock on record was the California gold rush, which started in 1848, and the Australian gold rush that began in 1851. Together, they contributed to a rise in prices globally of 26 per cent between 1849 and 1867. However, that equated to an average annual increase of only 1.3 per cent.[2]

Smaller Denominations

When the prices of stuff are falling, it means that money is becoming more valuable (i.e. it can buy more stuff). For example, say it costs one cent to buy a piece of gum, but then the gum companies discover more efficient ways of producing the gum, and, because they compete with each other, the price of gum reduces to half a cent. As we discussed earlier, this is easily solved by minting money into ever-smaller denominations as it becomes more valuable. New coins can be minted in half-cent denominations.[3] This is what happens when you have 'sound money.' This was the term used to describe gold or silver coins that you could actually hear clinking in your pocket and that gave you confidence that there was real value in the money you received in return for handing over your hard-earned capital. In stark contrast, paper money is as silent as the capital theft that occurs when central banks print more of it.[4] As paper money loses its value relentlessly as policymakers print more of it and redistribute your capital to others, smaller denominations eventually disappear. On the other hand, sound money, due to the productive investments of millions of people with skin in the game, becomes more valuable over time and can be reduced into smaller and smaller denominations. And even with a growing population, the amount of money in the economy does not need to be increased.

You would think that a situation where the prices of goods and services are becoming more affordable for people would be a good thing – and it is. It's known as *good* deflation. But policymakers seem to have convinced themselves and the citizenry that any sort of price decline is a bad thing.

Again, nothing could be further from the truth.

Bad Deflation

However, there is such a thing as *bad* deflation, and that is almost any scenario in which the supply of money is falling. And there were periods in the past when this happened, the most notable example being the Great Depression of the 1930s. Decreases in the money supply can happen when people are paying off their bank loans at a rate faster than those taking out new loans. It could also happen if the central bank reduced the total amount of reserves in the system to the point where banks no longer had any more reserves on which they could pyramid loans.[5]

Note that decreases in the prices of assets such as houses and stocks are not examples of bad deflation, unless they are happening due to a decrease in the money supply. A decrease in house or stock prices usually results after those prices have first been bid up to sky-high levels; a speculative frenzy. Their declines from such peaks simply represent the markets trying to return to normal or fair value. Of course, this is not pleasant for those who bought near the top, but it doesn't mean that policymakers should step in and prevent the decline from happening. However, this is exactly what they do and I discuss this in detail in the chapters on housing and stock markets.

Growing the Money Supply

A stable money supply is key to economic prosperity. But, of course, not everyone agrees with this, particularly governments. You'll soon see why. There are other schools of economic thought that prescribe various changes to the money supply. For instance, in the twentieth century, Milton Friedman, who is accredited with founding the economic school of thought known as monetarism, recommended a slow but steady increase in the supply of money (3 to 5% per annum, I believe) as the economy grows.

In the United States, the monetary base, which only the Federal Reserve can create, has increased at an annual rate of 7.5 per cent since 1959.[6] (Remember that the banking system creates deposits off the monetary base.) Over that same period, the increase in the prices of consumer goods (or inflation) as measured by the Consumer Price Index (CPI) has averaged around 3.7 per cent.[7] The reason prices didn't rise as fast as the supply of money was due to the fact that the amount of stuff being produced was growing faster than the money supply.

However, growth in productivity in the United States is not what it once was. Of course, it can be cyclical, depending on the development of new technologies, but looking longer term, you can see that productivity growth has slowed. The first slowing phase happened after the United States went off the gold standard in 1971.

Productivity growth by decade:[8]

Decade	Productivity Growth
1950s	2.7%
1960s	2.8%
1970s	2.0%
1980s	1.5%

With the dawn of the internet and, perhaps, globalisation, productivity then picked up again in the 1990s and 2000s, but since then, it has started to fall – and I believe a large contributor to this decline has been the financialisation of the economy:

Decade	Productivity Growth
1990s	2.3%
2000s	2.8%
2010s	1.2%
2020s	1.7%

Good Deflation: A Recent Example

One of my favourite examples of good deflation is flat screen televisions. When they first came out in the early 2000s, they were very expensive. They cost thousands of dollars. Consequentially, not many people could afford them and, thus, not a lot of them were produced. However, by investing in innovation and research and development, companies learned how to make flat screen televisions at a much lower cost, and they were also able to expand capacity so that they could mass-produce them. Those companies then made much more money because far more people could afford to buy their televisions.

However, the high profitability attracted competition from other companies, who entered the market and attracted customers by offering their television sets at lower prices. This forced the original television set producers to lower their prices. Th more productive the companies became, the more the prices of their television sets fell. Importantly, however, this can only happen if there is freedom of competition and no barriers to entry erected by governments (e.g. excessive regulation or import restrictions such as tariffs). Thus, the price of a flat screen television was driven down by competition eliminating high profitability. The productivity growth in the manufacturing of televisions was even faster than the increase of the money supply; therefore, their prices fell steadily over time. The lower prices made televisions more affordable, leading to an expanding market, which allowed the television manufacturing industry to make significantly more money despite the falling prices.

From a consumer perspective, I'm sure you would agree that this good deflation is to be welcomed. For instance, isn't it great that over the last couple of decades the prices of flat screen TVs went from thousands of dollars to a few hundred dollars today? And they're also better quality now. And note that if it hadn't been for the money supply increasing at an average rate of 7.5 per cent each year, the prices of those televisions today would have been even lower. And, finally, just a reminder that all of this great stuff happens not because of governments and central banks attempting to stimulate the economy but, increasingly, in spite of all that.

Of course, good deflation is a really good thing for consumers, but don't tell your local central banker. They believe that falling prices are bad for the economy. Their belief is related to what some policymakers and economists call 'the paradox of thrift'. I call it 'the paradox of the paradox of thrift', because it's an absurd doctrine.

The Paradox of Thrift

'Thrift' is simply a word for being careful with your money (i.e. not spending it recklessly). Most would think that this is a good thing. Spoiler alert: it is. And of course, the word 'paradox' means a contradiction, or something that does not mean what it seems at first glance. Thus, 'paradox of thrift' implies that being careful with your money is not actually a good thing. It goes something like this. Because any time you spend money it becomes someone else's income, many policymakers believe that consumer spending is the fount of all economic prosperity. And since saving is sort of the opposite of spending, they then conclude that saving must be detrimental to the health of the economy because your saving is depriving someone else of an income. As more people save and deprive others of income, companies see their sales decline; thus, they lay off employees, which results in even less money being spent and, thus, even less income for others in the economy – and even more layoffs. Eventually, so these people believe, the whole economy spirals downward into a black hole, never to return.

As usual with these sorts of things, some of the arguments seem to make sense. But as soon as you bother to even barely scratch below the surface, you quickly understand how absurd it is. The first thing that might pop into your mind if you believe in this sort of doctrine is that the more people consuming their capital, the better it would be for the economy. But most people understand that the whole world cannot consume its way to prosperity, despite the fact that many seem to try. Most people understand that the more you consume and the less you save, the less well off you are financially. But policymakers might respond that just because you're well off financially, with lots of savings in the bank, it doesn't mean that's good for the economy. Well, actually, it does. The key is this: just because you are saving your capital, that doesn't mean that it doesn't get spent. It does get spent, but there are two key differences. First, someone else is spending your capital for you. Secondly, the nature of that spending skews more to investment than consumption.

Because you've decided to forgo consuming some of the capital that you have produced and have, instead, saved it by depositing it in your bank account, your capital is then available to the bank to lend to others for investment purposes. And those borrowers can put your capital to work to create more capital. So you savings are still providing income for others, but the things they are producing may be intermediate goods that are not captured in GDP. Therefore, by delaying your own consumption of capital, you contribute indirectly to the creation of additional capital by others.

The second thing that might lead you to question the doctrine of paradox of thrift is that although consumption is the ultimate end-game of all investment, investment must happen before consumption, and investment can occur only after capital has been saved. The less capital that is saved, the less investment that can occur, and the less consumption that can happen in the future.

The Spiral

Policymakers' fearmongering about the horrors of deflation is related to this doctrine, and they believe, or at least tell you, that if people expect lower prices for things, then they will hold off purchasing those things until those prices fall. And again, as people reduce their spending, then companies will sell less stuff and make less money, so they will have to start laying off their employees; and those laid-off employees, in turn, will have less money to spend, which will lead to even lower profitability and more layoffs. Cue spiral.

Again, to understand how absurd this line of thinking is, all one needs to do is think of real-life examples of products that have fallen in price over many years. Not only did people not stop buying them and wait for lower prices, they bought more. People will continue to buy consumption goods in a slow deflationary environment despite the fact that they could save some money by waiting. This is because the amount of money you can save by forgoing a whole year of enjoying a product is usually not worth it.

As discussed earlier, people will hold off on purchasing assets such as houses if they are falling in price, but that's only because the house was probably ridiculously overpriced due to a housing bubble deliberately created by policymakers. Of course, if you are expecting a sale on sofas a week from now then it would be smart to delay your purchase, but that is a completely different matter to wait a week to buy something at half price versus waiting a whole year because there is slow and steady deflation in consumer prices.

No Spiral

Let's look at an example to help clarify why people won't delay their consumption in a deflationary environment (i.e. falling prices). Zero inflation – prices neither rising nor falling – is considered by many policymakers to be too low, as without the fear of prices rising, policymakers believe you won't be encouraged to go out and consume your capital. The response by central bankers is to increase the money supply by driving interest rates to zero and/or directly printing money (i.e. increasing bank reserves) to get prices rising by 2% per annum. Only then do they believe that you'll do the right thing with your capital and spend it.

Consider something even worse than no inflation. Assume a central banker's worst nightmare: actual price deflation of 2% (i.e. prices are falling 2% annually). Policymakers believe that in this sort of environment, consumer spending would grind to a halt, as everyone would simply wait for lower prices in a year's time. You're probably already starting to notice the absurdity of it all, but let's go through a couple of examples that expose how fallacious this doctrine is.

First, if your fridge or stove stopped working, you wouldn't care at all about what prices might be a year from now, because life without either appliance – or any other sort of necessity – would be pretty difficult. Prices being 2% lower in a year's time is not going to encourage you to delay you from buying a replacement. Okay, that's pretty obvious, as that's why those products are called *essential*. But what about non-essential items? Same result.

Assume that you already have a television and you are thinking of buying another one for the basement for your teenage kids. This would be more a luxury than an essential – although some parents might deem it an essential ☺. However, you notice that the prices of televisions have been falling 2% per annum. Policymakers believe you would wait a whole year to get a better deal on a television. And that, if in a year's time you expected prices to be another 2% lower the following year, you might delay your purchase another twelve months. Heck, if you expect 2% deflation to go on indefinitely, you may never buy that second television for your basement. Really? Let's do the maths.

Assume that the price of the television today is $300. With price deflation of 2%, next year that television will cost $294. So here are your choices: (1) buy the non-essential second television for the basement today for $300; or (2) wait twelve months and save yourself six dollars. Another way of thinking about it is that by purchasing the television today and not waiting twelve months, it would cost you fifty cents a month (11.5 cents per week; 1.6 cents per day) to have that television in the basement for the first year. (*Hey Dad, instead of listening to loud music in the living room, can I go watch television in the basement*? I'd say that is 1.6 cents well spent.)

Some Other Causes of Inflation

Over shorter periods, other things can contribute to inflation, for example, supply shocks that cause a decrease in the available goods for purchase, such as we experienced during the COVID pandemic. On its own, this may have led to some inflation. But, due to the fact that, at the same time, the central banks printed trillions of dollars that were effectively lent to the government who then handed it out to people to go and buy a diminished number of available goods, extremely high inflation was practically unavoidable. This was Scenario 1 above (supply of stuff falling and the supply of money increasing – rapidly). However, there wasn't a shortage of *all* goods during COVID. Yes, car manufacturing declined significantly, but on the other hand, the volume of goods going through the ports in California during the pandemic were at record levels because all of the consumer spending.

Port of Los Angeles Loaded Container Imports:[9]
1 July 2018 to 30 June 2019: 4.9 million

1 July 2019 to 30 June 2020: 4.4 million
1 July 2020 to 30 June 2021: 5.7 million

Note that it was March 2021 when the $1,400 stimulus cheques were sent out to US citizens.[10] Inflation by month in that year was as follows:

- February: 1.7%
- March: 2.6%
- April: 4.2%
- May: 5.0%

Stimulus cheque–driven demand resulted in record numbers of goods flowing through US ports.

Some believe that inflation results from greedy corporations who charge ever-higher prices for their products so that they can make more money. Of course, corporations will always attempt to maximise their profitability, and, to be sure, greedflation happens. But to continually raise your prices at the expense of the customer value proposition is to eventually sign your own death warrant as a going concern, as it opens the door for the competition to poach your customers.

Imagine if, all of a sudden, you decide to double the price of your bikes from $500 to $1,000, not because you've doubled the quality of the bikes but because you want to make more profit. The market system has a way of self-regulating such that greedflation doesn't last for long. Despite this, there are indeed companies that attempt to continually raise their prices to achieve excess profits. However, as companies always try to maximise profitability, it seems strange that over the last fifty years, greedflation has caused only around 2–3% inflation (according to the official numbers). Why was it that the only times greedflation led to very high levels of inflation was when the money supply was going through the roof (in the 1970s and, more recently, during COVID)? One answer might be that when it is well known by consumers that the economy is suffering from inflation, then those consumers may be more resigned to paying higher prices, and so companies will jack up their prices, whether or not such increases are warranted. So it may be that while greedflation can contribute to inflation it can only do so once policymakers have set the process in motion by exploding the money supply higher.

Velocity of Money

Other people believe that inflation is caused by the velocity of money, which refers to the number of times money is spent in the economy over a given period, usually a year. For example, if in our island economy there's a total of $15 on the island and that money changes hands ten times in a year, then the velocity of the money would be 10.

However, if the number of goods produced on the island were to double, the money would have to work twice as hard to facilitate the exchange all of those goods. The velocity of the money would increase; it would change hands more often. Some people believe that if money is being spent more often, then it will cause prices to rise. At first blush, that seems to make sense, but I'm not sure that it does. If money, the medium of exchange, is simply used to exchange real resources effectively, then how often those real resources change hands should not impact their prices.

Perhaps one way of thinking about how money can work harder as the medium of exchange for an increasing amount of goods without impacting their prices would be if, instead of a one island economy, we had two. One island, Liberty Island, is particularly good at producing a lot of fish, coconuts and water; the other island, The Island of Truth, is better at producing yams, leather and goat's milk. The people in our two island economies decide they want to exchange goods with one another, but there is no way of transporting goods to and from each island. So, they build a boat. In effect, the boat becomes a medium of exchange, because capital is temporarily stored on the boat. The boat is an agreed-upon mechanism that both sets of islanders can use to affect the exchange of the capital that they are all producing. This is similar to the role that money plays in a developed economy.

Now, both island economies are using the boat to exchange their goods. In the parlance that we have been using (borrowed from others), when the people of Liberty Island take their goods over to The Island of Truth to acquire theirs, the means of payment are fish, coconuts and water. The medium of exchange is the boat. So, the goods are the means of payment, or capital, and the boat is the medium of exchange, or money. The capital is temporarily stored up in the boat.

If the residents of the islands decide they want to consume more stuff, then each of them needs to do more work and save some of their capital and invest it to create more stuff. They can then exchange that extra stuff with the other island. But they wouldn't need to build another boat; it would simply make more trips. The velocity of the boat (the medium of exchange), would increase, but note that it doesn't result in prices increasing for the goods that the islands' residents are exchanging with each other. Instead, the boat just has to work harder because more stuff is being produced.

Note that if the island residents wanted to consume more stuff, it wouldn't do any good to simply build another boat – increase the money supply. The amount of capital (stuff) in the island economies would still be the same. Having two boats would simply mean that each boat would transport less stuff. There would be less stuff stored up in each boat – which, of course, is what happens when policymakers increase the money supply (the medium of exchange becomes less valuable; each unit of money stores less capital). Also note that now there are two boats doing the work, the velocity of the medium of exchange (the average number of trips per boat) would halve.[11]

Importantly, both capital (means of payment) and money (medium of exchange) are required for an economy to thrive, but it's only the expansion of capital that grows an economy, not growth in the money supply.

Now, in this analogy treating boats as the medium of exchange (i.e. the mechanism that exchanges capital between two parties), boats have a limitation that money doesn't have. If more and more capital keeps being produced, it might get to the point where the boats are constantly travelling between the two islands (note that the velocity of the medium of exchange is going up but the prices of the capital are not). Eventually it might get to the point where the amount of stuff being created on the two islands is more than the two boats can carry. In this case, more boats would need to be built. In contrast, money is different in that, if more and more capital is being produced, there is no limit to how much of it can be stored up in each unit of currency.

Let's go back to the island economy scenario where three fish, three coconuts and three litres of water are being produced each day. Assume that thirty shells are being used as money and each person starts the day with ten of them. You use your ten to buy a coconut and litre of water, each of which costs five shells. Now you're out of money. However, you catch three fish, keep one for yourself, and sell the other two for five shells each. You are back to ten shells. The prices per item are as follows:

- Fish: 5 shells
- Coconut: 5 shells
- Water: 5 shells

Now assume that each of you increases the amount of capital you produce by five times. You now produce the following:

- You: 15 fish
- Shirley: 15 coconuts
- Jane: 15 litres of water

What this means is that, because the money supply has not increased, each shell will now represent five times the capital it did before you all increased your productivity. For instance, you catch fifteen fish and eat five of them, which leaves you with ten fish to sell: five each to Shirley and Jane. Likewise, for Shirley and Jane, who each have ten coconuts and ten litres of water to sell, respectively. You start the day with ten shells and buy five coconuts and five litres of water, which means that the price of each item is one shell. The new prices per item are:

- Fish: 1 shell
- Coconut: 1 shell
- Water: 1 shell

Each fish now costs one shell instead of five. The greater the productivity of the economy, the more capital that can be stored up in each unit of money. Another way of thinking about it is that the prices are reducing in terms of the number of shells (good deflation).

However, policymakers want you to believe that deflation is a very bad thing, which justifies them rapidly increasing the money supply and causing inflation that robs you of your wealth.[12]

Disinflation

Disinflation describes a situation where the rate of inflation is falling. Policymakers will often congratulate themselves on achieving such an outcome. However, there is a big problem with this. Although the rate of inflation may be falling, prices are still rising, albeit a little less each year. For example, say a $5 cheeseburger increases in price by 10% in 2023, but in 2024 it only goes up 9% and in 2025 it only goes up 8%. Yes, there is disinflation; inflation is coming down. But prices are still rising. Here are how the prices would drop in the constantly disinflationary environment as described above:

2022: $5.00
2023: $5.50   (+10%)
2024: $6.00   (+9%)
2025: $6.48   (+8%)
2026: $6.93   (+7%)
2027: $7.35   (+6%)
2028: $7.71   (+5%)
2029: $8.02   (+4%)
2030: $8.26   (+3%)
2031: $8.42   (+2%)

As you can see, if the disinflationary environment were to last nine years, the price of cheeseburgers would increase by $3.42 (+69%) over that period. So, yes, policymakers may have successfully reduced the rate of inflation, but the price of cheeseburgers still continued rising each year – and by 2031, they are significantly more expensive than they were at the start of the disinflationary period.

You'll notice that I stopped in 2031 when the inflation rate got down to 2%. This is because once policymakers get prices increasing 2% per annum, they declare *mission accomplished*. But you're still getting ripped off by 2% every year. For instance, with 2% inflation, in 2032, the price of the cheeseburger would go up to $8.59; in 2033, it would be $8.76; and so on, until, in 2041, it would be $10.27 (an increase of 22% since 2031 – the year the policymakers declared victory). Not only that, but the 2% inflation rate becomes more and more punitive every year because it resulted in a larger absolute dollar increase. In 2031, 2% inflation on a $8.26 cheeseburger is an increase of 16.5 cents. But a 2% increase in 2041 when the price is $10.07 results in an increase of 20 cents. And that number keeps going up. The maths is simple: the higher the price, the more money is siphoned away from you by 2% inflation.

Disinflation Analogy

The way I like to think about disinflation is through an analogy, with cheeseburgers, pants size and health representing consumption, economic capacity and economic productivity, respectively. Assume that policymakers keep telling you that consumption is key to economic health and so they lower interest rates so you can afford to borrow more money and increase your consumption. You particularly like cheeseburgers and start binging on them, happy in the knowledge that you're providing an income to the owners of the burger joint. However, you start putting on weight. You need to buy a larger pair of pants. Policymakers are pleased with this outcome, as there was excess material (resources) in the economy that were not being used up. But now you find your health is deteriorating. Your productivity starts to fall. You decide to improve your health by consuming fewer cheeseburgers; instead, you start investing in your body via nutrition and exercise. You shed a few pounds, and now find that your pants are too big for you. Your happy conclusion is that you need to have your pants altered (i.e. your pants need to adjust to your improved health). However, some economists would view things the other way around. They would say that the slack in your slacks needs to be used up. Your pants have unused capacity, and increasing your consumption of cheeseburgers would be the best way to get that excess space in your pants back to work.

So now you go crazy eating cheeseburgers, and a week later, you've put on eight pounds. And sure enough, just as those economists promised, you find that some of the slack in your pants has gone. Your pant's underutilised capacity is being put back to work. The following week, you put on another nine pounds, and yet more slack is used up. By the third week, after you gain another ten pounds, you find that all of the slack has gone. There is now full employment in your pants (so to speak).

You decide you'd better stop increasing your cheeseburger consumption. But you're still putting on ten pounds a week, and you find that your pants are now getting a little snug. Your productivity starts to suffer as a result, so you decide you'd better actually cut back a bit on your cheeseburger consumption. In week two, you gain only nine pounds. Now your pants are really tight, so you decide to cut your cheeseburger consumption even more. You put on eight pounds in the third week. Now your pants are so tight that you can't even do up the button. You continue cutting back.

You're still gaining weight, but one pound less each week. Your weight gain is experiencing disinflation, but your health continues to deteriorate. Why? Because you're still gaining weight, only at a slower rate.

By week eleven, you're no longer putting on any more weight. You congratulate yourself on getting your weight inflation down to zero. The only problem: you're fifty-five pounds heavier than you were when you started cutting back on the cheeseburgers (10 + 9 + 8 + 7 + 6 + 5 + 4 + 3 + 2 + 1 = 55). Indeed, if you were a central banker, you would have declared mission accomplished once you got down to putting on two pounds per week.

A thriving and productive economy should be experiencing slow deflation as consumers benefit from productivity improvements and competition that competes away excess profits.

The real scourge of inflation is that it's asymmetrical: prices go up, but they rarely subsequently fall. Thus, anyone with savings or earning an unindexed income or wages that don't rise as fast as inflation suffers a permanent loss of capital/wealth from which someone else benefits.

Now let's have a look at why the real increase in consumer prices is much higher than official government numbers tell you they are.

ENDNOTES

[1] Economic journalist Henry Hazlitt differentiated between the two by calling an increase in the money supply *inflation* and an increase in prices *price inflation*.
[2] *Better Money. Gold, Fiat or Bitcoin?* Lawerence H. White. Cambridge University Press, 2023. pp. 65–6.
[3] Recall from the 'Evolution of Money' chapter that in the UK there used to be a coin called a farthing (a quarter of a penny).
[4] Note that paper money would also be sound were its quantity not increased at such prodigious rates.
[5] Note that the Federal Reserve has reduced reserves twice in the last ten years, but the starting point was outlandish excess reserves in the banking system that were a result of the Fed printing money to drive asset prices higher. In other words, commercial banks had far more reserves than they needed with which to make loans. More on this later.
[6] Federal Reserve Bank of St. Louis.
[7] Ibid.
[8] Nonfarm Business Sector: Labour Productivity (Output per Hour) for All Workers. St. Louis Federal Reserve and my calculations.
[9] Portoflosangeles.org
[10] Note that a married couple with two dependents could have received a cheque for $5,600.
[11] The velocity of money in the US plummeted when the Federal Reserve started quantitative easing in 2008 and then resumed it in 2020.
[12] For another explanation of why the velocity of money does not lead to inflation, see the earlier-cited Frank Shostak (https://www.cobdencentre.org/2022/09/the-velocity-of-money-circulation-myth/).

CHAPTER 13
INFLATION: HIGHER THAN YOU THINK

As long as we are plagued by false theories of what causes inflation, we will be plagued by false remedies.[1]

– Henry Hazlitt

[I]nflation must always end in a crisis and a slump, and that worse than the slump itself may be the public delusion that the slump has been caused, not by the previous inflation, but by the inherent defects of 'capitalism'.[2]

– Henry Hazlitt

Not What it Seems
Governments always seem to be at pains to understate the real rate of inflation. Why might this be? Understating inflation aids governments in obtaining capital. We'll have a look at why that is.

Obtaining Capital
There are several ways that one can obtain capital to fund one's spending. We'll look at three main methods here.

1. Create it
The first method, the only one that truly drives economic prosperity, is what we have already discussed at length: people produce some capital that others value and then sell it to those people, who give them money in exchange. But of course, this takes saving, investment, effort and, importantly, time, which may not coincide with an election cycle.

2. Borrow it
The next main method of obtaining capital is to borrow it. Of course, there's nothing wrong with borrowing, within reason. For most of us, without the ability to borrow, we would never be able to afford buying a home or a car. However, although most of us have probably borrowed at one time or

another to fund our general consumption – for example, clothes and dinners – this is generally not a good idea. But it seems that policymakers don't care what you spend your borrowed capital on, as long as you spend it. And if you're spending by borrowing capital, then the lower the interest rate on that borrowed capital, the more you can borrow and the more you can spend.

However, if inflation is too high, central banks will need to keep interest rates higher, which will lead to less debt-fuelled consumption. So, by making inflation appear lower than it really is, central banks can keep interest rates lower than they should be, thus enabling people to take on more debt and consume more – which helps inflate that GDP number. Recall that we have already discussed the hazards of manipulating interest rates to levels lower than the natural rate.

3. Receive it
A third way in which people can obtain capital is by having the government give it to them in such forms as social benefits, stimulus cheques and tax credits.

Government Obtaining Capital
The government obtains capital in three ways:

1. Taxation
2. Borrowing
3. Printing money

The first two methods are not initially inflationary. This is because they don't increase the money supply. However, over longer periods, high levels of taxation and borrowing lead to increased levels of inflation. Both methods involve taking capital from the producers of capital and giving it to consumers of capital; over time, both methods lead to a situation where the money in the system is chasing fewer goods than would otherwise have been produced.

The third way, printing money, is most definitely inflationary. As we discussed in the chapter on capital, every time the government increases the money supply, it extracts some of the capital you have stored up in your money and gives it to someone else. And again, the lower inflation appears to be, the more the government can get away with printing more money – extracting more of your capital.

As you can see, there are a number of reasons why policymakers would be motivated to make the official inflation number appear lower than it actually is (lower interest rates allow people and governments to take on more debt; governments can print more money; asset prices are propelled higher). It's a controversial subject. Some people say that the official inflation number *overstates* the real rate of inflation, but I find that hard to believe. The government subjects actual prices to a number of adjustments that always seem to result in a lower official inflation rate rather than a higher one.

Basket Case

To calculate the rate of inflation, policymakers determine a basket of goods that are regularly bought by consumers and then they track the prices of those goods. As you can imagine, that basket will slowly change over time as new products are developed and as consumer tastes evolve, so it makes sense for policymakers to occasionally adjust the basket accordingly. However, some believe that when they update the basket, policymakers use that as an opportunity to make inflation look lower than it really is. One point of possible evidence is that most of the times the basket was changed, it resulted in a lower official inflation rate. Economist Stephen Roach used to work for the Federal Reserve in the 1970s when it was led by Arthur Burns. Roach said that Burns wanted to create a gauge of core inflation, but '[h]e didn't like things that were going up, so month after month, we took out things like energy, food, and home ownership, and used cars, and women's jewelry, children's toys, you name it, we took it out, and if we didn't, we had job security to worry about at the same time.'[3]

The debate about whether inflation is being accurately measured was further fuelled by the decision to change how the most common measure of inflation – the Consumer Price Index (CPI) – is calculated. Historically, the CPI was a *cost of goods index* which measured the change in price over a given period of a fixed basket of goods. The same items were measured each period, and there was no flexibility to change any of the items in the basket, no accounting for any improvements in those goods. We've already discussed how it makes sense to change the basket if consumer tastes change. For instance, we probably don't need a hula hoop in the basket. However, the calculation was changed so that the CPI is now a *cost of living index*, which allows for greater flexibility. Policymakers can make assumptions about how the basket of goods may change in terms of not only products but also product quality. Such changes are implemented using tools called *substitution* and *hedonic adjustments*.

Substitution works like this. Consumer A has a choice between buying a flank steak or paying more for a higher-quality cut of meat such as filet mignon.[4] Consumer A prefers to pay the extra money, but when the prices of both items rise, the price of filet mignon rises more than that of flank steak. Consumer A might then decide to switch to buying flank steak. Policymakers will estimate how many consumers would decide to trade down to the flank steak because of its lesser price increase and reflect that in the CPI.

It also works the other way. Consumer B decides that they can't afford filet mignon, so they decide to buy flank steak instead. But then the price of flank steak increases faster than the price of filet mignon. Policymakers will estimate how many consumers would trade up to the filet mignon because of its lesser price increase, and they will reflect that estimate in the CPI. (However, I assume that this wouldn't happen much, as many people who choose flank steak over filet mignon simply cannot afford a more expensive cut. An increase in the price of flank steak would probably lead them to trade down to an even cheaper cut.)

In both of these scenarios, policymakers assume that Consumers A and B maintain a constant level of satisfaction by substituting to products with a lower relative price increase. And that's the price increase that gets reflected in the official inflation number. But how have those consumers been able to maintain the same level of satisfaction? Consumer A had initially chosen filet mignon over flank steak – because that choice gave them greater satisfaction – but now they are eating flank steak. So, even before the prices of the two steaks increased, switching to flank steak would have resulted in a lower level of satisfaction. And now that its price has gone up, the level of satisfaction would have been even lower.

Consumer A felt compelled to substitute their preferred purchase for something that had previously been less preferred, and they did this when the steaks had higher prices. In other words, the consumer substituted products because the price of filet mignon went up. I don't see how this consumer maintains their level of satisfaction.

Hedonic Adjustments

Hedonic adjustment is another way that policymakers seem to attempt to make inflation appear lower than it really is. As an example, if the price of a car rises by fifty per cent over time, but at the same time, the car's performance and safety improves by fifty per cent, the government might decide that the price didn't really go up – because the car you're buying is fifty per cent better. Apparently, you're getting just as much car per dollar, despite the fact that you may no longer be able to afford the car. This way, according to the government, despite the price of the car being fifty per cent higher, its impact on the official inflation number would be zero. It would look something like this:

Car Price Today	Car Price in 10 years	Price Increase	Hedonic Adjustment	Impact on Official Inflation Number
$20,000	$30,000	50%	-50%	Zero

So, despite the fact that you're out an additional $10,000, the government tells you that you're not.

To be fair, there are situations where the adjustments can go both ways. For instance, we have all witnessed a lot of shrinkflation recently. This might take the form of a company selling a box of thirty cookies for four dollars. However, the company might reduce the number of cookies to twenty-eight or make them smaller, or both, and still charge you four dollars. Now you're getting less cookie for your buck: inflation. The government would adjust for this and reflect it as an increase in the CPI.

However, a big problem with the rationale for making hedonic adjustments is the thinking that you should be paying higher rather than lower prices for product improvements over time. As discussed earlier, even though products get better over time, the prices of many of those products should be falling due to productivity improvements and competition. However, because the money supply increases rapidly at a rate faster than the rate of improvement of the products, you have to pay considerably higher prices for goods and services than you should. Not only that, but the government then adjusts those prices lower for its official inflation gauge to try to convince you that you're not actually paying that much more. And telling you through the official inflation number that prices are not going up as much as they really are, it enables the government to continue increasing the money supply, extracting your capital from your savings, and transferring it to others.

Let's look at a real-life example. From 1996 to 2008, five of the most popular vehicles in America were the Ford F-150, Toyota Camry, Honda Accord, Dodge Ram and Honda Civic.[5] Here is a table showing how their prices increased from 1996 to 2008.

Car	Model	1996	2008	Per cent Change	Annual Percent Change
Ford F-150	Regular Cab	$18,327	$22,360	22%	1.7%
Toyota Camry	LE Sedan 4D	$20,588	$23,124	12%	1.0%
Honda Accord	LX Sedan 4D	$19,270	$21,795	13%	1.0%
Dodge Ram	1500 Regular Cab	$18,032	$23,460	30%	2.2%
Honda Civic	DX Coupe 2D	$12,280	$15,445	26%	1.9%
Average		$17,699	$21,237	20%	1.5%

If we assume that these vehicles were representative of the overall US car industry at that time, we could say that the prices of cars over that twelve-year period rose on average 1.5% per year or by a total of 20%. However, when looking at the price progression of new cars over the same period, the Bureau of Labor Statistics (BLS) used hedonic adjustments to factor in quality improvements. In their mind, the prices of new cars *didn't* rise 1.5% per year (up 20% in total); rather, they *fell* 0.8% per annum (down 9% in total).[6] In other words, rather than reflect the reality of the average car price rising from $17,699 to $21,237, the BLS tells you they fell from $17,699 to $16,105 – they tell you that you were paying $5,132 less than you were really paying. So, the official inflation number factors in a falling price for new cars instead of a rising one. But, of course, when you went to buy a car in 2008, you were paying the real average price of $21,237 rather than the make-believe BLS price of $16,105.

Average Car Price 1996	Average Car Price 2008	Actual Price Increase	Price Increase according to the government
$17,699	$21,237	20%	-9%

Here's another way of thinking about it. The money supply (monetary base) over the same period increased at a rate of 6% per year.[7] And while not all products react immediately or to the same degree to new money being injected into the system (some react more, some less, some sooner, some later – and that can depend on how quickly loans are pyramided off that new money by the commercial banking system), let's assume the impact on the average price of a car was equal to the increase in the money supply. That would mean that the increase in the money supply led to an increase in the average price of a car of 6% each year.

However, remember that the actual average annual increase in the price of a car was 1.5%, not 6%. So, if the money supply hadn't impacted the average price by 6% per year, the price change would have been 6% lower than 1.5%; the average price would have fallen each year by 4.5%. That annual fall in average price, if it had been allowed to occur, would have been a result of saving and investment that resulted in innovation and productivity improvements (more cost-effective production) with competition taking away the resulting excess profitability. Instead, the price rose because the money supply increased at a rate faster than the productivity improvements for new cars. The increases in the money supply more than merely cancelled out any benefit you should have received (a better car for less money).

Or you can think about it this way. Productivity improvements should have resulted in the average price of a car falling 4.5% per year, but because the money supply increased every year and pushed prices 6.0% higher than they otherwise would have been, the price of the average car rose 1.5% per year.

To simplify things a bit, let's look at a hypothetical example. Assume the price of a new car is $20,000 in 2023. In a world with stable money, and productivity improvements of 3% per year, the price of a car would fall 3% per annum. The price progression over five years would look like this:

	2023	2024	2025	2026	2027
Price at Start of Year	$20,000	$19,400	$18,818	$18,253	$17,705
Productivity/ Competition: -3%	-$600	-$582	-$565	-$548	-$531
Price at End of Year	$19,400	$18,818	$18,253	$17,705	$17,174
Annual Decrease	-3%	-3%	-3%	-3%	-3%

So, with a stable money supply, the price of the car would have fallen 3% per year, and by the end of 2027 it would have fallen from $20,000 to $17,175 (14.1% cheaper). How great is that? And not only that, but it would be a better car.

However, if the money supply is increasing by 6% per year, the price of the car would progress as follows:

	2023	2024	2025	2026	2027
Price at Start of Year	$20,000	$20,600	$21,218	$21,855	$22,510
Productivity/ Competition: -3%	-$600	-$618	-$637	-$656	-$675
Increase in Money Supply: +6%	$1,200	$1,236	$1,273	$1,311	$1,351
Price at End of Year	$20,600	$21,218	$21,855	$22,510	$23,185
Annual Price Increase	3%	3%	3%	3%	3%

The increase in the money supply did worse than cancel out any benefit you received from productivity improvements and competition; instead of falling 14.1% over five years, from $20,000 down to $17,175, the price actually rose 15.9% – from $20,000 up to $23,185. Productivity and competition subtracted a total of $3,185 from the original $20,000 purchase price, but the increase in the money supply (inflation) increased the price by $6,371.

But remember, not only do companies invest to improve productivity and make products cheaper; they're also constantly innovating and making products better in an attempt to stay ahead of the competition. However, because the product has improved, the government says you're getting more product for your dollar. And so, when they calculate car price inflation, the government doesn't use the actual price. Instead, they hedonically adjust the actual price down for quality improvements. So, if, in addition to productivity and competition making the cars 3% cheaper, the quality of cars was increasing 4% per year; the inflation calculation by the government would look like this:

	2023	2024	2025	2026	2027
Price at Start of Year	$20,000	$19,800	$19,602	$19,406	$19,212
Productivity/Competition: -3%	-$600	-$594	-$588	-$582	-$576
Increase in Money Supply: +6%	$1,200	$1,188	$1,176	$1,164	$1,153
Hedonic Adjustment: -4%	-$800	-$792	-$784	-$776	-$768
Price After Hedonic Adjustment:	$19,800	$19,602	$19,406	$19,212	$19,020
Percent Change From Beginning of Year	-1%	-1%	-1%	-1%	-1%

Thus, when calculating the impact that car prices are having on the official inflation number, the government would factor in an annual decline in average car prices of 1% despite the fact that those prices were rising each year by 3.0%.

According to the Manheim Used Vehicle Index[8], the price of a used car in the United States rose by 55% from the beginning of 1998 to early 2020. However, through hedonic adjustment, the BLS will tell you that the prices of used cars and trucks actually fell by 5.1% over that same period.[9,10]

Despite the money supply increasing rapidly and driving the prices of most things much higher than they otherwise would have been, through hedonic adjustments made by the BLS, there is sometimes little or no reflection of the rising prices of many products in the official inflation number. This is one of the reasons that many people don't believe the official inflation numbers. People know they're paying considerably more year by year, but the official inflation numbers from the government tell them that they're not. Increasingly, consumers can no longer afford certain items – yet the government tells them they've never had it so good. At the very least, the government should be disclosing what the pre-hedonically adjusted number was and then how much they believe product quality has improved and let us make our own minds up as to whether or not prices are truly rising.

No Say in the Matter

The government hedonically adjusting prices down to account for quality improvements is one thing. But they can also make hedonic adjustments for improvements that you don't even want but you have no choice but to purchase if you want the product. To illustrate the point, think about those old cable TV bundle packages which offered you a bunch of channels to watch, but you were completely uninterested in most of them. For instance, you might have had a package of fifty channels that cost $50 per month, so in effect you were paying $1 per channel. However, if you're like most people, there might have only been five channels that you would watch on a regular basis. So, you were really paying $10 per channel per month ($50 cable bill ÷ 5 channels = $10 per channel).

Then, over the years, your cable company might have increased the price of your monthly cable bill while also informing you that they had added twenty-five more channels. Perhaps they increased your bill from $50 to $75 – a 50% increase. They might have justified the price increase by saying they increased the number of channels you could watch by 50% (from fifty to seventy-five). However, even if you had no interest in watching any of those new channels, you had no choice about the bill if you still wanted to watch your five channels. So, your cable bill just went up by $25 despite the fact that you were still only watching five of the channels that they offered. This meant that your price per channel just went up from $10 per channel to $15 ($75 cable bill ÷ 5 channels = $15 per channel).

However, the government might use hedonic adjustments to determine that there had been no increase in your monthly cable bill because, in their mind, you're paying the same price per channel ($75 for 75 channels is still $1 per channel, even though you never watch 70 of them). In fact, if the cable company added enough channels, the government might even determine that, like new cars from 1996 to 2008, your cable bill actually went down. For instance, if your cable company added another fifty channels that you never watched, increasing your number of channels to a hundred, and increased your cable bill from $50 to $75, your price per channel would go down from $1 to $0.75 ($75 cable bill ÷ 100 channels = $0.75). So, even though you're paying 50% more per month and more per channel that you actually watch ($100 ÷ 5 channels = $20 per channel), the official inflation number might reflect a decrease in cable bills.[11]

Real Cuts
Some people claim that governments prefer measures that understate the real inflation rate because some government (taxpayer) benefits such as social security are indexed to inflation (i.e. as inflation goes up so do the payments). If inflation is understated, then those benefits won't go up as quickly as prices, and, thus, the government will save money by paying out less in real terms.

Still others feel that if the official inflation number appears lower than it really is, then workers won't demand higher wages. Of course, this means that if the real inflation number is higher than reported, then workers could be suffering from a cut in their real wages – their wages don't go down in money terms, but those wages buy less stuff each year as the prices of things go up more than the government tells them they do.

It's Money and Stuff
Inflation is made to be a complex subject by focusing on the symptom of rising prices rather than the underlying cause of an increasing money supply and the amount of stuff being produced. For instance, if prices were rising at 2% per annum, that could mean that the money supply was staying constant but the amount of stuff being produced in the economy was falling 2% each year. Or it could mean that the amount of stuff being produced is the same each year, but the money supply is steadily increasing 2% per annum. Or – as in Scenario 2 in Chapter 12 – the amount of stuff being produced is growing, but the amount of money in the economy is growing at a rate 2% faster than that. So, if you simply focus on prices, then it's likely to go unnoticed that you're being ripped off – that the amount of stuff being produced grows each year and the only reason that you're not able to buy that stuff at lower prices is because the government is printing money at an even faster rate and transferring your hard-earned capital to someone else.

Two: The Magic Number
You will often hear central bankers claim that an inflation rate of around 2%

is needed to ensure the sustainable growth and health of the economy. It's quite amazing that this has been accepted as true by so many people. Does it really make sense that prices have to increase 2% per annum (translation: that 2% of your money wealth and income purchasing power needs to be taken from you annually) for an economy to be in good shape?

Now that central banks have convinced everyone that 2% inflation is needed to grow an economy and that inflation is rising prices rather than an increase in the money supply, everything is in place for central banks to continue increasing the money supply and transferring wealth within society. That's because central banks have convinced everyone – and themselves – that there are no consequences to printing money as long as inflation (price increases) doesn't exceed 2%.

Services Prices

By the way, the prices of services can also fall due to improvements in technology or management practices. But I believe they could also fall simply because the prices of goods are falling. I know that, at first glance, this might sound weird. If you are, say, a massage therapist, you can't really increase productivity by somehow doubling the number of massages give in the same amount of time – perhaps two customers at a time, one with each hand? And, when you master that, maybe three customers if you can use your feet to massage a third customer lying on the floor?

Remember that in the goods industry, if prices are falling across the board due to productivity improvements, then excess profitability will eventually be competed away. If the prices you charge for a massage don't change, then each year, your company will effectively become more profitable because the money you make will buy more stuff.

Assume that you employ three massage therapists who each earn $30 per hour. In an eight-hour day, each therapist gives five massages, for which you charge each customer $100 each. Total sales would be $1,500 and wages would be $720. Operating costs are $400. Your daily profit would look like this:

- Sales: $1,500
- Wages: $720
- Operating costs: $400
- Profit: $380

Now assume that the price of a TV last year was $380. After one day of business, you would have enough to buy a TV. However, because of investment in innovation and productivity, over the years, manufacturers have been able to produce the same TV at a lower cost, and high levels of competition have competed away the excess profitability of the industry. Therefore, the price of a TV has fallen from $380 to $350. The same goes for many other goods. Therefore, whereas your massage business would have initially made only enough profit in one day to buy a TV, it can now buy more.

The bottom line: in an economy of falling prices due to productivity gains and competition, owning a massage business becomes more profitable and, thus, more rewarding, not because of anything you have done, but because the rest of society has become more productive. This improvement in the profitability might attract competition in the massage industry. Meanwhile, your employees will continue to earn $30 an hour and benefit from the economy's productivity improvements.

However, there is a way in which you could increase your own productivity. Over time, the prices of items such as massage oil, soaps, and towels will fall. Thus, your operating costs might fall by $50 to $350, which would allow your profit to rise to $430. Again, this might attract competition, and competition would bid down the price of a massage.

Another thing that might drive down the price of the massages you offer is that your clients would notice that their dollars go a lot further buying other stuff than paying for a massage. There is always an opportunity cost to anything we do – if we spend our money on something, it can't be spent on something else. Whereas, initially, someone might decide to forgo buying a $100 sweater to have a massage instead, that is, they would prefer a massage to a sweater. But, if due to productivity improvements and competition, the price of the sweater now falls to $75, they might prefer to buy a sweater and a pair of $25 shorts rather than purchase a massage. Thus, the price of a massage would go up relative to goods, and you might want to consider dropping your prices so that a massage remains an attractive option.

The Pause That Refreshes

Policymakers will attempt to avert a slowdown in consumption at any cost, even if that cost is the future productive capacity of the economy. It is like saying that you need to sprint at the beginning of a marathon because otherwise you'll lose the lead. By sprinting at the beginning of a marathon, you may indeed end up leading the pack – but not for long. Yes, perhaps you'll get your name in the paper that you were leading at the one-mile mark; but you may also get your name in the paper for finishing last, or not at all. Rather, at the beginning of the race, you save some of your energy for the latter part of the race. You don't go as fast as you can; and, in a way, you are also investing time in the short term (not going as fast) to ensure continued performance later in the race. Without that investment of time to save energy, you wouldn't be able to finish the race.

Providing Others With an Income

Central banks want you to spend all of your money so that you provide others with income. In fact, they encourage you to borrow more and more so you can spend that, too, and thus provide others with even more income. As we discussed in the chapter on GDP, policymakers do this because they judge their own success on how much money is being spent in the economy on final consumption.

Of course, despite the best efforts of policymakers, many people don't spend all of their capital; instead, they save some of it in the form of money in the bank. That's when central banks come in and print money to extract some of that capital from that money. Then they'll give it to someone else who will do your duty for you and spend your capital.

You would think that policymakers would encourage people to responsibly save their money so they will have enough for retirement and, thus, be less reliant on the state (taxpayers) in their old age. (Or perhaps they like that people are reliant on the state extracting capital from taxpayers, which is how they get people's votes). So many people are struggling with the soaring cost of living and housing prices and rent as a result of central banks printing so much money to protect asset prices that comfortable retirement is becoming a near-impossibility for them. This is a modern-day crisis – all in the name of the wealth effect, that is, with the aim of driving the stock markets and housing prices higher.

The Inflation Impact of Absorbing Slack

As we saw earlier, a rationale that some policymakers might give you for printing money and extracting your capital from your money savings and giving it to others to spend is that some industries may have excess capacity, that is, they have overexpanded. Recall that excess capacity in the economy is called 'slack'.[12] Some people believe that you are somehow obligated to buy that industry's excess goods so that no one gets laid off. You can either spend your money directly (spend your savings) or indirectly (have someone else spend it for you).

Let's go back to our island economy. The residents have begun to believe that there are great health benefits to eating coconuts. Shirley can't keep up with the demand, so she hires Dave to climb trees and collect coconuts. The coconut business is thriving. But eventually, the coconut craze wanes, and people go back to their original level of consumption. However, now we have too much coconut-picking capacity in the coconut industry, and Dave is in danger of being laid off by Shirley. Economists would say that there is slack in the island economy, so they recommend that the central bank should lower rates or print money to get people to buy more coconuts and use up that slack. (More specifically, there is slack in the coconut industry, because Shirley and Dave are producing more coconuts than people wish to purchase.) So, policymakers would jump into action to lower interest rates and increase the money supply. This would extract capital from your money savings and redistribute it to others to encourage them to buy the excess coconuts. All of a sudden, coconut consumption increases. The coconut industry's slack is used up, and Dave gets to keep his job. The policymakers are pleased with themselves, and they take credit for saving Dave's job.

However, policymakers can't force people to buy 'only coconuts' (that day is eventually coming). People will increase their spending on all kinds of things, many of which had no slack in their respective industries. Prices in those other industries start to rise, leading to inflation in consumer prices.

The government will do its best to convince you that prices are not rising nearly as fast as you think they are. Regardless, you will find you have less money at the end of each month and you'll have to start cutting back on some of your discretionary spending. Not only that, but governments and central banks must also continue to take capital from you to fund others' spending on 'coconuts, to ensure the slack doesn't return to the coconut industry, meaning that Dave can keep his coconut-picking job'. Even worse, by extracting your saved capital for others to consume, your capital is no longer available to be used to invest in the future productive capacity of the economy. Again, by definition, more capital is being consumed than invested, which reduces the fundamental health of the economy. We've been experiencing this for many years, and it has had a deleterious impact on productivity.

Common Sense
Of course, a normal person would conclude that if no one wanted to buy the extra coconuts that Dave is collecting, then Dave should retrain and perhaps try doing something else that others value (e.g. building huts). Now, don't get me wrong: no one is claiming that this is much fun for Dave. He was quite happy working in the coconut industry and making a good income. But, for an economy to thrive, it's necessary that stuff be produced in response to what the consumer wants to buy (the consumer is sovereign), not what producers want to make. The consumer ultimately decides how much stuff gets produced and the prices at which it will be sold. Each person decides what they want to buy and how much they're willing to pay for it. It's a beautiful thing. So, any time there's slack in any part of the economy, it acts as a signal that either those parts of the economy have expanded too much or consumer tastes have changed. Either way, it's the industry that needs to adjust, not the spending of consumers – the production side of the economy must adjust to the demand side, not vice versa.

Uncommon Sense
The ultimate in all of this is a suggestion by economist John Maynard Keynes that during times of economic weakness, if all else fails, then governments should stuff money into bottles (I assume he means printed money) and then bury those bottles in disused coal mines, cover them all up with garbage and then allow the free market to dig up those bottles – and this would eliminate unemployment.[13] Of course, he doesn't mention that each time one of those bottles is dug up and opened, capital is transferred from you and into the pocket of whoever found the bottle.

No Inflation Without Money
Note that in our island economy, in the scenario where we have a direct-exchange barter economy, it is impossible for there to be a general rise in the prices of all goods. Remember that each commodity on the island was

priced in one unit of the other commodities (one fish equalled one coconut equalled one litre of fresh water).

Now assume that there is a supply shock in the coconut industry. Shirley has hurt her foot from continually kicking central bankers back into the surf as they attempt to scramble up onto the beach. Rather than collecting three coconuts per day, Shirley can climb the trees only every other day; thus, the supply of coconuts has gone down, which may push up the price of coconuts.

But because it is a barter economy, for the price of coconuts to go up, the price of fish and/or fresh water must go down. Perhaps the price of a coconut has doubled from one fish to two fish. That means that the price of fish has gone down from one coconut to half a coconut. The result is the same no matter what drives up the price of coconuts, including *animal spirits*.[14] Perhaps coconuts suddenly become valued simply because their price keeps going up, and a speculative coconut frenzy ensues. The result is the same: the prices of coconuts can only keep rising if the prices of fish and water continue to fall.

A sustained increase in the prices of all goods (price inflation) can only occur in an economy when two things happen. First, money needs to be used as a medium of exchange. Secondly, the supply of that money must increase (or there must be a sustained decrease in the production of goods).

Short-Term Inflation

General price increases can happen over shorter periods if people value their money less than goods. If people began spending cash that they had tucked away, this could drive prices higher. However, this sort of price inflation would be limited, as people don't typically have large cash balances. The higher prices would encourage people to hold on to their money again, and prices would fall. (And once price deflation occurred, this would encourage people to start spending their money again...)

Much has been written on the supposed causes of general price inflation – much of which is to deflect attention away from the real cause: an increase in the supply of money. In the spirit of Occam's razor[15], I think the famous economist Milton Friedman summed it up nicely in only thirty-two words: 'Inflation is always and everywhere a monetary phenomenon in the sense that it is and can be produced only by a more rapid increase in the quantity of money than in output.'

A Cancer

Persistent general inflation is a form of capital confiscation. However, when inflation is low – or appears low – it receives little, if any, resistance from the populace. It is a sort of theft that is hidden in plain sight. Indeed, not only have people been conned into believing that inflation is an unavoidable fact of everyday life, but policymakers have also convinced the general public that a little inflation is actually a net benefit to society, a crucial ingredient of a healthy and vibrant economy.

The truth is the exact opposite.

Not only does inflation *not* contribute to the fundamental health of the economy, but it instead detracts significantly from it.

> *When plunder becomes a way of life for a group of men living together in society, they create for themselves in the course of time a legal system that authorises it and a moral code that glorifies it.*
>
> – Frédéric Bastiat

Inflation prevents an economy from achieving its true wealth creation potential and, instead, acts like a cancer slowly eating away at the system from within. Not only does it result in slower growth, higher levels of debt, greater wealth disparity and financial crises, but it also results in a system where people increasingly gain at someone else's expense rather than via mutual benefit. Unsurprisingly, this leads to a more divided society with people looking for someone else to blame for the fact that, no matter how hard they work or study, they just can't seem to make ends meet – while they see others racing ahead in life.

So, no, inflation is not good for the economy and does not lead to permanently lower unemployment. In fact, it does just the opposite.

> *We have been misled by a false dichotomy: inflation or unemployment. That option is an illusion. The real option is whether we have higher unemployment as a result of higher inflation or as a temporary side effect of a cure for inflation.*[16]
>
> – Milton Friedman

Later we'll look at how an increasing money supply has inordinately benefited a small per centage of the population via the stock market and skyrocketing share prices. However, policymakers will tell you not to worry, because you will have benefited from the wealth effect that results from ultra-low interest rates. Which takes us to the next chapter.

ENDNOTES

[1] *Inflation for Beginners*. Henry Hazlitt. 12 June 2018. Mises.org.
[2] *What Is Inflation?* Henry Hazlitt. 11 March 2008. Mises.org.
[3] Rosenberg Research: *Webcast with Dave*, transcript, 14 July 2021.
[4] The Bureau of Labor Statistics uses the example of choosing between filet mignon and flank steak. See *Common Misconceptions about the Consumer Price Index: Questions and Answers*. John Greenlees and Robert McClelland. August 2008.
[5] They were in the top ten of the most popular cars in both 1996 and 2008 (*Best Selling Cars Blog*; prices from *Kelly Blue Book*).
[6] Data from the Federal Reserve of St. Louis. https://fred.stlouisfed.org/series/CUUR0000SETA01.
[7] I use the period of September 1996 to September 2008 to calculate the growth in the money supply. If I had used December, the growth would have been much quicker (over 11% per year) as the US central bank rapidly increased base money later in the year to bail out Wall Street.
[8] Manheim by Cox Automotive. https://www.coxautoinc.com/market-insights/mid-sept-2024-muvvi/.
[9] BLS data via the St. Louis Federal Reserve. https://fred.stlouisfed.org/series/CUSR0000SETA02.
[10] Note that the Manheim Used Vehicle Value Index captures wholesale prices at auction, while the BLS number reflects retail prices. However, I suspect that price changes for the two would be fairly similar, as wholesale price changes inevitably get passed through to retail prices.
[11] Note that the methods used by the BLS to calculate quality improvements is quite complex and my example is simply for illustrative purposes.
[12] Slack can also be determined by comparing GDP to potential GDP, but the issue here is having confidence in their ability to know what potential GDP is.
[13] The quote is from Keynes's book *The General Theory of Employment, Interest and Money*: 'If the Treasury were to fill old bottles with banknotes, bury them at suitable depths in disused coal mines which are then filled up to the surface with town rubbish, and leave to the private enterprise on well-tried principles of laissez-faire to dig the notes up again (the right to do so being obtained, of course, by tendering for leases of the note-bearing territory), there need be no more unemployment and, with the help of the repercussions, the real income of the community, and its capital wealth also, would probably become a good deal greater than it actually is. It would, indeed, be more sensible to build houses and the like: but if there are political and practical difficulties in the way of this, the above would be better than nothing.'
[14] This is key to Keynesian economic doctrine. If there is a lack of 'animal spirits' (too much prudence on the part of consumers), the government and central bank are expected to step in and spend people's money for them or redistribute it to someone who will.
[15] Named after a Franciscan friar, William of Ockham, and sometimes known as the law of parsimony, which basically says that given two hypotheses, the one with fewer assumptions is more likely to be correct.
[16] *Money Mischief*. 1994. p. 233.

CHAPTER 14
WEALTH EFFECT

Described

The wealth effect is the theory that people will spend more money if their assets have risen in value. Those assets could be in the form of investment portfolios or houses. As the prices of those assets rise, people will feel wealthier and are, thus, more likely to spend more of their money rather than save it. On the surface, this makes a lot of sense. You can imagine that if some of your assets were to double in value, you might decide to celebrate by treating yourself to a new car or a vacation. And why not?

The trouble with people spending more money because their assets have gone up in value is that it is only a good thing depending on why their values have increased.

In the case of stocks, a wealth effect can be a very good thing if the stocks are increasing in price due to companies investing and improving their productivity to create more wealth. However, a wealth effect in the housing market, as we'll see in the following chapters, is a result of wealth being redistributed, not created. There can be limited situations where houses increase in price because of true wealth creation. For example, prices might rise in certain areas as they become more favourable due to the construction of a new subway line. Things like that. Investment in an area effectively makes the homes in that area more valuable.[1] However, the number of people who benefit is limited and the rise in value is never to the detriment of the rest of society.

While wealth effects created through the stock market and the housing market were primarily a result of productivity and luck, respectively, central banks decided to concoct a new strategy that artificially drove those prices higher, creating a wealth effect in the stock market without all of the saving, investment, hard work and time required to increase productivity. It also created a housing wealth effect that was not enjoyed only by a lucky few but, instead, benefited a whole generation at the expense of our kids. This central bank strategy makes people feel wealthier, and then they benefit from wealth redistribution without any real wealth having been produced. Not only that, but over time it also actually results in less wealth being produced in society – and with much of that diminished wealth being owned by the top one per cent.

Stocks

Assume you bought 1,000 shares of Company A at $20 each, costing you $20,000. Now, five years later, the share price has gone up 50% to $30. The total value of your shares are now $30,000 (1,000 shares x $30 = $30,000). As you know, the difference between what your shares are currently worth and what you paid for them is called a capital gain. In this case, your capital gain was $10,000 ($30,000 – $20,000 = $10,000). You would likely experience a wealth effect if this happened; you would feel wealthier and, therefore, might decide to increase your spending. And you might do so in two different ways.

You could sell your Company A shares. However, if you did, you would have to pay a capital gains tax on the $10,000 that you made on your stock. Here in Canada, the capital gains tax is half of your personal tax rate. Assuming you are near the maximum tax bracket in Canada, which is around 50%, your capital gains tax would be about 25%. Therefore, your capital gains tax would be $2,500 ($10,000 × 25% = $2,500) which would leave you with $7,500 after tax, which you can now spend on stuff and do your bit to boost GDP (note the sarcasm).

Rather than selling your Company A shares, your financial advisor might recommend that you use those shares as collateral for a loan, and you could spend that money instead. The benefits of borrowing money on the value of your shares instead of selling them are twofold:

1. You don't incur a capital gains tax.
2. You get to participate in future share price appreciation of Company A's stock.

Of course, there are also consequences to borrowing on your Company A stock rather than selling them:

1. You have to pay interest on the loan. This can be particularly damaging if interest rates rise.

2. The price of your shares could fall to the point where their value is not enough to cover the amount of money you borrowed from the bank. Then you could suffer a margin call: your bank could require you to immediately pay back part of the loan so that the amount borrowed is not greater than the value of the shares.

Regardless of which course you choose, as long as Company A's share price is rising because the company is investing capital and becoming more productive, then the rising share price is reflecting increasing wealth in society. However, over the last twenty years, share prices have been rising far and above the amount of wealth that the underlying businesses have been creating. We will talk about this in the chapters on stock markets.

Housing

Now let's look at the wealth effect created by rising house prices.

Assume you want to buy a house worth $400,000, but you don't have enough money to pay for it. You would need to go to a bank and arrange a mortgage to purchase the house. The bank might agree to lend you only 75% of the value of the house: $300,000 You would need to fund the other 25% yourself; that would be your down payment. This $100,000 is also referred to as your equity, which is calculated by subtracting from the price the amount you owe to the bank. It would look like this:

House price:	$400,000
Mortgage (loan):	$300,000
Loan value as a percentage of the house price:	75% ($300,000 ÷ $400,000)
Your equity:	$100,000 ($400,000 − $300,000)

Now assume that a year after you purchased your house, its value has gone up 25% (by $100,000) to $500,000. The situation would now look as follows (to simplify things, I have assumed no mortgage payments):[2]

House value:	$500,000
Mortgage (loan):	$300,000

Loan value as a percentage
of the house value: 60% ($300,000 ÷ $500,000)
Your equity: $200,000 ($500,000 − $300,000)

Thus, with the value of your house going up 25%, or $100,000, your equity has doubled from $100,000 to $200,000 and the loan value as a per centage of the value of the house has dropped from 75% to 60%. In this case, your bank might offer to lend you more money, using the higher value of your house as collateral. If they lend you 75% of the value of your house, the situation would look like this:

House value: $500,000
Total the bank is willing to
lend you based on 75% of the
value of your house: $375,000 ($500,000 x 75%)
Existing mortgage (loan): $300,000
Additional loan amount: $75,000 ($375,000 − $300,000)

The bottom line is that you now have an extra $75,000 to spend. With millions of other homeowners also borrowing more money on the inflated values of their houses, spending in the economy will increase, boosting GDP.

So far so good. But in the chapters on housing, I'll explain why we should not be making money on our houses.

The Wealth Effect's Effect

The rationale behind the wealth effect and its impact on an economy is fairly straightforward: as people become wealthier, they are likely to spend more, and that spending then becomes someone else's income. For example, if you spend $500 on a new bike, then the person who sold you the bike has income of $500. They may then use that $500 to buy more parts to make more bikes, which then becomes income for the sellers of bike parts. The sellers of bike parts then spend their income, which in turn becomes someone else's income. When you think of it in those simple terms, given our propensity to spend, it's a wonder we're not all multimillionaires!

What central banks forgot, or never realised, is that a wealth *effect* is a symptom; thus, the term wealth effect rather than wealth *cause*. What causes wealth creation is saving, investment, innovation, risk-taking, hard work and time. Unfortunately, there is no way around this. However, the creation of wealth enables spending. Spending does not create wealth; it redistributes it. And spending and the redistribution of wealth have been the main focus of central banks over the last two decades. Not only that, but their policies, although well-intended, have resulted in less wealth being created than would have been otherwise.

Fake Wealth Effect

A minority has become wealthier at the expense of the majority, in an economy that was experiencing far weaker productivity growth than it should have. The reason this happened is because the wealth effect generated by central bank policy was a fake wealth effect. Share prices increased far in excess of the wealth that companies were creating and house prices increased much quicker than the general rate of inflation.

Therefore, the wealth effect policies of central banks ended up being a wealth *spending/redistribution* effect while at the same time having a detrimental impact on the productive capacity of the economy. The results?

- A redistribution of wealth leading to obscene levels of wealth inequality.
- A population burdened with staggering levels of debt.
- A younger generation that feels increasingly frustrated and cheated out of the same opportunities and lifestyle that were available to my generation.

One other consequence of a fake wealth effect concocted through stock markets by central banks is that investors have to pay tax on their capital gains, which means there is a tax on the wealth that is being redistributed. Thus, the government gets more of society's wealth, which, for the most part, is then consumed rather than invested.

In the next chapter we'll look at how the US Federal Reserve created a fake wealth effect in the housing market, the consequences of which we're still living with today. After that, we'll start looking at stock markets and then show how harmful to the economy the efforts of central banks to generate wealth effect are.

ENDNOTES

[1] Of course there can be some kinds of investment that may detract from a home's value: landfills or prisons perhaps?
[2] Don't think that that is so bizarre. During the housing boom of the mid-2000s, many people took on interest-only mortgages because that significantly reduced their monthly payments; others had negative amortisation loans, which actually increased the amounts they owed the banks.

CHAPTER 15

HOUSING PART 1

IN THE PREVIOUS chapter we discussed what a wealth effect is and how this can be a result of savings and investment over time. We also looked at how central banks decided they couldn't wait for a wealth effect to be created the old-fashioned way, so, instead, they created a fake wealth effect. They did it by manipulating interest rates far below the natural rate to drive asset prices higher in an attempt to boost GDP (final spending). However, in my opinion, these central bank policies only resulted in a redistribution of wealth that primarily went to those who don't need it (which doesn't mean those people didn't want it) while at the same time hampering the economy's wealth-producing capacity.

In this chapter I'll explain how, for the most part, none of us deserves to make money on our home and how utterly unfair that is to the next generation and new arrivals to our countries.

The Beginning

Many of my generation, including me, have benefited enormously from these central bank policies that have created a housing wealth effect. Although we may have played by the rules, we didn't deserve to make money on our homes.

It started with the technology-driven stock market bubble that raged during the late 1990s that finally peaked in 2000 and then duly plummeted. The dot-com boom was followed by the Tech Wreck. With the stock portfolios of investors falling significantly in value, the Federal Reserve was worried about a negative wealth effect (i.e. people feeling less wealthy and, thus, spending less, and the impact that that might have on GDP). Indeed, the US economy did experience a recession in 2001, albeit a very mild one. To counter the negative wealth effect of falling stock prices, a number of commentators recommended that the Federal Reserve create another wealth effect, but this time by driving housing prices higher. The Fed did this by driving interest rates down to make borrowing more affordable. However, you'll soon see how borrowing made more *affordable* makes houses more expensive.

US Housing Bubble

I'm sure many of you will remember the housing boom of the mid-2000s and how many people were making a lot of money speculating in the housing market.[1] Many people were also making money without speculating – many simply bought homes in which to live and then witnessed their prices soar. In fact, the whole housing market became so frenzied, and so many people were making so much money, that increasingly reckless behaviour was not only accepted but also actually encouraged by some policymakers and financial institutions.

Reckless Behaviour

In the chapter on the wealth effect, we discussed the mechanics of how it works with housing. In our example, we assumed a 25% down payment on your house. However, during the housing boom, some financial institutions kept lowering their down payment requirements so more people could join the frenzy. It got to the point where no down payment at all was required. Not only that, but some financial institutions were also lending more than the house was worth so the home buyer could afford to furnish it, as well. Payment terms were increasingly relaxed; for example, some financial institutions offered *interest-only* mortgages, which means that for a specified period, no repayment of the principal was required. This lowered the borrower's monthly repayment – meaning they could bid on a more expensive house.

But it gets worse. Some homeowners were taking out *negative amortisation mortgages*, which means that not only were they not making any monthly principal repayments, but they also weren't paying the full interest payment, either. For instance, the homebuyer might sign up for a mortgage with an interest rate of 6%, but for the first few years pay only 2% interest. The other 4% would be added to the mortgage, meaning that the amount of money owed to the bank would increase each month. Of course, banker and borrower alike were comfortable with this because they all believed that house prices would continue to soar – that the value of their home would increase endlessly and at a much faster rate than the debt owed to the bank.

Go Big or Go Home

Many home buyers who were speculating in the housing market were more than happy to purchase the most expensive house that they could, because that way they could make more money if the house appreciated in value. As an example, compare three houses, one priced at $200,000, one at $2 million and another at $20 million. Assume all three houses increase in value by 20%. The following shows how much each owner would benefit from such an increase in value:

Home 1:
Initial price: $200,000
Appreciation: 20%
New value: $240,000
Homeowner benefit: $40,000

Home 2:
Initial price: $2,000,000
Appreciation: 20%
New value: $2,400,000
Homeowner benefit: $400,000

Home 3:
Initial price: $20,000,000
Appreciation: 20%
New value: $24,000,000
Homeowner benefit : $4,000,000

While driving interest rates close to zero, central banks may have claimed that they were attempting to make housing more affordable, but their actions served to drive house prices significantly higher, making them less *affordable*. So, any savings from lower interest rates on the money borrowed to buy a home was offset by the increased amount of debt that was required to buy the same home. Similarly, with commercial banks reducing lending standards with interest-only or negative amortisation mortgages, they may have also argued that they were attempting to lower the monthly mortgage payments of homeowners. However, that came at the expense of more debt and higher house prices.

Housing vs. Wages

For the five-year period from the beginning of 2002 to the end of 2006, the median (the middle price in the range of prices)[2] house price in the US rose by approximately 36%. Some markets increased at a significantly faster rate. Over the same period, house prices in Florida increased by 99% – around 15% per year.[3] This compared with an average annual price appreciation in Florida of around 5% over the previous twenty-six years.[4] Over the years, house price appreciation far in excess of the increase in wages means that people have had to work longer to buy a house. In 1966, the median price of a house in the United States was $17,400. In today's dollars, adjusted for inflation, that would be equivalent to $179,772.

The median price of a house in the US in April 2023 was $416,100.

So, in inflation-adjusted terms, house prices are more than two times what they were in 1966. As wages have more or less kept up with inflation over that time[5], workers need to work twice as many hours as in 1966 to be able to purchase a home. To be sure, the median home today differs from the median home of 1966, particularly in terms of size. On the other hand, some will tell you that they don't build homes like they used to. Regardless, land values aside, technological improvements have made house building more efficient over the years, which should have helped to supress price increases.

Home ATM

Throughout the 2000s, as housing prices soared, US consumers were collectively extracting equity from their homes – borrowing hundreds of billions of dollars each year on the newly inflated values of their homes. Rather than paying off their mortgages and increasing their home equity, homeowners were, instead, withdrawing that equity and spending it. In effect, homeowners were consuming their homes. Millions were doing it.

A paper co-authored by former Federal Reserve chairman Alan Greenspan estimated that home equity extraction contributed close to 3% to annual personal consumption expenditure (PCE) from 2001 to 2005.[6] And policymakers were happy to encourage this behaviour. Of course, that sort of encouragement was all many people needed to hear to feel justified in borrowing more money as the prices of their homes increased. It made it that much easier to convince themselves that not only was it not reckless, but that it was also the sensible thing to do. Unfortunately, we don't need much encouragement to spend money. A University of Chicago Law School paper estimates that homeowners in the United States extracted a trillion dollars of equity from their homes from 2002 to 2005.[7]

Lower Interest Expense

In the past, homeowners would attempt to pay off their homes as quickly as possible. There are a number of benefits to this, one being that it significantly reduces the amount of interest you would have to pay to the bank over the life of the mortgage. In the chapter on the wealth effect, we assumed a house price of $400,000 with a 25% down payment, resulting in a mortgage of $300,000. If the mortgage had an interest rate of 5% and you paid it off over 30 years you would pay a total of $279,767 in interest expense to the bank on top of paying back the $300,000 mortgage – for a total of $579,767. However, were you to able to pay the mortgage off in fifteen years, instead, the total interest expense you would pay to the bank would be reduced to $127,029 – saving you $152,738.

Forced Saving

Another benefit of paying off your mortgage is that it is a form of forced saving. Saving your money is a voluntary action, but making monthly mortgage payments to the bank isn't. You're forced to do it or risk having the bank take your home away from you. But by making monthly mortgage payments, you're building equity in your home. For instance, once you've paid off your $300,000 mortgage on the above home, you would have $400,000 of equity in your home even if the value didn't rise. Again, because the equity belongs to you, you could sell your home and put the $400,000 of savings in your bank account. Equity in a home is often referred to as a nest egg. For many people, it's difficult to save a meaningful amount of money for retirement, but at the very least, if you owned a home and were able to pay off your mortgage over time, you would have the equity in your home to help fund your retirement.

Mortgage Burning

Years ago, once they had paid off their mortgages, some families would host mortgage-burning parties, during which they would ceremoniously burn the mortgage document to signify that they were free and clear of their debt burden to the bank. These days, far fewer people seem to be in a position to celebrate paying off their mortgages; for many, it's almost impossible to pay it off. Not only that, but house prices have risen so much that many people can't even qualify for a mortgage in the first place.

Upside Down

Starting in the 2000s, it became increasingly acceptable to add to one's mortgage rather than pay it off. If the value of their house increased, a homeowner's bank would encourage them to borrow more money, with the increased value of the house being used as collateral for the loan. Many people did this multiple times. Sadly, many Americans lost their homes during the housing crash of 2007 to 2009, and millions owed more to the bank than their homes were worth; this was known as being 'upside down on your mortgage' (the mortgage is under water) or in a negative equity position.[8]

In the above example, assume that the home you bought for $400,000 grew in price 20% per year for four years and you kept extracting the maximum equity from your home by borrowing from the bank. After four years, the situation would look like this:

> House value: $829,440
> Money owed to the bank (75% of the house price): $622,080
>
> – You originally owed the bank $300,000 but borrowed another $322,080 as the value of your house increased.
>
> Equity in your house (house value minus what you owe to the bank): $207,360

But then assume the value of your home fell 30%. You would now be in a negative equity position, and it would look as follows:

> House value: $580,608
> Money owed to the bank: $622,080
> Negative equity in your house (house value minus the debt owed to the bank): -$41,472

At one point, a significant percentage of mortgages in the US were in negative equity position. And as homeowners owed more to the bank than the house was worth, many simply walked away from their homes and mailed the keys to the bank (this was known as 'jingle mail'). This was the rational thing to do, as in many US states, mortgages are 'non-recourse', meaning that if you default on your mortgage, the bank can't go after your other assets to make up the shortfall.

For years, American consumers were sacrificing their future financial security in the name of validating the distorted consumption-based economic theories of central banks, and at the same time boosting the profits of banks and Wall Street.

Fake Wealth Effect

To be crystal clear on all of this, a wealth effect derived from rising housing prices that are distorted higher by central bank policy is not a net wealth benefit to society. House prices going higher does not create net wealth for society; it is, rather, a redistribution of wealth within it. We will see later that the same holds true for the stock market when it is goosed higher by dropping interest rates and/or quantitative easing. Rising house prices are simply a redistribution of wealth – taken in advance from the next generation and from immigrants – to people of my generation. We're the ones who were fortunate enough to have bought homes before the fake wealth effect era of zero interest rates and quantitative easing drove their prices skyward.

I'll use my own house as an example. My wife and I bought in a suburb of Toronto back in 2001. If we were to sell it today, we would get approximately four times what we paid for it. In real terms (adjusted for inflation), the value is two and a half times what we paid. We don't deserve a dime of that; we have not made our home two and a half times more productive than it was back in 2001. It's not two and a half times larger. And it certainly hasn't managed to magically relocate itself to a beautiful lakefront view.

The only reason we would make two and a half times (150%) what we paid for our home in inflation-adjusted terms is because a younger couple or immigrants are on the wrong side of central bank and government policies. Looking at it from a societal perspective, there would be no increase in capital when we made money on our home – there is no more capital in the economy. All that would have happened when we sold our home, effectively, is a first-time homebuyer would have had capital in their bank account transferred to ours. It's a transfer of wealth: no net wealth in the economy is created.

These policies were implemented because of the widespread belief that driving asset prices higher is good for the economy.

It's not.

Driving asset prices higher through artificial means such as lowering interest rates and printing money simply results in a redistribution of wealth within society. It's a zero-sum game, with winners and losers.

My wife and I are not going to be the ultimate beneficiaries of the increase in value of our home, because if we sell our house, we plan to give the proceeds to our children, so they will have some hope of buying an overpriced home from someone else. However, many young people are not fortunate enough to have parents who were lucky enough to have benefited at someone else's expense from the value of their home skyrocketing. Thus, the sage advice: 'Choose your parents wisely.' For many younger people whose parents were fortunate enough to have their house soar in value, it may be that their parents will need that bloated home equity to fund their retirement and, therefore, won't be able to afford to pass it to their children.

Intergenerational Wealth Transfer

The next generation is paying considerably more than my generation for what is, pretty much, the same asset. So, my generation wins and the next generation and immigrants lose. How is that fair? It's not. But it's very easy for me to convince myself that it is. After all, like any other homeowner out there, I played by the rules. I haven't broken any laws. Furthermore, it's not like I'm forcing that younger couple to buy my house; they're doing it of their own free will (well, sort of). And I can congratulate myself on the timing of my purchase and convince myself that I somehow had a knack for buying real estate at the right time, and, therefore, I'm smarter than other people and deserve to make all of this money on my home.

Borrowing from the great Frédéric Bastiat quotation earlier in the book, 'When plunder becomes a way of life for a group of people living together in society, they create for themselves in the course of time fallacious economic doctrine to justify it and a moral code that glorifies it.'

Trickle Down

Central banks might respond that their polices are for the next generation's and immigrants' own good and that, somehow, the benefits of zero interest rates and printing money will eventually trickle down to them in due course.

Spoiler alert: they won't.

Unless, of course, the next generation and immigrants are fortunate enough to, in turn, screw over the unfortunate suckers entering the housing market further down the road. In my opinion this is an immoral system, but the participants are not to blame, even though for decades many of those participants have been benefiting at someone else's expense. Another obvious thing to note is that, at some point, the maths of the beggar-thy-children policy of extracting wealth from the following generation simply doesn't work.

Incentives

Driving interest rates down enabled people to borrow that much more money and buy that much more house. Human nature being what it is, many people, when buying a home, don't decide on a size that makes sense and then determine if they can afford it. Instead, they calculate the maximum mortgage payment they can make on a monthly basis and buy as big a house as they can ('Here's how much I can afford every month; how much house can you get me for that?'). Of course, home buyers are cheered on by some in the banking and real estate industries, as both will make more money if you purchase a more expensive home. And while there are many honest bankers and real estate agents who will serve you well, there are also some unscrupulous variants of both who will attempt to convince you that you should buy more home than you really need. The more you borrow from the bank, the more interest expense you pay over the life of a mortgage; and the more expensive the home, the more the real estate agent makes in commission. Obviously, they're not doing anything illegal; they're all playing by the rules; but like all of us, their behaviour is driven by their incentives. It's the rules that are flawed, not the people.

With homeowners borrowing more on their homes each time they rise in value, and spending that borrowed money on things like wide-screen televisions or all-inclusive trips or an SUV, what is essentially happening is that all of that spending is being funded by the next generation and immigrants. When homeowners eventually sell their homes, they sell them at ludicrously high prices to the next generation and immigrants, and with the proceeds from those sales, they are then able to pay off all of the debt they have accumulated over the years.

Best-Laid Plans

Over the years, I've heard a number of policymakers claim that they were simply driving interest rates to zero to help make life more affordable for the average consumer. However, the result was just the opposite – and, in particular, these policies inordinately hurt lower-income households. They hurt them in three ways.

First, a lot of lower-income households aren't able to access loans because they don't score well on the banks' credit rating systems.

Secondly, when lower-income households do manage to borrow money, they typically pay far higher rates of interest than the wealthy. For instance, a lot of lower-income people effectively borrow by maintaining outstanding balances on their credit cards, which tend to have much higher rates than other forms of loans. And although interest rates were at near-record lows, the interest rates on outstanding credit card balances were near all-time highs.

Thirdly, although record low interest rates make it easier to service debt (i.e. your interest payments are lower), that's only true if you're talking about the same amount of debt. The problem for anyone who doesn't own a home is that with the Federal Reserve driving interest rates to zero to create a wealth effect (by driving housing prices higher), you need to borrow that much more money if you want any chance of being able to purchase a home.

Less Means More

In 1992, the median price (of a home in the United States was $121,375, and you could get a thirty-year mortgage at a rate of 8.40%.[9] Your total payments over the life of that mortgage (assuming no down payment) would have been $332,885, which consists of the $121,375 you paid for the house and $211,510 in interest expense to the bank.

1996

House Price:	$121,375
Mortgage Rate:	8.40%
Interest payments over the life of the mortgage:	$211,510
Total Payments:	**$332,885**

Inflation adjusting the 1996 payments to 2022 dollars the total would be $497,279.[10]

By March 2022, the median price of a house had risen to $413,500, and the thirty-year mortgage rate had fallen to 4.67%. Now your total payments for the life of the mortgage (also assuming no down payment) will be $769,362, consisting of the $413,500 purchase price plus $355,862 of interest expense.

2022
House price:	$413,500
Mortgage rate:	4.67%
Interest payments over the life of the mortgage:	$355,862
Total payments:	**$769,362**

So, while lowering interest rates may initially reduce the monthly mortgage payments for homebuyers, over time, it increases the total amount of payments they will need to make over the terms of their mortgages, as the higher house prices offset the lower interest rates.

Who Benefits the Most?

Not only do the wealthy own more expensive houses but they also own the lion's share of stocks and other financial assets, which benefit from the same wealth effect policies. Thus, amongst citizens, the wealthy have been the largest beneficiaries of the actions of central banks.

Finally, because they are, by far, the biggest borrowers of money, governments and corporations benefit the most from record low interest rates.

ENDNOTES

[1] A great book on this topic (later turned into a movie) is *The Big Short* by Michael Lewis.
[2] Average prices can be very different from median prices. For instance, with three houses priced at $10 million, $400,000 and $300,000, the median price is the middle price or $400,000, but the average price would be $3.6 million.
[3] This is the all-transactions house price index from the St. Louis Federal Reserve (I couldn't find the median price).
[4] Data is from the St. Louis Federal Reserve.
[5] A report from the Pew Research Center by Drew DeSilver shows that inflation-adjusted wages in 2018 were $22.65 per hour, versus $20.27 in 1964. So, wages slightly outperformed inflation if you believe the official inflation numbers.
[6] Alan Greenspan & James Kennedy, 'Sources and Uses of Equity Extracted from Homes' (Finance and Economics Discussion Series, 2007) p. 10.
[7] Neil Bhutta & Benjamin Keys, 'Interest Rates and Equity Extraction during the Housing Boom' (Kreisman Working Papers Series in Housing Law and Policy No. 3, 2014).

[8] There were even stories of people with underwater mortgages buying second homes in their neighbourhoods before defaulting on their existing homes. Their reasoning: if they had a mortgage for $300,000 but their home was worth only $200,000, it was better to buy a similarly priced home with a new $200,000 mortgage. Of course, their credit rating would take a hit, but they just saved themselves $100,000.

[9] House prices and mortgage rates are from the Federal Reserve Bank of St. Louis website.

[10] Each mortgage payment needs to be inflation-adjusted separately as later payments are less impacted by inflation than earlier payments. I assumed annual payments instead of monthly to make things simpler, but the numbers should be close enough.

CHAPTER 16

HOUSING PART 2

Too Much of a Good Thing

In some countries, governments join central banks in driving housing prices higher by allowing immigration at rates far in excess of their countries' abilities to increase their housing stock. That is especially true here in Canada. I should state at the outset that immigration is a wonderful thing that truly adds to the wealth and culture of a country. Many of my best friends are immigrants or second-generation immigrants. I'm Welsh, and my wife is from the Philippines. I'm proud to be Canadian, in part, because we welcome people from all over the world. And I'm particularly proud to be living in the greater Toronto area as it must be one of the most culturally diverse areas in the world. Canada is made up of people from all over the world. It not only accepts other cultures but also celebrates them.

However, like anything, there are limits, and too much of a good thing can be harmful. Immigration must be aligned with the ability of a country's infrastructure to handle it, including its ability to house the new arrivals. In recent years, annual immigration here in Canada has far outstripped the increase in available housing and, as you know, demand in excess of supply drives prices higher (which I think was the plan). The result is that so many young people are unable to afford the price of a home anywhere near the neighbourhood in which they grew up, and, thus, are often forced to move far away from their roots, away from their family and friends. In some cases, people feel they have to leave the country.

Piling On

In parts of Vancouver and Toronto, some houses are bought simply for investment, with no one living in them. This is what happens when investors can rely on policymakers to deliberately drive housing prices higher. By increasing the population at record rates and faster than the nation's housing stock could grow, house prices soared due to the excess demand. This juiced the wealth effect that was already taking place due to ultra-low interest rates.

Per Capita

Of course, policymakers are happy to see population growth contributing to the GDP number, as immigration results in higher overall spending. I've already discussed why policymakers focusing on simply driving spending higher at any cost is a bad idea. But even worse is if it's simply being driven higher by increasing the population. GDP (final spending) should always be looked at on a per-capita basis. The GDP number might be rising in a country with a rapidly growing population, but it could still fall on a per-person basis. Consider this very simple hypothetical example:

GDP:	$1 trillion
Population:	20 million
GDP per capita:	$50,000

Assume GDP grows by 5% due to a 10% rise in the population (perhaps due to immigrants with initially less money to spend, as well as existing citizens spending less). The situation would then look this:

GDP:	$1.05 trillion
Population:	22 million
GDP per capita:	$47,727

In this situation, all you would hear from politicians and some in the financial press is that the economy grew by 5%, because they measure growth in the economy by adding up all final spending. But average spending per person actually declined $2,273 per person; on average, each person is spending 4.5% less than they were the year before.

Note that at the time of writing, GDP per capita in Canada has been falling.

Roadblocks

Building houses at scale can be fraught with challenges, for example, preserving green spaces and saving buildings of historic importance. Another issue is the NIMBY ('not in my back yard') attitude; often, people don't want new developments to be located near where they live – they want them built somewhere else. I'm not trying to belittle some of the challenges of increasing a nation's housing stock, but the government doesn't help things with onerous taxes and fees on the construction of new houses. Two separate studies here in Canada point to government fees and taxes accounting for almost a third of the cost of building a new home in Toronto and Vancouver.[1] Not only that, but the higher house prices rise, the more the government takes from you in property taxes – the more wealth that is transferred from the productive private sector to the unproductive public sector. And while governments increasingly benefit from these growing taxes and fees, the impact from the resulting higher house prices is that fewer houses are built, as fewer buyers can afford them.

Immigration is a great thing, but when too much of it contributes to redistributing wealth from those very immigrants and the next generation to those who already own houses and to the government, it only leads to anger and frustration for a sizable segment of the population. Plus, it could lead to an unfair, anti-immigration mindset taking hold.

Delusion

We can all attempt to convince ourselves that we do deserve to make money on our homes despite them having made zero contributions to society, but it's simply delusional and self-serving to think that way. I've suggested this to many of my clients over the years, and most of them have immediately understood. However, once in a while, I will come across a client who takes great exception to what I'm saying. They believe they deserved to make money on their house, and they don't like being told otherwise. It reminds me of a line from many years ago by the journalist Upton Sinclair: 'It's difficult to get a man to understand something when his salary depends upon him not understanding it.'

For some people, it's just too painful to admit that the wealth they made by owning a home came at the expense of someone else. I understand how they feel, as most people have accepted that real estate simply goes up over time, and when you sell your home, you're not coercing someone to buy it from you. And, to be sure, there are instances when the value of a house can increase if real demand changes and/or the neighbourhood changes (in which case, the house is no longer the same level of economic good).

Corporate Buyers

As you may have guessed, I am a free-market advocate when it comes to most things; but there are certain markets that I feel need protection from large corporations, and housing is one of them. In the business world, most people have a choice about whether or not to compete or participate. Unlike the business world, people have no choice about needing some form of accommodation; they *have* to live somewhere.

In the housing market, large corporations have been buying up tens of thousands of houses. Due to their size they obtain cheaper funding than is available to the average person, thus enabling them to outbid people for houses. This contributes to skyrocketing house prices, making houses unaffordable for the average person. Those houses are then put on the rental market, and because so many people can't afford to buy a home, they're forced to rent – which drives up rental prices.

Companies should be able to freely compete to build houses, and consumers should be able to buy them at prices they consider appropriate, but companies should not be allowed to outbid people for the purchasing of houses. For some reason, policymakers seem uninterested in dealing with this issue. Perhaps this is because it results in higher house prices, which they believe is good for the economy due to the wealth effect – and because it boosts their tax revenues via property taxes.

Large corporations in many areas of finance will often justify their actions with claims that they're providing liquidity to the market by buying assets when no one else wants them and helping to avoid a price collapse. I've always been sceptical of such a rationale, but it certainly doesn't apply in the housing market, with corporations competing with potential homeowners and driving prices higher. An in-depth analysis of this topic is beyond the scope of this book, but, in my opinion, it's a problem that needs dealing with.[2]

Less Than Net Zero

Another way of thinking of the net zero-sum game that results from a wealth effect policy is to consider the net emotional impact within society. All those who benefit (primarily my generation) feel pretty good about themselves; they have a much better chance of being financially secure. In contrast, all those getting screwed by buying overpriced houses worry about ever being able to retire comfortably.

Meanwhile, many others who can't afford overpriced homes stay in the rental market (rental prices are now also going through the roof) and wonder if they'll ever be able to buy a house in which they can raise a family.[3]

For the younger generation, this leads to feelings of anger, frustration and hopelessness. So, within society, my generation's smug, misplaced feelings of accomplishment are offset by those of the next generation and immigrants. It's an emotional zero-sum game where the anger of the losers is offset by the joy of the winners.

However, longer term, it all becomes a significant net negative effect, as it increasingly leads to an 'Us vs. Them' type of society with populist movements forming and (rightly) demanding change. The big risk is that those suffering don't fully understand how they're being screwed. The result being that they misdiagnose the economic problems and then, if they get into power, they prescribe the wrong medicine – for example, socialism. In this system government takes over ownership of the production of everything and provides all services deciding who gets what and how much. (In that case, the cure would be even worse than the disease – hard to believe though that may be.) We are not there yet, but are steadily moving closer to greater and greater government involvement in the economy which further and further detracts from its ability to function.

As if all of this weren't bad enough, there is one final thing to note about why driving housing prices higher is terrible for the economy. As most people have become accustomed to seeing the value of their home soar, they start factoring their home's value into their retirement plans; they will view the value of their home as a retirement nest egg. The problem is this: the more people see the values of their homes increase, the less they are likely to save money for retirement; instead, they will rely on the value of their home. Thus, soaring house prices lead to greater consumption at the expense of saving and investment. And, as you know, the greater consumption juices the shorter-term GDP (final spending) number, to the satisfaction of policymakers, but it reduces the productive capacity of the economy over time.

Building Pyramids

You'll sometimes hear people say that they want to get onto the housing ladder. They plan to buy a house, wait for its value to soar, then buy a more expensive one with the proceeds from the sale of the first, and then do it again. Eventually, they will retire with a bundle of money made without having made any contribution to society – such a fortune having been funded by those who are at the bottom of the ladder. Of course this is one way of off-setting central banks extracting capital from your savings when they print money; taking money from one pocket and putting it in the other. But for those who decide to rent or can't afford to buy a home there is no off-set.

Doesn't this sound like a pyramid scheme?

ENDNOTES

[1] Urban Development Institute. *Taxing Growth: Analysing the Taxes and Fees on New Housing Development*. And Canadian Centre for Economic Analysis (CANCEA). *An Uncomfortable Contradiction: Taxation of Ontario Housing*. 27 June 2023.
[2] Ryan Dezember has written on this subject (*Underwater: How Our American Dream of Homeownership Became a Nightmare*).
[3] Note that there is absolutely nothing wrong with someone who *decides* that they would rather rent their accommodation than purchase a home.

CHAPTER 17
CORPORATE CULTURE

Real Wealth Effect

Companies are the lifeblood of our economy. They produce capital and provide employment for millions of people. They are able to do this because they put capital to productive use in an attempt to provide consumers with a superior customer value proposition. The very successful ones will save some of their capital and invest it in innovative ways to continuously improve their products to attract even more customers. This is a real wealth effect, because wealth truly is being created.

However, some companies are better than others. I believe that corporate culture is key in determining which companies will thrive and which will die a slow death. In this chapter we'll take a look at what corporate culture is and how it has deteriorated over time. The decisions being made by some corporations, and the motives driving them, are not dissimilar to those of some policymakers in managing the economy. The result is that both are detracting from productive capacity. We'll explore how they are related.

Defined

Every company has a corporate culture. Some are good; some are bad. As you might expect, for a company to have a good chance of achieving long-term success, it must have a great corporate culture.[1]

Corporate cultures have generally evolved in line with the culture of a society. How could they not? The reason these things are related is simple: companies, just like economies, are made up of people, and people make decisions. That's why economics is a social science, like psychology and sociology, and not a natural science, like chemistry and physics. Unfortunately, however, because many economists try to apply natural science methods (e.g. formulas and equations) and, thus, effectively treat people like numbers, the manipulation of people for well-intended economic reasons is one of the things that ails society today.

Competitive Advantage

It is not usually too difficult to identify a company that has a strong competitive advantage. More often than not, it's reflected in its financials. Even if you don't know what a company does, or the products it makes or services it provides, you can get a pretty good idea if it is a decent business just by looking at its financial statements. Strong financials will likely indicate that those sovereign consumers are willingly and increasingly purchasing the company's products and/or services. My old boss used to say that when analysing a company, he liked to begin by reading the company's annual report, starting at the back. In the back are all of the financials. Reading them first will give you a good idea as to whether or not the business is any good and if the management team knows what they're doing.

At the front of the annual report is the commentary by the management team. It's a sort of proclamation of how successful they have been: Chairman's Letter, CEO's Letter, and then a report on the finances by the Chief Financial Officer. These letters tend to gloss over the bad stuff and can be very persuasive. But if you've already gone through the financials, you'll be in a much better position to judge the commentary and keep your emotions in check. It's kind of like making an assessment of a person's success by simply looking at the size of their house or how fancy their car is. These things their 'proclamations' of how successful they have been. But looking at their financial statements would give you a much better idea of their success, at least in terms of how much capital they are making – or are they borrowing it?

There are many aspects of the financials you could look at, but, generally, if you see steady sales growth, a reasonable level of profitability, a good return on capital, strong cash flow, and a healthy balance sheet, then that company is probably pretty good at doing something.

Sustainability

Regardless of what a company's competitive advantage is, the most important (and more difficult) thing is to determine whether or not that competitive advantage is durable. The future landscape of a particular industry and future consumer preferences are unknown, and they are difficult to predict.

It's tough to make predictions, especially about the future.

— Yogi Berra

However, one thing you have a better chance of predicting is management behaviour. Having a good understanding of who the management of a company are and what they stand for in terms of things such as belief systems, values and objectives can help you predict how they will respond to a range of possible future events, none of which you can know for certain will happen. If you have the right management team, they will readily acknowledge that they don't know what the future will look like. They won't make an all-in bet with the company's capital. They won't attempt to position the business assuming that they do.

Parenting

When I think of corporate culture, I think of how my wife and I raised our three daughters. Throughout their lives, we strived to instil in them principles such as manners, courtesy, respect, empathy, honesty and hard work (while, unfortunately, not always setting the best example). As any parent will tell you, that's a lot of work, and it requires a big investment of your time and effort. There are days when you just don't feel up to it, and one of the reasons for that is that there is no immediate payback or benefit for your efforts. Reminding your kids fifteen hundred times to say 'thank you' is exhausting and thankless. Even worse is taking back a treat because your child (once again!) forgot to say 'thank you'. Now your child is upset at you, because they don't truly understand why good manners are necessary. So, the temptation is often to give in just a little bit. And why not? You convince yourself that things will probably work out just fine and that you still have plenty of time to set things right. Better to enjoy the moment today with our kids. YOLO.

As your children grow, the efforts required on your part change from the teaching of basic manners to helping them with decision-making. These decisions are not about what career to pursue or whom to date; they are about keeping them out of trouble or harm's way. The reason they often have trouble with these decisions is that, while there may be a real immediate benefit from making a particular decision, the harmful consequences of that decision may occur further into the future: the potential harm may be a longer-term consequence and, perhaps, two or three steps removed from the initial decision – or it may not even occur at all.

I believe this is related to why policymakers often make the decisions that they do. Not only are the short-term benefits enormous to certain parts of the citizenry in terms of wealth and to the policymakers themselves in terms of popularity (as in the previously discussed case of former French President President François Mitterrand lowering the retirement age from sixty-five years to sixty), but those who actually provide the wealth (have it taken from them) also don't realise it's happening (or they do, but don't know how it's happening). In addition, sometimes, the consequences of the bad decisions only become visible some time in the future and so it's difficult for people to connect the dots between cause and effect. Because of this, the architects of many of the economic problems we're currently dealing with today are able to keep their reputations intact.[2]

Adding Alcohol

An analogy I have used with my clients in the past goes something like this. Your teenage children are drinking alcohol at home with their friends. Later in the evening, one of your kids asks you if they can borrow the car to go to a party. You say no. Well, as you can imagine – or may have experienced – that message doesn't go over too well with your kids, especially now that you have embarrassed them in front of their friends. The result is that there may be a week-long recession going on in your household as your kids sulk and slam bedroom doors. Nevertheless, it was, of course, the right decision to make, even though the consequences of that decision were immediately felt by everyone.

And while central bankers would of course make similar decisions with respect to their kids, they have effectively, thrown car keys to inebriated global stock and housing markets, sending them on reckless and precarious trips up steeply sloping roads – and that has already had terrible consequences. The cars are swerving dangerously to and fro and are only being kept on the road by the enormous and increasing efforts of people like you due to your ability and work ethic. But if things don't change soon, the efforts of the people will not be enough to keep the cars on the road and they'll eventually end up in a ditch or wrapped around a tree.

Letting Go

Apart from the required investment of time and effort on your part when raising your children, the other difficult thing to do is let go. And I don't mean the part about them finally moving out of the house and going to university, or moving into their own apartment, which is a very emotional time for most parents. I'm talking about avoiding being a control-freak parent, which tends to start when the children are very young. Although you attempt to instil certain principles within your children, it is just as important to not force them in the direction you want them to go. We've all seen those parents who try to control every aspect of their kids' lives to give them the best chance of success, in areas such as education, sport, arts, and business. But these efforts often represent the dreams of the parents, not the kids.

To be fair, these parents are only doing what they think is best for their kids. Yes, it may earn them bragging rights, but it's probably an attempt to give their kids better lives than they had. Looking back, it can be tempting to tell ourselves 'If I'd just committed myself to this or that and put more effort into it, then perhaps I'd be in a much better and happier place today. If only my parents had told me what to do or forced me instead of letting me goof off.' Regardless of the reasons, we all know who these parents are. And even if their actions are well-intended (like policymakers), for some reason, they can't see that only their kids can know what is truly best for them.

Never Work

Find a job you enjoy doing, and you will never have to work a day in your life.
– Mark Twain (no relation to Shania)

If you are fortunate enough to enjoy what you do for a living, then you tend to be more successful at it. And you will be happy, and, after all, isn't that the main objective for all of us? I've always thought that money follows passion a lot easier than passion follows money. And if you can't find a job you love, sometimes, sticking with the one you have can turn it into something you do love. If you have a good work ethic, I believe you can find good things in most jobs.

I know I've gone off on what might seem like a bit of a tangent here, but this is all closely related to corporate culture and, also, the culture of our financial system.

Let's look now at what I believe are the specific characteristics of a good corporate culture company and contrast them with those that represent a bad one. I came to this over the years by attempting to assess whether or not a company had a decent chance of being successful in the long term and whether or not I should risk allocating some of my clients' capital to that business (at the right price, of course).

Good Corporate Culture

A great corporate culture starts at the top. My experience is that it is almost always entrepreneurial in nature. Entrepreneurialism is often thought of as being small in scale, but I think of it more in terms of attitude. It can mean running a business and putting your own capital at risk, but it can also signify innovation and creativity. These management teams typically live to wow their customers or clients with better and better products and/or services.

Because they love what they do, it's constantly on their mind, and they don't consider it work. It can even be something that the rest of us would consider pretty mundane stuff. I'm sure many of you have met people like this who are very successful because they love what they do, but what they do is something you could never imagine doing yourself. Yet when these people wake up in the morning, the first thing they think about is the business and/or the customer, and they can't wait to get at it. Of course, this alone is no guarantee of success, but if you were to invest your capital in a company, the presence of this sort of attitude would be a pretty good starting point.

Reinvestment

Because entrepreneurial management teams love what they do and can't imagine doing anything else, they're afraid of the competition catching up and overtaking them. So, to help ensure their customer value proposition keeps them ahead of the competition, they constantly reinvest in their business to make even better products or make the same products even cheaper. This reinvestment in the business takes many forms: research and development, product innovation, up-to-date capital equipment, the latest IT systems, and the best employees. Of course, all of this costs money, which means the company has to spend more today to help ensure the strength of the business in the future. This reinvestment reduces the profitability of the business in the short term, and the lower profitability may lead to a lower share price. But the management teams don't care about that, because their main goal is to win the sovereign customer. They know that if they continue to be successful in winning the customer, then, over time, profit will follow and so will the share price. These management teams are very strategic in their thinking; they take a long-term view.

Everyone Wins

Another important characteristic of a great corporate culture is that all the constituents benefit from the business model, not just the senior executives and the shareholders. The other constituents are the suppliers, the employees, the community at large, and, of course, lastly and most importantly, the customer. The customer is the most important because they are the only constituent of the business model that pays; all the others get paid by the customer. The management of companies with great corporate cultures like seeing everyone benefit from their efforts. Apart from feeling good about seeing all of the constituents of a business model succeed, there is an even more important reason for sharing in the success of the business. If any of the above constituent groups are not benefiting from being part of this business, or, even worse, are suffering as a result, then they would likely decide they no longer want to be a part of it. Therefore, the business model in its current form would not survive.

Organic Risk Control

An entrepreneurial management team doesn't try to micromanage their staff and restrict their behaviour with all sorts of rules. They also don't have a 'My way or the highway' type of attitude; rather, they invite diverse opinions and are open to being wrong. They do this because they know that such an approach will improve the business and give them a greater chance of success. I remember one company saying that their corporate culture was their best risk control. What they meant was that if everyone in the company is on board with the corporate mission and shares the same principles and belief system, then you don't have to have all sorts of rules to stop people from doing stupid things. Of course, every company has employment standards and the like and templates for success that everyone can follow, but, apart from that, everyone in a company with a great corporate culture just gets on with their job, not worrying that their colleagues are goofing off or going in a different direction. Corporate culture is incredibly empowering in this regard. It tends to bring out the best in people.

Characteristics of a good corporate culture include the following:

- An ability to let go
- A focus on fundamentals
- A long-term mindset
- Leadership by example
- Humility
- Hard-working
- 'Everybody wins'
- 'Everything starts with the customer'
- Strong principles

There are many companies out there who simply pay lip service to corporate culture or simply do things that make them look like good corporate citizens, for example, donating to charities, talking about how they're going to lower greenhouse gas emissions or organise a bunch of employee team-building exercises. These are all good things, but unless the main focus is on the customer, all of that other stuff is for naught, as, eventually, the company won't have any customers and, thus, won't be in a position to do all of those other things.

Here are a couple of examples of the many companies out there with great corporate cultures and that employ thousands of people.

Costco
I know many of you are familiar with this business. Every time you walk into one of their stores, you get great customer service. This is because Costco's employees tend to be happier than most. They're happy because their management treats them well in a number of ways – and pay is just one of those ways. Employees at Costco make much more than employees at most other retailers. As a result, Costco has one of the lowest, if not *the* lowest, levels of employee theft[3] in the retail industry. That's the risk control benefit of a great corporate culture. The level of employee theft is not low because Costco is constantly watching their employees to make sure they don't' steal anything. It's low because their employees like working there.

Another great aspect of their corporate culture is always giving the customer the best value possible. For example, if Costco is able to negotiate a better deal with their suppliers to purchase products at a lower price, Costco lowers the price of those products on the shelf for their customers. Other companies might maintain the original higher price for their customers and keep the cost savings for themselves (i.e. boost their profit).

Hot Dogs
Some years ago, during a visit to the Costco head office, I asked the CFO about their corporate culture. He gave a great example of how fanatical Costco is about ensuring their customers get the best value possible (such enthusiasm in talking about the customer is always a good sign of a great corporate culture). As you may know, Costco sells great hot dogs. The price is the same in every store in the United States, and it has never changed: $1.50.

However, several years earlier, when the CEO was visiting a Canadian store, he noticed that the price of their hot dogs was two Canadian dollars instead of $1.50. He asked why, and was told that it was because of what the exchange rate had been when the store had first opened. But at the time of the CEO's visit, the Canadian and US dollars were almost equal in value. The CEO ordered the price of hot dogs in all stores in Canada to be lowered to $1.50. The CFO said that the impact of that decision on Costco's annual sales in Canada was in the millions of dollars.

Now, importantly, the CEO was not expecting to offset the sales hit from the lower hot dog price by selling that more hot dogs. He knew it would impact profit in the short term. However, it's part of the Costco promise to its customers to always give them the best value possible. It's about trust and brand equity that is built over many years with decisions just like that. Undoubtedly, there will have been countless decisions made over the years by Costco people that have contributed to their great corporate culture.

Fastenal
Fastenal is a wholesale distribution business of industrial supplies, things such as fasteners. Not terribly exciting, but it is a company with a great corporate culture. We toured one of their plants, and I was amazed at the enthusiasm of the plant manager who was taking us around. They distribute things as mundane as screws, but listening to this guy, you'd have thought they were about to land a rocket ship on the moon.

We also chatted briefly with a few of the other employees on the plant floor, and they all said how much they loved working there. They said their management never had to worry about making sure everyone was doing their job, because if anyone dared to goof off, the other employees would pull them in line. They said they felt that the company belonged to all of them.

I asked the plant manager why he liked working there so much. He said it was really down to management and ownership. Those at the top would often ask for the opinions of the rank and file, and they would often put those opinions into action. And, importantly, the employees got to share in the success of the business; it didn't all go to the executives.

He then gave a great example of why they all loved working at Fastenal. The CEO was the founder of the business, and he owned about a third of the company. His wife had passed away some years earlier, and she had also owned a considerable number of shares. After her passing, the CEO distributed her shares to his employees. Not only that, but he also paid the capital gains tax out of his own pocket.

Bad Corporate Culture

While there are many more companies out there like Costco and Fastenal than you think there are, not all companies have a great corporate culture. Companies with bad corporate cultures tend not to be entrepreneurial in nature, and the executives usually don't have any skin in the game (i.e. there is none or little of their own capital invested in the business). They are also less concerned with innovation and creativity, except when it comes to driving their company's share price higher. (On this score, some of them can, indeed, get quite creative.)

As you can't possibly forecast the challenges a company will encounter in the future (just like for your children), you want to have confidence that its management team will be prepared and able to respond to any of those unknown challenges in the best manner possible. You also want to ensure that the management team is not being delusional about the potential longer-term consequences that might result from their shorter-term *beneficial* actions. This means you want to ensure that the management team is not arrogant. I've actually heard some people proclaim proudly that they are arrogant. They seem to have a misconception of what 'arrogant' means. It's probably because they've been called arrogant so many times that they've convinced themselves it must be a good thing. According to Merriam-Webster, one definition of 'arrogance' is 'An *attitude* of superiority manifested in an overbearing manner' [emphasis mine]. That pretty much sums it up.

Full Steam Ahead

People who think they are smarter than others, combined with an overbearing manner, are less likely to consider the error of their ways and, thus, they don't learn from their mistakes. In other words, they're not as smart as they think they are. A line frequently used to describe these people is 'Often wrong, but never in doubt.' As a result, people who are arrogant will often unwaveringly charge full steam ahead with whatever course of action they deem best without ever stopping to consider that they might be wrong. And if it doesn't seem to be working, they just do more of it (see the chapter on central banks).

Companies with poor corporate cultures typically focus on the short-term performances of their share prices, and the actions taken to drive that short-term performance can often come at the expense of the long-term strength of the business model. For instance, rather than maintaining a strong balance sheet by paying off their debt, these companies will often take on considerable amounts of debt and use that to drive their share prices higher (explained later). Of course, in this process, the management team can reap significant financial rewards by cashing in their stock options (explained in the stock market chapters), but if you are a long-term investor, you will be the one left to pick up the pieces.

It Takes Time and Effort

Sometimes you can have a management team with good intentions who really do want to have a great corporate culture, but they go about it the wrong way. Creating a great corporate culture requires a lot of letting go. However, many times, I've seen companies attempt to force great corporate cultures upon their people. Although the motives may be good, it can't be done. You cannot impose or plan a great corporate culture; it's something that has to evolve organically. It doesn't happen overnight. I believe it always starts at the top and filters its way down as the organisation slowly grows over time.

Employees see the senior management leading by example, and they take their cues (good or bad) from their bosses. Corporate culture grows over time through actions. It results from doing things for the right reasons: working hard, being trustworthy, being pleasant, making mistakes and learning from them, satisfying the customer, and, finally, sharing the profits with the company's constituents, commensurate with their contributions. It's powerful stuff. Rather than putting in place a plan to create a great corporate culture, I believe it can only happen if you establish the right conditions or environment in which it can, hopefully, evolve organically over time.

However, it's very tempting to try to create a great corporate culture by edict and get it done quickly, as it's obvious to many people what the benefits would be if management were successful. And there are a lot of books and consultants out there ready to lend a helping hand. It always sounds good on paper. I'm not saying that there is no benefit in attempting to do it; however, I don't believe that will achieve what most people are looking for.

Deteriorating Economic Culture

Policymakers dealing with an economy face a choice similar to that facing a management team running a business. Central banks and politicians can either take actions that will result in a stronger economy in the long term but that are possibly at the expense of GDP or the stock market in the short term, or drive GDP and stock markets higher today at the expense of the economy over the long term. Of course, if policymakers opt for the latter, then the stock market will also suffer in the long-term, but by then the economy will likely be someone else's problem. Or if they do acknowledge the longer-term consequences of today's decisions, they may hope that something will eventually come out of left field to save the day.

As we have already seen, policymakers have been driving GDP higher in the short term via the wealth effect. They have been driving stock markets and house prices higher via ultra-low interest rates and printing money. Asset prices have been boosted far above the levels that market forces would otherwise dictate. This has resulted in malinvestment, or misallocation of capital, as the price discovery mechanism is no longer working properly. In the short term, there is no obvious negative impact to the economy, particularly if one focuses solely on GDP to determine whether or not an economy is in good shape. However, the distortion of asset prices harms long-term economic fundamentals: productivity growth suffers, which leads to less wealth creation in the future. In addition, the world's balance sheet gets distorted with significant levels of debt.

Some policymakers – like some career executives – exhibit very poor corporate culture behaviour. This is because it's much easier to positively impact short-term symptoms and take credit for them than to help establish the conditions that drive long-term fundamentals, which in great part requires them to let go.

Now it's time to talk about stock markets.

ENDNOTES

[1] Or be in a government-granted monopoly position, which is good for the company but not for anyone else.
[2] In fact, many policymakers don't believe they bear any responsibility for our current situation. I'll get to that later.
[3] The industry term for this is *shrink*.

CHAPTER 18
STOCK MARKETS: SETTING THE SCENE

Lubricant

The finance industry consists of a whole array of entities such as commercial banks, investment banks, mutual fund companies, pension funds and insurance companies. You may think that most of these companies are intimidating and/or boring – and to some extent, you'd be right. However, those entities have a very important role to play in facilitating and ensuring the smooth functioning of the real economy, which is where all wealth is created. Through the careful allocation of capital, proper accounting, insuring against loss, helping people to plan for their retirement, and numerous other functions, the finance industry adds significantly to our general prosperity.

But note that the finance industry's role, like that of government, is primarily to facilitate the creation of wealth. No wealth is really created by the finance industry itself. I kind of think of it like engine oil for your car: not terribly exciting, or expensive, and not top of mind when you're thinking about how comfortable your car is, how it looks, or how it performs; but without it, your car could not function.[1] Likewise, the economy could not function without the facilitator role played by finance.

The Blob

However, there is a major problem. Increasingly, over time, parts of the finance industry, and, in particular, stock markets, on which I will focus, are *becoming* the economy rather than playing the facilitator role for which they were designed. In my opinion, the reason this has happened is that smart people can make significant amounts of money and can do it a lot faster in the finance industry than they can in the real economy. But the main problem with this is that as the finance industry grew to grotesque levels, it began to have some negative impacts on society and, thus, detract from the positive role that it played.

Because Wall Street is becoming a larger part of the economy but doesn't actually produce anything, that means it's taking more and more from the real economy; those in the real economy have less and less capital than they otherwise would have had with which to produce more stuff. Therefore, much of the enormous wealth that many in the finance industry have achieved in recent years has not been earned but, rather, redistributed to them from others.

The Real Economy

I spent my whole career in the finance industry, and I was an investor. The investments I made, although I believe they were very important, were very different from the investments being made in the real economy. When deciding to invest my clients' capital, I would scour the globe for companies that I believed would best put that capital to use and, thus, produce more capital in the most efficient manner.[2] Investing in this manner, undertaken by my team and thousands of other investors around the globe, helps to ensure that only the best companies have access to capital and that basket-case companies don't get the opportunity to destroy any more of it. However, none of us ever actually put capital to productive use: that's the job of the companies in which we invest.

In the real economy, individual entrepreneurs as well as large corporations need to successfully invest capital that has been saved, by themselves or others, to produce goods and/or services that they believe other people or companies will want to purchase. This takes time, and, importantly, comes with risk, as others may decide they don't want what has been produced – in which case, the invested capital would be lost.

Successful entrepreneurs or companies can, over time, generate a significant amount of wealth if people want to buy their products. Notice that in this situation, both parties will benefit: the producer by receiving money from the buyer and the buyer by receiving a good or service from the producer – a fair exchange.

The Siphon

The finance industry is an important facilitator in this wealth creation process, primarily by helping channel capital from savers to investors. However, over the years, the industry discovered that, with the help of central banks, it was much easier to make a fortune by siphoning off wealth that had already been created. Why bother going through the trouble of facilitating the time-consuming and risky wealth creation process within the real economy? One consequence of this has been that more and more of the best and brightest university graduates have wanted to work on Wall Street rather than in the real economy.[3] The result: too many smart people who would have otherwise been applying their abilities to help create wealth in the real economy have, instead, been focusing their energies on extracting wealth from it.[4]

Fairly Obtained Wealth

Most people working in the finance industry are hard-working and honest people, just like in any other industry. But while most of them contribute to society's wealth creation process through their facilitator role, there is a minority within it who are simply benefiting at the expense of someone else – and the extent to which they benefit is enormous. I suspect that most of this minority are unaware of their negative impact on society, and they are not breaking any laws, as far as I know. Naturally, they would view their wealth as being fairly earned; but wealth is only earned if it's a result of contributing to the creation of real wealth rather than its redistribution. Therefore, instead of being fairly earned, much of their wealth has been fairly *obtained*.

Winning Wealth

Increasingly, stock markets have been moving further away from their intended facilitator role and instead, they are becoming a shell game where wealth is moved around rather than created. The way wealth is obtained by many working on Wall Street resembles more what happens in a casino than in a real economy. In a casino, wealth is *won* rather than earned. No net wealth is created; it is simply redistributed between the people gambling at the casino with the house taking a considerable stake. And this is also increasingly what is happening in the housing market. It's like one big game of poker, and, unfortunately, in a game of poker, it's not like everyone walks away from the poker table with more wealth than when they arrived. There is no net wealth creation at the table. Wealth is redistributed at the table, and the end result is that there is usually one winner and a bunch of losers. Sound familiar?

Also, notice that in a game of poker the one who ends up with all the wealth is the winner. They won the money; they didn't earn it. Of course, there's nothing wrong with this and there are a number of people out there who are very good poker players and successfully make a living winning money from others. But because they win money from others, that means there are a bunch of people out there who lose money. And there are a lot more losers than winners. In poker, the winner wins at someone else's expense. Again, there is nothing wrong with this as long as all of the players are participating voluntarily (and don't have gambling addictions) and are aware of the purpose of a game of poker.

Losing Wealth

While the redistribution of wealth at a casino is increasingly similar to that of the current distorted role of the stock market, there are a number of differences that make the latter immoral. Players in a casino are there voluntarily. They are willing to lose their wealth for the chance – albeit slim – of winning big, as well as for the thrill and entertainment. However, much of the wealth being redistributed to Wall Street and corporate executives actually comes from people who have purposely decided to not invest in the stock market. Despite not being willing to risk losing their wealth by investing in the stock market, their wealth is still taken from them, indirectly. Some have called this 'social security for the top 1%, with the other 99% footing the bill'. Not only that, but most people are unaware that it's happening, although they *are* aware that they seem to be working harder and harder simply to maintain their current standard of living. Many people are aware the system is working against them; they're just not sure how.

The Good

Let's explore how and why all of this happens, and how the consequences go far beyond an involuntary and unfair redistribution of wealth. But, first, it's important to understand the good role that a stock market plays in a thriving economy.

Back to your bike business. Because you have been riding for so long, you are very aware of the differences between a good bike and a bad bike, as well as possible improvements that might be made that cyclists would value and be willing to pay for. Your bikes are very popular, and demand for your bikes is increasing. You decide to hire someone and train them to make bikes. But rather than each of you producing a bike in its entirety you divide up the work. You make the frame and the gears, and your employee makes the wheels and the tyres.[5]

Over the years, you come up with new ideas for the design of the frames, and your sales keep growing. However, making more bikes requires you to invest in more tools and equipment to make those bikes, and you access that capital by borrowing from your bank. You hire more and more employees to help you make the bikes, then you have to buy a larger building for all of your equipment and inventory. This necessitates even more borrowing from your bank.

Note that this is all works because of your fanatical devotion to providing your customers with the best bikes at the best prices. You are providing a great customer value proposition. You are successful because you are adding value to society by making bikes that people will choose to part with some of their wealth to purchase.

Your employees choose to work for you because you pay them a fair wage. Ideally, you would offer them a percentage of the profit in your business, so that the more successful your business is, the more everyone in your business benefits. You reinvest some of the wealth you've created to create even more wealth in the future.

Mutual Benefit

Notice here that no one is winning at the expense of someone else. The only losers are those who are making lousy bikes, but this encourages the right sort of behaviour from them. First, they could try to improve the quality of their bikes so that people will want to buy them. Secondly, they could decide that they're not good enough to compete with you, so they might decide to start a business that makes, say, shovels that are better than those currently being sold. Thirdly, they could decide that they are going to try to invent something completely new. Fourthly, they could decide they no longer want to be an entrepreneur and, instead, get a job with another entrepreneur/business. Assuming they are successful at any one of the four choices they make, society will be better off. Of course, failure is not much fun and change can mean great uncertainty, but protecting bad businesses reduces everyone's wealth.

Equity

Your bike business is growing nicely, and you want to keep investing capital in it. However, you're becoming a little uncomfortable with your level of bank debt and the interest that they are charging you. Therefore, instead of borrowing more money to expand your business, you decide to see if your friend Jill is interested in investing in your company. In return for that investment, you will give her a *share* of whatever profit the company makes. That investment is Jill's equity, which simply means her level of ownership in your business (similar to your equity in your home).

Let's assume that the total value of your company less any liabilities you owe is $1,000,000; this is your equity in your business.[6] Jill has offered to invest $500,000, so now the equity of the business goes up to $1,500,000 (your equity plus Jill's). Jill now owns one-third of the business; she has a one-third equity share in your company (total equity $1,500,000 ÷ $500,000 = 1/3 or 33.3%). You issue Jill a share certificate that proves she owns a third of the business and is entitled to a third of all of the profits your company makes. This is why stocks, or equities are also called shares; a stock is your share in the equity of the business.

Now let's assume that you have successfully invested Jill's capital. Word of your great bikes has now begun to reach other countries, and you now wish to start exporting them. To do this, you need significantly more capital to build a very large factory, invest in tools, equipment and supplies, and hire hundreds of employees. So far, you've been able to grow the business by reinvesting some of your profits back into the business, borrowing some money from the bank and getting a capital injection from Jill in return for part-ownership of your business. However, in order to get your hands on the large amount of capital that's needed to take your company to the next level, you contact an investment bank. Which leads us to the next chapter on stock markets.

ENDNOTES

[1] Not an issue for electric vehicles.
[2] And, very importantly, I sought evidence that the businesses were valued fairly.
[3] In more recent years, many of the very best have been entering the technology sector, which benefits us all.
[4] Note that there are instances where much of the wealth obtained by executives running companies that operate in the real economy is also not earned but, rather, redistributed from those who created it. We'll get to that later.
[5] In reality, you would probably not bother making the gears and wheels yourself. You would purchase those from other suppliers. Your expertise in making bikes is mainly about the shape and design of the bike frame.

[6] Note that valuing a company is a complex exercise. It is not necessary to understand to follow what I'm trying to explain here, but you can think of it as determining what assets your business currently has, such as cash, inventory, buildings and equipment minus what you owe (to banks, suppliers or others) plus the present value of all the money the company is expected to earn in the future (discounted cash flow models will forecast cash flows out to ten years and discount them back to the present along with the discounted terminal value of the business in ten year's time).

CHAPTER 19
STOCK MARKETS: SOME OF THE BASICS

IN THIS CHAPTER we'll look at some stock market terminology, why stock markets are important, and how your company gets listed on a stock market. If you find some of the stuff in this chapter too detailed, or you are already well-versed in this stuff, then you could skip it and move on to chapter 20 and come back to it as reference for things like return on equity (ROE), stock options and price discovery.

Return On Equity (ROE)

As the years go by, you continue to reinvest most of your profit back into your business. This increases the equity in your business, which is much like when you pay down your mortgage – injecting capital increases your equity in your home. And because both you and Jill have claims to the profits of the business, each time profits are ploughed back into the company, the equity ownership for both of you increases. Thus, if the total equity has now increased to $12 million, then two-thirds, or $8 million, would be owned by you; a third, or $4 million, would be owned by Jill. Now if we assume that your company is earning $1.2 million dollars after tax, then the return on equity or ROE would be 10%.

$1.2 million profit ÷ $12 million equity = 10%

You own two-thirds of the equity; thus, you get two-thirds of the profit, or $800,000 (2/3 x $1.2 million = $800,000); Jill, with one-third ownership, is entitled to $400,000. ROE essentially tells you how profitable your equity investment is or how much it is earning every year.

Initial Public Offering (IPO)

So far so good, but now you believe that your company could earn significantly more money if you were able to get your hands on more capital to invest to expand your business even more. You contact an investment bank, and they take your company public, which is also known as an initial public offering, or IPO (don't worry, it's not complicated).

When Jill invested in your company, that was a private transaction not offered to the public at large. You didn't publish an ad calling for interested parties to invest in your business. That is what the investment bank will now do. They will ask their clients if any of them would be interested in purchasing shares of your company, and those shares will subsequently be listed on a public market or stock exchange. It's the first, or *initial* time your company is offering shares to the public and that's why it's called an initial public offering, or IPO.

By going public, you will no longer be able to dictate who owns shares in your business. First, you don't know who the investment bank will find to invest in your business. Secondly, once your shares are listed on a stock market, the investors in your business can sell those shares any time they want to whomever they want. In fact, they won't even know who the buyers of their shares are, and the buyers may even include some of your competitors. You may end up getting shareholders who have very different ideas about how your business should be run. However, as long as you control the majority of the shares, you can't be forced to change how you run the business.[1]

Perhaps, after talking to the investment bank, you decide to raise $3 million dollars from other investors. That $3 million plus yours and Jill's original $12 million will result in total capital of $15 million. The investment bank might decide to create 1.5 million shares in your business; thus, each share would be worth $10.[2] This is calculated by taking the total of $15 million in equity in the business and dividing it by 1.5 million shares. Note here that your ownership stake in your business has gone down, but you still have a majority ownership position: you own $8 million or 53.3% of equity versus 26.7% owned by Jill and 20% by the public.

	Equity Value	Shares: $10 per share	% of Total
You	$8 million	800,000	53.3%
Jill	$4 million	400,000	26.7%
Public	$3 million	300,000	20.0%
Total	$15 million	1.5 million	100%

So, from now on you will be entitled to only 53.3% of the profit that your company generates, and Jill, 26.7%. The other investors, who own 300,000 shares of your company, will be entitled to 20% of your company's profit. However, despite the fact that you are now entitled to only 53.3% of the profit, rather than the 66.7% entitlement you had before the IPO, there is that much more equity in the business. You still own $8 million of equity and, thus, will continue to earn $800,000 as long as the ROE remains at 10%.

However, as you reinvest more capital into your business, you are able to do things more efficiently. Over time, you improve your company's ROE to 20%, which equates to $3 million profit. As 53.3% of that profit belongs to you, $1.6 million belongs to you – double your previous share of $800,000.

By accessing more capital from investors and sharing with them the success of your business, you were able to make more money.

Earnings Per Share (EPS)

EPS is calculated by dividing the total earnings of the business by the number of shares outstanding[3]. In this case, the new profit of your company is $3 million and the total number of shares outstanding is 1,500,000; therefore, the earnings per share are $2 per share.

Price Earnings Multiple (PE)

It's now necessary to talk about the Price Earnings Multiple (PE). Again, it's not that complicated. First, the calculation: you simply divide the share price by the earnings per share (EPS).

In our example, assume that because you have improved the ROE from 10% to 20%, the price of your shares has grown from $10 to $20. As your company is currently earning $2 per share, the PE is 10× ($20 ÷ $2 = 10). The PE gives the multiple of earnings per share that must be paid if someone want to buy shares in your company. However, given the higher efficiency of the invested capital and the anticipation of stronger earnings growth, investors may be willing to pay a higher price for those earnings. If the price increased to $40, the PE would be 20× ($40 ÷ $2 = 20).

PE ratios will differ from company to company. Usually, that is because of different assumptions about how companies will be able to grow their earnings per share over time. For instance, if your company was growing EPS at 10%, then a 20× PE multiple may be appropriate; however, if it wasn't growing earnings at all, then the PE of your company would be much lower. All else being equal, the faster the earnings of a company are growing, the higher the PE multiple, which is very intuitive. However, not all else is equal, and there are other things that can impact the PE of a stock. For instance, if the company has a strong balance sheet (i.e. less debt) or a more predictable earnings stream, then it might command a higher PE multiple. Importantly, just because you might have to pay a higher PE for a stock doesn't mean it's more expensive than a low-PE stock. That is because of the different assumptions about growth. For instance, if you had the choice to pay a PE of 15× for a business that was not able to grow its earnings versus a 20× PE for a company that was growing its earnings at 10%, you could make a lot more money buying the 20x PE stock. Yes, its PE multiple is higher, but the faster earnings growth makes it a cheaper stock

Market Capitalisation

Market capitalisation ('market cap' for short), is simply the total value of your company as determined by investors. It is calculated by multiplying the share price by the number of shares outstanding.

The 1.5 million shares outstanding represent the total investment of $15 million; remember that each share is priced at $10. We saw that when the ROE of your company increased to 20%, the share price rose to $40. The market cap of your company can be calculated by multiplying the $40 share price by 1.5 million shares, giving you $60 million.

Dividends

Companies also usually pay dividends to their shareholders. A dividend is a percentage of the profits that are paid out to shareholders. For instance, if your company decided to retain half of its profits for reinvestment, it could pay out the other half as dividends. Thus, each share would be entitled to a dividend of $1: half of the profit ($1.5 million) is divided by the total shares outstanding (1.5 million). A share's dividend yield is the dividend divided by the share price. In this case, $1 divided by $40 gives a dividend yield of 2.5%.

Price Discovery

Okay, so now you have a publicly listed company, which means your shares are listed and trading on a stock market. And now some of the investors who bought your shares during the IPO may decide that they no longer want to own those shares. Publicly listed shares are easy to sell to other investors. The stock market plays a very important role by coordinating buyers and sellers of your company's stock through the price discovery process.

Price discovery describes the process by which investors analyse all aspects of a business and develop their expectations of what the business might look like in the future. They do this to determine the price they think would be fair to pay. Meanwhile, sellers are doing the same thing to determine at what price they'd be willing to sell their shares. When a buyer and seller agree on a price, the exchange happens, and that becomes the new price for the shares of your company.

Say the last price of your company's shares traded at the end of a day – the closing price – was $40. When the market opens the next day, others will likely buy and sell your company's shares. If there has been no significant news about your company or the economy, then most trades will probably happen within a narrow range of that closing price of $40. This is happening with thousands of stocks every day; literally billions of transactions are taking place. The wisdom of crowds is usually pretty good at determining the price that best reflects the intrinsic value of a stock.

The wisdom of crowds is nicely demonstrated by Victor Saenger. He filled a jar with 490 jellybeans. He then asked thirty people to guess how many jellybeans were in the jar. Six people were very close to the actual number. The other twenty-four were way off. But the average of all the guesses came to 487 – only missed it by 0.6%! Am I the only one amazed at this sort of stuff?

Risk and Return

Investors analyse the risk/return trade-off to determine what they consider to be a fair price for a stock. Another way of putting it is *How much risk am I taking on for the expected return*? Typically, if the risk is low, you should also expect a lower return, and vice versa. For instance, depositing your money in a bank account is low risk (apart from the risk of central banks debasing your money's purchasing power by printing money); therefore, you will typically receive a low (or no) return, and the return is often negative in real terms (i.e. the inflation rate is higher than the rate of interest you earn on your money). In terms of stocks, if you invested your money in a utility company, you should probably expect a low return, as the earnings and cashflow pattern of a utility company are more predictable (utilities are not without risk, but they have lower risk than other types of companies). If instead you invested your money in a company that had a less predictable earnings stream you would likely pay a lower price and thus have the potential to make more money. In a nutshell, the more predictable the future cash flow and earnings of a business, the lower the distribution of potential outcomes and the higher the price you would be willing to pay for those outcomes – which means you would have a lower expected return because you paid a higher price. And, of course, the opposite is true: paying a lower price for less certainty can result in a greater return on your investment.

Notice that the return is an *expected* return, not a guaranteed return. Obviously, if the returns were guaranteed, everyone would select the option with the higher return. Returns have dispersions, or ranges, of outcomes – they will be plus or minus whatever the expectation is. For instance, if a stock has an expected return of 10%, the dispersion of outcomes might range from 5% to 15%. That is, the return you receive could be anywhere in that range, the average of which is 10%. A lower-risk stock might have an expected return of 8% with a dispersion of 7% to 9%; a higher-risk stock might have an expected return of 50%, with a dispersion of zero to 100%.

We'll see later why it's very important that true price discovery by those with skin in the game be allowed to unfold – and why, due to central banks, less and less of this is happening today.

The Sovereign Consumer, Again

So why does all of this matter, and how does it help create real wealth for society? The stock market is made up of thousands of companies like your bike company, all producing different things and offering different services. But they all have one of thing in common: if they want their share price to grow, they need to grow the earnings of their business and give investors confidence that the company's earnings growth is sustainable. In order to grow their earnings, companies need to save some of their earnings (retained earnings), and continuously reinvest those retained earnings in their business. This enables the company to provide better products and services, and more of them (to improve or maintain their competitive advantage), to their customers and clients. Think of how every couple of years Apple launches a new iPhone model that is a bit better than the previous version. This doesn't happen by accident. Apple spends billions of dollars every year reinvesting in their business to create better and better products. In 2023, they spent around $30 billion on research and development, as well as another $11 billion on fixed equipment.

A company like Apple will continuously reinvest in their business in order to ensure they are able to make products that their customers value. We will buy Apple products only if we think it's worth it to do so. It's our capital (or what's left of it after taxation and currency debasement), and we have the right to determine what we buy and at what price. We might want an iPhone but find that it's too expensive. If so, we are free to choose not to buy one.

Cause and Effect

Employees help their companies develop products that they hope consumers will value, and the employees themselves are consumers using the money they have been paid. It's a virtuous circle in which real wealth is being produced by companies, consumers are purchasing their products, and the companies are paying their employees, who then have the means to purchase things from other companies. A byproduct of this is that successful companies will see their profits increase. And, as we have seen, the higher the profits of a company, and the more confident investors are that profitability will continue, the higher the share price. As stock markets are made up of thousands of companies, if most of the companies are successfully creating wealth, then the stock market will rise to reflect that fact.[4]

Through the price discovery process, investors continuously determine the fair prices at which to buy and sell stocks, based on how successful they think companies will be at satisfying the demands of the sovereign consumer.

The Importance of Price Discovery

Why is it important that the price discovery process be allowed to determine fair prices? There are several reasons.[5]

Companies Selling New Shares

First, some companies, even though they may have already raised capital through IPOs and are, thus, publicly listed, may wish to raise more equity (seek more capital from more investors) to further expand their business. This is done via a secondary offering of shares, and the price of the new shares will be very close (usually offered at a small discount) to the last closing price of the shares that are already listed on the stock market. If the price discovery mechanism isn't functioning properly and the shares are trading at a price much higher than the intrinsic value of the business, then the new investors will be paying too much for their shares – they'll be getting screwed.[6,7] The company will be selling its shares to the new investors at a price higher than warranted by the success of the business; thus, those new investors will not be fairly rewarded for the risks they are taking on. This is effectively a transfer of wealth from the new investors to the existing shareholders.[8]

Price discovery is also important because when other companies do their IPOs, the prices at which their shares are offered to prospective investors are, in part, derived from the prices of similar businesses that are already trading on the stock market. For example, assume a trucking company wants to raise capital via an IPO. Part of the process for determining a fair price will be to look at the share prices, or, rather, the valuations of trucking companies that are already publicly listed. If the shares of trucking companies are trading at an average PE multiple of 20x and, on average, their earnings are growing at a rate of 10%, then, if the trucking company going public also has earnings growth of 10%, they will likely also offer their shares to the public at a similar PE multiple of 20×.[9]

Now assume that, because of a broken price discovery mechanism, the share prices of all of those trucking companies are trading at price earnings multiples well over their intrinsic values, perhaps 30×. In this case, if the new trucking company was able to price its IPO shares at a similar multiple, the new providers of capital would be paying 50% more for their shares than they would have had true price discovery been allowed to take place. The new investors are overpaying for their shares and the existing owners of the company are making more than they should on the IPO – a transfer of wealth from the new investors to the existing investors.

Stock Options

Executives of many large companies receive stock options as part of their compensation. The value of a stock option is determined by the price of the company's stock. If the stock price increases, the value of the options also increases, but in multiples of the increase in the share price.

Here's how it works. Assume the price of a company share is $100 on the day that the CEO has been granted a million stock options. They give the CEO the right to buy up to a million shares at $100 per share at any time over the next ten years. The CEO did not have to buy the options from the company; they were simply a part of their compensation.

Now assume that over the next year, the price of the company's shares increased by 10% to $110. This might be because the company is growing its profit at a good rate, or it might simply be because investors are in a bullish mood and it is driving the share prices of all companies higher (even those that aren't growing their profits or that don't have any profit at all i.e. zombies). If the CEO exercises their options now, they could buy a million shares from the company for $100 and then immediately sell them in the stock market to other investors for $110, yielding a $10 profit per share.

Thus, exercising their million stock options would give the CEO $10 million. Not bad for one year. Typically, executives are not allowed to exercise their options in the first few years after they have received them, but consider how much money they would make if they held on to those options until the share price doubled. They would make $100 per share, and selling all their options would net them $100 million. They would get that money even if the stock markets were simply going up because the central banks were driving them higher via quantitative easing (discussed soon).

Even when price discovery is allowed to happen and a company's share price truly reflects its intrinsic value, stock options represent a massive transfer of wealth from shareholders to executives. However, the shareholders usually won't mind because it means the value of their shares are going up and everyone's making money. However, if the share price is being driven higher by management in an unsustainable fashion, then ultimately the shareholders will be screwed: the executives are benefiting at the expense of the shareholders.

Now imagine how much money executives can make from stock options when true price discovery is not allowed to take place and, thanks to central banks, shares are trading at levels way above their intrinsic values.

Shares as Currency

Another reason why price discovery is so important is that companies will sometimes use their shares as currency – as a type of money –to acquire other businesses. For example, if one company wanted to take over another company, they would have to buy the equity (the shares) of that business. To buy that equity, the acquiring company has two broad alternatives: it could use cash, or it could offer its own shares as a form of payment. As you can imagine, true price discovery plays a very important role here for both the company using its shares as currency and the company whose shares are being bought.

The share price is supposed to be a symptom of the underlying health of a business. The more profitable and the higher the growth, all else being equal, the higher the share price.[10]

The bottom line is that if true price discovery is not allowed to occur, then capital gets misallocated in unfair ways that are not based on fundamentals or intrinsic value. This means some people are benefiting at the expense of others rather than the parties both benefiting from a fair deal. This serves to reduce trust in the market system.

True price discovery has deteriorated over the years as many companies began, instead, to focus on driving their company's share prices higher in the short term rather than through the costly, lengthy and risky reinvestment process. Central banks then joined in the fray. We'll discuss that soon.

Although the stock market still provides enormous benefits to society, it has started to also contribute significant negatives. It's not the stock markets themselves that are faulty; rather, it's how they are being distorted. But before we get to that, let's look at a few more aspects of stock markets.

ENDNOTES

[1] Shareholders are allowed to vote each year on how a company should be operated. Decisions are based on a majority vote; therefore, if you own more than 50%, you will always be able to decide how the business is run. However, corporate executives often own a very small percentage of their company's shares and so can come under enormous pressure from other short-term investors who gang up and vote for actions which benefit the share price in the short term – which often comes at the expense of the long-term health of the business. More on this later.

[2] Note that share are typically priced higher than the value of the equity in the business or book value.

[3] Shares that are outstanding are held by shareholders. However, shares can also be held in treasury (treasury shares) and these are not entitled to earnings (dividends) of the business.

[4] Sometimes a small number of companies can become so large that they have an overbearing influence on the stock market. In that scenario, the behaviour of the stock market may not be representative of what is going on generally within the economy.

[5] And price discovery applies not only to stock markets, but also at such times as when purchasing something or applying for a job.

[6] If the price discovery process is not working properly, it almost always means that stocks are trading at much higher prices, not much lower prices.

7. Note that this means that investors are voluntarily buying overpriced stocks. This happens when active managers fear they would be jeopardising their careers if they don't participate in stocks that grow ever more expensive or passive funds that are price indiscriminate (will pay any price).
8. How much of a wealth transfer this is will be determined by how effectively the company puts that new capital to use. If the money is wasted with no return, then the existing shareholders will be worse off with their shareholdings being diluted.
9. There are many more things to consider when determining the offering price for new shares, but all else being equal, the valuations of similar businesses already listed in the stock market play an important role.
10. Prevailing interest rates can also impact the share price of a business and do so fairly as long as those rates are determined *naturally*.

CHAPTER 20
STOCK MARKETS: A FEW MORE THINGS

Stock Market Wealth Is Not Money Wealth

One misunderstanding that some people seem to suffer from is equating stock market wealth with money wealth. While your holding of shares in a company represents wealth of a kind, that wealth can disappear overnight. The value of a share is representative of the wealth that the underlying company is producing and is expected to produce in the future. However, stock market wealth can go up very quickly not because there is more wealth being produced by companies but because investors are willing to pay more for that wealth creation. And it can also go in reverse. Also, things can change, and a company can go bankrupt, wiping out wealth: the share price can go to zero.

Over the last few decades, share prices have, on average, been much higher than their intrinsic values (i.e. the amount of wealth they are expected to produce). For instance, the price to sales ratio for the S&P 500 Stock Index has been rising steadily as central banks increasingly back-stop the stock market. Here is the average price to sales according to DQYDJ[1] and the cyclically adjusted price earnings ratio CAPE[2] by decade (both for the S&P 500 stock index):

	Price to Sales	CAPE
1980s	0.6×	11.5×
1990s	1.1×	25.3
2000s	1.5×	26.7
2010s	1.7×	25.6
2020s	2.6×	32.4

This is a result of policymakers taking actions to drive asset prices higher or prevent them from falling to their true values.[3] Of course, those prices could fall at any time. Any shares you own are not money wealth until you sell them– until you monetise them. When you monetise them, that gives central banks the opportunity to extract your capital from you by printing money, but at least your wealth can't evaporate overnight like it can in the stock market.

Share prices rise during a bull market, and in extreme cases, they can bid up to ridiculous levels, with all of the shareholders believing they have become wealthy. However, that kind of share wealth usually doesn't last long, as shares will eventually return to fair value or lower.

Money Doesn't Disappear in Stock Markets

I remember during the stock market technology bubble of the late 1990s (the dot-com boom) and the ensuing tech wreck that commentators were saying that trillions of dollars had disappeared as a result of the stock market implosion. I remember thinking to myself, 'How on earth can money just disappear other than by putting your cash in a pile and burning it?'[4] The truth is that not a single dollar had disappeared due to falling share prices; the stock market wealth that had been lost was not the same as money wealth. The lost wealth was simply representative of the outlandish expectations of so many investors; it was faux wealth.

Why does money not disappear when stock markets implode? Because when investors buy shares, it doesn't result in a whole bunch of cash sitting in the stock market. Thus, when the market crashes, it doesn't result in a whole bunch of money evaporating – because the money's not there in the first place. Every time an investor uses cash to buy a share in the market, they buy it from another investor who takes that cash and puts it in their bank account.[5] In other words, when people lose their money because of plummeting stocks, that money hasn't disappeared; someone else has it.

Basketcase.com

Let's use a hypothetical example to better explain the concept. It's the year 2000. You own a thousand shares of a new internet company called Basketcase.com. The share price is about $120; thus, the value of your shareholding is $120,000. Fred, an optimistic investor, decides he wants to jump on the stock market bandwagon. He offers you $120,000 for your shares, and you accept. Fred now has an asset worth $120,000.

However, over the next few years, the company's business model didn't play out as planned, and the company eventually declared bankruptcy. The share price dropped to zero.[6] Fred has seen his $120,000 share value evaporate. But no actual dollars disappeared. There was a transfer of real wealth in 2000, from Fred to you, of $120,000 (the amount of money that he took from his bank account and gave to you in return for your Basketcase. com shares). That money was never *in the market*; instead, that money that used to be in Fred's bank account had been put safely into yours.

Pricing Stocks

Stock market wealth can change very quickly, up or down – not because of changes in what the companies are producing, but, rather, based on investors' expectations. This is because whatever the value of the most recent buy/sell transaction is for a share, all the other outstanding shares of that company will be valued at that price. And the prices of stocks can get bid to extremely high levels based on a market frenzy.

We can go back to our island economy to help explain this even further. Assume the economy has grown. There are more inhabitants and more activities. For some reason, the residents develop a particular fondness for conch shells. They begin to buy them up, and a mania ensues. The price of conch shells explodes, and fortunes are made. A 'you conch lose' attitude takes over.

But there is little real value in a conch shell. Fortunes are being made simply because people are buying conch shells for the sole purpose of on-selling them for a higher price.[7] Fortunes are not being *earned*; no real wealth is being created. Rather, it is being redistributed within the economy. The higher prices that people continue to expect are not a result of the conch shells becoming more productive. They are simply due to a mania that has developed because people think that they can make a fortune buying and selling conch shells. Few people bother to question the rationale of the prices skyrocketing to the moon, probably because they want to believe it will continue forever.

Let's say the residents own a total of one hundred conch shells and they are using dollars as a medium of exchange. The price per shell started at $10; thus, the total value of conch shells was $1,000. But following the frenzy of buying and selling, a conch shell is sold for $100. Now all of the other shells are considered to be worth $100, as well. The total wealth in conch shells has risen from $1,000 to $10,000. Not only that, but the island's economists and policymakers point to the enormous growth in the household wealth of the economy. However, no real wealth was created. There are still only a hundred conch shells on the island. All that changed was the price people were willing to pay for them.

Here Today, Gone Tomorrow
What if the next shell sells for a much lower price? Consider this scenario. People begin to worry that they won't be able to find others to pay higher prices for their shells. They decide to cash out by selling their shells. But now that the frenzy has ended, no one wants to buy the shells. The price plummets, and the next shell sells for $5. Thus, the value of every shell drops to $5. The total wealth in conch shells plummets from $10,000 to $500 – all because one person sold their shell for $5.

We see this sort of thing – the idea of a growth in wealth where no real wealth is being created – in the real world in the area of household wealth. Some economists and policymakers enthusiastically point to how much household wealth is increasing due to rising house prices and stock markets. However, as we have seen, rising house prices do not contribute any net wealth to society any more than the rising prices of conch shells did to the island's economy. Rising stock markets contribute real net wealth to society only if they rise due to companies putting capital to productive use. If they are driven higher by artificial means, then there is no net wealth creation, and the wealth people think they have can disappear very quickly.

Ponzi
Stock markets driven upwards artificially are classic Ponzi or pyramid schemes. And it can result in a significant redistribution of wealth amongst the participants. And the early participants get richer at the expense of the newcomers. Another downside is that as each trade triggers a capital gain which then gets taxed, more money ends up in governments' hands, to be consumed. One might argue that because much of the money is traded back and forth and not invested, there's no real harm done. But from a societal perspective, this is yet another redistribution of capital within the system.

These days, many people who invest in stock markets have no idea what they're invested in – and they don't even care. A lot of people invest in index funds which contain hundreds or even thousands of different stocks. Investors in these types of funds would have no idea whether they are overpaying for the stocks in their funds.[8] Instead, they assume that there are enough investors out there who are correctly valuing those underlying stocks based on their assessments of each company's ability to grow in a profitable way over time. However, there is less of that going on than there used to be. Not only that, but the popularity of index (passive) funds may also be driving stock markets higher.[9]

There are other forces at work that drive stock market valuations far above their intrinsic values. We'll look at them in the next chapter.

ENDNOTES

[1] DQYDJ (Don't Quit Your Day Job). https://dqydj.com/sp-500-ps-ratio/
[2] Shiller Data. https://shillerdata.com/
[3] Note that valuations can also be impacted by what sorts of businesses are in the index. For instance, if the index has a higher proportion of higher growth industries then the valuation metrics, all else equal, will be higher. On the other hand, economic growth has slowed over the last forty years.
[4] Note that money can disappear when borrowers repay their bank loans, or when the central bank sells assets.
[5] Note that, at times, investors can purchase shares not from other investors but from the companies themselves in the aforementioned IPOs or secondary offerings. However, the result is still the same: the money that you use to buy shares from the company ends up in that company's bank account. This happened a lot during the dot-com boom. Many basket-case companies went public, raising hundreds of millions of dollars from investors; and then some of those companies went bankrupt. But the investors' money didn't *disappear*. It was in the bank accounts of the founders of those companies.
[6] This happened numerous times during the Tech Wreck of 2000–2002.
[7] This is known in the investment industry as the *greater fool theory* ('I know I'm a fool to be buying this stock at such a high price, but I know there's an even greater fool somewhere out there who will buy it off me at an even higher price').
[8] Index funds are *price indiscriminate* when they buy stocks.
[9] Several podcasts feature market strategist Michael Green discussing this phenomenon. His theory is that the largest stocks are inelastic in terms of their trading liquidity versus the number of stocks that passive funds are required to buy.

CHAPTER 21
STOCK MARKETS AND EXECUTIVES

The Good
There are still lots of great things happening, and real wealth being created, with the help of stock markets. However, as already discussed, over the years, stock markets have become more and more like giant games of poker – less about helping to create real wealth and more about redistributing existing wealth amongst the participants.

Many investors still make decisions based on the traditional price discovery process (i.e. analysing a company's prospects for long-term growth, profitability and risk and then paying accordingly). However, an increasing number of investors don't. And when more and more people treat the stock market like a big game of poker, less wealth gets produced, because capital is being misallocated and fewer people in the real economy are producing things than there would be otherwise.

The Not So Good
The facilitator role of the finance industry has come at a greater and greater cost as it steadily increases as a per centage of the total economy. According to a paper by the Bank for International Settlements, once finance becomes too big, the 'growth of a country's financial system [becomes] a drag on productivity growth'.[1] And according to an ECB member, the finance industry's share of GDP in the United States almost quadrupled to 8% over a sixty-year period.[2]

The purposes of investing and capital markets are becoming increasingly distorted. Many people are already paying a steep price for this distortion, and it's only going to get worse. And the real crisis is that the people most negatively impacted are those who don't even participate in the markets – who don't even own a single share.

Zombie Management Teams
Let's look at one example of how the distortion of the price discovery process can reduce productivity.

Assume that you want to acquire the bike company Spin-Cycle. You've noticed that Spin-Cycle has underinvested in its business for many years. It has lost its way and is no longer making any money. It has become a 'zombie'. (Zombie companies don't produce enough profit to cover the interest expense on their debt.) However, Spin-Cycle still has a lot of good employees, a well-recognised bike brand and manufacturing capacity. You believe that you could put those assets to much better use and derive much more value from them than Spin-Cycle has. So, you approach their management and offer to buy the company.

However, despite the company being mismanaged and losing money, Spin-Cycle was able to constantly gain access to more and more low-cost capital because interest rates were being relentlessly distorted downwards by central banks. As investors were no longer able to earn money on very safe investments, they were *reaching for yield*. By having driven interest rates to zero, the central banks have essentially forced investors to take on more risk if they want to earn any sort of return.[3]

Gaining more access to capital did nothing to fix Spin-Cycle's business model. It continued to lose money. And the very actions of central banks made it unnecessary for the company to mend its ways. The zombie bike company's inept management team refuses to sell their company to you because they know they would likely lose their jobs if they did. Instead, they continue to destroy capital as long as they can continue to access more of it. By not being able to purchase Spin-Cycle, you lose the change to create more capital with those assets and possibly hire more people. The mismanagement of Spin-Cycle continues to contribute to the declining productivity growth we have been experiencing for many years.

What is the impact of all of this on the global economy? In a nutshell, a lot of capital is misallocated at improper prices to the wrong businesses and, thus, not put to its most productive uses. Not only that, but a lot of that capital doesn't even go into investment in the businesses; rather, it ends up in the pockets of the executives. Remember that the executives of a company are usually not the founders; thus, they don't own the majority of the company. Yet, they will still own some shares and often a large number of stock options, which, as we have seen, are a leveraged bet on the share price going higher.

Therefore, executives can make a lot more money in the short term by taking measures that drive their company's share price higher rather than investing in the business. The result? A higher share price today at the expense of the success of the business in the future, which ultimately leads to a lower share price, which, of course, is detrimental to the long-term shareholders (owners).

Treating Symptoms

If true price discovery is allowed to take place, then the stock market has a much better chance of being a true barometer of the health of an economy. However, it's important to understand that the stock market – and, thus, the stock prices of all of the companies in the stock market – are merely symptoms of what's going on. Just as a fever can be the symptom of a virus or a headache the symptom of a hangover. The fundamental issues are the virus and drinking too much, respectively. Treating the symptoms does not address the underlying causes and will not lead to long-term health. Trying to eliminate bad symptoms (e.g. falling share prices or GDP) while ignoring the real causes leads to a steady deterioration of health over time (a weaker economy).

We would all like to be convinced that there's an easy way out. And central banks are only too happy to do the convincing. They are the key perpetrators in promising politicians and the electorate that their magic money-printing elixir is all that's needed to fix any bad symptoms from which we may be suffering. As a result, not only are the real problems not addressed, but they also continue to fester and grow unabated. This leads to more bad symptoms, which then requires even more money-printing. This is exactly what has been happening in the global economy in recent years. The symptom-soothing potion administered by central banks has not only blinded people from the disease that is slowly destroying the productive capacity of our economy, but it has also created probably the greatest redistribution of wealth since the United States became a republic around 250 years ago.

Shortcut

As we have seen, creating real wealth is costly and uncertain, and it takes time. And making sure all of the constituents of a business model are benefiting is a lot of work. And all of the work that helps ensure the strength of a business model in the long-term can negatively impact growth and profitability in the short term. Not only that, but the future benefits are uncertain. As a result, many companies have resorted to other means to drive their share prices higher. These other means are more certain and immediate; however, they are short-term in nature and ultimately harm the company's ability to compete in the long term. Some people have used the analogy of an athlete using performance-enhancing steroids. In the short term, it leads to better symptoms of greater speed or strength, and one may be led to conclude that those athletes are very healthy. However, longer term, those steroids make the athlete less healthy.

Unfortunately, not all businesses are run by people who get a kick out of wowing their customers. Some are in it solely for the money. Rather than benefiting alongside their customers, they seek to benefit at the *expense* of their customers. These companies tend to have bad corporate cultures, and, unfortunately, it seems there are more and more of them. This has led to the financialisation of the global economy. Executives of companies with poor corporate culture become fixated on the share price of their businesses, because that is what they are incentivised to do. They invest not only the firm's capital but also their own emotional capital into increasing the share price. Thinking of ways to invest in the business itself takes a back seat. If a management team believed that the only way they could increase their company's share price (and thus increase their compensation) was by increasing the true intrinsic value of their business, then they would focus on reinvesting in the business rather than the share price.

Share Buybacks

Share buybacks are one way in which corporate executives can drive their company's share price higher. You will have heard about these in the press. They have become a real symbol of the financialisation of corporate America. A quick explanation of what they are is necessary.

Let's go back to your bike company. As a reminder, these are some of the basic financials for your company.

>Equity in the business: $15 million
>There are 1.5 million shares outstanding.
>The price of those shares is $40
>Earnings equal $3 million
>Earnings per share are $2.00 ($3 million of profit divided by 1.5 million shares outstanding).

The price earnings multiple of your stock is 20x ($40 share price divided by $2.00 of earnings per share)

That's all you really need to know to understand the explanation of how share buybacks work.

A share buyback means just that. You initially sold shares to investors at $10 a share to raise capital, but now that your company is making more money, you don't need all of that capital. So, you decide you want to ~~drive your share price higher~~ give some of that capital back and you do so by buying back some of the shares you had originally sold to the investors. The only problem for you is that due to the success of the business, you have to pay the original investors (or whoever it is who currently holds the shares) $40, which is four times the price that they paid you. Regardless, if your company has excess capital, which means even after you have reinvested capital in your business, then it might make sense to buy some of those shares back. The benefit being that you will no longer have to share any of your company's profit with those investors.

Excess Capital

Let's assume that you decide to buy back 10% of the shares outstanding in your business – 150,000 shares. At $40 a share, that would cost the company $6 million. But the $6 million was just sitting in your company's bank account, anyway, earning little interest. Or maybe you were even being charged a negative interest rate like back in 2019 when there was around $18 trillion of debt globally with an interest rate less than zero.

So, let's see what that does to the earnings per share of your company, which were sitting at $2.00. We have the same earnings of $3 million, but now instead of 1.5 million shares outstanding, there are only 1.35 million shares. The earnings per share has gone up, because the profit is the same but there are now fewer shares. That is, the numerator (earnings) is the same, but the denominator (shares) has gone down. The new earnings per share of the business would be $2.22 ($3 million profit ÷ 1,350,000 shares), an increase of 11%.

But there is another benefit to buying back your own shares, and that benefit is the prime motivator for many companies buying back their own shares. As your shares currently trade at a 20× earnings multiple, your company's share price will go up, because the 20× multiple will now be applied to a higher earnings per share. So, a 20× multiple on earnings per share of $2.22 would give a new share price of $44.40 (20 × $2.22 = $44.40). So, even though you didn't help the company grow faster by making and selling more bikes, you were able to increase the share price by 11% ($44.40 ÷ $40 − 1 = 0.11).

All the Wrong Reasons

As I said earlier, there is nothing wrong with doing this if you have excess capital (i.e. capital left over after you have invested in the business to help ensure its long-term success). And it also makes a lot of sense if the price of your shares is not very expensive. Unfortunately, for a lot of companies that have been spending billions of dollars on share buybacks over the last number of years, neither of these two situations has been the case. First, many companies don't have excess capital for share buybacks; instead, they borrow the money to buy back shares. Not only that, many of them are buying back their own shares at very expensive prices. But even buying back shares at expensive prices increases the earnings per share of your business and, in turn, the share price. The result is that many companies that once had very strong balance sheets, and in many cases no debt, all of a sudden have developed very poor balance sheets because they have taken on so much debt to buy back their shares.

Incentives

Do this for three to five years and executives can have so much money that they won't have to worry about whether the business succeeds or not, as they'll be in a position to retire. Either that or move on to another company and then load its balance sheet up with debt and buy back shares. Many of us might do the same thing if we were in their shoes, the rewards for doing this are staggering, and no one's breaking any laws. Not only that, but there are a whole host of investors, Wall Street analysts and 'bubblevision' types cheering them on. As investor Charlie Munger liked to say, 'Show me the incentive and I'll show you the outcome.'[4]

Executives of corporations should be incentivised to grow their businesses in a long-term sustainable fashion, with a rising share price being the symptom of that. But just like some policymakers put spending (GDP) ahead of saving and investment and central bankers target a rising stock market over efficient allocation of capital, some management teams focus on their companies' share prices at the expense of investing in the businesses. All of this has diminished the productive capacity of the global economy while at the same time contributing to the world's grotesque levels of wealth inequality.

Boeing

An example of all of this is Boeing, which employs a lot of talented people doing great things and is still a great business, but over the years, the company seems to have lost its way and its focus. It had been a company run by engineers who lived and breathed the manufacturing of aircraft. However, over the years, it started to be run by non-engineers whose expertise was more in the area of finance.

In 2001, the executive team even moved the head office from Seattle to Chicago, far away from where the planes were being made. Some believe that this change in corporate culture contributed to a steady deterioration in standards within the business and an increasing focus on the share price. One glaring example of this was share buybacks, which had never been a large part of their business model until 1998, which was around the time the corporate culture started to change.[5] Things kicked into overdrive starting in 2013, and from that year through to 2019, the company spent approximately $43 billion buying back their own shares.

In 2013, the company had a very strong balance sheet in a net cash position – the company had more cash than debt (think of your own balance sheet and how comfortable you would be if you had more cash than debt rather than vice versa). This is always a good place to be in, especially for a business in a cyclical industry like airplane manufacturing. Business can be very good in a strong economy but not so good in a weak one. But because the company was borrowing money to buy back its own shares, Boeing's cash kept declining, and their debt kept increasing until in 2018 their balance sheet was in a net debt position (i.e. they had more debt than cash).

And then there were those two tragic 737 MAX airline crashes, which were then followed by COVID. Naturally, no one could have predicted these events, but there are all sorts of events you can't predict. And it's not a good idea to presume that nothing bad will ever happen. By the end of

2020, Boeing was in a net debt position of approximately $38 billion, versus a net cash position of around $5.6 billion back in 2013.

In 2017 and 2018, Boeing spent $3.2 billion and $3.3 billion, respectively, on research and development and $9.3 billion and $9.0 billion, respectively, on share buybacks. Throughout this period, Boeing did grow their sales, profit and cashflow, and they reinvested in the business, but we will never know the counterfactual – how much would they have reinvested had the share price not been such a focus. With share buybacks driving EPS growth higher, excited investors then drove the PE multiple of the company from around 15x in 2012 to a peak of around 30x in early 2018. This further increased the value of Boeing's stock and, thus, pushed the value of executive stock options significantly higher.

General Electric

Let's have a quick look at General Electric (GE) to see how their share buyback plan worked out for shareholders versus the company's top executives. From 2010 to 2017, GE bought back approximately $42 billion in shares. In 2016 alone, they bought back over $21 billion worth of shares.[6]

Over that period, the company's balance sheet was severely weakened, to the point that in 2017 and 2018 it was barely producing enough profit to pay the interest expense on its debt; and that was with near-record-low interest rates.[7] Its share price peaked in 2016 at around $150. By July 2022, it had fallen to just over $38 – a drop of around 75%. (In fact, at the time, its share price was back to where it had been in 1994; not exactly a great outcome for shareholders.) Meanwhile, for the five-year period from 2013 to 2017 the top executives (five to six of them, depending on the year) were paid a total of around $333 million.[8]

I decided to focus on Boeing and GE as they are both very high-profile businesses. But they are by no means alone in their focus on their share price It is possible that both companies have now changed direction. They both continue to do great things and employ a lot of capable and hard-working people. But incentives matter, and we shouldn't be surprised when people act accordingly.

So, these are some of the issues with today's stock markets that have arisen because they are increasingly about wealth redistribution rather than wealth creation. Some investors and executives focus more on the share price than on the underlying business fundamentals, and this approach is negatively affecting the economy's productivity. It's all part of the financialisation of the economy. Not only that, but policymakers have also increasingly been focusing on share prices, and as a result, stock markets have been driven far above their intrinsic values. Thus, those with wealth tied up in stocks don't have nearly as much wealth as they think they do, unless policymakers can continue to extract capital from the rest of the economy and keep stock markets soaring. We now turn to this latter issue.

ENDNOTES

1 Stephen G Cecchetti & Enisse Kharroubi, 2015. 'Why does financial sector growth crowd out real economic growth?', BIS Working Papers 490, Bank for International Settlements.
2 'Has the financial sector grown too big?' Speech by Lorenzo Bini Smaghi, Member of the Executive Board, European Central Bank, Nomura seminar *The paradigm shift after the financial crisis*, Kyoto, 15 April 2010.
3 This is also referred to as forcing investors up the risk curve.
4 I talk more about share buybacks and policymakers in the next chapter.
5 To be fair, many companies began to target share buybacks in the late 1990s.
6 After leaving GE, CEO Jeff Immelt wrote a book about his time at GE. I didn't read it, but there was a review on it in the *Wall Street Journal* (Saturday, 20 February 2021). There's a telling part in the review: 'Looking back, he says that he wishes he had said "I don't know" more often: "There's a certain sense of vulnerability to saying I haven't figured this out yet. But there are a few times when that would've served me better."' It's a shame that, for many of us, it's only after we've been in a position of influence that we start figuring things out.
7 Even after adjusting for goodwill impairments both years. These impairments were related to their acquisition of Alstom's power and grid business back in 2015 i.e. they overpaid for the business. When a company has goodwill impairments which are subtracted from profits, those losses are often ignored to give one a better sense of the ongoing profitability of the business i.e. it's assumed impairments won't reoccur in coming years. Regardless, it's an indication of the management's capital allocation abilities.
8 The share price has since rebounded to $189 (September 2024), in large part because one of the best CEOs in North America, Larry Culp, is turning around the business.

CHAPTER 22
STOCK MARKETS AND POLICYMAKERS

People who get their feet wet must learn to take their medicine.
— Mary Poppins

IN THIS CHAPTER we'll talk about how policymakers have shifted their focus from the economy to stock markets, and the consequences of that shift. It's not just corporate executives who are obsessed with stock prices.

I've talked about how stock markets seem to be more about redistributing wealth amongst the participants rather than creating wealth. In this chapter and the next, I'll talk about how policymakers have contributed to all of this.

Many corporate executives will rationalise their exorbitantly high compensation by claiming they've created value through a higher share price. However, those higher share prices have been, in part, determined by financial wizardry by said corporate executives and policymakers. These actions give the illusion of value in the short term at the expense of true value in the future.

Why Do Stock Markets Go Up?

It's perfectly natural for people to focus on the symptoms of a rising share price and stock market as an indicator of the health of a business and the economy, respectively. It was never perfect, but, more often than not, it worked – because that's how it's supposed to work.[1] If you look at a long-term chart of the US stock market vs. GDP (no longer a great measure of economic health, but it will suffice for these purposes), you can see that over longer periods, when GDP was growing, stock markets were strong, and when GDP was contracting (recessions), stock markets were weak.[2] In fact, the Wilshire 5000 Stock Index, which is a very broad representation of companies in America, has had a 92% correlation with nominal GDP since 1971.[3] Going back to 1947, the correlation between the Down Jones Industrial Average and nominal GDP is 96%.[4]

However, despite this relationship, the growth of stock markets is becoming increasingly disconnected from that of the economy. Looking at the annual growth rate of GDP vs. the stock market, we can split it into two periods: that before Quantitative Easing (QE) and that after.

Pre-QE: 1971–2009:
- GDP: 7%
- Stocks: 10%

Post-QE: 2009–2023:
- GDP: 5%
- Stocks: 15%

So, even though economic growth slowed after QE, stock market growth actually accelerated.

Backstop

Since 2009, whenever the economy has weakened, central banks have announced that they will print even more money (i.e. extract wealth from savers and stable income earners) and use it to drive asset prices higher. Thus, we have the perverse situation of investors often hoping for a negative economic announcement so that central banks will print more money and, thus, drive stocks higher. This sentiment is known in the industry as *bad news is good news*. Bad news for workers is good news for Wall Street. However, from an individual company's perspective, bad news is still bad news, because even the Federal Reserve can't justify printing money just because one company has suffered a loss – at least, not yet.

What Leads to Sustainable GDP and Earnings Growth?

Over time, GDP growth should be a symptom of strong earnings growth at corporations, as the people they employ are themselves consumers. And that strong earnings growth will lead to growth in stock markets. And if that earnings growth is a result of companies continuously increasing investment in their businesses, leading to rising productivity growth, then rising GDP and stock markets are likely to continue (i.e. the growth will be sustainable).

However, if GDP is rising because of large government deficit spending enabled by borrowing trillions of dollars, then it's not likely to be sustainable. In that case, the rising GDP would be a symptom of debt rather than the creation of capital. Similarly, if a company is growing its earnings per share simply because it is borrowing billions of dollars to buy back its shares, then that growth will eventually stop and then decline (because that approach is unsustainable). In both cases, the growth is a result of debt rather than the creation of more stuff. And that debt eventually starts to suck the lifeblood out of the company and the economy.

Skipping the Middleman

Stock markets have been driven higher, in large part, by debt. But they have also been driven up by central banks' explicit focus on driving asset prices higher by extracting wealth from savers through the money-printing process. It has happened despite deteriorating economic fundamentals (productivity growth, sales growth and balance sheet). The problem is that we have all learnt that a strong stock price or stock market is supposed to be symptomatic of strong company or economic fundamentals, so it's natural for people to come to those conclusions. However, policymakers have changed the rules. Rather than focusing on fundamentals, which takes far too long to have an impact on the symptoms of GDP or stock markets, they have decided to skip the middleman and focus directly on symptoms.

With the ability to source large amounts of capital through stock markets, companies have been able to invest far more capital than they would have done otherwise. That investment has resulted in incredible amounts of innovation and ingenuity that have led to so many great things that we all benefit from, things like life-saving medicines, smartphones, electric cars, gaming and streaming. But the role of stock markets is to help facilitate what entrepreneurs are doing in the real economy. The market helps provide the people doing these great things with the capital they need to invest to do even more great things. It also helps to ensure that those who are not really providing anything of value to society are soon encouraged to change their ways, for example, zombie companies. It's extremely important that zombies that destroy capital rather than creating it do not get access to more capital. If they do, not only do they not contribute to the overall wealth of our society, but they also detract from it by being net beneficiaries of the great redistribution shell game. Their contribution is negative because they take more from society than they contribute.

Fair But Not Equal

Remember that for an economy to truly thrive and for all people to benefit the most from the wealth produced, the distribution of that wealth needs to be fair but not equal. (The equal part comes in terms of opportunity, which, as we have discussed, is also not happening to the degree that it should be. Moving closer to that will be of enormous benefit to all of us.) Imagine that you're a server in a restaurant providing very efficient and friendly service to its customers, who, as a result, are loyal regulars. One of your colleagues provides terrible service with a bad attitude, driving diners away from the restaurant. Should the two of you be compensated fairly, or should the compensation be equal?

Or consider a great musician whose music you enjoy listening to and are happy to purchase with some of your hard-earned wealth. Compare that with someone who thinks that they are a great musician, but no one wants to listen to their music. Should the compensation for the efforts of these two musicians be fair or equal? Most people would argue for a *fair* distribution of wealth based on productive efforts rather than an *equal* distribution based on entitlement. And because an economy thrives so much on the former, society is then in a position to provide wealth to those who, for whatever reason, are unable to provide for themselves or are in a transition period (perhaps the lousy musician is retraining to become a software developer). The problem, however, is that much of the distribution is no longer fair and is even much further away from equal than it was in the past.

Distorted Markets

I believe that many, or most, of those benefiting from these distorted stock markets are unaware that their success comes at someone else's expense (similarly to those benefiting from the wealth redistribution in the housing market). Human nature being what it is, it's very easy for us to assume that our success is a result of our ability or genius and that we somehow deserve the wealth that has come our way. It's only when we lose that we start reflecting on how unfair the result is. And so, by definition, as stock markets continue to drive relentlessly higher, there is less reflection about what's actually going on and more self-congratulatory and entitled attitudes from people who attempt to justify and rationalise their good fortune. These attitudes are self-serving and delusional, but many of us would do exactly the same thing if we were making millions of dollars as a result of stock markets soaring ever higher.

The chief culprits or enablers of all of this are central banks. Without them, the redistribution of your wealth to the top ten per cent would not occur. This is because there would be no way to force you to hand over your capital that you have temporarily stored up in your money savings to enrich those who are the largest owners of stocks. However, central banks do take your wealth and give it to investors in stocks. Here's how it happens.

For many years, central banks have influenced the prices of stocks, but in the past, they did so more indirectly, through moral suasion.[5] For instance, if stock markets started to fall in response to economic weakness, the central banks might make announcements saying that they were getting ready to lower interest rates or inject liquidity into the system. They would essentially remind investors who might be nervous about an upcoming recession that the central bank would be ready to lower interest rates to make borrowing more affordable so people could go out and spend more or companies could roll over their debt at lower interest rates.[6]

Unfortunately, as we have seen, recessions are not things to be avoided or prevented. They are the necessary healing processes that the economy must go through to cleanse itself of past mistakes. This then sets the foundation for the next stage of growth. A recession is the process that helps to ensure that misallocated capital doesn't continue to be a deadweight hindering the economy from moving forward. Today, we have the opposite: when the symptoms of distorted markets begin to appear, rather than allow the economy to heal, policymakers will distort the markets even further. Would you avoid having surgery to remove a tumour just so you could continue going to work and, thus, spend more money?[7]

> *The financial public, too, believes that the Fed can control interest rates, and that belief has spread to the Treasury and Congress. As a result, every recession brings calls from the Treasury, the White House, Congress, and Wall Street for the Fed to 'bring down interest rates.' Counterbalancing pleas, at times of expansion, for the Fed to raise interest rates are notable by their absence.*[8]
>
> – Milton Friedman

Let's look at a couple of more direct ways in which policymakers have helped to drive stock markets higher.

Regulation and Deregulation

For capital markets to play their role in contributing to the creation of sustainable, true wealth generation for all, there needs to be a clear set of rules. And those rules need to be followed and firmly enforced. However, although there must be strict rules in place, the market must remain unhampered, which means that policymakers must not interfere in any way with the risk/return decisions of entrepreneurs and market participants.

But, more important than this, the rules put in place need to truly represent principles of fair play; otherwise, there's no point in having rules. In some cases, rules that have been established and have done a good job of upholding certain principles can, over time, become hopelessly outdated and, thus, abused. Not only that, but if policymakers don't like the restrictions imposed upon them by rules that they have previously put in place, they will simply change the rules.

Deregulation in capital markets had been going on for a number of years, such as when the Glass-Steagall Act was repealed in 1999. This rule had originally been put in place during the Great Depression back in the 1930s. The Act made it illegal for banks to engage in both commercial banking and investment banking activities. Thus, banks were not allowed to put their depositors' capital at risk in traditional investment banking–type business. This was important, because deposits were only protected for the first $100,000 of their deposits.[9] Anything more than that and it would be taxpayers who were on the hook if banks went bust. The elimination of Glass-Steagall in 1999 allowed commercial banks to speculate with deposits effectively putting taxpayers at risk if investment banking businesses experienced catastrophic losses on their risky bets.

Share Buybacks

In the last chapter, we talked about how share buybacks (companies buying back their shares, often with borrowed money) can drive stock prices higher. Interestingly, before 1982, most companies did not buy back their own shares, because they were afraid of being accused by the Securities and Exchange Commission (SEC) of manipulating their own shares higher.

Makes sense. Then, in 1982 the SEC put in place a 'safe harbour provision'.[10] This provision meant that as long as companies followed a set number of rules when buying back their own shares, the SEC would not accuse them of stock price manipulation.

However, the rules are now hopelessly outdated, and I suspect that the potential for share price manipulation is significant. For instance, one of the rules says that when buying back their own shares, companies' purchases cannot constitute more than 25% of the average daily volume (because trying to buy a significant number of shares in a short period would drive the share price higher). The problem is that, whereas in 1982 buying 25% of the shares on offer might not have moved the share price, it most certainly would do that today.

Today, stock markets seem to be dominated by hedge funds and high-frequency traders who use sophisticated trading tactics and algorithms to make money within the market. One such tactic of high- frequency traders is to pay stock exchanges to get quicker access to trades that are happening on the stock exchange. It's rather complex, but the bottom line is that if you are trying to buy shares in a company, high-frequency traders might see your order coming in and quickly buy the shares before you so they can then sell them to you at a slightly higher price than what they paid for them.

It would be like if you were to go online to buy a new coat for $200, but soon after you click on the Buy button, you receive a message saying that they are out of stock. But then you receive another message saying that the same coat is now available for sale on this other website for $201. Someone with a sophisticated algorithm saw your order come in for the coat and quickly bought it before you could, then they added a dollar to the price before on-selling it to you. You've just been ripped off $1, which might not sound like a lot. In the same way, high-frequency traders make only small profits on each trade, but when you're transacting in billions of shares, those small amounts quickly add up to meaningful amounts of money.[11]

And while you might object to paying an extra dollar for your coat, corporate executives might not care about paying more for their shares. First, they're not using their own money, and, secondly, a rising share price increases their wealth. So, not only might corporate executives not worry about being detected by high-frequency traders when buying back their own shares, but it could also be that these companies very much want to be detected, because they would much rather see their share price rising than falling.

If high-frequency traders are legally front-running companies buying back their own shares, and if companies are legally buying back amounts of shares that are easily detected by those traders, then is it any wonder that stock markets have grown so much faster than the economy? As a professional investor, whenever we were trying to purchase shares in a company, our purchases would be far less than 25% of the daily average volume. In fact, we had to be considerably less than 10% of the volume; otherwise, we'd end up paying a lot more for those shares.

I still don't understand why the 25% rule is still in place. Perhaps I'm missing something and maybe this only has a temporary impact on stock markets. However, it seems to me that people don't mind if stock prices are being manipulated, just as long as those prices are manipulated higher rather than lower.

While all of this is bad enough, that there were two actions by policymakers that I think have truly undermined the free-market process and significantly contributed to falling productivity growth and growing wealth disparity.

Plunge Protection Team

The first action was in 1988 when President Reagan, by executive order,[12] established The President's Working Group On Financial Markets, better known as the Plunge Protection Team (PPT). The PPT is made up of the Secretary of the Treasury, the head of the Federal Reserve, the head of the SEC and the head of the Commodity Futures Trading Commission. President Reagan issued this executive order in response to the stock market crash of October 1987, which wiped out over 20% of the market's value in one day.[13] It was deemed that various new and sophisticated trading strategies had been responsible for the market plummeting so quickly – nothing to do with economic fundamentals. However, before the market started rolling over a few days before the crash, it had soared over 40% since the beginning of the year, and the Federal Reserve had started increasing interest rates. The role of the PPT was ostensibly to help ensure that stock markets were *efficient* at reflecting true underlying fundamentals rather than some sophisticated (or unsophisticated) trading strategies gone haywire. Makes sense. However, ever since PPT was put in place, many people have assumed that the PPT no longer plays the role it was originally designed for and that, instead. it does the exact opposite. Thus, the PPT intervenes only when stock markets *are* efficient – when they are falling and attempting to truly reflect the underlying state of the economy. Note that there is no government team in place to protect stock markets from rocketing skyward.

Sunlight

No one knows for sure (apart from the government) what the PPT does or has done in the past, because it is unaccountable to the public. When looking at a business to assess whether or not to invest in its shares, it is useful to remember the truism that companies typically don't hide good news; why would they? It would make sense that the same wisdom applies to governments and, thus, also the PPT.

> *If the broad light of day could be let in upon men's actions, it would purify them as the sun disinfects.*
> – Louis Brandeis[14]

If there has been nothing untoward going on, then you would think that they would willingly disclose past actions. Naturally, the fact that they refuse to makes people suspicious.

Of course, they'll come up with reasons why they need to act in secrecy – keep market forces from anticipating future actions, perhaps. And it may be that just the knowledge that the PPT stands ready to manipulate stock markets higher is enough to encourage stock market participants to bid stocks higher all on their own. Regardless, many feel that the government needs to come clean on the PPT.

PPT in Action?

A recent example of the PPT possibly intervening in stock markets was 24 December 2018. After peaking on 21 September, the S&P 500 stock index had started to fall, and by 24 December it was down 19.7%. As a stock market fall of 20% is deemed to be a bear market, another day's decline in stocks could have taken the market down into bear market territory. That would not make for good headlines. So, that day, Christmas Eve, it was announced that the PPT had been convened. But there was no announcement on what actions the PPT was taking. When markets reopened on 26 December, they started rising again, and over the next twelve months, the S&P500 was up 37%. Mission accomplished.[15]

In my opinion, the main consequence of the formation of the PPT is that the government started explicitly influencing stock prices and, thus, hampering the price discovery process, which has contributed to slower productivity growth.

But Even Worse

There have certainly been other key examples of government influencing stock markets to the detriment of the long-term health of the economy, for example, the orchestrated bailout of Long-Term Capital Management in 1998. However, I believe that perhaps the worst and most damaging action of all was when the US Federal Reserve embarked on its Quantitative Easing campaigns starting in late 2008, which was the dawn of monumental wealth confiscation.

I believe central banks taking interest rates to zero and printing money to create a wealth effect has caused the most damage to the price discovery mechanism and is, thus, most responsible for capital being misallocated and the increasing wealth disparity. We have already discussed the hazards of manipulating interest rates to extremely low levels. It's now time to talk about QE.

ENDNOTES

1 For evidence on how both stock markets and the term structure of interest rates anticipate output growth in the economy, see *Predicting GDP Growth with Stock and Bond Markets: Do They Contain Different Information?* by David G. McMillan, Division of Accounting and Finance, University of Stirling. February 2019.

2 Note that there can be periods when correlations are weak (e.g. when the starting point for the stock market is one of extreme overvaluation or vice versa).

3 Data from St. Louis Federal Reserve. As stock markets tend to anticipate GDP growth, I compare the stock market with GDP the following year.

4 Data from St. Louis Federal Reserve and Samuel H. Williamson, 'Daily Closing Value of the Dow Jones Average, 1885 to Present,' Measuring Worth, 2024.

5 According to *Oxford Reference*, moral suasion is '[a] regulatory body's use of argument and persuasion, rather than coercion or legislation, to influence the activities of those within its purview'. The term is often applied to the efforts of the Federal Reserve Board (see Federal Reserve System) to persuade its members to comply with its policies.' Increasingly, authorities believe they have the right to influence your behaviour, that you are incapable of deciding what's in your own best interest. A more fitting description might be 'immoral suasion'.

[6] In the wake of COVID, some policymakers were saying that interest rates would remain extremely low for a considerable period. This had the hoped-for impact: stock markets and house prices soared.

[7] I will explore this analogy in the next chapter, which is on stock markets and quantitative easing.

[8] *Money Mischief*, Milton Friedman. p. 209.

[9] See chapter 26 for a discussion of the Federal Deposit Insurance Corporation or FDIC.

[10] US Securities & Exchange Commission (SEC) Rule 10b – 18.

[11] For a great description of this, read *Flash Boys* by Michael Lewis.

[12] An executive order is a discretionary power that allows the President of the United States to make certain decisions without the approval of Congress. One of the most infamous of these was Executive Order 6102 by President Franklin D. Roosevelt back in 1933 that prohibited the private ownership of gold. You were required to sell your gold to the government at a price of $20.67 an ounce, and if you didn't, you could be slapped with a $10,000 fine or face ten years in prison. This was done because the government believed that the only way they could end the Great Depression was by printing money, but the US was on a gold standard at the time, which prevented it from doing so. In 1934, Roosevelt changed the price of an ounce of gold from $20.67 to $35, thus significantly devaluing the dollar against gold. The rapid expansion of the money supply did drive GDP (spending) higher, but as we have seen, it's investment that creates wealth, not consumption. Five years after the devaluation of the dollar, the unemployment rate in the United States was still higher than 17%, despite the money supply increasing more than 50% over the same period (M2 number from San Jose State University Department of Economics). It wasn't until 1974 that President Ford signed a bill that allowed US citizens to legally hold gold. However, by this time, the US dollar no longer had any link with gold, or real money, because President Nixon took the US fully off the gold standard in 1971, which effectively removed any constraint on the Federal Reserve from printing as much money (confiscating your wealth) as they wanted and which ultimately ushered in a decade of stagflation: rising prices, slow economic growth and high unemployment.

[13] That day, when the S&P 500 Index fell 20.4%, is known as Black Monday. This wasn't just an American event; it was global in nature. Stock markets tumbled all over the world. The Hong Kong index fell over 45%!

[14] A Supreme Court Judge from 1916 to 1939.

[15] Some believe that the PPT sprang into action because of new debt issuance drying up. Maybe. However, they had plenty of opportunity to act before 24 December. The PPT was convened only once the headlines in the press were possibly one day away from declaring a bear market.

CHAPTER 23

STOCK MARKETS AND QUANTITATIVE EASING

I'VE MENTIONED QUANTITATIVE Easing (QE) a few times so far, and how it was used to drive stock markets higher. We'll now look at it in a little more detail and use a couple of analogies which will, hopefully, give you a good understanding of why QE is so harmful to the economy – as well as being terribly unfair. Note that while I will be talking about why I believe central banks embarked on this misguided policy, of course, I don't know exactly what they were thinking. However, while policymakers are intelligent and, I believe, had good intentions, I feel that the mistakes were driven by short-termism and hubris. But more on that later.

The Beginning

Quantitative Easing came into being in the United States[1] during the Global Financial Crisis of 2008, which, as we saw earlier, was a consequence of easy monetary policy attempting to create a wealth effect. And QE has been with us ever since. In my opinion, this is perhaps the most destructive form of monetary policy in the history of central banking, and it has had many consequences, including the current obscene levels of society's wealth disparity.

As we saw in the Evolution of Money chapter, the Federal Reserve creates money reserves (monetary base, or M0) which the commercial banking system then uses to pyramid loans to its customers (these loans are called fiduciary media as there are more loans outstanding than the amount of base reserves). However, the problems facing the US economy during the Global Financial Crisis were not that people were not borrowing enough money. In fact, it was actually the opposite: many people had already borrowed far too much. The problem was that easy money had created bubbles in housing and stock markets – and those bubbles were now bursting.

Prices were plummeting from unnaturally high levels that had not been a result of economic fundamentals. Both asset categories (as well as many others) had been driven higher by the Fed's abnormally low interest rates and the excessive borrowing that resulted. This was all part of the Fed's attempt to create a wealth effect by distorting asset prices higher so people would feel wealthier.

With asset prices descending to healthy and fair levels, I suppose the US Federal Reserve believed that this was creating a significantly negative wealth effect. No one likes seeing asset prices decline. The US central bank believed that they needed a plan to drive those prices back up to unnaturally high levels. However, central banks effectively have two related tools to implement monetary policy: they can change interest rates, and they can change the money supply.[2] Lowering interest rates, all else being equal, drives asset price higher. However, interest rates were already at zero and, thus, couldn't be lowered any further. But the Federal Reserve could still print money. If market players were not willing or able to buy assets and drive those prices higher, the US Federal Reserve decided it would do it itself. Enter quantitative easing.

Description

What is quantitative easing? Here is a description from Investopedia.[3]

> Quantitative easing (QE) is a form of monetary policy in which a central bank, like the U.S. Federal Reserve, purchases securities in the open market to reduce interest rates and increase the money supply.
>
> Quantitative easing creates new bank reserves, providing banks with more liquidity and encouraging lending and investment. In the United States, the Federal Reserve implements QE policies.

For the first part of the definition, it should say *longer-term* interest rates. QE is usually enacted when short-term interest rates are already very low.

In my opinion, the second part of the definition is misleading because I don't believe that the goal of QE was to increase the number of bank reserves so banks would increase their lending. The last thing the Federal Reserve wanted was more money in the economy. I'll explain why as we go along. I believe that the primary goal of QE was to drive asset prices higher. The Fed started printing trillions of dollars and buying longer-maturity government bonds, as well as mortgage-backed securities. The central bank used primary dealers/commercial banks as conduits to buy the securities from non-bank institutions such as pension funds, insurance companies and hedge funds.[4]

Portfolio Effect

The idea was that printing money and buying those securities would force their prices to rise and the yield or interest rate to fall. For instance, if you have a bond worth $1,000 that pays interest of $100 per year, then the interest rate or yield on that bond is 10% ($100 ÷ $1,000 = 0.10). However, if the price of the bond rises to $1,100, but it still only pays $100 in interest, then the yield falls to 9% ($100 ÷ $1,100 = 0.09). Driving prices higher and, thus, yields lower would force investors to go out into the marketplace and look for higher yields; and when they bought those securities, their actions would, in turn, drive those prices higher and yields lower. These actions would cascade through the capital markets, eventually reaching stocks. This is referred to as the portfolio effect.

Paid Not to Lend

However, the Federal Reserve still had a problem in that the act of purchasing all of those trillions of dollars in assets from financial institutions resulted in trillions of new bank reserves being created. And remember from the Evolution of Money chapter that when reserves are created, banks can increase the amount of their lending. However, far too much money had already been lent to borrowers with dodgy credit ratings who were now unable to pay the money back. In fact, in the years leading to the crisis, bank lending in the US had been growing at around 10% per annum, versus an average rate of around 5% in the 1990s.[5]

But the Fed had another problem. Even if banks were successful in finding creditworthy borrowers, the new fiduciary media created from the enormous number of new reserves could have resulted in rampant inflation. If that had happened, the Federal Reserve would have been forced to raise interest rates, which would have put downward pressure on asset prices – which would have defeated the whole purpose of QE.[6]

The Fed needed a way to increase the money supply and bid up the prices of assets without the resulting bank reserves being used to make more loans and causing inflation to explode higher. A law change allowed the Federal Reserve to pay the banks interest on the reserves that they did not use to make loans.[7] Tens of billions of dollars of Interest On Excess Reserves (IOER) were being paid by the Fed each year to commercial banks to encourage them not to lend. Thus, the US central bank was able to print trillions of dollars to buy securities without causing consumer price inflation to soar because of higher bank lending.

Stealth Inflation Impact

But that didn't stop QE from impacting inflation; it just impacted it less than it would have done otherwise. Inflation was slowly seeping into the economy. Each time the Fed printed money to buy a security (indirectly) from a non-bank financial institution, that money ended up in the bank account of that institution. However, money being injected into the economy in that way did not result immediately in consumer price inflation.

For instance, if the Fed had bought a billion dollars of assets from one of the mutual funds that I was managing at the time, the cash position in that fund would have gone up by a billion dollars. However, that wouldn't have meant that my clients would have all rushed out to buy shaving cream and donuts. What it would have done was drive asset prices higher; I would have had to go out into the marketplace and use that new cash to find other assets to take the place of the bonds we had just sold to the Fed.[8] Over time, as asset prices soar, the owners of those assets will feel wealthier and spend more, which could increase consumer prices, particularly the prices of more expensive things like houses, yachts, fine wines and art. But that money gradually seeps into the general economy, impacting lower-priced goods, as well.

The Fed was also indirectly financing the government's spending with newly printed money. If the government borrows to spend, that typically doesn't lead to inflation (at least not in the short term), as it doesn't increase the money supply (a person or institution lends money to the government, and the government will spend it instead of the lender). However, with QE, trillions of new reserves were created, indirectly financing government spending.[9]

QE also gradually drove house prices higher with the Fed printing money and buying mortgage-backed securities. This pushed mortgage rates much lower than they would have been in an unhampered market. With much lower interest rates, house prices increased as people took on much larger mortgages. And in my opinion, there can be no excuse for printing money to buy mortgage-backed securities during the COVID crisis and driving mortgage rates to record low levels, an action that has resulted in soaring house prices that many young people can no longer afford.

A Whole Raft of Consequences

However, the main problem with all of this is that the US central bank was driving asset prices to levels much higher than would be dictated by free market forces (i.e. by those with skin in the game who had something to lose). The Fed had no skin in the game; if it lost money, it would simply print more.[10] As discussed earlier, price discovery in an unhampered market is crucial to sustain the economy's productive capacity. QE significantly hampered the market such that capital was misallocated in the marketplace on a monumental scale. And as we have seen, it has resulted in a whole raft of negative consequences:

- An army of debt-laden zombie companies roaming the earth and destroying capital.
- Declining productivity growth.
- Obscene levels of wealth disparity as the rich benefited inordinately from soaring asset prices.
- Monumental levels of debt (individual, corporate and sovereign).
- Moral hazard within the financial community, where market players are encouraged to seek higher profits by taking on more risk, knowing that if they get into trouble, the central bank will come to their rescue.
- Housing prices that are unaffordable for a large part of the population.
- People focused on trying to make money from each other in the marketplace rather than making real contributions in the real economy.

No Time Like the Present

The crux of the matter is that central banks around the world have joined (led?) the short-termism crowd. They no longer have the patience to allow for the time that it takes for productive investment to improve economic fundamentals and drive stock markets higher more holistically. That takes too much time. Better to print money and drive the prices higher now, rather than wait for those prices to respond to improved productivity.

Sclerotic

Although the economic recovery since the financial crisis was the longest in modern history, it was also the slowest. It was the slowest because each time the stock market started to weaken, the Federal Reserve would step in and print more money to keep asset prices rising. They were afraid that a falling stock market would cause a recession due to a negative wealth effect. But as we have seen, this is misguided thinking on two measures. First, an economy is supposed to be the ultimate driver of the stock market, not vice versa. Secondly, a recession is the economy's effort to heal itself from misallocated capital during the boom phase. If central banks had not been so active in causing the boom phase in the first place, the recession phase would have been very mild.[11]

The Healing Process

Some people think that those who don't think a recession should be prevented from happening are malicious and cold-hearted, because they don't care if people lose their jobs. I don't believe that anyone takes pleasure in seeing others lose their job. Obviously that is a very traumatic thing to go through. That's why people like me caution against causing an artificial wealth effect in the first place. Unfortunately, job losses during a recession are part of the necessary healing process. Preventing this healing from happening not only ensures the disease is not cured, but it also actually makes the disease that much worse and leads to even slower growth in the next boom phase – and, eventually, even more job losses.

Even More

The slow recovery has not been confined to the United States. All developed economies are suffering from much slower growth compared to what was experienced prior to 2008. Most of them have been printing money on a reckless scale over this time, but they will tell you that they are not responsible for the slowest recovery on record. (If, on the other hand, the economic recovery had been strong, they'd be taking all the credit, no doubt.) They simply respond with one of those unproven counterfactuals, for example, the recovery would have been even slower if not for their actions, and, in fact, the recovery would have been stronger had they not been prevented from printing even more money. However, the opposite is true. QE is responsible for the slowing growth we are experiencing because it focuses on the symptom of prices at the expense of the fundamental health of the economy.

An Analogy

As discussed, two paragraphs earlier, recession is an economy healing itself, and preventing the healing process from happening only makes things worse. The following is an analogy I've been using with my clients since around 2011. (I've seen others use similar analogies.)

Assume that you are having a successful career making bikes because your products are highly valued by your customers. You are being rewarded with wealth that your customers have themselves created. (In this analogy, you are the economy.) But you develop a pain in your stomach, and you begin to be less productive than you were in the past. (The economy starts to slow.) Your doctor tells you that you are suffering from a tumour. (Some capital has been misallocated in the economy; thus, the productive capacity of the economy is suffering.)

The doctor tells you that you will require serious surgery to remove the tumour. There will be a lengthy rehabilitation period of up to eighteen months. Throughout this period, you will not be able to work. Thus, economically, you will be taking a step backwards. (Recession.) Not only that, but there will be contagion: through no fault of their own, your family members are all going to have to tighten their belts while you heal.

Anyone recommending to a loved one that they should go ahead with the major surgery and the rehab that follows would not be labelled malicious and cold-hearted − unlike those who recommend that money should not be printed to prevent a recession. Both are trying to address an underlying malaise and fix what's wrong. Unfortunately, in both situations, the cure is extremely unpleasant. But doing the opposite is worse.

While surgery and a lengthy rehab is bad news, the doctor also has some good news for you. After the eighteen months, you will be completely healed. You will still have your experience, your work ethic and your education, and you will be able to make bikes again. However, it's not up to the doctor to decide how much money you should make and then spend when you go back to work. Or even if you should go back to work at all; that's completely up to you. The doctor's job is to bring you back to fundamental health, so you are in a position to decide what's best for you. You decide what you want to do and how much money you want to earn and spend.

You decide to go ahead with the operation. As they're wheeling you into surgery, a quick-fix doctor (central banker) enters the operating room and asks what's going on. You tell them that your doctor has told you that you have a tumour, and that you need surgery that will require a lengthy rehabilitation period. The quick-fix doctor (QFD) tells you your doctor is a quack. The QFD has magic pills that will make you feel better than you've ever felt before. Not only that, but the pills act immediately. (When central banks bail out stock markets they immediately soar higher.) You'll be able to go back to work the very next day. And the pills will make you feel so good that you'll be able to make even more money than before. (Stock markets will climb even higher.)

You start to get excited, but being sceptical of people who tell you that you can take the easy way out without suffering any consequences, you ask the QFD if the pills will actually get rid of the tumour. They tell you that the pills won't work *directly* on curing your tumour. But they will make your body feel so good that there will be a *health effect*: your body will cure the tumour all on its own. This sounds better all the time. But then you ask how much the pills cost; you assume they must be very expensive. No, they're absolutely free. (Just print like hell and buy anything that isn't nailed down.)

This is all you need to hear. You jump off the gurney and take one of the QFD's magic pills. Just like they said, you do feel better than you have ever felt before, and you immediately go back to work, making more money than ever. (Soaring stock markets are what central bankers and politicians point to to validate that printing money and buying assets was the right thing to do.)

Ever since you took the central banker's magic QE1 pills, life has been very good: bigger house, fancier car, new friends. Nine to twelve months later, however, the pain in your stomach returns, and your productivity resumes its downward trend. (The economy starts to slow again.) You go back to the first doctor, who tells you that not only is the tumour still there, but it's also bigger. The doctor can still operate and bring you back to fundamental health; however, the rehabilitation period will now be three years instead of eighteen months.

So now the consequences of taking the right course of action are that much more severe. It's even more difficult now to do the right thing. You kick yourself for not following through on your initial decision to undergo surgery. You knew (gut feel) that you should have dealt with the issue then and there – and you were going to do that. But, instead, you let some fancy-talking quick-fix doctor convince you with words that you didn't really understand, but sounded pretty good: that you could take the easy way out and there wouldn't be any consequences.[12]

Despite the consequences of the surgery now being that much more severe, you decide to finally do the right thing and deal with the issue. However, as they're wheeling you into surgery, the QFD once again arrives out of nowhere and offers you QE2 pills. These are much bigger than the QE1 pills and so they should now do the trick.

Again, the QFD's smooth talking convinces you to take the easy way out. And the result is exactly the same as when you took the QE1 pills. You initially feel great and quickly return to work, making even more money, only for your productivity to once again wane. However, this time it takes only six to nine months until you're back at the hospital – with the QFD now prescribing a round of QE3 pills. (Each round of money printing serves to further weaken the fundamental health of the economy.)

Hopefully, it is obvious that the QE pills don't work because they don't deal with the underlying fundamental health issue: your tumour. Instead, they simply make you feel good. From the outside, anyone seeing you would assume you must be healed, because you look great and your energy levels are off the charts. These are symptoms, not your fundamental health itself. (Similarly, printing money focuses on the symptoms of rising stock markets, house prices and GDP, thus giving everyone the impression that the underlying economy must be in great shape. However, the truth is that the health of the economy is steadily deteriorating.)

Contagion

It's never easy to make difficult decisions in which you suffer short-term pain for long-term gain. And today, it seems that many decisions offer short-term gain at the expense of long-term pain. Scare tactics are used to convince people that policymakers need to intervene immediately to drive the symptom of stock markets higher. One such scare tactic is to highlight the risk of *contagion*.

Contagion was often the excuse given by policymakers regarding why they couldn't do what was necessary to fix the economy during the Global Financial Crisis, as many innocent people would have suffered. For instance, if the Fed didn't print trillions of dollars to bail out the stock market and, instead, allowed insolvent or basket-case companies to fail, then that would have resulted in the employees of those companies losing their jobs. In addition, investors in the shares of those companies would have suffered, as this would have had a negative effect on the values of people's 401(k) accounts (retirement plans). True. But this was more of a ruse by central banks to bail themselves out as they were responsible for the Global Financial Crisis in the first place.

Regardless, those negative effects would have been shorter-term in nature. Longer-term, as long as those 401(k) accounts were being managed by competent portfolio managers who were primarily investing in good businesses at appropriate prices and the Fed wasn't destroying the economy, then those accounts would eventually resume growing. But, importantly, the value of the 401(k) accounts would grow because of the strength of the underlying economy, which is driven by the success of the businesses in which those accounts are invested.

As we have seen, an economy can only thrive as long as those companies that are destroying capital are allowed to fail. However, by bailing out insolvent and basket-case businesses, central banks not only harm the productive capacity of the economy but they also bail out the basket-case investors who decided to invest in those capital-destroying businesses in the first place. This bailing-out enables those investors to continue making capital-destructive investments that further harm the economy. Central banks take your wealth from one pocket by printing money, only to partially, and temporarily, increase your wealth in the other by levitating the prices of any basket-case or insolvent businesses in which your 401(k) may be invested. However, many people have only one pocket; thus, their pockets are picked, with no offsetting temporary benefits. Also, as these actions harm the economy, eventually, the stocks in your 401(k) will start falling again, requiring the Fed to confiscate even more wealth from savers to, yet again, temporarily save your 401(k) account.

Trickle Down

Rather than destroying the economy to temporarily levitate the values of 401(k) accounts, the US government should have considered bailing out the owners of those 401(k) accounts directly by injecting capital into them. It wasn't the fault of workers that the Fed blew up the economy. Any basket-case portfolio managers of those 401(k)s should have lost their jobs. Instead, the Fed and Wall Street convinced people that indirectly bailing out 401(k)s by extracting trillions of dollars of wealth from savers and purchasing power from the middle class was in their own best interests and that the benefits would eventually trickle down to them (savers and middle class). Of course, the fact that Wall Street and the top one per cent would be the overwhelming beneficiaries of all of this was never mentioned.

Fortunately, despite our failing to deal with the root causes of our economic malaise, the situation is not terminal. However, it does mean that the consequences of finally doing the right thing will be particularly severe. I believe that we can all get through this together. I'll explain in the 'How Do We Fix Things?' chapter.

Fed Money Creation

I mentioned earlier that I don't believe that the Fed wanted banks to create more money by making loans on the newly created trillions of dollars of reserves. As evidence of the money-printing through QE not leading to more loans, one can look at the history of loans versus deposits in the commercial banking system. As deposits are created each time a bank makes a loan, one would expect that, over time, the total amount of loans in the system would very closely match the total number amount of deposits. And up until 2008, that was true. But as you can see in the following graph, once QE took off, so

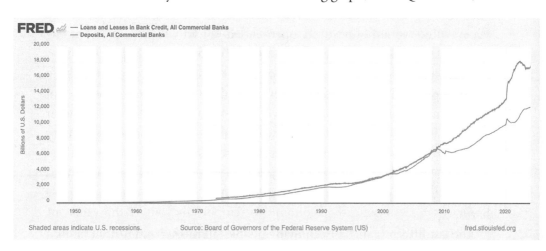

did the dollar value of deposits. But the number of loans didn't; in fact, they initially went down. The same thing happened, but even more dramatically, after COVID. That's because, through QE, the Fed prints money and buys assets from financial institutions and then those institutions deposit that money in their bank accounts. The deposits were created by the Fed printing money rather than a commercial bank making a loan.

Solvency Crisis

The Federal Reserve initially claimed that QE was a temporary emergency measure that was required to help get the economy through what they termed a *liquidity crisis*, where confidence in the financial system had been shaken. However, it was a *solvency crisis*. Some banks were technically bankrupt because the prices of so many of their assets had fallen precipitously. Printing money and extracting your wealth from you and using it to buy government bonds was to help governments decrease their borrowing costs, to help them get their (our) finances in order. At the same time, QE raised the prices of banks' assets, making them solvent again.[13]

Responding to Stock Markets

Once the crisis had passed, QE (redistributing wealth) was supposed to no longer be required. However, as QE was ending in 2010, stock markets started to fall, so the Federal Reserve came storming back with a second round (QE2). But once again, as QE2 was ending, stock markets started to fall, so the Federal Reserve tried a variant of QE called Operation Twist.[14] However, by the summer of 2012, stocks were once again falling, so the Federal Reserve announced an open-ended round of quantitative easing (QE3). As QE3 ended, the European Central Bank picked up the money-printing baton to keep global liquidity flush and drive asset prices higher.

During COVID, the Federal Reserve returned to QE, and while one can be sympathetic given the circumstances, they kept printing money long after the crisis had passed. That, combined with outrageous government spending, caused the highest inflation we had seen in over forty years.

Rather than being a temporary emergency measure, QE has been with us almost constantly for the last fifteen years. And it has done unimaginable harm.

The last fifteen years has seen many people fall further and further behind as asset prices soared skyward. Any attempt by stock prices to gravitate back down to levels that economic fundamentals would dictate is quickly halted by the Federal Reserve printing money and using your capital/wealth to keep those prices elevated.

Another Analogy

Another way I like to think about it is by using the analogy of a hot air balloon drifting safely over the landscape, providing a nice view for its occupants. Suddenly, a central banker comes along and convinces everyone that it would be better if the balloon travelled at a higher altitude, because by ascending higher and higher into the sky, it would provide its occupants with better views (the wealth effect).

Now imagine that the balloon springs a leak at high altitude and starts to descend back down to earth. The prudent and safe thing to do would be to allow that descent (recession) to happen and use that opportunity to fix the leak. Once the balloon has been fixed, it can safely ascend again (economic growth) to its previous safe height.

But the central banker should be prevented from trying to take the balloon up to an unsafe height.

However, policymakers don't like the balloon coming back down to earth, because they've convinced everyone that if the balloons are high in the sky, then that means we should all be thankful for how well they're *managing* our economy. A deflated balloon sitting on the ground signifies failure on their part. Of course, a deflated balloon (recession) provides an opportunity to fix things and prepare for the next journey forward. But in a world of short-termism, which comes from central bankers convincing people, or at least some politicians, that you can get something for nothing, fewer people now have the patience or willingness to go through what is necessary to create true economic wealth. Also, from a politician's perspective, it can be terribly inconvenient if the balloon is sitting on the ground and getting fixed during the run-up to an election.

Rather than taking the prudent action that would help ensure the long-term fundamentals of the economy by allowing it to slow, or allowing stock prices to reflect underlying economic fundamentals, central banks will simply create more 'hot air'. In the process, they burn through your savings to blow hot air into the balloon to compensate (and more) for the hot air that is still leaking out. Meanwhile, the unrelenting force of gravity (price discovery) continues, attempting to pull the balloon back down to earth to reflect reality. The hole in the balloon expands and thus requires ever-increasing amounts of hot air (your capital, burned) to keep the balloon aloft.

The 'hot air' created by the Federal Reserve, benefits the few sitting in the balloon. But it comes at the expense of everyone else down here on earth, as the amount of savings been burnt up to create the 'hot air' leaves too little for the economy to create real wealth for society at large. So much capital is burnt that the oxygen is sucked out of the atmosphere. People don't understand why it's getting increasingly more difficult to breathe, but they know that they're suffering as they watch the top one per cent rise higher into the sky. Meanwhile, central banks and politicians will turn a blind eye to the growing wealth disparity and congratulate themselves on their success – while convincing you that you've never had it so good. They will tell you to stop complaining about higher prices, and they'll draw your attention to the colourful balloon and its ever-increasing altitude.

A Fire Hose of Sugar

Some policymakers believe that driving stock markets higher is good for the economy.

It's not.

Stock markets should move higher only as a result of companies investing, innovating and improving productivity, and all to the benefit of the consumer. If less of that is happening, then stock markets need to fall so that prices reflect the underlying deteriorating fundamentals.

While Mary Poppins would say that those who put their capital at risk must, from time to time, learn to take their medicine, she also said that a spoonful of sugar helps the medicine go down. However, central banks replaced the spoon with a fire hose spewing syrup across global stock markets, sending the world on a years-long sugar rush. The sugar has overwhelmed the effects of the medicine, and the patient (the global economy) not only remains unhealthy but is also sicker than ever.

I don't blame most politicians for falling for much of the fallacious economic doctrines that are offered as sure-fire cures for economic slowdowns. Part of the problem is that policymakers feel the need to be seen to be doing something when an economy weakens, as most voters believe that doing something is what they should be doing. However, there are a lot of things policymakers can do to help restore our economic system to one that more fairly rewards effort, and in so doing, lessen the divisiveness that seems to be tearing society apart. We'll look at that later, but first we'll look at what many people believe is the main cause of our economic malaise: capitalism.

ENDNOTES

[1] Japan had already been doing Quantitative Easing for a number of years: since 2001.
[2] Traditionally, the Federal Reserve would move interest rates up or down by decreasing or increasing the amount of reserves (monetary base).
[3] Quantitative Easing (QE): What It Is and How It Works. https://www.investopedia.com/terms/q/quantitative-easing.asp
[4] According to a 2013 paper by the US Federal Reserve, more than half of these assets were bought from hedge funds, or what the Federal Reserve calls *families* – which sounds a lot better. I discussed this on a conference call years ago with Seth Carpenter, who had worked for the US Federal Reserve (Deputy Director of the Division of Monetary Affairs) and who co-wrote the paper 'Analyzing Federal Reserve Asset Purchases: From Whom Does the Fed Buy?' Federalreserve.gov April 2013.
[5] St. Louis Federal Reserve.
[6] Raising interest rates curbs inflation by making borrowing more expensive. As it becomes more expensive, people borrow less; thus, there are fewer fiduciary media being created that can then be used to drive the prices of goods higher.
[7] This was originally supposed to take effect in 2011, but it was brought forward because of the crisis.
[8] As I was managing money in Canada, the Fed was not indirectly buying any of our assets.
[9] From August 2008 to August 2009 the monetary base more than doubled, but inflation was not high in 2009, as much of the indirectly financed increase in government spending went to bail out Wall Street and commercial banks curtailed their lending.
[10] Note that as of writing the Federal Reserve had lost $200 billion (accumulated negative net income), but it doesn't even recognize it as a loss and instead treats it as a deferred asset on its balance sheet (Federal Reserve Balance Sheet Developments. December 2024.
[11] As discussed, there were recessions before central banks came along, so it's not entirely their fault. Some people believe those pre–central bank recessions were caused by the fractional reserve banking system; others believe they resulted from poor government policy/regulation.
[12] This is what some policymakers and some on Wall Street do on a regular basis: they appeal to your ego and convince you that you are special, smarter than others, and entitled. Who doesn't like hearing that? Human nature being what it is, many of us fall for it – hook, line and sinker. It's all part of the something-for-nothing disease that is killing our economy and leading to the haves vs. have-nots.
[13] There were a myriad of government and central bank actions taken to bail out Wall Street.
[14] Selling shorter-dated Treasuries and buying longer-dated ones.

CHAPTER 24
WHAT'S WRONG WITH CAPITALISM? PART 1

Perception

Many people hate the word 'capitalism'. It conjures up so many negative images in people's minds: greed, evil, unfairness, lack of compassion. However, these words are human traits that better represent how the system has been abused and distorted (just like money) by many of its participants.

In fact, the very word itself, capitalism, was conjured up as a pejorative term by its Marxist enemies back in the 1800s to give the impression that a free market, competitive system benefits only the providers of capital.[1]

One of the main issues is that there is a wide and long-standing *perception* about what capitalism is and what it does. As the Austrian school economist Fredrich A. Hayek said, 'The widespread emotional aversion to "capitalism" is closely connected with this belief that the undeniable growth of wealth which the competitive order has produced was purchased at the price of depressing the standard of life of the weakest elements of society.'[2] He also noted that:

> *Most people would be greatly surprised to learn that most of what they believe about these subjects are not safely established facts but myths, launched from political motifs and then spread by people of good will into whose general beliefs they fitted ... most of what is commonly believed on these questions, not merely by radicals but also by many conservatives, is not history but political legend.*[3]

Even worse is that, in more recent years, some policymakers and market players have increasingly distorted the system for short-term benefits which are resulting in grave longer-term consequences. This has led to less wealth creation than there otherwise would have been and an unfair distribution of that diminished wealth, leading people to rightly question the fairness of our economic system.

So, what is capitalism supposed to be? The Merriam-Webster definition of capitalism is 'An economic system characterized by private or corporate ownership of capital goods, by investments that are determined by private decision, and by prices, production and the distribution of goods that are determined mainly by competition in a free market.'

Progress, Eventually

For the last two hundred years or so, the capitalist system has created more wealth than any other system before it. Below is how global GDP per capita (final spending per person), has grown over the last few thousand years.

Historical Levels of GDP Per Capita[5]

Year	GDP Per Capita, World Average
1000 BC	$160
AD 1	$135
1000	$165
1500	$175
1800	$250
1900	$850
1950	$2,030
1975	$4,640
2000	$8,175

For centuries there was effectively no progress on this number, that is, until we reach around 1800 when the industrial revolution took large parts of the Western world by storm. Many countries adopted the capitalist system to varying degrees. Over the next century, global GDP per capita increased threefold after having barely budged for 2,500 years.

On the following page is the GDP per capita for the United States.[6]

Year	Real GDP Per Capita	10-Year Growth
1949	$15,162	
1959	$19,265	27%
1969	$26,175	36%
1979	$32,323	23%
1989	$38,893	22%
1999	$48,485	23%
2009	$53,213	10%
2019	$62,606	18%

The US has experienced very strong GDP per capita growth over the years. However, I don't believe that it is quite as impressive as it looks, as, over the last few decades, final spending has increasingly been funded with debt. It has required a monumental amount of debt to keep driving that GDP (final spending) number higher, which effectively borrows from the future.

Allocating Scarce Resources

In a free market system, there are millions of entrepreneurs making their own risk/reward decisions with their own capital (skin in the game). It is beyond dispute that this system results in the most efficient allocation of capital or scarce resources. When government officials allocate taxpayer dollars to certain projects or spend/print to *stimulate* the economy, it will always be done less efficiently than decisions made in the private sector.

First, government spending has no measuring stick to make sure it's efficient; it has no real accountability regarding how wisely that money was spent. In contrast, spending by a private business needs to result in a profit (i.e. sales must exceed expenses), otherwise it will go out of business. Secondly, government obtains the capital it spends through taxation, borrowing and printing money; in other words, the capital they're spending is not their own. For a company, the capital that it spends is owned by the shareholders and that capital first had to be *earned*. If the management of the business spends that shareholder capital recklessly, they will be held accountable (fired). Don't get me wrong, I don't believe that government attracts those who don't give a damn about how efficiently money is spent. Rather, it's the *system* that creates that behaviour, because there is little incentive to do otherwise. And I believe many of us would be motivated to behave in a similar manner if we were in their shoes.

It's Not Capitalism

Within the system of capitalism, there are businesses that are run by all types of different people with different values (some good and some bad), belief systems, temperaments, and time horizons. Capitalism has no say on how business owners *should* treat their employees, or what sort of product or service they should provide, or what quality. However, as we saw with our examples of Fastenal and Costco, long-term business success is usually a result of companies treating their employees very well and providing their customers with great value propositions.

> *I don't pay good wages because I have a lot of money; I have a lot of money because I pay good wages.*
>
> – Robert Bosch

On the other hand, if one is simply interested in short-term business success, that can be obtained at the expense of employees and the customer – and, unfortunately, we seem to see much more of this these days. However, although things have deteriorated, I believe that the majority of companies do what's necessary for long-term success. That is why there are still so many great things going on in this world despite the system being distorted by some for short-term gain. But things could, and should, be a lot better.

The Most Productive System

Profits, in general, are a very good thing; they are a sign that companies are producing capital that others value. It's only sustained high profits that can become an issue, because that might mean that something is preventing consumers from benefiting by having those high profits competed away. As we have seen, the ultimate beneficiary of productivity growth and competition is the consumer, through declining prices – good deflation. Thus, even if your income is stagnant, you become wealthier in real terms, because, every year, you can buy more stuff with the same amount of money.

Distortion

However, the system we now have morphed in another direction. I believe the main reason for this is that some have attempted via debt-fuelled spending or printing money to *stimulate* the economy to grow faster than its natural rate. We've already discussed the consequences of this. Many are getting poorer in real terms as prices rise faster (particularly housing and rent) than their earnings while those who own stocks and expensive homes get richer and richer. But instead of blaming those distorting the system, people often direct their anger at capitalism.

Those who do believe in greater government spending do themselves and others a disservice by restricting capitalism. It's through capitalism that we are able to take care of the less fortunate in our society. Actions by many well-intending policymakers unfortunately boost consumption at the expense of investment or distort the crucial price discovery mechanism of capital markets, leading to misallocated capital. These actions serve to transfer unearned wealth to some who are already very rich and make the world poorer – or not as rich as it would have been otherwise.

Rules

For capitalism and markets to work most effectively, they need to be free and unhampered, which means policymakers must not interfere with the risk/return decisions of entrepreneurs and market players with skin in the game. But let's be clear: unhampered doesn't mean no rules. As I mentioned earlier, for capitalism and capital markets to play their role in contributing to the creation of sustainable and true wealth generation for all, there needs to be a clear set of rules. Those rules need to be followed – and, importantly, they need to be enforced!

Hockey Analogy

Rules that help with the smooth functioning of capital markets are not unlike rules in sports. The rules are there to give everyone an equal opportunity to excel – but not to ensure everyone excels equally. We can use a hockey analogy. Becoming a professional hockey player requires a significant investment of time and effort over many years. The result is incredibly fit and talented athletes entertaining millions of people who are willing to spend some of their capital to be entertained by them.

But can you imagine what attempts at equalisation of outcomes would do to the game of hockey? For instance, what would happen if one player was a faster skater than everyone else? The referee might then require that player to wear a thirty-pound backpack to slow him or her down and give the others a chance. What would happen if the referee attempted to equalise things in this way? Well, there would be no incentive for anyone to practice, because as soon as you improved, your advantage would be taken away from you by the referee.

In fact, you would be incentivised to not practice at all, because, like anything that you do, practicing has opportunity costs; you could be doing something else, instead. Those who practise/train all of their lives to become professional hockey players make all sorts of compromises, for example, not watching as much TV, not eating as many cheeseburgers. But there would be no cost to not practicing or eating lots of cheeseburgers if referees could always be counted on to equalise things by taking away any advantages that other players had worked for.

If you didn't practise/train and someone else did, their superior fitness or skill would be taken away from them so that you would not be at a disadvantage. Everyone else would stop practising/training, too, because there would be no advantage in trying to improve. Eventually, you would have a hockey league full of overweight, unskilled and unmotivated players that no one would be willing to pay to watch (sounds like my over-40s soccer team). So, while the referee would ensure equality within the hockey league, he or she would also condemn it to economic disaster.

You Can Only Take So Much

This is the ultimate endgame of socialism. While it might seem like a nice idea to spread most of the wealth around, it's really bad for the economy and, ultimately, even for those who are receiving the handouts. Those putting in all of the effort to produce the wealth that gets redistributed will become less incentivised to invest the time, capital and effort that is required to produce that wealth. Why would they want to, when they see more and more of it taken from them? Human nature being what it is, when people are taxed more, they are less incentivised to work. Meanwhile, those who receive taxpayer handouts are also less incentivised to work. Again, this is not a criticism, simply a comment on human nature.

There are some extreme historical examples of this, but the one that always sticks out in my mind occurred in the United Kingdom in the 1970s. In 1974, the top tax rate on earned income over £20,000 (equivalent to approximately £260,000 in 2024) was 83%. Not only that, but a surcharge of 15% brought the top tax rate for investment income over £20,000 to 98%![7] This resulted in what they called the 'brain drain'. Many of the brightest and most successful people in the UK left the country for more tax-accommodating places such as the United States and Switzerland. I remember as a kid wondering why so many famous British people such as rock bands and actors left the UK. A top tax rate of 98% will do it.

Some may attempt to stop the brain drain by ensuring that *all* countries have very high tax rates – so there's no point in leaving your country. However, that would actually make things worse, because, then, people would not have a destination where they could put their productive ability to work. So, not only would the productivity of your own country spiral downwards, but the whole world would also do the same; everyone would be equally poor.

When able-bodied people can easily receive capital from others while doing nothing, they are disincentivized to work and, thus, a risk that they don't add to the productive capacity of the economy. Just like an athlete without the incentive to excel would stop practising/training and become less fit, the economy would become flabby and less dynamic. The first stop on this path is global secular stagnation. We are a good deal of the way there already. However, stagnation would not be the worst of it. Ultimately, it would lead to economic contraction. In times past, it has led to violence. Hopefully, things can change long before we reach that point.

Just Rewards

In capitalism, as in hockey or any other sport, there *should* be inequality of performance and results. But the inequality should be determined by effort and ability, not by special favours or corruption. I believe that most people don't begrudge those who benefit commensurately from the results of their actions. I think that most people would agree that one's rewards should, more or less, equal their contributions. This is the same as you making a bike and then selling it so you can use that money to buy a suit. You earned a suit, and if the tailor then uses that money to buy a TV, then they effectively earned a TV. You both *earned* something by creating capital which means it did not come at the expense of someone else. *Net* wealth creation occurred in the economy through you and the tailor. First, there was no bike or suit, and now there is one of each. Having sold what you have made, you are now both wealthier and satisfying various of your needs and wants. And, importantly, not at the expense of a single soul.

Not everyone thinks this way, and there is a minority of people out there who *do* begrudge the success of other people or are angry that the world hasn't recognised *their* own greatness. Unfortunately, these people who suffer from envy are increasingly flexing their muscles and recommending that more capital should be extracted from the successful people that they resent. This comes in the form of higher tax rates, wealth taxes and capital gains taxes. By redistributing successful people's capital, these people receive the accolades that they were not able to obtain by creating capital themselves. The answer is not to unfairly extract increasing amounts of capital from those who fairly earned it but to stop implementing policies that inordinately and unfairly benefit the top one per cent.

The way I like to think of things is that if you don't have any debt, then whatever material wealth you have or have consumed should be approximately equal to the wealth that you have created for others (i.e. whatever you decided to produce: a good, a service, or hours of work for a company) that they were willing to purchase in a fair exchange with whatever capital they produced. As should be obvious from this example, in a truly capitalist market system where rules that define and protect property rights are obeyed and enforced, it's not as easy for people to obtain wealth at the expense of others. It doesn't mean it doesn't happen but it's more difficult. And corporations benefiting from regulatory capture is not capitalism. There are many nuances but generally a system with strict rules that are enforced and where there is voluntary participation will result in the fairest and greatest outcomes. Of course, it's not perfect and unfortunately some will still seek to take advantage of others and this is where the state can intervene: while often obvious, defining what is and isn't fair can sometimes be tricky.[8]

Slowing Growth

A fairer redistribution of wealth should be the goal, but 'fair' means 'based on what you have produced' (the capital you have created directly or indirectly). However, many today believe in simply spreading around more evenly the capital that other people have produced. I can only assume that these people don't believe that this will result in less wealth being available, including for those on the receiving end of the redistribution.

These people couldn't be more wrong.

And sticking their heads in the sand and refusing to acknowledge the terrible economic consequences of all of this is, in my opinion, irresponsible. Again, this doesn't mean that no capital should be redistributed, but it must be based on real need, not wants. And definitely not to buy votes.

The first stop on our current path is a global economy that experiences slowing growth. That is, there is still growth, but it's not as fast as it was in the past. This is what we are experiencing now. Since 1960, the US economy has grown at the following rates each decade:

US Real GDP Per Capita Growth Rate by Decade[9]

Decade	Average Annual GDP Growth Rate
1950s	2.3%
1960s	2.8%
1970s	2.2%
1980s	2.2%
1990s	2.0%
2000s	0.8%
2010s	1.5%

Again, note that the GDP per capita growth rate in the US over the last twenty years has been much slower than it was in prior decades. It picked up a little over the last ten years only because a monumental amount of debt was taken on to fund final spending. This debt will slow the economy even further. So, not only will this monumental liability be thrown on the backs of the next generation, but they'll have to somehow pay it back by finding a job in an economy that will be even weaker than it is today. It's patently unfair that the previous generation and mine took on debt in a strong economy to live a lifestyle far beyond our contributions, and that they will leave it to the next generation to pick up the tab.

Misdiagnosis

Today's system is structurally flawed. Even worse, yet predictably, this led to populist (socialist) movements around the globe, as well as anger and resentment.[10] And while the ultimate motives of most socialists might appear noble, their policies will only eventually impoverish everyone. However, socialists don't believe that their means of redistributing wealth are ignoble. I believe that's because many of them don't understand the true nature of a free market system and how it's supposed to work. It may be that many socialists don't understand how the current market-based system is rigged and is moving further and further from what a capitalist system is meant to foster. As a result, socialists have misdiagnosed the patient and they are prescribing the wrong medicine. I believe that their *cure*, which would initially reduce wealth disparity and, thus, look like it's working, would, ultimately, mortally wound the patient, making everyone considerably worse off than they could even imagine.

Referees

People's frustration about the current state of the world should not be focused on a system of capitalism, rather, on those who have distorted the system for short-term gain. In particular, people should be frustrated with the referees of the system, because it was they who allowed the rules to be disregarded or bent, who went against the very principles of the rules. When policymakers use taxpayer dollars to bail out poor investment decisions on Wall Street or distort interest rates to keep zombie companies alive, that is the opposite of capitalism.

I believe those in charge have been taking these actions because they have convinced themselves that the avoidance of short-term pain that is achieved by distorting capitalism is good for the economy.

It's not.

Their action treats symptoms at the expense of society in the long term. And the cost is not just in economic terms but also in the form of deteriorating social cohesion.

Another Hockey Analogy

Assume that the owners of a hockey league decide that there is more money to be made for the whole league if teams from big cities such as New York and Los Angeles always made it to the playoffs. More people would be interested in watching those games, and there would be more money to be made from the media rights.

The league owners start instructing referees to make decisions that favour the big-city teams. They justify their actions by saying that, yes, although the bigger city teams will make more money, the whole league will benefit, as the extra money will eventually trickle down to the teams from smaller cities.

It all makes sense on paper. However, as time goes on, the bigger teams just keep getting richer and richer. And not only do the benefits not trickle down to the smaller teams, but fans of the smaller teams also stop paying to watch the games because their teams always lose. The smaller teams fall further and further behind, and their fans become resentful when they realise that the rules have been stacked against them. They come to the conclusion that hockey is an unfair sport. But, of course, it's not the sport (capitalism) that's unfair but how the system has been distorted by misguided economic theories that have benefited the few at the expense of everyone else.[11]

Striking the Right Balance

All wealth and prosperity are created by the investment of time, effort, ingenuity and capital. However, there are many people in this world, and increasingly so, who don't create wealth but take it from those who do. And they do this because it's quicker and easier than creating it.

The most obvious and open form of wealth redistribution happens through taxation, where a percentage of your productive efforts are collected by the government and spent or handed out to other people. And as we have seen, there are also other forms of wealth redistribution.

As discussed earlier, I believe that most would agree that redistributing some wealth from those who have been successful to those who are in need is a good thing to do. And aspects of the welfare system can contribute to economic growth, for example, unemployment benefits that give people time to regroup after having been laid off and to possibly even find a better job. The main questions, and where people will differ significantly, in terms of the redistribution of wealth is how much, for how long, and to whom? There are political/economic extremes on both sides (e.g. communism, where all all property is owned by the state and then disbursed as they see fit, to socialism where the means of production are owned by the state but other private property rights still exists, to capitalism to libertarianism whose proponents believe there should be extremely little or even no taxation, that you own everything you produce, and all services in society should be provided by private enterprise).[12]

Connecting the Dots

I believe that some policymakers suffer from a lack of understanding of how and why capitalism really works and how true wealth is created. It may be that they simply succumb to the enormous pressure of the requirement to be seen to be doing something to help the economy. Regardless, once again, I believe that it's a result of focusing on short-term symptoms rather than long-term fundamentals.

It would be easy for anyone to fall into this trap and convince themselves it's the right thing to do. The reason for this is that boosting short-term symptoms feels good. Many people benefit from those symptoms improving. Not only that, but the fundamental consequences of those actions are also usually borne by someone else, or they are further into the future, and most people are not able to connect the dots between the short-term cause and the long-term effect. *How can the actions of the central bank driving the stock market higher result in slower productivity growth ten years later?*

For instance, many have pointed to the rebound of stock markets after the Global Financial Crisis as proof that the US Federal Reserve did the right thing in bailing out Wall Street. Markets fell over fifty per cent but then they quickly started rising again and, eventually, far exceeded their prior peaks. However, this was achieved at the expense of most people through a process known as financial repression. Most people's savings were hit by government policies enacted to reduce government interest payments on their gargantuan levels of debt and drive stock markets higher, which I believe has been the main contributor to society's obscene levels of wealth inequality.

Phase one of the financial repression strategy used to bail out Wall Street was driving interest rates to zero; stock prices, all else being equal, go higher as interest rates fall. Phase two was printing money, or quantitative easing, which drives asset prices higher through the portfolio effect. The result was a double-whammy negative impact on savers. For years, savers were receiving zero interest rates on their savings, and in some instances interest rates were even negative. Literally trillions of dollars that should have been earned by savers as interest income didn't get to them. Instead, the money went to governments and corporations as the trillions of dollars of interest expense on their debt that they didn't have to pay to those who lent them the money (i.e. you). But it gets worse, because not only did you not earn the interest income on your savings that you were entitled to, because interest rates were zero, but the real value of your savings also went down due to all of the money that was printed. That lost value went to someone else: holders of assets like stocks and those who owed you money, such as corporations or governments.

Trampoline

I like to think of it this way. During the Global Financial Crisis, the US stock market fell off a cliff. What should have happened is there should have been a reckoning once stocks hit the ground: poor investment decision–makers exposed and fired; same for incompetent bankers; bad investments should have been unwound and capital reallocated. Most importantly, there should have been an admission that zero interest rates and central bank wealth effect strategies had not only been ineffective but had also caused great harm.

Of course, it was unlikely that those who had implemented the strategy would ever have had the courage to admit such a thing – which is why it was such a disastrous decision to put them back in charge after the crisis happened. Unsurprisingly, these people simply doubled down on their policies that had caused the problems in the first place, as doing anything else would have been an admission of fault. One can imagine that, because these people had been at the helm all those years, they were deemed to be indispensable in fixing the problems. However, as the old saying goes, graveyards are full of indispensable people.

As a result, there was no real reckoning for those who had caused the crisis, nor for those who had benefited the most from the boom years. In fact, the reckless behaviour got worse over the ensuing thirteen years. Again, policymakers pointed to the stock market rebounding higher as proof that they were doing the right thing. But this rebound was at the expense of all those who were not heavily invested in the stock market. Rather than crashing on the ground at the foot of the cliff, those who owned stocks rebounded off a giant trampoline and soared skyward again. The trampoline was made up of savers being financially repressed (earning no interest income on their savings and watching the value of their savings being eroded). This is what sent asset holders soaring through the stratosphere and what led to a significant increase in wealth inequality.

ENDNOTES

[1] Henry Hazlitt. *Foundations of Morality*. Chapter 30.
[2] *Capitalism and the Historians* (Chicago: University of Chicago Press, 1954, p. 10).
[3] Ibid. p. 9.
[4] Note that, in the past, GDP was driven less by debt and more by actual productivity and was, thus, a more meaningful measure of an economy's progression (or regression).
[5] From Arnold Kling and Nick Schulz. *Invisible Wealth: The Hidden Story of How Markets Work*. Chapter 2, 'Economics 2.0 In Practice.' Their source was J. Bradford DeLong, *Macroeconomics*. McGraw-Hill Irwin, 2002. Chapter 5, 'The Reality of Economic Growth: History and Prospect.' His source was from Joel Cohen, *How Many People Can the Earth Support?* (New York: Norton, 1995).
[6] Federal Reserve of St. Louis. Chained 2017 dollars. These numbers are not comparable with the previous table i.e. global GDP per capita over the centuries.
[7] Just a reminder that with a progressive tax system the first part of your income is taxed at a lower rate and then increases progressively. In 1974/75 the tax rates in the UK were as follows: First £4,500: 33%, £4,500 to £5,000: 38%, £5,000 to £6,000: 43% and so on (sourced from Stanford University).
[8] One example might be where a company is the only employer left in a small town and decides that they can get away with offering lower wages. Now the only alternative for those employees would be to quite and move to another town with better employment opportunities. And perhaps leaving behind their parents, friends and roots which of course can come with social and emotional costs. Although technically voluntary, it hardly seems fair or right.
[9] Federal Reserve of St. Louis.
[10] By 2023/2024 the pendulum started to swing the other way in countries like Argentina and the United States.
[11] The National Hockey League (NHL) is one of the greatest examples of how a sports league should be run. Teams have salary caps and, thus, no matter how much a team makes, they can spend only so much on players' salaries. This results in a great deal of parity within a league that has very few consecutive winners.
[12] Note that there are differences with respect to personal freedom vs. economic freedom. See *How Does One Define "Libertarian"?* Stephen Apolito. 09/15/2023. www.mises.org

CHAPTER 25

WHAT'S WRONG WITH CAPITALISM? PART 2

No Coercion

So far, we have discussed what capitalism is and what it is not. Let's see how it works from the perspective of your bike company.

When you started your company, you decided to save your money and take a chance by investing in what was required to start your business. You make all the decisions and take on all of the risks. If your business is growing, then it's your decision whether or not you to hire employees. You decide how much you will pay them and you know that it simply makes good long-term business sense to pay them a fair or even above market wage – and they decide whether or not you're paying them enough. Your success is determined by your ability, efforts and willingness to take a chance with your own capital (skin in the game). And all of this is done with one goal in mind: providing a great value proposition that customers are willing to pay for. As the entrepreneur and risk-taker, you are the one who potentially benefits from your business's success – or suffers from its failure. Note that, in all of this, everything is voluntary, from your decision to start a business and how to run it, to your employees' decisions to work there, to the customers' willingness to buy your bikes. There is no coercion.

No one is winning at the expense of someone else, or put more accurately, your company is not winning at the expense of the customer, or the employees. No one is forced to purchase your bikes or work at your company. Rather, your success is a result of satisfying customers and treating your employees well.[1]

Competitors

However, there is someone who is suffering here: anyone who makes lousy bikes or, at least, doesn't strive to improve their bikes by reinvesting in their business and paying up for the best employees. Too bad. No one buys an inferior bike if they know they can easily get a better bike for a similar price. These companies could consider reducing the prices of their lousy bikes to encourage people to buy them. Every bike has its price. However, lowering the price may not generate enough sales to cover all of their costs, and they may start losing money. Earlier, we discussed four options for the maker of lousy bikes: reinvest in their business to make better bikes, make another product (e.g. a shovel), develop a completely new product, or go work for another company.

This is how capitalism is supposed to work and, indeed, still does to a great extent – but there is obviously room for improvement. Admittedly, it's not much fun for the maker of lousy bikes. They were doing just fine before you came along with your cool bikes, however, if the company isn't willing or able to be competitive then it makes no sense for policymakers to attempt to keep that company in business. Yes, it will initially save jobs which is a good thing, but it does so by taking capital from the private sector to keep in business a suboptimal operator (zombie): throwing good money after bad.

Not Capitalism

An anti-capitalist alternative for the maker of lousy bikes might be to go talk to his brother-in-law, who is the town's mayor. He may convince his brother-in-law that you are ruthlessly driving him out of business with your amazing bikes, and if that happens, his staff will end up being unemployed. The mayor might then impose a regulation making it illegal for you to charge a certain price for your bikes, thus forcing you to raise your prices, which then allows the maker of lousy bikes to increase his prices and stay in business. Price controls such as that price floor[2] may be advertised as protecting jobs; however, ultimately, they protect the executives and owners of lousy businesses. They do so by forcing other companies to charge consumers more for their products than they otherwise would.[3] Good companies and consumers get screwed to protect basket-case businesses. Some would label a person who advocates such an approach a capitalist, but they're not. In fact, it's the opposite of capitalism because it involves government entering the fray to decide winners and losers, and it comes at the expense of the consumer.

Zombies

Over the last fifteen years, central banks have created the conditions that have enabled basket-case companies to continue destroying capital, which has resulted in declining productivity growth. Zombie companies are steadily growing as a per centage of publicly listed firms. According to the Bank for

International Settlements, the percentage of zombie companies rose from around 4% in the 1980s to 15% in 2017.[4] It's likely higher than that today given today's rising interest rates and post-COVID government (taxpayer) support programmes.

Executive Pay

One of the issues is that total earnings for some executives have risen to outlandish levels while those of their employees have grown much more slowly. It does makes sense that executives should be paid more based on their ability to successfully run a business. For instance, if an executive makes fifty times what the average employee at the company earns, it's not as if fifty employees working together would know how to do the executive's job. You'd just have fifty people who don't know how to run a business. However, there are limits to how much more executives should be making than the rank and file. According to a report by the Economic Policy Institute[5], the ratio of the compensation of CEOs to that of the typical worker has gone through the roof over the last fifty years:

- 1965: 20 to 1
- 1989: 59 to 1
- 2021: 399 to 1

As we have seen, executives have benefited enormously from central banks driving stock markets higher. And most of the increase in the multiple of CEO pay to that of the average worker is due to stock compensation. However, if one just looked at cash compensation, the multiple would still have increased. And while it's hard to justify some CEO salaries, they often don't really come at the expense of the employees. For instance, in 2021, Tim Cook, the CEO of Apple, made $16.4 million in cash compensation. While one could question whether or not Tim Cook made $16.4 million worth of contributions to the business, his compensation didn't really come at the expense of the other employees at Apple. Around 154,000 people worked at Apple at the time, so if the company paid Tim Cook zero that year and, instead, distributed his pay to the rest of the employees, they would have all received around $106 each. The total cash compensation of the top five executives was $36.5 million; distributing this to everyone else in the firm would have come to $237 per employee. So, yes, receiving another couple hundred bucks a year would be nice, but it's hardly going to change one's lifestyle.

Creative Destruction

The term 'creative destruction' associated with economist Joseph Schumpeter, refers to the idea that new innovations make past ones obsolete. That is, the creation of something new and better effectively destroys what came before it. Change is a constant in a dynamic economy, and people and corporations must be allowed to fail. Business formations – a statistic that measures the number of businesses that have payrolls within a year of submitting a business application – averaged about 280,000 per year from 2009 to 2017.

Destructive Bailouts

Of course, not only are people starting businesses, but they're also going out of business. According to the American Bankruptcy Institute, during the 1980s, on average, around 65,000 businesses went bankrupt each year. But starting in the 1990s – coinciding with falling interest rates – annual business bankruptcies averaged around 56,000. As interest rates continued to fall, so did the number of bankruptcies. In the years shortly before COVID, they averaged around 23,000. In 2022, they had fallen to just over 13,000.[6]

It's natural to feel that a company going bankrupt is not a good thing – and it certainly isn't for the employees of that business and whoever invested money in that business. It's also natural to think that a significant decline in the number of bankruptcies over the decades is a good thing.

It's not.

Remember from the table above that GDP per capita growth in the US is lower now than it was back in the 1980s when the number of bankruptcies was higher. Creative destruction is not happening to the extent that it should be. As a result, not only mediocre but also failing businesses are propped up by central banks and governments using other people's money. The result: those companies can continue to destroy capital and do things that few people value. This supresses the productive ability of the economy and also drains it of its innovative drive.

Misleading Averages

The numbers of jobs gained and lost are very fluid measures. However, the numbers that you see can be very misleading about what's going on, as they often only show a net figure. This masks the fluidity and dynamism present in the US labour market. For instance, according to the US Bureau of Labor Statistics, in 2019 there were 2.2 million jobs gained in the United States. However, that number nets out the number of *hires* (70.0 million) and the number of *separations* (67.8 million). Again, this demonstrates how simply looking at net numbers, or averages, can skew your perception of what is really going on.[7] Average numbers are often used by policymakers or those on financial TV. They talk about how strong the average company balance sheet is in the US, or what the average savings rate is for Americans. Some companies with very large and strong balance sheets offset the many with lousy balance sheets. And the very high savings of wealthy people more than offset the fact that many people have no savings at all.

Not Equal

A great tragedy is that there are people who are not in a position to obtain the skills or education necessary to fairly compete in a given field. There are millions of lower-income people who don't receive the same quality of education, or perhaps they come from broken families or dangerous neighbourhoods where they can't benefit from the limited education that may be available to them. I'm sure that great efforts have been made by many people and billions of dollars have been spent trying to fix these sorts of problems, and poverty certainly has fallen to very low levels in most developed economies (of course the goal should be zero poverty).

However, many still suffer from disadvantage when trying to make their way in the world. Not only that, but, even within the ranks of those who are not considered lower-income, there are some who are greatly advantaged over others, for example, wealthy families who can afford the best schools for their kids. It's important to remember that although there are people who never get a fair shot, this is not the reason others succeed in an unhampered market. Our goal should not be to punish successful people but ensure that we increasingly level the playing field in terms of *opportunity*. Levelling the field would see many more successful people with that much more wealth being created, so it's in all of our interests to do what we can to make that happen.

More Level Than You Think

Some might believe that socialism is the answer, but I think that the problems are much deeper than simply giving people more money, particularly when that can become a disincentive. In fact, government benefits are already considerable for lower-income earners. When government economists calculate income quintiles for households in the US (divide them into bands of one fifth each), they don't take into account government benefits or taxes. And so, the government will tell you that the top 20% of households make more than 16x than the bottom 20%. But once you add all the government benefits to the bottom 20% and subtract the taxes from the top 20%, then the difference is 4×.

Here is the after-tax income by quintile after accounting for all government benefits and taxes:[8]

Bottom:	$49,613
Second:	$53,924
Third:	$65,631
Fourth:	$88,132
Top:	$197,034

Earned Wealth

When people see a movie star or athlete driving around in an expensive car or buying an expensive mansion, for the most part, they don't begrudge them their wealth. The reason for that is we can see what their contributions to society are in terms of adding value to our leisure time. Many of us are willing to pay to see those actors and athletes perform, and we think it only fair that they end up making a lot of money.

I'm sure there are some out there who don't agree with this. However, even those people would have to admit that any money actors and athletes make is a result of providing entertainment for which others are willing to pay. These people become wealthy because they provide a service that many people value; they do not become wealthy at the *expense* of someone else. For instance, you might sell one of your bikes and use the proceeds to watch a whole lot of movies. The actors receive their capital from you, and you receive capital from them in the form of their performances.

When I see multimillion-dollar homes, I don't resent the people who were fortunate enough to own them because I don't believe that their success has come at my expense (assuming of course that their wealth reflects their contributions to society rather than central banks transferring wealth to them from others). Nor do I feel that if their homes were taken away from them, that would somehow enrich my life. Of course, that doesn't mean I wouldn't love to be able to afford to live in one of those houses, but I can't because my contributions to society have not been enough such that I have enough money to buy one (I haven't created enough means of payment stored up in the medium of exchange called money).

Some might argue that the residents of those mansions may have had an advantaged upbringing. Perhaps they took over a family business or inherited a lot of money, but, often, those people still have had a lot to do to be successful. However, many didn't have an unfair advantage, and they still managed to make it on their own. Regardless, however other people may have become successful, as long as it was achieved fairly through the creation of capital then none of that had a negative impact on me regarding where I ended up in my life, so why would I begrudge them their success? Nor has their success come at the expense of many others who, sadly, never had the opportunity to achieve such wealth. Therefore, I don't believe the answer to helping the disadvantaged is to punish those who have been successful.

How would taking the luxury homes away from the wealthy enrich my life? It wouldn't. Although some would advocate for this for no other reason than satisfying the horrible human emotion of envy. There's an old tale about a Russian farmer who owns a cow but is envious that his neighbour owns two cows. A sorcerer approaches him and grants him one wish. Rather than wish for another cow, the farmer tells the sorcerer to kill one of his neighbour's cows. Envy is a horrible human emotion, and the resulting destruction of other people's wealth is often justified by some who believe they're fighting on the side of social justice. And while there is a lot to be angry about with some people benefiting enormously at the expense of others, we need to be careful not to throw out the free market baby with the something for nothing fallacious economic doctrine bathwater.

Unearned Wealth
When people see wealthy corporate executives lounging on their multi-

million-dollar yachts while making four or five hundred times what the average workers make, then resentment naturally builds. But only because people don't believe that those executives earned the money as an entrepreneur would have done: by putting their own capital at risk and providing a true customer value proposition. Instead, people can see that many of today's billionaires have become wealthy by being financial engineers and by playing the system. These people are sometimes referred to as fiat billionaires (i.e. their wealth accumulation would not have been possible in a hard currency system).

Don't get me wrong. Many corporate executives are often very capable, hardworking people who make significant contributions to society and deserve to be well compensated. However, in some instances, their wealth can far exceed their contributions, which means much of their wealth (not all) has come at the expense of someone else (i.e. you). And, as should hopefully now be clear, that is not capitalism.

Many view capitalism as an unfair system that favours the few at the expense of the many – shareholders and senior executives at the expense of the average worker. And there's good reason for this view, because this sort of thing seems to be happening more often. Some refer to this as the financialisation of capitalism, but this is not true capitalism. Why should we begrudge an entrepreneur benefiting from their efforts as long as their customers feel they are getting true value for their money and that the entrepreneur was truly responsible for that value proposition?

People who build up businesses over many years who invest significant amounts of their own time and risk their own capital to try and make a go of it deserve the success they achieve, if they achieve it. In addition, they usually end up providing livelihoods for all sorts of other people, livelihoods that would not have existed were it not for the willingness of the entrepreneur to take a chance. Similarly, executives who take over from entrepreneurs can also add significant value to a business and often grow it to much greater heights than an entrepreneur ever could. Where people get angry is when short term–focused career executives waltz into a business and, despite the fact that they had nothing to do with its founding, they start to extract value from that business and do so at the expense of the employees, customers, suppliers and society at large.

From Great to Bad

Success requires a long-term mindset and considerable patience and perseverance. And success is not guaranteed; nor should it be. Countless setbacks are encountered along the way, but the ones that succeed are the ones that don't give up when they stumble.

It usually doesn't happen overnight. When an entrepreneur suddenly bursts onto the scene with a great new product, they're often labelled an 'overnight success'. However, what people didn't see was the many years of investment, toil and failure that happened before they finally made it.

Comedian Eddie Cantor said it best: '*It takes twenty years to make an overnight success.*'

I know someone who owns a brewery. It took eight years before his business began to generate positive cashflow, and this was after re-mortgaging his house and maxing out all of his credit cards just to keep the business going. He is now very successful, but there are countless others who gave up long before they were able to succeed. Those who don't succeed often have just as much passion and the work ethic required for success, but you need a lot of things to go right for a business to succeed, and, sometimes, you might simply run out of money before you can come up with that winning customer value proposition.

Someone might have a true passion for something, but they're just not very good at what they want to do. In these cases, the sooner these people realise this the better. Then those people can go and find something else to be passionate about. For example, if someone is passionate about being an artist but can't paint anything anyone is willing to buy, that's not society's fault. Yes, that person can continue to paint, but if society doesn't value what is being painted, then that artist has no right to demand anything in return from society. The wannabe artist needs to find another way of making a living and, perhaps, paint only as a hobby.

We discussed earlier how entrepreneurs can be extremely passionate about their businesses, but I have found that they also tend to treat their employees extremely well. I think this may be because when an entrepreneur starts a business, they often do so on their own and, thus, they end up doing every type of task that's required to make the business successful. For this reason, they may tend to have more empathy for their employees who are doing the jobs the entrepreneur used to do; the entrepreneur can better understand some of the challenges that those employees may be going through. Over time, I've found that success often follows this mindset.

Career executives are typically groomed more from a financial perspective than an entrepreneurial one. They don't know what it's like to start a business and go through all of the thrills, ups and downs, anguish and perseverance that it takes to succeed from the ground up. (Few of us do.) This can result in some career executives who focus more on the numbers than on the customer or their employees. It's not that they're bad people or that they don't care about customers and employees; it's just that their training and expertise is often numbers-based. When these executives meet with analysts, the questions they get are often of the following nature:

- What will your profit margin be next quarter?
- Do you expect to reduce your tax rate?
- What are your cost reduction plans?
- How much debt will you be taking on to buy back shares?

If your main focus is numbers and the share price, you may be tempted to look for ways to extract from the customer value proposition. This can be done by either increasing the price or reducing the quality of the product. Both ways, you make more money. However, the extra profit is short-lived because your customers aren't stupid, and, eventually, they'll see they're getting ripped off and will take their business elsewhere. Similarly, if you attempt to extract value from your employees by not paying them enough or not investing in a safe and pleasant work environment, eventually, you'll either find it hard to attract and keep employees or the quality of their work will suffer.

Again, this is not to denigrate all career executives. I have met and I know many incredibly talented career executives who do understand that the customer needs to come first and how important their employees are to the long-term success of their businesses and who truly do make a difference. However, I've met a number of the opposite ilk.

A Moral Issue
While capitalism does better enable a society to take care of the less fortunate, this is not the justification for why the capitalist system should be defended

at all costs. Its importance is based on property rights and freedom. However, our rights and our freedom are increasingly being trampled upon because policymakers believe that we will, ultimately, be better off as the wealth they distribute to the top one per cent will eventually trickle down to everyone else (i.e. the means justify the ends). However, it's up to us to decide if we are okay with their means. Not only that, but their means won't lead to the ends they expect.

Best-Laid Plans

As I have said many times, I believe that the actions of policymakers are well intended but terribly misguided. Perhaps they do this because they want to believe so badly that there is such a thing as a free lunch. Or they simply can't wait for the time that it would take to focus on fundamentals such as saving and investment; instead, they focus on the symptoms in the hope that something will eventually come out of left field to save the day. Otherwise known as kicking the can down the road.

Most people don't know what capitalism is. They only know our current system, which is a distorted form of capitalism which, in many ways, is unfair, destructive and divisive. I'm not sure if there is a perfect system, but I believe that if more people really understood what capitalism is supposed to be, they would see it as the best system we know of that can provide the best opportunity to create the most wealth for the most people. And that it does this in the fairest way possible, while at the same time helping to safeguard property rights and freedom. If they understood this, they could then vote for the form of fiscal policy that best aligned with their own beliefs regarding how much of their own productive efforts (rather than other people's productive efforts) they believe should be distributed to others. But unless we mend our ways, there will be less and less to share.

So, my answer to the title of the last two chapters, 'What's Wrong With Capitalism?' is 'Not a hell of a lot.'

What's wrong is that the system has been distorted and there is a widespread misunderstanding with respect to how the system is supposed to work. Our current system works for some, but many do not benefit to the extent that they should.

Perhaps we could modify the previous quote from John Wesley: *Do not impute to capitalism the faults of human nature.*

Too many people are not benefitting from our current system. But socialism is definitely not the answer as the initial *fairer* distribution of wealth would inevitably result in significantly less wealth for all. I like the old quip: 'Socialism works fine until you run out of other people's money.' And the reason you run out of other people's money is those other people stop creating capital.

Unsurprisingly, Winston Churchill had a great way of explaining capitalism versus socialism: 'The inherent vice of capitalism is the unequal sharing of blessings; the inherent virtue of socialism is the equal sharing of miseries.'

Fix What We Have

So, if socialism isn't the answer, what are we to do? I believe that the best course of action would be to fix our current system. Changing things won't be easy, as so many people have been benefiting from our current distorted system, and others have been benefiting from society's more recent pivot towards socialism. And many of those who are suffering don't realise that these distortions and recent pivot are only making things worse. Unfortunately, there's no way of fixing things without first going through a difficult and uncertain adjustment period. However, there is a way forward but before we discuss that, let's take a quick review of how we got to where we are.

ENDNOTES

[1] Of course, I'm not saying that all situations are like this and as mentioned earlier, there are circumstances in which employees feel they have no choice but to accept suboptimal employment conditions.

[2] Most price controls are price ceilings which limit the ability of companies to raise prices. They usually lead to product shortages.

[3] Tariffs can also cause this although they may be put in place for a number of different reasons.

[4] The BIS definition of a zombie is a company that doesn't make enough money to pay the interest on its debt and has a low equity valuation. They look at companies in 14 developed economies. BIS Working Papers No 882. *Corporate zombies: Anatomy and life cycle*. Ryan Banerjee and Boris Hofmann. September 2020 (revised January 2022).

[5] Josh Bivens and Jori Kandra. *CEO pay has skyrocketed 1,460% since 1978*. Economic Policy Institute. 4 October, 2022.

[6] American Bankruptcy Institute
https://abi-org.s3.amazonaws.com/Newsroom/Bankruptcy_Statistics/QUARTERLY-BUSINESS-1980-PRESENT.pdf.

[7] US Bureau of Labor Statistic: Job Openings and Labor Turnover – 2019
https://www.bls.gov/news.release/archives/jolts_02112020.pdf.

[8] All data from *The Myth of American Inequality: How Government Biases Policy Debate*. Phil Gramm, Robert Ekelund and John Early. Roman & Littlefield. 2022.

CHAPTER 26
HOW WE GOT HERE

The ultimate result of shielding men from the effects of folly is to fill the world with fools.

– Herbert Spencer

Now that we've gone through the basics on money and capital, the economy and markets and differentiated between wealth creation and wealth redistribution, let's go on a quick journey of the last fifty years to see how we got to the precarious situation in which we now find ourselves. What you will see is that, despite the fact that policymakers didn't intend to get us to this point, it's no accident that we now live in a world of record debt, sky-high asset prices, declining productivity growth and record wealth inequality – all of those things leading to anger, frustration and division.

Some Saw It Coming
Economic doctrine based on longer-term second- and third-order consequences of actions, as well as realistic, if unpopular, thinking, long predicted that we would eventually end up in this unholy mess. On the other hand, those who espoused an economic philosophy based solely on short-term immediate effects and a very popular something-for-nothing free-lunch doctrine, by definition, had no way of seeing this coming. Once economic stagnation became too obvious to ignore, rather than revisiting their economic policies to determine whether or not they may have contributed in any way to our economic malaise, they instead looked elsewhere for anything they could find to help explain away any role they may have unintentionally played in making the economy worse.

Some like to blame *global secular stagnation*, which they claim is caused in part by demographics (ageing population), wealth inequality (which they caused – which they don't claim), and, more recently, trade tensions. But in my opinion, this serves only to deflect attention from the real causes that I have outlined in this book.

The bottom line is that, unfortunately, we now find ourselves in a position from which there is quite simply no easy way out.

But there *is* a way out, which we'll get to in the next chapter.

Started With Soft Money?

Some might point out that the treacherous path we are on actually started more than fifty years ago, in 1971, when the United States went off the hard money gold standard and ushered in the free-lunch era of fiat currency. That certainly was a game-changer which, ultimately, enabled much of the reckless behaviour that was to come.

Dual Mandate

Others might point to the Federal Reserve Reform Act of 1977, which gave the Fed a dual mandate to promote maximum employment, stable prices, and moderate long-term interest rates (seems like a treble mandate to me). It's worth spending a little bit of time on this.

Full Employment

First, let's look at the full employment mandate. In my mind, again, it boils down to symptoms versus fundamentals. Providing cheap credit and increasing the money supply to keep people consuming and enable companies with poor business models (zombies) to remain solvent definitely helps with the mandate of maximum employment – in the short term. But due to its negative impact on economic fundamentals via increased consumption and malinvestment, longer-term, maximum employment becomes more difficult to achieve. And if it is achieved, then employment becomes far less productive and, in the extreme case, it's akin to what economist John Maynard Keynes recommended (i.e. have unemployed people dig up bottles full of printed money). Yes, maximum employment, but no contribution to society whatsoever, which means that that new Fed-induced employment would be *taking* from society.

If the Fed were concerned about the quality of employment, then they would want that employment to be productive. That sort of employment is first and foremost produced via free-market forces with skin in the game. And it must happen in an unhampered market system where players use a market-derived interest rate to determine the risk/reward trade-off for potential investments. All that goes out the window with a Fed-distorted interest rate set to a level that will encourage maximum employment. No matter how well-intended, this will always lead to less efficient employment and less capital than otherwise would have been produced, not to mention distorted asset prices.

Stable Prices

Now let's have a look at the second mandate: stable prices. Again, on the surface, it seems to make sense. No one wants runaway inflation. Stable prices would make it much easier for people and businesses to plan for the future. But as discussed, when a market economy is functioning properly through productivity growth and freedom of competition, falling prices, not stable prices, should be the natural order of things. The only reason there is any risk of runaway inflation in the first place is because the Federal Reserve rapidly increases the money supply. So, when the Federal Reserve increases the money supply to maintain stable, rather than falling, prices, they're robbing you of the lower prices from which you should benefit. We've already discussed how the paradox of thrift argument for preventing prices from falling is completely fallacious. Therefore, with the stable prices mandate, you end up paying more for products than you otherwise should.

Moderate Long-Term Interest Rates

Finally, we come to the Fed's responsibility to ensure moderate long-term interest rates. Again, there doesn't appear to be anything sinister in this. However, as we have already discussed, interest rates need to be naturally determined by unhampered market forces with skin in the game so that those interest rates can perform their function of most efficiently allocating capital to its most productive uses. There's no way the Federal Reserve or any other organisation could possibly know what that rate should be. At a particular time, it might need to move higher, based on the collective time preferences of market players; at other times, it might need to move lower.

The obligation of policymakers should not be to question why that rate is what it is, but to ensure it's not manipulated to a level that temporarily benefits one group at the expense of another. Of course, the timing of higher interest rates may come at an extremely inconvenient times for policymakers, corporations or individuals – and this is where the trouble starts. Policymakers believe that they have the ability, and the right, to steer the economy in the direction that they deem best.

I don't think that they have the ability, and I don't believe they should have the right, no matter how well intended they may be.

Somehow, they believe that by forcing people to pay more for consumer products, by encouraging people to spend more and more by taking on more and more debt, and by driving stocks prices and housing prices higher, everyone will be much better off and that, somehow, the benefits of all of this will trickle down to everyone. However, the result has been that people cannot afford to buy as much stuff as they otherwise could have, and there's trillions of dollars of debt outstanding acting like an anchor to prevent people, corporations and countries from moving forward as fast as they should be. And wealth inequality is hitting new highs.

Get Out of the Way

When I look at the Fed's mandate from Congress, I believe that the aims of two aspects of the mandate would, ironically, be achieved much more readily and sustainably by doing the exact opposite of what the Fed currently does to try to comply with its mandate: stop manipulating the money supply. If it were to do that, there would be more efficient allocation of capital and greater productivity and, thus, stronger and higher quality employment. It would likely also lead to lower interest rates by encouraging saving and investment rather than consumption; it would lower society's time preference. It wouldn't result in stable prices, though: prices, in general, would slowly deflate.

The GOAT[1]

So, many of the root causes of today's problems go back a long way. However, after the Fed's mandate changed in 1977, Americans were fortunate they had the greatest central banker in history in charge of the money supply: Paul Volcker. To kill off the high inflation of the 1970s and early 1980s, he took interest rates up towards 20%. This contributed to two severe recessions in the early 1980s, but Volcker was willing to do the right, albeit painful, thing in the short term as it was best for the country in the long-term. A truly courageous central banker.

Goat[2]

However, after Volcker's departure, things started to change, and policymakers became particularly emboldened in their attempts to steer the economy by engineering higher asset prices. This was not in the best long-term interests of the economy, as it hampered its ability to boost its productive capacity or, subsequently, fairly redistribute the wealth created. The focus of the policymakers turned to short-term symptoms rather than long-term fundamentals, and, in my opinion, it was the beginning of the end.

The Birth of the Wealth Effect?

I have already talked about the formation of the Plunge Protection Team in the late 1980s. The next blatant interference with the market process was the New York Federal Reserve helping broker a private bank–sponsored bailout of failing hedge fund Long Term Capital Management in 1998. However, shortly after the deal was announced, stocks started falling again, and so the Federal Reserve quickly lowered interest rates. But they did so not because the economy was weak but to get stock markets moving up again. That set the stage for a stock market melt-up[3] in 1999, with the Nasdaq Composite index rising over 85% that year. The stock markets were nearing the apex of the dot-com bubble, and policymakers believed it was contributing to a wealth effect that was encouraging consumers to borrow more money and spend.

Dot-com

Like many stock market bubbles, the dot-com bubble was based on something that was very real. In this case, it was the dawn of the Internet age. I imagine it's difficult for younger people to comprehend a world without websites, social media platforms and smartphones. But the world was a very different place before all of this, and it was a very exciting time of change.

As usual, people tend to get carried away with the potential of any change when they believe there's money to be made. The frenzy that ensued in the late 1990s was unlike anything anyone had seen since the stock market bubble of the late 1920s.[4] Any company that ended its name with '.com' witnessed its share price driven dramatically higher by speculators who saw a quick way to easy riches – even though many of those speculators had no idea what the company actually did.

Meanwhile, many non-dot-com businesses were largely ignored in the gold rush mentality of the late 1990s. Their share prices languished far behind the stocks of the *new economy* companies. If you had listed your bike company on the stock market in the late 1990s you likely wouldn't have received a very high price for your shares, because a bike company wouldn't have sounded very exciting. However, if you had changed the name to 'Bikes.com', your share price would have gone through the roof.

While Alan Greenspan, the head of the Federal Reserve at the time, was initially concerned about 'irrational exuberance' in the stock market, he eventually convinced himself that productivity improvements justified high stock prices. He also stated that it was impossible to know when the stock market was fairly valued and, thus, that no one could know if the market was in bubble territory. (As we'll soon see, when markets crashed, he apparently *was* able to discern fair value.)

Pop

The dot-com bubble popped in early 2000. Over the next two and a half years, stock markets fell approximately 50%. The tech-heavy Nasdaq Composite index fell 78%, and the S&P 500 fell 49%. As discussed in earlier chapters, when stock prices are rising because of speculation rather than actual productivity, then no net wealth is being created in the market system. Instead, it's simply being redistributed within it. Again, this is similar to what happens in a casino, the only difference being that at a casino, you know very quickly when you are losing – you see your money leaving your pocket, and unless your luck changes, you don't expect to get that money back.

When stocks come crashing down like they did during the Tech Wreck of 2000–2002, no real wealth disappeared, just as there was no real wealth created when the stocks were being driven higher through speculation. It was simply a redistribution of wealth from those who bought stocks to those who sold them.

Origins of the Crash by Roger Lowenstein is a good account of the dot-com bubble. Here are two quotations from that book:

> By the late 1990s, America had become more sensitive to markets, more *ruled* by markets, than any country on earth.[5]

> But it is in the nature of people to ascribe a permanence to the latest trend, no matter how numerous the previous trends that have since collapsed.[6]

The first quotation supports my belief that policymakers had become inordinately influenced by what was going on in stock markets and would, thus, set interest rates that were more beneficial to asset prices than the general economy. They did this because they convinced themselves that higher asset prices would eventually be good for the economy.

The second quotation really speaks to human nature, particularly during bull markets. If you are benefiting from a trend like this, it can be very alluring and intoxicating. And it can be very easy to rationalise why it's the new normal and will go on forever: some people call this view 'hopium'. Of course, the beneficiaries claim that the naysayers just don't get it or that they are resentful because they have not been benefiting from the irrational frenzy. To them, it's just a case of sour grapes on the part of the critics.

Wasted Opportunity

The popping of the dot-com bubble provided a real opportunity to return to a market system of real wealth being created through hard work and longer-term investment in productivity improvements, as well as a fairer distribution of that real wealth (based on the contributions of those creating that wealth: workers, investors, entrepreneurs). However, in response to the plummeting stock market, the Federal Reserve slashed interest rates to near-record lows. It seems that although central bankers believed investors know best in valuing stocks when markets were soaring, it was a different story when markets were falling. Policymakers have convinced themselves that investors value stocks accurately in a bubble but undervalue them in a crash.

Double Down

The wasted opportunity to return to a fairer system was bad enough. Instead, the Federal Reserve made things even worse by doubling down on their short-term, trickle-down stock market wealth effect doctrine by driving housing prices higher, too. Housing became the tool of choice to encourage consumers to embark on even more debt-driven consumption. Policymakers drove house prices higher in an attempt to drive higher aggregate demand (final spending), which policymakers continued to believe was the magic elixir for economic prosperity.

After a very mild recession in 2001, the Federal Reserve kept interest at a ridiculously low level of 1% for another two years, despite the fact that the economy had resumed its growth path. Before this period, seeing interest rates as low as 1%, one would have assumed that the economy was in recession – or even depression. However, during this period, interest rates were at 'emergency' levels, but not because the economy was in trouble. Instead, rates were on the floor because central banks had decided to take a much more aggressive approach in interfering with the decisions of market players (stocks and housing) with skin in the game.

Government agencies like Fannie Mae and Freddie Mac did their part for the housing bubble by lowering their lending standards (effectively putting taxpayers on the hook for more and more mortgages that were unlikely to be paid back). And Wall Street also joined the fray by packaging up higher-risk mortgages and selling them to the government agencies.

Housing Boom

Many of you will remember the euphoria of the housing boom in the early to mid-2000s. Like most booms, it seemed like it would go on forever. It seemed that way because so many people on TV were telling you that it would continue indefinitely. Policymakers stated that house prices were rising so quickly because it was a reflection of how healthy the US economy was. Ben Bernanke, who would soon be appointed as the new head of the Federal Reserve, had this to say in October 2005:

> House prices have risen by nearly 25 per cent over the past two years. Although speculative activity has increased in some areas, at a national level these price increases largely reflect strong economic fundamentals, including robust growth in jobs and incomes, low mortgage rates, steady rates of household formation, and factors that limit the expansion of housing supply in some areas.[7]

As I have discussed, there is no reason for a strong economy to drive house prices higher. A strong economy that is producing more capital builds more houses. And as we previously discussed, a house is not a productive asset. Also, if people were actually producing more capital and could then afford to purchase rather than rent, you would expect to see rental prices in the US fall, but they didn't; they actually went up in 2006. And there have been plenty of periods of economic growth in the US that were far stronger than the period from 2001 to 2006, yet those periods didn't result in housing bubbles. And, finally, the six-year housing bubble did not occur during a period of particularly strong economic growth. In fact, 2000–2006 was one of the slowest six-year periods of economic growth in real terms since the late 1940s.

Six-year growth rate in US real GDP:[8]

- 1947 to 1999 average: 23% (3.5% per year)
- 2000 to 2006:   16% (2.5% per year)

But the mania was not restricted to the United States. Countries such as the UK (Bank of England), Ireland and Spain (European Central Bank) also continued reducing rates into 2003, setting off their own housing bubbles. Also through something called the carry-trade, investors could borrow in low interest rate countries, convert that money into US dollars, and then use that to drive up asset prices in the US.

It's Working!

As per usual, at first, it appeared that the central bank strategy for boosting the economy was working. People increasingly borrowed more money. The higher the prices of their homes would rise, the more those homeowners would borrow, using their homes as collateral. Homeowners would spend this borrowed money, thus boosting GDP. Complacency sets in the longer bubbles continue, and more and more people start to believe they will never end; thus, people will take on more and more risk to make more and more money. Euphoria took root as everyone was making out like bandits. They were receiving wealth without creating it and, ultimately, receiving it at the expense of others rather than through mutual benefit. Homeowners saw the values of their homes soar, and that allowed them to buy more and more stuff.

Banks lowered their lending standards and increased their exposure to subprime loans (loans made to people who are considered a higher risk based on their ability to pay the loan back). Because of the higher risk to banks, they charged subprime borrowers a higher rate of interest and, thus, made more money from the borrower (that is, as long as the borrower paid the money back).

Blamestorming

But of course, the party couldn't last. Trees don't grow to the sky. By 2008, the whole housing edifice came crashing down, bringing stock markets down with it. Some people blamed greedy Wall Street, which had, no doubt, played a significant role by taking on more and more risk with more and more debt. Others blamed the US government for not bailing out Lehman Brothers, a large investment bank that had got into financial trouble and gone bankrupt. Still others blamed policymakers for steadily reducing regulation over the financial services industry by getting rid of some rules that had been put in place in the 1930s – rules that were established to prevent another Great Depression. Capitalism was also blamed for the crisis.

However, my opinion is that the Federal Reserve had set the stage and conditions for all of this to happen. They kept interest rates far too low for far too long and encouraged the very type of high risk–taking behaviour that was so successfully driving house prices and stock markets higher and, thus, creating a wealth effect that was contributing to GDP growth.

Until it didn't.

The ensuing collapse in the US economy was the largest since the Great Depression of the 1930s. Housing prices collapsed, leaving many homeowners in the unenviable position of owing more on their mortgage than their house was worth. The sudden downturn in asset prices threatened to drive some of the largest banks in the world into bankruptcy. Some people were fearful that the whole financial system would implode.

Contained

While there were many people to blame for the housing crisis, this couldn't have happened had the Federal Reserve not established the conditions for it to happen. The Fed also encouraged the sort of housing bubble mentality that they believed was doing so much good for the economy. When questioned about the risks of such a policy, the central bank denied that there was any risk of a nationwide decline in housing prices and that any potential damage resulting from the riskiest mortgages (subprime) would likely be 'contained'.

Taxpayers to the Rescue

However, the US did experience a nationwide decline in house price, and the impact from subprime mortgages was not contained. Once the crisis hit, the Federal Reserve enacted a cornucopia of bailouts in an attempt to save the financial system. Through the Federal Reserve and the Treasury, American taxpayers bailed out many institutions and individuals who didn't deserve to be bailed out. For years, many people and corporations had made millions, or billions, of dollars, and as soon as they got into trouble, the rest of the country – those who hadn't made millions or billions of dollars – had to come to the rescue. Some argue that, at that moment in time, the Federal Reserve didn't have any choice. And, as distasteful as it was to bail out Wall Street, it needed to be done to save the financial system. I have my suspicions about whether or not it was necessary. I believe that, to a large extent, it was just as much about bailing out reputations, but, of course, that's an unprovable counterfactual – it's impossible to know what would have happened had Wall Street not been bailed out.

My Fix

In my opinion, any financial institution that was technically bankrupt at that time should have been nationalised. Shareholders would have been wiped out and bondholders would have taken significant haircuts on their bonds. People who had their savings deposited in those banks would have had up to $100,000 of their savings protected by the Federal Deposit Insurance Corporation (FDIC). The FDIC charges banks an annual fee and keeps those funds as a sort of insurance policy for the banks in case they go bankrupt. However, if too many banks go bankrupt at once and the FDIC doesn't have enough money to protect the savings of all of the depositors in those banks, then the FDIC can borrow money from the government – which means that part of the cost would, ultimately, have come at the expense of taxpayers.[9]

Once nationalised, senior management of those companies should have been fired. The rest of the employees and management would have retained their jobs and continued to run the businesses. At the same time, the government should have injected enough capital into the banks to make them solvent (but not enough to repay the obligations of those financial institutions to other banks, such as the backdoor bailout of Goldman Sachs through AIG).[10] In this way, the banking system would not have collapsed, particularly with people knowing it had the backing of the US government (taxpayers).

After, say, five years, the banks should have been broken up into separate, smaller entities – similarly to what was done during the Great Depression –

and then re-privatised. The whole process would, no doubt, have been very painful, but it would have created a much stronger and fairer foundation for the next growth phase of the US and global economy. The rallying cry from government should have been 'We're now all in this together, and we'll never again allow Wall Street banks to get so big that they threaten to hold taxpayers hostage for more bailouts after having previously made billions of dollars!'

Conflict of Interest

Of course, Wall Street and central bankers who were in charge at the time would have come up with every reason they could think of as to why nationalising the insolvent banks wouldn't have worked. However, it makes no sense to listen to anyone's opinion about how public money should be spent when those people would be the prime beneficiaries of such actions. Others would argue that these people were the smartest in the land and were, therefore, indispensable for getting the world out of the financial mess in which it had found itself. However, given that they were the ones who had caused the crisis in the first place, that should have given politicians some pause in seeking advice from them.

Naturally, Wall Street would tell you that bailing them out was for your own good. They'd also remind politicians that the 401(k)s (retirement accounts) of the average taxpayer would have taken a significant hit had taxpayer dollars not been used to bail out Wall Street and get stock prices moving higher again. And, not surprisingly, the Federal Reserve didn't need much convincing that they needed to take extraordinary measures to effectively bail themselves out of their failed housing wealth effect experiment.

In my opinion, during the depths of the Global Financial Crisis, there were more than just the two options of 'bailout or Armageddon' available to policymakers. However, when bailouts save the wealth of Wall Street and the reputations of central bankers, and politicians were generally reliant on them for answers, it's not surprising that Washington went the bailout route. This is what made the false dichotomy of 'bailout or Armageddon' so readily accepted and, indeed, welcomed by so many.

Rational Behaviour

When people are bailed out of making risky bets that have failed, it results in the moral hazard that we talked about earlier. If people know that someone else will bear the cost of a failed bet, then those people will make larger and riskier bets. Imagine if you went to Las Vegas and knew that no matter how much money you lost, you wouldn't be required to pay up, as the bill would be passed on to someone else. The rational thing for you to do in that scenario would be to make the biggest bets you could on the things that had the highest odds. That way, you could make the most amount of money in the shortest time. If you got lucky, you would walk away wealthy. If you were unlucky, someone else would foot the bill.

For years, Wall Street was making very large and risky bets. This resulted in billions of dollars being paid out in the form of bonuses. However, when they and the Fed blew up the world's financial system, hundreds of billions of taxpayer dollars were used to cover the banks' losses. But the bankers got to keep their previous winnings.

Excuses

Some people advised against bailing out Wall Street because of the moral hazard issues such a measure would engender, but, of course, anyone who stood to benefit from the bailouts warned that 'this was no time to worry about moral hazard' (you might as well say that this is no time to worry about property rights or free speech). However, by definition, the time to worry about moral hazard will always be when things have gone wrong and someone will undoubtedly suffer the consequences of their own actions. Yes, there undoubtedly would have been innocent people who would also have felt the effects of Wall Street not being bailed out (that contagion we talked about earlier), but that's where government can and should have been ready to step in with assistance for them with taxpayer dollars.

The government directly bailed out Wall Street, thus creating massive moral hazard, which contributed mightily to the current precarious situation in which we find ourselves fifteen years later. Supporters of the bailouts will point to their eventual low cost, but this resulted only because the Federal Reserve reverted to the most reckless monetary policy in its history. They drove the prices of most assets in the financial system higher so that the government losses were reduced. However, this came at the enormous expense of extracting wealth from savers and pensioners, harming the productive capacity of the economy and creating a world of debt serfs. And it was directly responsible for the obscene levels of wealth disparity we're currently experiencing. As you would expect, this is leading to a sort of class war between those who unfairly benefit from these policies and those who unfairly pay for them. Naturally, there are many people who are angry at this situation. But it wasn't caused by capitalism.

One and Done
To be sure, these were scary times, and swift action needed to be taken. A taxpayer bailout for banks that were truly suffering from a liquidity crisis could have been entirely justified. But not for insolvent institutions. It would have given one hope had the Fed admitted their role in establishing the conditions for the catastrophe and committed to never going down that path again. Wall Street would then know that they would never again be allowed to get to the place where they could hold the world hostage for a taxpayer bailout.

If At Second You Don't Succeed
Instead, after doubling down on their wealth effect stock bubble of the late 1990s that ended in disaster – leading to an even more disastrous housing crisis – the Federal Reserve *tripled* down on what is now known as the 'everything bubble'. The main tools used to create the everything bubble were zero interest rates and quantitative easing. I can understand to a degree why some felt that the first round of QE was justified, but there can be absolutely no excuse for the trillions of dollars that were printed through subsequent rounds of QE when there was no emergency – financial, economic, geopolitical or otherwise.

Lost Opportunity
Once the financial system had settled down in the aftermath of the Global Financial Crisis, it was the chance of a lifetime to return to a fairer market system where what one earns is a reflection of what one has contributed. Instead, we went the opposite way, and each time the stock market showed signs of slowing or reversing as the sugar highs from money printing started to wear off, the Federal Reserve instituted another round of QE to keep the party going.

How we got here really comes down to human nature and the willingness of policymakers to delude themselves about what really makes an economy grow. They delude themselves because that allows them to avoid making unpopular decisions. It allows them to continue being heroes with other people's capital and convincing the populace that you can have your cake and eat it, too – and that deficits and debt don't matter.

The Blobs

Then we find the virtue that possession would not show us.
— William Shakespeare

As mentioned, both government and finance don't produce anything themselves. They are meant to facilitate market players with skin in the game who can drive the economy forward. For many years, it worked very well (if not perfectly); indeed, if it's working properly, then the roles played by government and finance are hardly noticed. It's sort of like officiating in professional sports. If the referee or umpire has a great game, it's almost like they're not even there. It's only when they start making bad calls and influencing the outcome of the game that they get noticed. We never knew how good we had it and slowly but surely, over the last few decades, both government and finance have exploded as a per centage of the total economy. And they are strangling its productive capabilities. This is the reason why economic growth is stalling. This is the cause of the global secular stagnation.

Eyes Opening?

We got here by policymakers believing in something-for-nothing economic doctrine, by relying on complex mathematical formulas that take themselves and others ever further from the truth. And it's easier to believe, because the process of printing money very visibly drives asset prices higher in the short term, enriching some. Whereas the consequences, and where the capital actually comes from to make that happen, are less clear or further down the road.

While it's often said that the people always get the government they deserve[11], that can only be true if the people know what's actually going on. Many have benefited from this charade, but most have suffered. And the maths is becoming increasingly obvious, to the point that many policymakers are beginning to understand that the path we're on is not only unsustainable but also terribly unfair. In the final chapter, we'll look at the path that I believe will lead to the least painful fix for the past decades of fallacious economic doctrine.

ENDNOTES

[1] Greatest Of All Time.
[2] Goat: A farm animal often associated with stubbornness.
[3] A melt-up is a rapid surge in asset prices usually from already very high prices or valuations.
[4] The Nifty Fifty craze of the late 1960s and early 1970s was also nuts.
[5] *Origins of the Crash*, Roger Lowenstein, 2004. Chapter 1, p. 3.
[6] *Origins of the Crash*, Roger Lowenstein, 2004. Chapter 5, p. 98.
[7] Council of Economic Advisors. *The Economic Outlook*. By Ben S. Bernanke. Chairman, President's Council of Economic Advisors. 20 October 2005.
[8] Federal Reserve of St. Louis.
[9] In 2008, the amount of savings guaranteed by the FDIC was *temporarily* increased to $250,000 but that figure was then made permanent in 2010. This higher level of insurance allows banks to take on even more risk (and make even more money) without savers questioning the riskiness of the bets being made with their deposits..
[10] AIG is a large insurance company that had started dealing in all kinds of risky financial instruments. They were effectively bankrupt during the GFC and owed billions of dollars to other financial institutions. Policymakers used taxpayer dollars to provide AIG with billions of dollars so AIG could then, in turn, pay billions of dollars to all of those financial institutions who had made reckless bets with them.
[11] Thomas Jefferson: 'The government you elect is the government you deserve.' Joseph de Maistre: 'Each country has the government it deserves.' I suppose one could argue that the majority gets the government they deserve while the minority doesn't. Of course, this doesn't mean that what the minority wants wouldn't be worse. And as there are times when there are poor voter turnouts, a party can win power with a minority of the population's vote.

CHAPTER 27

HOW DO WE FIX THINGS?

While it won't be easy, we most certainly can fix our economy, and I believe the fix would result in the following:

- A fair system where one's wealth is more representative of one's contributions to society.
- Lesser wealth disparity.
- Lower levels of debt, particularly that of government.
- Greater productivity growth.
- Affordable housing.
- A persistent increase in the real wages of workers.

I truly believe all of this is possible, but it will all start only once we demand that policymakers start focusing on longer-term fundamentals instead of shorter-term symptoms.

Here is my ten-step solution.[1]

1. Stop Rapidly Increasing the Money Supply

The first step on the road to healing, prosperity, fairness and freedom would be to stop increasing the money supply at such high rates. Whether it would be better for the money supply to remain stable or increase very slowly I really couldn't say, but either scenario would be a significant improvement on what we have been experiencing for many decades.

This would result in the elimination of price inflation and would, instead, likely lead to good price deflation for many things. Thus, even if your income were to never increase, you would become wealthier each year as your stable earnings or pension would buy more and more stuff each year.

I believe that this first step is probably the most important one, as it leads to so many positive things. Here is Howard Buffett, former member of Congress and father of famed investor Warren Buffett, talking about the benefits of a hard currency:

But when you recall that one of the first moves by Lenin, Mussolini and Hitler was to outlaw individual ownership of gold, you begin to sense that there may be some connection between money, redeemable in gold, and the rare prize known as human liberty.

Also, when you find that Lenin declared and demonstrated that a sure way to overturn the existing social order and bring about communism was by printing press paper money, then again you are impressed with the possibility of a relationship between a gold-backed money and human freedom.

The gold standard acted as a silent watchdog to prevent unlimited public spending.

But, unless you are willing to surrender your children and your country to galloping inflation, war and slavery, then this cause demands your support. For if human liberty is to survive in America, we must win the battle to restore honest money. There is no more important challenge facing us than this issue – the restoration of your freedom to secure gold in exchange for the fruits of your labors.[2]

2. Let Interest Rates Be Determined by Market Forces

The next step on the road to a fair society would be for central banks to stop distorting the most important price in the world: interest rates. Allowing interest rates to be determined by the natural rate and not the neutral rate would return the economy to the levels of productivity growth it enjoyed back in the days before the US abandoned the gold standard in 1971.

This would also make housing more affordable and allow the younger generation to enjoy the same housing opportunities this and previous generations did. Of course, more affordable housing means prices declining to fair value, and this would be tough for recent first-time home buyers. For them, and only them, a temporary government (taxpayer) programme could be put in place to help them out if they suffer a loss when they sell their home.

Perhaps this assistance could be funded with a 10% tax on the enormous gains my generation enjoys when we sell our principal residence.[3] But the tax needs to be small, as many people are relying on the equity in their home to fund their retirement. Even though this money was not earned, I still don't think it's fair to put in place a policy that significantly detracts from the financial security of those nearing retirement. But the proceeds of this 10% tax would need to be ringfenced from other government revenue and earmarked specifically for those first-time home buyers who suffer a loss through no fault of their own. (And once the programme was announced, it would only apply to people who had bought a home prior to the announcement.)

Anyway, this is just one idea. And, of course, it would be subject to abuse. Strict rules and regulations would need to be in place. I'm sure there are other ways of dealing with the consequences of falling home prices for first time homebuyers. However, while most people will still have made a bundle on their homes, even with prices declining, some would lose out, and they would need to be helped.

3. No More Bailouts

A third step on the road to recovery would be to stop using taxpayer dollars to bail out financial institutions, or any other institution for that matter, that get into trouble due to mismanagement. Companies that fail are destroyers of capital. The longer they are kept alive in zombie form by the state, the more capital that gets consumed instead of invested. This would be painful in the short term, as basket-case companies that fail would need to lay off their employees. But in the long run, those employees will end up at productive businesses that contribute to the economy. Sustainable employment that doesn't come at the expense of the rest of society should be the goal.

4. Stop Manipulating Stock Markets Higher

Fourth would be to ensure stock market prices are determined by the price discovery mechanism of free market participants with skin in the game – not by an implicit or explicit central bank backstop. This will have a significant impact on reducing wealth inequality and increasing the productive capacity of the economy.

5. Shrink the Financial Sector

Fifth, Wall Street needs to shrink as a per centage of the economy. A lot of what Wall Street does is crucial for a thriving economy, but a lot of what it does isn't. In fact, parts of it are becoming a drag on economic activity. Reducing Wall Street's footprint would not only remove a significant weight off the economy's back, but it would also release many very bright people into the real economy to start making real contributions.

Wall Street should not be forced by policymakers to shrink. However, if policymakers were to implement the first four steps, Step 5 would happen all on its own – and fairly quickly.

6. Shrink Government

Sixth would be shrinking the government in terms of the number of civil servants and cutting spending so that the government runs a balanced budget. This would not necessarily require government workers to be laid off; but it might, as the size of government has grown so rapidly since COVID. But, hopefully, most of the shrinking of government could be done by not hiring new workers when existing government employees retire. Perhaps we could even get to the point where the government is running budget surpluses. But one step at a time. A balanced budget would steadily reduce the country's debt over time.

As I mentioned earlier, government is extremely important. I'm a believer in the welfare state for those who really need help: the sick, temporarily unemployed, those in need. But taxpayers should only be expected to temporarily fund able-bodied people to stay at home. Of course, at times, no matter how hard one might try, it may be extremely difficult to find a job. There should always be a minimum level of taxpayer support, but that support should not be at a level which disincentivizes work.

One could easily make the case that people live more fulfilled lives when they are working and, thus, know they are making contributions to society, and are not living their lives at the expense of others. However, it's not for others to tell people they should live more fulfilled lives, and perhaps a lot of people don't even care. But we all have something to say about enabling it when we're the ones funding it.

Regardless, despite all of the important things governments do, they are far too large. They need to shrink. This is not about demonising anyone. While government employees do tend to have far greater job security and more generous pension plans than the average private worker, I don't think it makes sense to reduce those benefits, particularly for older workers. Government workers, like private workers, have played by the rules and have planned their retirement finances accordingly.

I don't think it's the case that government worker pensions need to shrink. But rather private pensions that need to increase. Policies should be put in place to encourage companies to offer employees defined benefit programmes rather than defined contribution plans.

As mentioned in the second chapter on Government, current government workers and retirees should realise that unless government starts shrinking as a per centage of the economy, their own pensions will not be affordable. Meaning they eventually *will* be reduced. In fact, a lot of the future benefits for the populace that governments are promising are not affordable and, therefore, will not be paid in full. And it's no use getting upset about it; the maths simply doesn't work. For instance, according to the Social Security Board of Trustees, by 2035 the combined Social Security and Disability insurance fund in the US will be insolvent. This would require a 17% cut in benefits.[4]

The problem is that, understandably, no politician is willing to deal with the situation – and for obvious reasons. If they told people that their benefits needed to be cut, or contributions increased, or that people needed to work a few years longer, that wouldn't go down very well with voters and their chances during the next election would suffer. This is particularly so when other politicians are out there telling people it's all affordable.

It's not. Those are the facts.

But it's much easier to kick the can down the road and make it someone else's problem long into the future. But the day is getting closer when we won't be able to kick the can any further, and the longer we put off dealing with the problem, the worse things will get.

7. Reduce Central Planning

Seventh, related to number six, governments should expunge from their minds the idea that they should be doing *anything* to stimulate the economy to achieve a higher rate of economic growth, other than through things like reasonable unemployment insurance. The government has a very important role to play in *facilitating* economic prosperity, ensuring our safety from foreign nations (the armed forces), safety from nutcases (the police and border security), the veracity of contract law (the courts), working with other nations in areas such as lowering tariffs and encouraging free trade. The very important role of welfare for those in need should be viewed as a humanitarian function and not as a means of juicing the economy, for example, via stimulus cheques. Government stimulus results in a short-term increase in spending, but it does that at the longer-term expense of the productive capacity of the economy.

8. Reduce Taxes
Eighth, and also related to number six, is lowering taxes and fees of all kinds. This should be done steadily and relentlessly over time. I have no idea what the ultimate and optimal level of taxation should be, but it's certainly a lot lower than it is today.

9. Reduce Regulations and Bureaucracy
Ninth is reducing regulations and as much bureaucracy and government red tape as possible. This is another tough one, as many government employees rely on the continuance of all of this to justify their careers, and many will fight to maintain things as they are. If we were in their shoes, we would do the same thing, so I'm sympathetic. Don't get me wrong. I am a believer in appropriate regulation, but the number of rules and regulations currently in place are strangling the economy and holding it back from achieving its true potential – a potential that is a result of entrepreneurial spirit, saving, investment, hard work, honesty, trial and error, all on an infrastructure of government-enforced defence of property rights, rule of law, appropriate regulation and freedom.

10. Stop Believing in the Something-For-Nothing Myth
For far too long, far too many people have been propagating the free-lunch doctrine. Why they do this I'm not sure. Whether they are envious of others who are successful or they attempt to bend the laws of economics to how they wish things were rather than how they really are, I couldn't say. But we need to stop giving airtime to people who have no desire to fix things but, instead, are hell-bent on preserving their cherished something-for-nothing fantasy. Some of these people respond very badly when confronted with a reality that threatens their 'Everyone-gets-a-pony' land of make-believe. They will sometimes resort to ad hominem attacks – attacking you rather than your doctrine.

A silly example to illustrate:

> You are on a stage explaining the importance of a hard currency and natural interest rates to a something-for-nothinger (SFN). Rather

than carefully listening to you to understand what you have to say, they start getting increasingly angry with you. As you're explaining that we can't consume our way to riches, the SFN interrupts you.
SFN: I heard that you like broccoli.
You: I'm not sure of the relevance of my liking broccoli to a free and fair world, but, yeah, I do like broccoli.
SFN: Do you know who else liked broccoli?
You: Who?
SFN: Hitler.
The crowd gasps. They begin to wonder what else you and Hitler might have in common. (And they're all secretly relieved that nobody knows that they also like broccoli.)

An ad hominem approach is a form of intellectual dishonesty. It is a very strong and mean-spirited attack on someone. It is the lowest, basest form of argument and it signifies weakness, a lack of character, insecurity and arrogance. You should avoid listening to people who deploy such arguments, as the only welfare they're interested in is their own.

> *The aim of argument or discussion should not be victory but progress.*
> *– Joseph Joubert*

The something-for-nothing crowd are not all like this. Many of them are very polite. Regardless, we all need to stop deluding ourselves about free lunches. They don't exist. If you receive something for free, someone else paid for it.

Wrapping Things Up
So, there you have it. My prescription for what ails us. Of course, none of these measures will be easy to execute, and many will meet with stiff resistance from those who have a vested interest in seeing things continue as they are. But I believe that this medicine will set the economy and society onto a path of fairness and prosperity. Once we stop deluding ourselves about the short-term, something-for-nothing mentality that has increasingly pervaded society for so long, the necessary steps will be much easier. And they will act – if you will – as a spoonful of sugar.

The time is always right to do what is right.

— Martin Luther King, Jr.

Unfortunately, as long as there are people of influence out there who believe that spending is what leads to economic prosperity; that house prices and stock prices artificially driven higher by policymakers is good for the economy; that using taxpayer dollars to bail out basket-case companies to temporarily save jobs is sound economic doctrine; and that inflation is not caused by a rapid increase in the money supply and, regardless, is good for the economy, it will be extremely difficult to effect change. This is particularly so when many of those who have the power to allow this to happen would suffer a significant reduction in wealth if they did the right thing. This makes it even more difficult to convince policymakers that the policies that they have personally been benefiting from are so destructive and unfair for so many people. It's natural that many of them fall victim to the easy-way-out economic doctrines from the we-can-have-our-cake-and-eat-it-too gang. I believe that there are many politicians out there with the courage to act and do the right thing, but I don't think it will happen unless the people first demand it.

I have great faith in humanity, and I believe that if people are given a straight bill of goods by policymakers, then most people will vote to do the right thing. They're not stupid. However, it's hard for people to make sense of what's truly troubling the world when so many authoritative people seem to be trying to deflect attention from the real problems. It could be that policymakers don't want to have to make the right, but unpopular, decisions. Or they don't want to see people suffer from the steps that must be taken.

Whatever the reasons, it makes no sense to get angry at the economics or the maths of it all, because it is what it is. Some have likened it to getting angry at the law of gravity or making claims that gravity has been unfairly targeting minorities. That is obviously nonsensical, but no more nonsensical than believing in the something-for-nothing myth. Too many people have been sticking their heads in the sand for far too long. Although things continue to worsen, it's not too late to act.

Unfortunately, there is no way of avoiding the pain and loss of wealth for many in society, as prices of stocks and houses would need to fall to their natural levels. I know that it's small solace knowing that much of the wealth that would be lost was obtained without having creating it and was, thus, not earned or deserved. If there were a better way of fixing things, then I'd be all for it. But beware of those giving you easy solutions, because there aren't any. We've had decades of so-called 'easy fixes' that have made policymakers and academics popular. But those things were what got us into this mess.

For instance, as discussed in the chapter on housing, my wife and I have benefited tremendously with the value of our house quadrupling since we bought it. If the value of our home was halved, our net wealth would suffer, but we didn't deserve that wealth – we did nothing to earn it.

Allowing prices to return to their natural level is an unavoidable step in returning some of the unearned wealth back to those who have been paying for it. But remember that if we do take this path, while it's true that your asset wealth would be lower, the prices of the things you would eventually buy with that asset wealth will also be lower. Not only that, but your earnings and savings would be worth more.

Policymakers need to be brave and stop leading us down the primrose path. Of course, it's much easier to talk about doing these things than being the one responsible for taking action. And when the consequences of the necessary actions start to rear their ugly heads, it will be very tempting for policymakers to reverse course.

> *No plan survives contact with the enemy.*[5]
> – Helmuth von Moltke

Therefore, it's crucial that policymakers have our unstinting support. Importantly, we must all be in this together. Given those conditions, I think that this ten-point plan would get us to where we need to be.

ENDNOTES

[1] It just so happens to be ten. I say that because I'm always suspicious when I see nice round numbers like that. I get the sense that the person came up with a couple more ideas just to hit a pre-set target rather than that those ideas are very helpful.

[2] 'Human Freedom Rests on Gold Redeemable Money'. *The Commercial and Financial Chronicle*. 6 May 1948, Vol. 167, No. 4696.

[3] Maybe it's only on gains over and above a certain amount e.g. $1 million.
[4] Social Security Press Office. *Strong Economy, Low Unemployment, and Higher Job and Wage Growth Extend Social Security Trust Funds to 2035*. Mark Hinkle, Press Officer. Monday 6 May 2024. https://www.ssa.gov/news/press/releases/2024/#5-2024-1
[5] Boxer Mike Tyson famously said that 'Everyone has a plan until they get punched in the mouth.'

CONCLUSION

Correct Diagnosis

In my opinion, the disease from which we currently suffer is not capitalism, but a short-term, 'free-lunch,' delusional, bailout mentality that has pervaded Wall Street and policymakers for far too long. Some refer to it as cronyism and this is the disease that needs curing. Socialists are right to be angry, but abandoning the concept of free-market economics because cronyism is suffocating capitalism would be a big mistake.

Disease Symptoms

The disease that needs curing is central banks interfering with interest rates and exploding the money supply higher, which have the effect of:

- Driving asset prices higher and redistributing wealth within society.
  - Creating housing affordability crises.
  - Widening wealth disparity.
- Enabling reckless spending by governments.
- Bailing out poor decisions by Wall Street; thus, they privatise their profits and socialise their losses.
- Creating moral hazard, giving rise to even more reckless speculation.
- Sustaining zombie companies that suck the lifeblood out of an economy.

Already Failed

I've heard some people say that policymakers can't allow the stock market or the housing market to fail – that they can't allow prices to fall. However, both markets have already failed. The stock market used to be a very efficient tool for allocating scarce resources within the economy, which contributed to strong productivity growth for many decades. For years, a family earning an average income could expect to be able to afford a home in which they could raise a family. However, due to policymakers manipulating prices of both stocks and houses higher, both markets have failed. The stock market is failing the economy, and the housing market is failing young families.

Race to the Bottom

The obscene wealth obtained by some by driving asset prices higher is more like the spoils of a distorted economic system. However, under socialism, the wealth-producing capacity of the economy would be significantly impaired and although we might all end up more equal in terms of wealth under socialism, no matter who you are, your wealth would eventually be a fraction of what it is now. A socialist system would be devastating in its impact on innovation and progress.

Much better would be to fix our current system, which will not be easy as there are some who would suffer in so doing. But the overwhelming majority would benefit, particularly over time. Doing the right thing would certainly not be easy, but policies could be put in place to help those with real losses. As long as there's a sense of us all being in this together, I do believe that we could revert to a system that is not only significantly fairer but that also leads to even greater wealth creation.

Policymakers' inability, or unwillingness, to understand the economic consequences of their actions; their fear of being blamed for what happens if they do the right thing; their belief that you truly can get something for nothing; and their belief that the benefits will eventually trickle down to everyone are taking us down a treacherous path.

The Road to Hell

As mentioned at the beginning of the book, 'The road to hell is paved with good intentions.' Some people may feel that that destination has already been reached. However, as Winston Churchill once said, 'If you're going through hell, keep going.' As long as you don't give up, you'll eventually come out the other side. I firmly believe that we will come out the other side of this divisive and unfair situation.

However, as long as policymakers remain on the current path, society will be burdened with ever-larger piles of debt, productivity growth will continue to grind lower and eventually turn negative, wealth disparity will get even worse, and society will become increasingly divided.

Some point to the slowing growth in the global economy as something that came out of left field.

It didn't.

It's a result of decades of bad policy.

You're the One Paddling

The more that the facilitators take, the harder the real economy has to work to keep the whole thing growing. In the words of the former head of Canada's central bank, Steven Poloz, 'We're steering the ship, we're not paddling.'[1] And while he meant that in a different context, I think it's an apt description of what's been going on in earnest for the last few decades. Government and Wall Street continue to grow as a per centage of the economy, making the economic boat heavier and heavier. There are more and more facilitators up on the bridge steering the ship (not producing anything), and fewer and fewer people down in the engine room working their butts off to keep the ship moving (making all the contributions). Our economic ship is becoming top-heavy and is in danger of capsizing.

There's Still Time

So far, we're at a point where we can still grow, albeit at a much slower pace than we should be. This is the unseen wealth you would have had, and because it's unseen, it makes it easier for policymakers to convince you (and themselves) that they're not to blame for the precarious situation in which we find ourselves.

Government welfare programmes are important, but they must be funded solely through taxation, not through borrowing from the future (the next generation) or extracting capital from people's savings by printing money. Policymakers also need to stop trying to manage the economy by taking your money and giving it to others to consume to achieve a level of final spending that they believe is appropriate for the economy.

Play by the Rules

They'll point to examples of how unfettered capitalism brought the world to its knees. The Great Depression. The Global Financial Crisis. How governments and central banks are there to protect the world from reckless behaviour by capitalists. Yet, both of those economic disasters were caused by governments and central banks creating the very conditions needed for that reckless behaviour to occur. By turning a blind eye to rules of engagement being broken; by reducing regulation that had been put in place to protect against the consequences of rampant speculation spilling over into the broader economy; by reducing interest rates to allow for monumental debt accumulation by governments, corporations and individuals to keep spending going; by increasing the money supply, which erodes the productive capacity of the economy; and then by bailing out the bad behaviour that all of these actions engendered, policymakers have unwittingly sent the world on a path toward economic stagnation.

Whatever it Takes

Due to their short-term focus and their desire to be seen fixing things now, central banks bail out poor and reckless behaviour, which helps to ensure more of the very same, while governments siphon capital from the productive side of the economy to the consumptive side, which even further diminishes the economy's productive capacity. But they are successful in getting GDP (final spending) growing again, and so, in their minds, its mission accomplished. However, the final spending is done by someone else – and it's being done with your capital. So, when you hear a central banker say that they will do 'whatever it takes', what they are saying is they will expropriate as much of your capital as is necessary to levitate asset prices or enable continued reckless government spending.

Hair of the Dog

Fiscal deficits– governments borrowing money on your behalf (or so you don't have to) and spending it – as well as central banks printing money will always have a short- to medium-term positive impact on spending. How could it not? But increased spending doesn't mean improved economic health. In fact, if it's a result of policymakers extracting capital from the productive side of the economy, then it means economic fundamentals will worsen. Eventually, the diminished productive capacity of the economy will lead to a hangover of lower spending. Policymakers will rush to the rescue again, with more stimulus to keep the party going, and the citizenry will then suffer an even greater hangover. (I know a thing or two about hangovers.)

What's even worse is that the efforts of policymakers to keep this whole charade afloat has resulted in two other things that will have terrible and lasting consequences. First is the false perception of how wealthy people believe they are when looking at the current values of their homes or investment portfolios. Much of that wealth can disappear overnight (the portion that's not truly reflective of fundamentals). House prices should not have increased at all.

The values of investment portfolios have skyrocketed without the economy's productivity rising in the same manner. Secondly, the resulting grotesque wealth inequality that angers people who see one part of society benefiting at the expense of another. It's completely unfair, and people should be angry.

Haves and Have-Nots

When I talk like this to people that I know, some will acknowledge that it may be happening to some degree (others are in denial), but they believe that as long as they mind their own business, they won't come to any financial harm.

Nothing could be further from the truth.

Many of us are already paying the price for these policies through slower growth, but even worse is the extent to which those policies are tearing society apart as the 'have-nots' increasingly despair at never being able to enjoy the same kind of lifestyle as the 'haves'. Much of the lifestyle of the 'haves' comes at the expense of the 'have-nots', and it's just not fair. Not only that, but the 'have-nots' have become the 'had-enoughs'.

The situation in which we find ourselves is fixable, but not without significant pain for many – primarily the 'haves'. Policymakers are increasingly talking about introducing wealth taxes to redistribute capital within society. Although I can understand why this would seem appealing to governments as they play the role of a modern-day 'Robbing Hood', extracting wealth from the 'greedy capitalists' and redistributing it to the 'have-nots', I have a number of issues with such an approach.

First, it leaves in place the broken system that allowed so many to become so filthy rich in the first place. Secondly, it puts more money in the hands of government, which will result in an even greater deterioration in the economy's productive capacity – and, ironically, over time, there will be less wealth for the government to confiscate. Thirdly, not all of the rich have achieved their wealth unfairly. Fourthly, simply taking the wealth of the rich would be nowhere near enough to address the inequality in the system; deteriorating productivity growth is also part of the problem.

Therefore, the cutoff for those targeted by the wealth tax would steadily decline. I could easily see it falling to $1 million in assets. This would affect significantly more people than you think. For instance, if you are sixty-five years old and receiving an annual pension of around $100,000 per year, then the net present value of the assets required to pay your pension until you are ninety is around $1.4 million.[2] Therefore, if an annual wealth tax of 2% were to be imposed on those with assets of $1 million or more, then in the first year you would have to return $28,000 of your $100,000 pension to the government.

Therefore, the wealth tax would increasing be applied to those who are not rich and who fairly earned their pension. This would engender resentment from those who do the producing and live their lives responsibly – within their means – and who already have a significant portion of their efforts taxed away by the government. As they see even more of their wealth taken from them and given to others who don't produce and don't live within their means, it would result in even more division within society. The incentive for those producing would be to stop producing and live irresponsibly – not within their means – and thus become beneficiaries of the government's Robbing Hood policies. This would indeed be the road to ruin.

We Can Do It

In the last chapter, I discussed the steps that I believe we should take to start setting things right. There will be short-term pain for many people, and it could lead to a severe economic slowdown. There will be extremely important roles for government to play by using taxpayer dollars to help those most in need, as well as protecting individual and property rights and ensuring that there are no dramatic declines in the money supply. However, for the economy to heal, it would be imperative that policymakers avoid trying to steer the economy and influence prices. If they are not stopped from doing that, then we could face a global depression, and it would last far longer than necessary.[3]

We've become accustomed to letting policymakers figure things out for us and let us know what's best for our financial well-being. That is exactly how they like it. But it's time we all started taking more responsibility for our own lives, and it can only start by having a good understanding of what's going on. This was the motivating force for me in writing this book. People are smart. Most of us have skin in the game and are, thus, both able and motivated to help fix the economy and put it on a much better and sustainable path. A free-market system works only for all when prices are not being distorted by driving interest rates far below the natural rate and if policymakers are prevented from bailing out risky, capital-destructive behaviour.

I truly believe we can get there, but I can't see any policymaker having the courage to act unless we all demand it. Perhaps we need a courageous modern-day Paul Volcker. But people like this are hard to come by, and they won't come forward unless they are confident that policymakers and society at large will support their prescription for what ails us. On the other hand, given that today there is far more debt outstanding than in Volcker's day and that the consequences of changing direction will likely be more severe, perhaps even he would have found it difficult to do the right thing.

> *Dark times lie ahead of us and there will be a time when we must choose between what is easy and what is right.*
> – Albus Dumbledore

Unfortunately, I suspect that the only way we can start to fix things is by first experiencing a crisis. I hope I'm wrong but this would be the most opportune, and possibly last, chance to fix things before social upheaval results in a new economic system that would take us back hundreds of years. We wasted the last crisis. It's imperative that if we have another one that we don't waste it. Otherwise, we and our children will bear a terrible cost. Borrowing from President John F. Kennedy:

'Ask not what your country can do for you…'

- Ask *not* what you can do for your country. Ask what you can do for yourself while at the same time ensuring you inflict no harm on anyone else.

Once you're able to take care of yourself and your family:

- Ask what you can do to help others take better care of themselves.
- Ask how you can help more people enjoy the benefits of being part of a loving family.
- Ask how you can help others benefit from the opportunities you were fortunate enough to have and that helped get you to where you are today.
- Ask how you can help those around you who, for whatever reason, have fallen on hard times.

It's a Wrap

No one intentionally got us to this unfortunate place. So, once we can agree on how we got here, I think it's important to avoid the blame game, to stop pointing fingers and move on (I know I've done a lot of fingerpointing in this book). Many of those currently in charge may be well suited to help get us out of this morass, but only if they're willing to admit the destructive nature of their previous policies. Anyone defending their reputation or holding on to the old ways out of stubbornness must be told to step aside. I believe that people generally want to do the right thing. Yes, we're all capable of rationalising away our bad behaviour, and we all have our 'not finer moments'. A poor environment or system tends to bring out the worst in people. The opposite is also true.

This is the first time in decades that children can expect to be worse off economically than their parents. This is the legacy we are leaving them, and it's absolutely shameful and inexcusable. People are becoming exasperated as they see governments growing and racking up debt piles that increasingly burden all of us but even more so the next generation. And division and conflict continue to grow, as most people seem to find it harder to get by.

We are a long way down this path. However, it's not too late to turn things around. I believe that because people are smart, and they will know that not only is it the moral thing to do but it will also eventually result in all of us being much better off. It will free up the ingenuity, work ethic, enthusiasm and compassion within all of us. Oh yeah, and world peace 😊.

Okay, maybe you think I'm getting a little carried away here, but I really do believe all of this. I have great faith in people, and I believe this is all possible. We've been moving away from a fair economy for far too long. We need to abandon our current delusional, something-for-nothing, free-lunch policies. Instead, we must go back to an economic system based on realism and truth, where people benefit only by creating capital and then voluntarily exchanging it through a medium of exchange (money) that can be trusted. Not only is it the most moral system, but it's also the one that would generate the most wealth for all of us, to better enable us to help those in need and lead to a fairer and less-divided world.

ENDNOTES

[1] Rosenberg Research: *Webcast with Dave*, 14 February 2022.
[2] Discount rate of 5%.
[3] Many of the well-intended actions of policymakers during the Great Depression served only to lengthen and make worse the economic downturn.

ACKNOWLEDGEMENTS

There are many people who have played an important role, whether they like it or not, in helping make this book possible.

For over twenty years I worked with a small investment team at Mackenzie Investments called Ivy. The Ivy Team's intellectually honest approach to investing taught me the importance of objectivity and how to be more aware of my own biases. I owe a great debt of gratitude to all of my Ivy Team colleagues, past and present.

I am very fortunate to have a lot of great friends, of all stripes, who were kind enough to take the time to read my book and provide careful and considered feedback. It resulted in a book that is much improved from the one they first read.

I've always thought that if you want to understand how an economy works you should try starting your own business. Entrepreneurs truly understand that success is a result of hard work, passion, skin in the game and creating real value for your customers. There have been many who have inspired me, but in particular, Tom and Joanne who own a family butcher shop, Kate with her bakery, Bike shop owner JP, clock shop owners Roman and Robert, and Maria and Rocco with their family pizzeria.

There are many economists and investors whose writings have helped me in my understanding of how an economy works and it would be impossible to list them all. But a few stand out. The first one is Stephen Roach who used to work for Morgan Stanley. I always appreciated his honest and straightforward approach, and he was the one who first got me interested in economics. There are three economists who have had a significant impact on me, and they come from three different economic schools of thought: Steven Kates, Robert Murphy and George Selgin. All three of them are more eager to educate than impress. Of course, they will not agree with everything in this book and I apologize for any misinterpretations of their work.

I thank my parents for instilling in me the importance of family and honesty and my siblings who as part of our family influenced who I am today. Our three amazing daughters have been a great support through this process, and I have learned much from each of them as we discussed things over the years.

But most of all I couldn't have done this without my wife Cynne. I've read a lot of acknowledgements over the years with the author often saying they couldn't have written the book without the support of their spouse. I never really understood why until I wrote my own book. There are a lot of ups and downs when writing a book and self-doubt can creep in from time to time. It was a six-year process with most of the writing being done on vacations and weekends. My wife not only never complained but also provided unwavering support and encouragement and constantly reminded me how much she believed in my book.

I cannot overstate how important all of this support has been.

INDEX

Page numbers containing 'n' ref to notes

A
abuses 77
accountability 290, 310
accounting (accountants) 170 *see also* stock markets (stocks)
actions 248
Adams, John 18
adding value 327
advantage: absolute 101–2; comparative 102–3
affordability 182, 219, 221, 360
agencies, government 341
alcoholism 137–8
alcoholism, as analogy 137–8, 240
algorithms 288
American Bankruptcy Institute 325
Anderson, Benjamin M 168
apathy 20–1
Apple 262–3
argumentum ad verecundian 107
arrogance 247
assets 338, 340, 358, 360–1; capital 114; capitalism 319; corporate culture 248; governments 143, 157; housing 225, 229; inflation 180, 207; stock markets 284, 293–7; wealth effect 213
attitudes: self-serving 285; societal 232
averages, misleading 325–6

B
bad deflation 180–1
Bagehot, Walter 11

bailing out (bail outs) 64, 344–7, 360, 363, 365; capitalism 317, 325; fixing 352, 357; GDP 96; quantitative easing 302–3
Bank for International Settlements 273, 323–4
Bank of Japan 175
banknotes 36, 37
bankruptcies 325, 343, 344
banks, central 39–40, 64, 341–2, 360; capital 117; corporate culture 236, 248; evolution of 36–7; executives and stock markets 274; fractional reserve banking 44–5; GDP 85–6, 95, 106; governments 144; housing 221, 225; inflation 180, 205, 207; interest rates 126, 131, 133–6; policymakers and stock markets 286–7; quantitative easing 294, 306; stock markets 251, 269; wealth effect 213, 217
barter 21–3, 31, 77
base money 47
baskets (of goods) 196–7
Bastiat, Frédéric 64, 211, 226
behaviours 97; rational 345–6
beliefs 332
benefits 204, 327, 354; governments 148, 157, 163, 169, 174 stock markets (stocks) 253–4 *see also* support programmes, governmental; welfare programmes
Bernanke, Ben 341
Berra, Yogi 238
blamestorming 343

INDEX

blindness, wilful 106–7
Boeing 279–80
borrowers 75, 125, 131
borrowing 133–4, 194–5, 254, 310, 342; governments 149–51, 162, 164–5
Bosch, Robert 311
brain drain 314
brand quality 245
bread analogy 115–17
broken window fallacy 64–6
bubbles 293
Buffett, Howard 350
Buffett, Warren 72
bull markets 269, 340
Bureau of Economic Analysis (BEA) 79
Bureau of Labor Statistics 147, 199, 202, 326
bureaucracy, reduction in 355
buybacks, share 276–7, 287–9

C

Canada 48, 145, 159, 167, 231, 233
Cantor, Eddie 330
capacity, productive 83, 87
capital 238, 306; bread analogy 115–17; consuming 113–14; definition 111; disingenuous response 120–1; economics 65–6; exchanging 111–12; GDP 96–7; governments 142–3, 162; governments obtaining 195–6; inflation 184, 189, 208–9; interest rates 138; misallocation of 248, 266; money 112–13; money printing 115; obtaining 114–15, 194–5; shell game 117–18; shell-shocked 120; the sting 119–20; and time 61–2; too much 118–19 *see also* stock markets (stocks)

capital consumption 87–9, 111
capital, excess 277–8
capital exchange 113–14
capital, misallocation of 273, 274, 286, 291, 298, 312
capital redistribution 114
capitalisation, market 260
capitalism 63, 95, 100, 343; analogies 312–13, 317–18; best-laid plans 332–3; competitors 322–3; connecting the dots 319–20; creative destruction 325; destructive bailouts 325; distortion 312; earned wealth 327–8; executive pay 324–5; fix what we have 333; from good to bad 330–1; just rewards 314–15; misdiagnosis 317; misleading averages 325–6; moral issue 331–2; more level than you think 327; most productive system 311; no coercion 322; not equal 326; perception 308–9; progress 309–10; referees 317; resource allocation 310–11; rules 312; slowing growth 315–16; striking the right balance 318–19; trampoline 320–1; unearned wealth 328–9; you can only take so much 313–14; zombie companies 323–4
car industry 199–201
career executives 57, 329, 331
carry-trade 342
cash 138–40
cash flows 262
casinos 252
charities 173
cheques 36, 40–1
Churchill, Winston 333, 361
cigarettes 32

371

coal production 102
coercion 114, 322
coincidence of wants 23–4, 26
coins 180
collateral 214, 216, 224, 342
commission 227
commodity monies 31–2, 33
commodity theory 20
common sense 209
communication 11–12
companies 128, 234 *see also* corporate culture; corporations
compassion 146, 367
competition (competitors) 83, 100, 238, 336; capitalism 308, 311, 322–3; economics 55–6, 58–9, 62 *see also* inflation
conflict of interest 345
Congressional Budget Office 145
consent 114
construction, houses 232
Consumer Price Index (CPI) 181, 196, 198
consumer tastes 196
consumers 134, 148, 234, 238; capitalism 311, 323; economics 56–7, 60–1, 63; GDP 97–100; inflation 183, 187, 197, 202, 209; sovereign 262–3; US 225 *see also* saving and investment; sovereign consumer
consumption 87–9, 335, 337, 340; economics 60–2, 64; inflation 184, 206; interest rates 123, 125, 135 *see also* Gross Domestic Product (GDP)
consumption, capital 87–9, 111
contagion 301–2
control 241
Cook, Tim 324

corporate culture 276, 279; adding alcohol 240; bad 246–7; competitive advantage 238; Costco 244–5; definition 237; deteriorating economic culture 248–9; everyone wins 243; Fastenal 245–6; full steam ahead 247; good 242; hot dogs 245; letting go 240–1; never work 241–2; organic risk control 243–4; parenting 239–40; real wealth effect 237; reinvestment 242–3; sustainability 238–9; time and effort 247–8
corporations 138, 187, 229, 320; buyers 233–4 *see also* companies
cost of living index 196
Costco 244–5, 311
costs, borrowing 125–6
COVID pandemic (crisis) 186, 279, 297, 304; governments 144–5, 151, 159, 168; money 40, 47
crashes, airline 279
creativity 242, 246
credit 228, 335
crimes 173
culture, corporate *see* corporate culture
currency, shares as 265–6
customers 57–8, 276, 322, 329, 331; corporate culture 243–4, 248

D

debasement 32–3
debt, global 9, 90, 94
debts 75, 337, 346, 361, 363; capitalism 310, 316, 320; corporate culture 249; global 90, 94; governments 151, 165–7, 174; housing 221; inflation 211; interest rates 134–5, 137, 140; quantitative easing 297; stock markets

(stocks) 278–9, 283–4; wealth effect 217 *see also* Gross Domestic Product (GDP)
debts, government 47, 113; GDP 91, 94n8; governments 151–7, 165, 174–5; interest rates 128, 130
decisions, unpopular 348
default, governmental 155
deficit spending 149, 152, 154, 161, 163, 283
deficits 149–50, 152–3, 159, 160, 163
deflation 176, 177–9; bad 180–1; good 179, 182–3
deflation, good 36, 100
demands 97
demographics 334
denominations, smaller 179–80
deposits 43
Descartes, René 7
destruction 64–5, 66; creative 325; money 73–5
developments, housing 232
direct exchange 27
discretionary incomes 85–6
diseases 56
disinflation 190–3; analogy 192–3
distortion 333, 351, 365
dividends 260
divisibility 25, 26
division of labour *see* labour, division of
divisiveness 307
do-no-harm attitude 11
dot-com bubble (boom) 219, 338–40
double coincidence of wants 23–4
dual mandate 335
Dumbledore, Albus 366

E
earned (unearned) wealth 327–9
earnings 67, 262, 283–4, 312, 358
earnings per share (ESP) 259
economic growth 48, 69, 82, 348
Economic Organization of a P.O.W. Camp, The 31
economic philosophy 10
Economic Policy Institute 324
economic productive health analogy 83–4
economic productivity growth 9
economics 51–2; benefits of failing 62–3; broken window fallacy 64–6; capital and time 61–2; competition 55–6, 58–9; entrepreneurs 56–7; fair share 57–8; free choice 53–4; how much should people earn 67; introducing money 54–5; invisible hand 52–3; island economies 52; real vs. nominal 61; saving and investment 59–60; shot-circuiting the system 64; sovereign consumer 60–1; time preference 62
efficiency 58, 76, 131, 310
effort 247–8
Einstein, Albert 11
emergencies 76
emotional impact, societal 234
empathy 330
employees 81, 183–4, 337, 352; capitalism 311, 322, 324, 329–31; corporate culture 244, 246, 248; economics 57–8, 67; governments 353, 355; public servants 142, 163; stock markets (stocks) 254, 263
employment 134, 243, 335–6, 352
enthusiasm 245, 367

entitlement 285
entrepreneurs (entrepreneurialism) 140, 172, 329–30; capitalism 310, 322; corporate culture 242, 246; economics 56–7, 62; GDP 84, 96, 105; stock markets (stocks) 251, 254, 287
envy 328
equality (inequality) 146–7, 313–14
equity 215–16, 223, 226, 265; negative 224; stock markets (stocks) 254–5
equity extraction 222
European Central Bank 304
everything bubble 347
exchange 21, 27
exchange, medium of 22, 111, 188–9, 367 *see also* money
excuses 106, 346–7
executive pay 324–5
executives 328–9
executives and stock markets 273; Boeing 279–80; excess capital 277–8; General Electric (GE) 280–1; incentives 278–9; share buybacks 276–7; shortcut 275–6; treating systems 275; wrong reasons 278; zombie management teams 273–5
executives, career 57, 329, 331
executives, corporate 56, 67, 246, 264, 265, 288
expectations, investors 269–70
Expenditure Approach to GDP 80

F

facilitators 362
failure 62–3, 96, 254, 305
fair share 57–8
fairness (unfairness) 72, 345, 349–51, 361, 367; capitalism 315, 328, 332–3; governments 146; policymakers 285, 287; quantitative easing 293, 307; stock markets (stocks) 266 *see also* unfairness
Fannie Mae 341
Fastenal 245–6, 311
Federal Deposit Insurance Corporation (FDIC) 344
Federal Reserve Bank (Federal Reserve) 336, 340, 343–7; capitalism 319; governments 155–6; housing 228; inflation 196; interest rates 133; money 38, 44–6 *see also* Quantitative Easing (QE)
Federal Reserve Reform Act 335
fees 232, 233, 355
fiat billionaires 329
fiat currency 46–7, 335
fiat fractional banking 76
fiduciary media 42
final consumption 207
final spending 64, 90–1, 107, 109, 135, 363
financial crises 211
financial industry *see* stock markets (stocks)
financial institutions 220
financial repression 319
financial services industry (sector) 343, 352–3
financialisation 276, 281, 329
fiscal policy 144 *see also* government spending
forgery 36
fractional reserve banking 37, 40, 43, 44–5
France 143

fraud 28, 29
Freddie Mac 341
free choice 53–4
free markets 84, 297, 310, 335, 365
freedoms 13, 332
Friedman, Milton 76, 181, 210, 211, 286
funding 234
fungibility 26–7

G

Galbraith, John Kenneth 19
gambling 253
GDP 64–5, 66
General Electric (GE) 280–1
generations, future 316, 367; governments 150–1, 156; housing 226, 227, 233, 235; wealth effect 213, 217
generations, future (next) 165
generosity 147
gifts 156
Glass-Steagall Act 287
global debt 9
global depression 365
global economy 276, 279
Global Financial Crises (GFC) 10, 345, 347, 362; capitalism 319–20; GDP 95; interest rates 126, 136; quantitative easing 293, 302
global secular stagnation 348
globalisation 182
gold 32–5, 43, 45–6, 179
gold coins 42–3
gold standard 33, 36, 76, 88, 181, 335
good deflation 179, 180; recent example 182–3
government bonds 130, 153, 174–5, 294, 304
government borrowing 94n5, 114
government debt 47, 91, 113; interest rates 128, 130, 135–6 *see also* governments
government growth 163
government spending 363; capitalism 310, 312; GDP 80–2, 87, 108; interest rates 130, 134; quantitative easing 296, 304
governments 75, 217, 229, 346, 362; backdoor tax 153–4; the blob 163; borrowing from the future 150–1; but it's free 155–6; capitalism 320, 323; debt: redistribution of wealth 165–7; debt tsunami 154–5; default 155; deficits 149–50; deficits matter 152–3; economics 53, 60; equality 146–7; GDP 89–91, 95, 104–6; go-between 147–8; gross 167; incentives 145–6; interest rates 129, 138; less bang for debt buck 156–7; making it clear 173–4; motives 145; obtaining capital 142–3; path of least resistance 174–5; PPT 289–91; private sector funding 144; progressive taxation 170–3; question of degree 145; saved money is spent 169; shrinkage 353–4; skin in the game 159–60; someone always pays 143–4; tautologies 160; team effort 151; trickery 160–3; trust 167–9; we don't owe it all to ourselves 165; we owe it to ourselves 164–5; who decides? 148–9; who pays? 170; withholding tax 163–4
Great Depression 95, 99, 180, 287, 343–4, 362
greedflation 187
Greenspan, Alan 222, 339

Gross Domestic Product (GDP) 160, 248, 363; absolute advantage 101–2; analogies 83–4, 91–3; basics 80–2; capital consumption 87–9; central banks 85–6; comparative advantage 102–3; debts 84–5; definition 79; governments 89–91; gross output 107–8; historic levels 309; incentives 95–7; intermediate spending 79–80; investment 108–9; micromanaging 95; my way or the highway 93–4; no tariffs 100; not satisfied 104–5; per capita 232; prosperity 103; seed corn 103–4; shopping 97; slack 86–7; spending 82; sustainability 283–4; tariffs 98–9; things should be a lot better 105–6; tit for tat 99–100; US 310, 316; want vs. demand 97; we all lose 106; wilful blindness 106–7
gross output 107–8
growth 211, 275, 364; slowing 315–16
growth, sustainable 205

H

hard work 11 *see also* work ethics
Hayek, Fredrich A. 308
healing 298
health, economic 79
hedge funds 295
hedonic adjustments 198–203
Hero Syndrome 12
heroes 89, 146, 164, 348
high-frequency traders 288–9
high time preference 62
hoarding 71
hockey analogy 312–13
honesty 11
house prices 144, 341, 357

households 271, 327; lower income 228
housing 207, 337, 340, 351, 360; the beginning 219; best-laid plans 227–8; building pyramids 235–6; corporate buyers 233–4; delusion 233; fake wealth effect 225–6; forced saving 223; go big or go home 220–1; governments 144, 160; home ATM 222; incentives 227; intergenerational wealth transfer 226; less means more 228–9; less than net zero 234–5; lower interest expense 223; mortgage burning 223; per capita 232; piling on 231; quantitative easing 293, 296, 297; reckless behaviour 220; roadblocks 232–3; stock markets (stocks) 252, 271; too much of a good thing 231; trickle down 226–7; upside down 224–5; US housing bubble 220; vs. wages 221–2; wealth effect 213, 215–16; who benefits the most 229
housing boom 341–2
housing bubble 185, 342
housing crisis 343
hubris 12
human nature 148, 169, 285, 313, 340, 347
humanitarianism 168
Hume, David 176
humility 244
hyperinflation 153

I

immediate gratification 97
immigration (immigrants) 143–4, 225–7, 231–3, 235
improvements 60, 205; technological 222

incentives 227, 278–80, 365; capitalism 311, 313; GDP 95–6, 105; governments 145–6, 168–9
Income Approach to GDP 80
incomes 207; discretionary 85–6 *see also* wages
independent thought 11
index funds 272
indirect exchange 23, 27
inequality 326, 364
inflation 54, 152–3, 336, 357; bad deflation 180–1; basket case 196–7; a cancer 211–12; capital 112, 116; common sense 209; disinflation 190–3; good deflation 179; good deflation: recent example 182–3; government obtaining capital 195–6; hedonic adjustments 198–203; inflation/deflation scenarios 177–9; inflation impact of adsorbing slack 207–9; interest rates 127, 131, 135, 137; it's money and stuff 204; money 36–7, 43, 46–7, 75; money supply 181–2; muddying the waters 176–7; no inflation without money 209–10; no say in the matter 203–4; no spiral 185–6; not what it seems 194; obtaining capital 194–5; other causes 186–7; paradox of thrift 183–4; the pause that refreshes 206–7; providing others with an income 207; quantitative easing 295–6, 304; real cuts 204; resignation 176; services prices 205–6; short-term inflation 210; smaller denominations 179–80; the spiral 184–5; two: magic number 204–5; uncommon sense 209; velocity of money 188–90

infrastructure 95, 144
ingenuity 59, 60, 105, 284, 367
inheritance 114
initial public offering (IPO) 257–9
innovation 93, 284, 325; corporate culture 242, 246; economics 58, 62; inflation 182, 200–1
insolvency 44
insurance: unemployment 167–8 *see also* stock markets (stocks)
interest expense 223, 227
Interest On Excess Reserves (IOER) 296
interest rates 120–1, 214, 340–1, 343, 347, 360; capitalism 319–20, 335; fixing 351–2; GDP 72, 86, 96, 100; governments 156, 174; housing 219, 221, 226–9; inflation 185, 208; lowering of, analogy 91–3; moderate, long-term 336–7; quantitative easing 294–6
interest rates, natural 122–4; determining 125–7; economy's natural regulator 131–2; example 129; inflation 131; low rates and least productive 129–30; risk 128; time 127–8; time preference 124–5
interest rates, neutral 133; absurdity 135–6; definition 133–4; functioning alcoholic 137–8; GDP focus 134; no more cash 138–40; push me pull you 135; race to the bottomS 134; robbed 138; short run is someone else's long run 136–7
intermediate spending 107–8
International Institute of Finance (IIF) 90
International Monetary Fund (IMF) 82, 108

Internet 338
investment 213, 239, 332, 337; economics 56, 59–60, 62; GDP 90, 104, 108–9; housing 231, 235; inflation 180, 184, 200, 206–7; interest rates 130, 139; stock markets (stocks) 251, 279, 284 *see also* governments
Investopedia 294
investors 219, 302, 340, 342; stock markets (stocks) and executives 273–5, 280; stock markets (stocks) and policymakers 286
Ireland 56
island economies 52

J
jingle mail 224
job losses 102, 298, 302
job security 148, 353
jobs 323
Joubert, Joseph 356
Judson, Ruth 38

K
Kennedy, John F., President 366
Keynes, John Maynard 19, 136, 209, 335
King, Martin Luther, Jr. 357

L
labour, division of 21
labour markets, US 326
layoffs 183, 184
leadership 244
Lee, Bruce 16
legal tender 46
Lehman Brothers 343
lenders 75, 131, 150, 174

lending standards 342
liabilities, government 161
Lincoln, Abraham 46
liquidity theory 126
living standards 64
loan duration 136
loan repayments 47
loans 75, 127, 162, 180, 214, 228; quantitative easing 295, 303–4
Long Term Capital Management 338
losing 106
low time preference 62
Lowenstein, Roger 339
luck 114

M
malinvestment 248, 335
management (teams) 239, 243, 246, 248, 279; zombie 273–5
managers, professional 57
Manheim Used Vehicle Index 202
manufacturers, local 99
market forces 351–2
McKinsey 138
means of payment 22
Merriam-Webster 308
micromanaging 95, 243
misallocation of capital 248
Mises, Ludwig von 123, 127
mistakes 247, 248, 286, 293
Mitterand, Francois 143
Moltke, Helmuth von 358
monetarism 181
monetary base (M0) 37–9
monetary systems 13
money 112–13; blaming 77; creation 37–9; definition 16–19; destruction 73–5; governments 149, 152, 167;

hoarding 71; inflation 179, 210; not the economy 69; other stores of value 73; problems solved 23–7; role of 27; saved is still spent 70–1; stable money principle 75–6; stable money supply 71–2; stock markets (stocks) 268–9; store of value 70; velocity of 188–90

money, evolution of: bank reserves 39–40; banks 36–7; clearing cheques 40–1; commodity money 31–2; fiat currency 46–7; fractional reserve banking 44–5; gold 33–5, 45–6; gold coins as reserves 42–3; how much is enough? 48–9; introducing 54–5; money creation 39; money supply 37–9; money supply contraction 47; money supply growth 47; names 33; re-lending money 41–2; silver and gold 32–3; today's bank reserves 43–4; true money 35–6

money printing 347, 362; capital 112–13, 115, 120; capitalism 310, 312, 319–20; GDP 97; housing 226, 236; inflation 185, 195, 204–5, 207–8; interest rates 130, 134, 136–7; quantitative easing 294, 298, 303, 305; stock markets (stocks) 269, 275, 283–4 *see also* governments

money supply 69, 76, 335–7, 360; evolution of 37–9, 47; fixing 350–1; governments 142; inflation 179–82, 200–1, 204, 210; interest rates 134; quantitative easing 294–5

morality (immorality) 227, 297, 345–6, 360, 367; capitalism 331–2; governments 147, 175; money 20, 77

mortgages 223, 229, 296–7, 341; interest-only 221; non-recourse 224

Munger, Charlie 278

N
Nasdaq Composite 339
national security 102
nationalisation 344, 345
natural disasters 65, 66
needs 316
negative amortisation mortgages 220–1
negative equity 224
net investment 160–1, 162–3

O
opportunities 146, 173, 174, 326, 328
Origins of the Crash 339
ownership 257–9

P
paper money 180
paradox of thrift 183–4
parenting 239–40
participants 10
Pascal, Blaise 12
passion 330
patience 11, 305, 330
payment, means of 27–8
penalties 173
pension benefits 163
pension funds 295
pension plans 138, 143, 353–4
pensioners 346
pensions 365
personal consumption expenditure (PCE) 222
philosophy, economic 10
planning, central 354–5
plunge protection team (PPT) 289–91, 338
policies 315

policymakers 9–10, 12–13, 336–8, 340, 343, 347–8; capital 116; capitalism 312, 317, 319–20, 332; conclusion 361, 365; corporate culture 239–40, 249; economics 51, 53, 55, 64; fixing 357–8; housing 227, 234; inflation 176, 180; interest rates 126, 134, 136–9; money 48; quantitative easing 306–7; stock markets (stocks) 268, 281 *see also* governments; Gross Domestic Product (GDP)

policymakers and stock markets 282; backstop 283; but even worse 291; distorted markets 285–7; fair but not equal 285; middlemen 284; plunge protection team (PPT) 289–90; PPT in action 290–1; regulation and deregulation 287; share buybacks 287–9; sunlight 290; sustainable GDP and earnings growth 283–4; why markets go up and down 282–3

politicians 11, 106, 248, 345; fixing 354, 357; governments 142, 147, 159, 163–4; stock markets (stocks) 275, 305–6

Poloz, Steven 362

Ponzi schemes 271–2

populist movements 235

population growth 179, 180, 232

populist movements 317

portability 25–6, 27

portfolio effect 319

poverty 326

POW camps 31, 32

preferences, personal 93

price deflation 350

price discovery 260–1, 273, 275, 291, 297, 312

price earnings multiple (PE) 259–60

price floor 323

price increases 47

prices 175, 296, 312, 337, 358; capital 112, 120; economics 55, 60; GDP 85, 96; interest rates 125, 134; money 24–5, 72, 74 *see also* inflation

prices, stable 336

pricing 270–1

prisoners 31

private companies 156

private sector 148, 154, 160–1, 162, 163

private sector funding 144

producers 60

product improvements 198

product quality 203

Production Approach to GDP 80

productive capacity 206, 235, 314, 338, 346, 363; GDP 83, 96, 101; global 88; governments 147, 157; interest rates 131, 135; quantitative easing 297, 302; stock markets (stocks) 275, 279

productivity 72, 151, 298, 337, 339–40; economics 55–6, 59–60; GDP 83–4, 87, 100, 109; inflation 193, 200–2, 206, 209; interest rates 128, 129, 139; wealth effect 213, 217

productivity growth 249, 336, 360–1, 364; capitalism 311, 323; GDP 94, 106; governments 154, 175; inflation 181; interest rates 131, 137, 140; quantitative easing 297; stock markets (stocks) 273, 283, 289, 291

profit-sharing 57

profit sharing 248

profitability 58, 129, 238, 242; inflation 187, 200, 205–6; stock markets (stocks) 263, 275

profits 148, 311
property rights 88, 365; capitalism 315, 332; governments 171–2, 175; money 20, 22
prosperity 69, 103, 107
public servants 145
purchasing power 22, 74
pyramid building 235–6
pyramid schemes 271–2

Q
quality improvements 199
quantitative easing (QE) 47, 265, 283, 291, 319, 347; analogies 299–301, 305–6; the beginning 293–4; contagion 301–2; description 294–5; even more 298–9; Fed money creation 303–4; fire hose of sugar 306–7; healing 298; no time like the present 297–8; paid not to lend 295–6; portfolio effect 295; raft of consequences 297; responding to stock markets 304–5; sclerotic 298; solvency crisis 304; stealth inflation impact 296–7; trickle down 302–3

R
Radford, R.A. 31
re-lending money 41–2
recessions 219, 340; GDP 89, 96; interest rates 133, 135; quantitative easing 298–9; stock markets (stocks) 282, 286
reckoning 320
redistribution, capital 114
referees 317
regulations 96, 323, 343, 352, 362; and deregulation 287; reduction in 355
reinvestment 83, 242–3, 263
reputations 345
reserve ratio 40
reserves 180
reserves, bank 295
resources 70–1, 96, 150, 188, 310–11; interest rates 125, 128–9
retained earnings 169
retirement 207, 223, 226, 235, 250, 351
retirement benefits 143
return on equity (ROE) 257
returns, risk and 261–2
rewards 19, 314–15
Ricardo, David 48, 176
rights 13
risk and return 261–2
risk control, organic 243–4
risks (risk-taking) 56, 128, 136
Roach, Stephen 196
Roosevelt, Franklin D. 28
rules 343, 352; capitalism 312–13, 317; GDP 96; housing 227; money 76; stock markets (stocks) 287–8

S
S&P 500 339
Saenger, Victor 261
sales growth 238
satisfaction 197; governmental 104–5
saving 70
saving and investment 59–60, 82
savings, private sector 162
savings (savers) 61, 235, 337, 346, 358; capitalism 319–20, 332; forced 223; GDP 88, 104, 109; inflation 183–4, 193, 200, 208; interest rates 124–6, 138–9; stock markets (stocks) 279, 284, 302–3 *see also* governments

Say, Jean-Baptiste (Say's Law) 52, 79
scams 115
scare tactics 301
Schopenhauer, Arthur 106
Schumpeter, Joseph 325
sclerotic 298
Second World War 31
Securities and Exchange Commission (SEC) 287–8
seed corn analogy 103–4
self-sufficiency 21
services prices 205
Shakespeare, William 348
share buybacks 287–9
share prices 247
shareholders 56, 260, 264–5, 275, 280, 329
shares, IPO 257–9
shopping 97
short-term inflation 210
Shostak, Frank 27
shrinkflation 198
silver 32–3
Sinclair, Upton 233
skin in the game 335, 365; capitalism 312, 322; corporate culture 246; economics 53; fixing 352; GDP 86; governments 159–60; inflation 180; interest rates 136; quantitative easing 297; stock markets (stocks) 262
Skousen, Mark 36, 107–8
slack 86–7, 97, 207–9
Smith, Adam 53
Smoot-Hawley Tariff 99
social cohesion 317
Social Security Board of Trustees 354
socialism 313, 333, 361
socialist movements 318

societal divisions 365
societal well-being 19, 234
society, divided 211
soft money 335
solvency crisis 304
something-for-nothing mindset (myth) 84, 355–6
sound money 180
sovereign consumer 60–1, 63, 98, 100, 262–3
Sowell, Thomas 159
speculation 96, 338, 339, 362
spending 360; economics 66; fixing 357; GDP 81–2, 87, 97, 103; governments 143; inflation 210; interest rates 124–6, 134, 137, 139; intermediate 79–80; stock markets (stocks) 278; wealth effect 217 *see also* final spending
spending, government 149
stagnation, economic 96, 314, 334
stealing *see* theft (stealing)
steel production 102
stock markets (stocks) 160, 207, 337–9, 360; basketcase.com 269–70; blob 250–1; cause and effect 263; companies selling new shares 263–4; corporate culture 248; dividends 260; earnings per share (ESP) 259; equity 254–5; fairly obtained wealth 252; fixing 352; good role 253–4; here today, gone tomorrow 271; housing 219, 229; initial public offering (IPO) 257–9; losing wealth 253; lubricant 250; market capitalisation 260; money doesn't disappear 269; mutual benefit 254; not money wealth 268–9; Ponzi schemes 271–2; price discovery 260–1, 263; price earnings

multiple (PE) 259–60; pricing 270–1; real economy 251; return on equity (ROE) 257; risk and return 261–2; shares as currency 265–6; siphon 251–2; sovereign consumer 262–3; stock options 264–5; wealth effect 213–15; winning wealth 252–3 *see also* executives and stock markets; policymakers and stock markets
subsidies 174
substitution 197
supply 52, 186
support programmes, governmental 173–4, 324
sustainability (unsustainability) 348, 365; capitalism 312; corporate culture 238–9; GDP 84, 90–1, 93, 109; governments 148, 157; stock markets (stocks) 265, 278, 283

T
Taleb, Nassim 53
tariffs 98–100, 182
taxation 362; capital 114, 116; capitalism 310, 314–15, 318; GDP 88, 92, 95, 97–8, 104; housing 232–4; inflation 195; interest rates 129, 136; progressive 170–3; reduction in 355; stock markets (stocks) 271; wealth effect 217; withholding 163–4 *see also* governments
taxpayers 287, 343–4
Tech Wreck 219, 269, 339
technologies 205, 219, 269
televisions 182, 183
term structure, interest rates 127
terminology (language) 10, 11, 19, 107
theft (stealing) 55, 115, 142; employees 244

thrift 183–4
time 62, 127–8, 247–8, 297–8
time preference 122–3, 124–5, 136, 337
time value of money 123
trade 20, 45, 102, 334; global 99
transfer payments 82
trickle down 226–7, 302–3, 332, 337
true money 35–6
trust 266, 367; corporate culture 245, 248; governments 148, 167–8; money 19, 29
Twain, Mark 241

U
uncommon sense 209
underinvestment 83
unemployment: benefits 169; insurance 167–8
unfairness 58, 122, 357 *see also* fairness (unfairness)
United Kingdom (UK) 36, 102, 138, 172
United States of America (US) 146, 149, 151, 156, 167, 170; GDP 102; housing 221–2 *see also* housing inflation 179, 181, 202; interest rates 138; money 36, 38, 40, 46; productivity growth 88–9
units of account 24–5, 26
University of Chicago Law School 222
upside down on your mortgage 224

V
value (wealth) 28–9, 32; store of 26, 27
value (worth) 10; capital 118–20; capitalism 320; governments 152–3, 173; money 21, 48, 72; stock markets (stocks) 282, 284; store of 70, 73

violence 114
Volcker, Paul 135, 337, 366
voluntary decisions (participation) 54, 253, 315, 322
voters 149, 307, 354

W

wages 61, 100, 204, 221–2, 254; governments 147, 153 *see also* incomes
Wall Street 250, 252–3, 341, 344–7, 362; capitalism 317, 319; executives 278; fixing 352–3; policymakers 283; quantitative easing 303
want vs. demand 97
wants coincidence of 23–4
war on cash 138
wars 65, 66
wealth 61, 312; earned (unearned) 327–9; real 340; stock markets (stocks) 252–3, 268–9
wealth creation 251–2, 270–1, 280, 308, 361
wealth disparity 9, 346, 360–1; capital 106; GDP 94; governments 175; inflation 211; money 20, 47; quantitative easing 297, 306; stock markets (stocks) 289, 291
wealth distribution 10, 308, 333 *see also* wealth redistribution
wealth effect 216–17, 320, 338, 343; described 213–14; fake 217, 225–6; housing 215–16; stocks 214–15
wealth extraction 32–3, 252
wealth inequality 137, 217, 279, 334, 364; capitalism 319, 321
wealth redistribution 96, 116–17, 140, 338–9; capitalism 317–18; economics 51–2, 66; governments 156, 165–7; housing 225–6, 233; money 48, 75; wealth effect 213, 217 *see also* stock markets (stocks)
wealth taxes 364
wealth transfer 140, 205; governments 150, 154, 156; housing 225, 233; intergenerational 226; stock markets (stocks) 264–5
welfare programmes (systems) 95, 104, 318, 362
Wesley, John 77, 332
White, Lawrence H. 76, 179
Wilshire 5000 Stock Index 282
winnings 114
work ethics 140, 241, 244, 330, 367
work, hard 11, 13, 239–40, 355; money 19–20, 27–8; wealth effect 213, 217
workers 204, 283, 324, 329; government 147–8, 163

Z

zombie companies 64, 85, 284, 297, 335, 360; capitalism 317, 323–4
zombie management teams 273–5